Nought to Sixty was a six-month programme of exhibitions and events at the Institute of Contemporary Arts, London, held to celebrate the organisation's sixtieth anniversary. It presented sixty projects by artists, artists' groups and commentators from the emerging art scenes in Britain and Ireland, including a large number of week-long exhibitions, but also performances, gigs, screenings, talks, publications, off-site projects and social events. Most of the artists were under thirty-five, few of them had had significant commercial exposure, and in most cases this was their first opportunity to mount a solo project in a major public space. The season was not intended to announce any new generation or style, but to build up a multifaceted portrait of the emerging art scenes in the two countries, and to build on the ICA's history as a club for artists and a laboratory for experimentation. This book is a record of an extraordinary six months.

Nought to Sixty

60 projects

6 months

Institute of Contemporary Arts, London

Contents

Introductory material

Project texts

Numbers in parenthesis indicate project number within overall sequence

Additional texts

Introduction

This book is a record of *Nought to Sixty*, a six-month season of sixty projects by emerging artists based in Britain and Ireland. *Nought to Sixty* was one of the major components in the ICA's 60th anniversary celebrations, and was designed to build on the institute's long-standing role as a champion of emerging art and artists. Many aspects of the art world have changed in the decades since the ICA was founded, but we have always offered an alternative to the established art structures, and operated as a club for artists and a laboratory for experimentation, and it was in this spirit that we approached *Nought to Sixty*.

When selecting projects for *Nought to Sixty* we looked for artists who we felt were at the forefront of art practice in Britain and Ireland. Most of the artists were young, and few had had much commercial exposure. Most of them had been born in Britain or Ireland, but we did also include people who had settled in these countries. Our research took us to the cities in this area that are major art centres, and we also asked many artists and artist-led organisations to give us advice. Our intention was not to document a new generation or style, and we tried to reflect a range of practices, but our choices were essentially subjective – governed by our own enthusiasms, and reflecting a network of shared energies.

The most common model for showing emerging artists is the group show, including annual prize-giving events such as the ICA's former *Beck's Futures*. However, when developing *Nought to Sixty* we decided that it would be better to do a programme in which each artist was given the opportunity to stage an autonomous project, and in which we did away with the element of competition. The result was a massive programme of events reflecting the diversity of art practice: including a large number of week-long exhibitions in the ICA's upper galleries; screenings and performances in our theatre, cinemas and other spaces; as well publications, off-site projects and other interventions.

Nought to Sixty was also intended as a space where the communal and discursive aspects of art practice could be emphasised – things that were sometimes neglected in the recent art boom. Exhibition openings and events were held every Monday night, creating a strong social dynamic. Each month we printed a magazine, which included texts on the individual artists, as well as longer essays, and a gazetteer that gathered together information on artist-led and non-profit initiatives. Finally, the sixty projects included a number of panel discussions which, like the essays, were intended to encourage debate about the range of forces that make up a healthy art scene. In such ways the ICA attempted to play its part in fostering a critical community of artists.

This book gathers together the texts that were commissioned for the *Nought to Sixty* magazine, but it also includes installation shots and other documentation of the exhibitions and projects, a complete list of works, edited transcripts of the panel discussions and an expanded gazetteer. It is not easy to document the range of activity within *Nought to Sixty*, but we hope that this book suggests some of the excitement of the programme, as well as revealing some of its recurring strands – the latter also addressed by Melissa Gronlund in a new extended essay.

The speed and churn of *Nought to Sixty* is not unique in the London art world, and this style of curating has its dangers, including the temptation to stress quantity over quality, or to emphasise the over-arching curatorial agenda over those of the individual participants. However, we tried hard to avoid these pitfalls, and to allow each artist or group to find its own pace. In addition, a number of the artists' projects, as well as the interventions in the discursive programme, explored the ICA's history and the issue of institutional responsibility towards emerging practice. Finally, a number of the artists chose to interrupt the flow of the programme, disrupting its fulfilment of our cultural imperative of consumption and speed.

Research for *Nought to Sixty* was led by the ICA's Richard Birkett, who managed the season with the help of Isla Leaver-Yap, and I would like to say a big thank you to both of them, and to everyone at the ICA who worked so hard, including Silvia Tramontana, Zoë Franklin, Trevor Hall, Kenji Takahashi and the installation crew. On behalf of the ICA I would like to thank all of our partners: including our regular funder Arts Council England; our season funders Scottish Arts Council, Culture Ireland and the Henry Moore Foundation; our season collaborators *Afterall*, *Art Review* and LUX; and our season sponsor Kirin. Finally, I would like to thank the artists, whose goodwill made this extraordinary project possible.

The ICA's Brandon Room, where some of the *Nought to Sixty* events took place, is named after Linda Brandon, who was the organisation's Director of Talks in the early nineties, before her untimely death. Linda was also my first landlady after I graduated from college and returned to London, and she introduced me to some of the artists – such as Cerith Wyn Evans – who were part of the ICA scene at that time. Linda was sociable, critical and inspirational, and brought out these important aspects of the organisation. I think Linda would have enjoyed *Nought to Sixty*, and this book is dedicated to her memory.

Mark Sladen
Director of Exhibitions
Institute of Contemporary Arts, London

Mapping *Nought to Sixty*

Melissa Gronlund

The ICA's *Nought to Sixty* season was a sprawling beast, installed on a rotating basis over six months. Scattered with events, any movement 'through it' was necessarily temporal, rather than linear. Who could make it to all the projects? The visitor caught some and missed others, and the diversity of art practices represented was impressively vast in terms of media, subject and style. The unifying elements were national and generational, but only obliquely: emerging artists working in Britain and Ireland, which meant youngish artists who were sometimes also transplants from other countries. This essay is tasked with finding the thread or locating the themes that would run through these works if they could somehow be shown together. The aim is to distil from sixty projects some general modes of practice and exhibition. Part of the difficulty of such an exercise is created not by the refusal of the works to cohere into trends – which cannily exist if you look for them – but by one of the main assumptions of the works themselves: a refusal of generality and a move away from authority.

The idea of art-making as something wider than studio- and gallery-based practice was crucial to *Nought to Sixty*. This was true on the level of curation, because of the ICA's decision to include panel discussions, events and criticism as part of its programme; but it was especially true on the level of production, since many of the artists chose to use their programme to create collaborative projects, or to curate other programmes – whether in film, music or performance. The result was an 'art world' configured as an expansive network of self-organised and multimedia platforms: from Mark Aerial Waller's film practice, which includes the staging of theatrical events in which 'cinema' is heralded as a ritual experience; to the recording label Junior Aspirin Records, whose members – artists and writers – produce albums as well as artworks and lectures.

In one of *Nought to Sixty*'s monthly salon discussions, entitled 'You talkin' to me? Why art is turning to education', artist Dave Beech connected the so-called educational impulse – in which an institution devotes a portion of its programming and budget to promoting dialogue in the form of talks, symposia, book projects and events – to Nicolas Bourriaud's notion of convivial collectivity and the quality of socially 'relational' behaviour that it ideally elicits from the audience. This terminology to an extent formalises what was ever so – the social aspect of making, exhibiting and discussing work; or perhaps it seeks to reinstate a sense of community that has been lost in the art world's expansion. But it also draws attention to the key element of shared experience in *Nought to Sixty*, which took place over a period of six months, punctuated by Monday night openings and events – rather than being the trim on the pillowcase, these openings were integral to the season, giving a structure to the project and setting its rhythm.

In addition to this curatorial backdrop of participatory audiences, much of the work itself also reflects Bourriaud's idea of postproduction, in particular the selection and recombination of pre-existent material (images, songs, artistic clichés). Bourriaud links this to larger trends: in *Postproduction* (2002), for example, he notes the relationship between modes of art production and contemporaneous modes of commodity production. For the 1990s artists he was specifically writing about, these affinities were reflected in their interest in social practices such as supermarket shopping and file shareware. The principles of eclecticism and individual choice promised by the latter modes, however, are tempered in reality. If the principle of Google, for example, is to provide access to all material published on the Internet, the company in actuality has to contend with national laws limiting free expression, meaning sites are blocked in various countries (France and Germany, where the sale of Nazi memorabilia is banned; Turkey, where insults to Ataturk are outlawed; Thailand, where it is illegal to ridicule the king).[1]

1. Jeffrey Rosen, 'Google's Gatekeepers', *New York Times Magazine*, 30 November 2008.

This recognition of local restrictions qualifies theoretical notions of free-market selection and consumption; and it was such a notion of these limitations that many artists' projects in *Nought to Sixty* sought to explore. Sarah Pierce, for instance, showed the archive as physically embedded in its mode of preservation and viewing. The artist brought together material on two well-known events in the ICA's history – the exhibition *When Attitudes Become Form* (1969) and *The State of British Art, A Debate* (1978), a conference organised by Peter Fuller, Richard Cork, John Tagg and Andrew Brighton – and displayed the papers and photographs in vitrines belonging to the institution.[2] In contrast to the emancipatory potential of archive material that can be infinitely reproduced, as for example in such works as Gerhard Richter's *Atlas* (1962–ongoing), or Hanne Darboven's *Kulturgeschichte 1880–1980* (1980–1983), Pierce's archive highlights instead its attachment to its place of display, suggesting a curtailing or even circumscribing of the archive's scope.

2. Pierce also showed the same archive in de Appel, Amsterdam (2008), and FOUR, Dublin (2008), with the infrastructure each time coming from the host institution.

Other touchstones in *Nought to Sixty* included the figurative and the body, and the implication of the human limits of an infinite horizon of delegated authority or Web-like iterability. Bodily limitation was the explicit subject of Alastair MacKinven's work, which complemented paintings based on MC Escher's 'endless staircase' etching with guardrails that help the elderly climb stairs. Tris Vonna-Michell sited performances (for audiences of two) in the projection booth of one of the ICA's cinemas, replacing the notion of the reproducible, public filmic illusion with the artist's unique, intimately delivered narratives. James Richards similarly effected a transfer from a publicly available to a privately devotional experience. His *Active Negative Programme* (2008) was exhibited in the gallery space and took the form of a video essay, comprised of clips culled from a diverse range of public and personal sources and assembled according to a private logic – as if, as curator Richard Birkett has suggested, the video were a mix tape.

Like Richards, many of the artists utilised archival or curatorial formats to form portraits of others through their outward effects – trading an evocation of subjectivity for the documentation of objectivity, in a manner reminiscent of French *nouveaux romanciers* such as Georges Perec or Alain Robbe-Grillet, who similarly sketched characters through their external attributes. This strategy resulted in an array of minor archives spread through the season, operating as sites of collective memory and active recuperation. Ruth Ewan, for example, has frequently dealt with the histories and representation of protest movements, in a practice that mines the notion of contingency – events that might or might not have happened, or which did not contribute causally to the configuration of the 'present'. Her piece for *Nought to Sixty* located this contingency in Fang, an eccentric London artist, activist and folk singer. In the free CD and booklet *Fang Sang* (2008), Ewan assembled recordings of songs Fang remembers from his childhood or has learned along the way, presenting this repertoire as a portrait of a man whose exploits might otherwise have fallen through the cracks of conventional history.

Ewan's *Fang Sang* uses its institutional platform as a way of operating in the world: retrieving these songs (folk or protest songs that might easily be lost) and returning them to circulation – in a follow-up project Fang reunited with members of a folk group that he used to perform with, singing at an open mic night in North London. A similar spirit of recuperation was visible in the work of the Open Music Archive, led by Eileen Simpson and Ben White, which sources and digitises copyright-free recordings – blues, jazz, music hall – and posts them on their website for download. For *Nought to Sixty*, the Open Music Archive put together a night where different musicians and DJs covered material from their archive, performing these rare songs for the ICA audience. Alun Rowlands, meanwhile, produced *Communiqué § 4* (2008), a pamphlet that documented the little-known 1970s London anarchist-socialist group The Angry Brigade, and distributed it free via the ICA and its website.

The shift towards the minor or contingent was mirrored in other projects, which evidenced a wish to share agency with the audience and collaborators, and to emphasise the role of personal resonance or relationships in the execution of a work. What emerged was the desire of the artist to remain immanent within the field sketched out by the artwork, participating within it rather than directing it from the outside. One example was Juliette Blightman's *Please water the plant and feed the fish* (2008), for which the artist set a fishbowl and a plant by a window in the gallery, and asked her brother Charlie to execute the work's title every day at 3pm. The latter is a significant hour in Blightman's practice, which she has used as the starting point of a number of film works – it is the hour, she says, when nothing happens.

Mike Cooter's installation was based on a chance sighting of a statue of the Maltese Falcon – an object likewise significant to his practice, one that he has based a previous work on – in the background of a television interview. The resultant work included a series of letters exchanged with the film's interviewee, the former US Supreme Court nominee Robert Bork, which attempted to coax the latter into offering his own opinion of the Maltese Falcon. Alexander Heim, whose work was shown during the same week as Cooter's, has used found objects that are accidental by-products of the urban landscape – clipped-off car wing mirrors, cracks in the pavement – elevating them to a high-art status. His exhibition included a video titled *Three Seasons* (2007), a modernised pastoral which looked for patterns in social behaviour: the change in the seasons illustrated, for example, by shifting levels of gym attendance. Ben Rivers, whose work includes film portraits of recluses and those living outside the mainstream, used the work of others to present his own concerns: his screening programme included a selection of films made by artists who, like him, explore different approaches to ethnographic filmmaking.

This emphasis on the archive as strategy, and on the activity of others (itself sometimes archivally presented), allowed curious features to emerge. As in the *nouveaux romanciers*, many projects in *Nought to Sixty* created portraits or characters through objective attributes, communicating personal likes and dislikes – songs, films, work – through objective effects in the public domain. Moreover, it was not only portraits of collaborators that appeared, but self-portraits of the artists – with figures such as Richards, Cooter and Rivers becoming a focus within their own work. And just as these pieces countered notions of universalism through their use of specific or personal ties, so they also suggested the artist's own lived experience – 3pm boredom, TV scanning, people watching – as reflected in shared concerns.

Stephen Sutcliffe's work, based on his own archive of recorded television and film footage, explored the relationship – intimated throughout *Nought to Sixty* – between personal and institutional authority. Sutcliffe excerpted TV images of actors from the 1970s and 80s, looping their short speeches on four monitors facing one another in the gallery. The arrangement of the monitors was intended to disconcert the encircled viewer, with each actor appearing on screen one at a time in random order. Sutcliffe has said about this era:

> This period is fascinating, as the protagonists represent a time when speaking as a figure of authority was still acceptable (Ian McKellan is presenting a Royal Shakespeare Company master class) without that much negotiation with the audience. This isn't to say that I am criticising this approach (in some respects I quite miss it); it is just that I can't help feeling that even during this period the artist must have been struggling with doubt but, as an authority, had a greater need not to make this visible – making the dichotomy, for my purposes, more intense.[3]

3. Email to the author, 2 December 2008.

The authoritative declaration 'this is how it is' became, throughout the *Nought to Sixty* projects, qualified by the dispersion of authority, and the branching of possibilities, between the artists, their collaborators and the visitors. It is as if the audience assumes control of the master class and promptly gets into an argument about what they will do next. Juliette Blightman's brother, perhaps, is held up in traffic and waters the plants at a quarter past three. Robert Bork decides he'd rather not participate in a Conceptual artwork and ends communication. Fang reunites with his band mates, but then decides he wants to sing alone. In this level playing field (almost utopian in character), disruption makes constant appearances: a single act creates scenarios of ever greater complexity; risking, or even courting, anarchy (the definitive condition of equally distributed power).[4] What is interesting about Sutcliffe's piece is his probing of exactly this scenario. He explores the shift between McKellan's institutional authority and a more voguish 'negotiation' with an audience, while also undercutting the latter – since the installation ultimately obstructs viewer participation and actively seeks to unsettle the visitor.

4. Artur Zmijewski's *Them* (2007), a key work in this participatory vein, would be another example.

Nought to Sixty's aim was partly retrospective, marking sixty years of the ICA by emphasising its roots as a centre for young artists. It was, in many ways, the reluctant embodiment of McKellan's authoritative stance, in its institutionalising function. This point was made in a number of the commissioned essays, as well as by David Osbaldeston's series of past ICA invitation cards rendered as etchings, marking the history of the ICA by revealing its 'young artists' as now established names. A few works took the form of an institutional inventory, though direct reflection on the ICA was, interestingly, largely bypassed by the artists' projects for a more abstract analysis of dispersed authority. Matthew Darbyshire's installation in the ICA's foyers and public spaces offered a veiled critique of its host: suggesting equivalences between the art centre and such apparently divergent organisations as estate agents and nurseries, based on their shared design values.

A number of sculptural works and videos looked at the relationship between the style and status of an object: the question of being able to 'recognise' an artwork simply through its appearance or framing. Modernist formalism, for example, was portrayed as a historically specific design language to be both represented and deployed. Giles Round set two scruffy chairs in front of an elegant formalist sculpture, framing the work as something 'to be looked at', or the passive object of a gaze. The Hut Project, a collective comprised of three artists, curated their own output, installing previous works of art (made both as a collective and individually) in a project entitled *Old Kunst* (2008). The title could be read as a reference to Germany's hegemony in post-War art, while the assembly of works tracked The Hut Project's own emergence as if they were already the canonised and traded subjects of Hans Haacke's provenance examinations.

In Ursula Mayer's exhibited film, *The Crystal Gaze* (2007), attractive women circle around an art deco interior, while the camera treats both people and objects with aloof attention – a reversal signalled in Mayer's title, which locates reification both in the gaze and its object. Jesse Jones's *Spectre and the*

Sphere (2008), meanwhile, depicts a luxurious theatre in Ghent, over which a soundtrack whispers the opening lines of Marx's *Communist Manifesto*: Marxism is reduced to a formless seductive whisper, a phenomenon that exists only as 'spectre' (in a play on the title of Derrida's *Spectres of Marx*, 1994), but one which haunts the art world (torn as the latter is between luxury commodification and radical critique). This tethering of art to visibility forcefully countered the relational and aleatory thrust of other *Nought to Sixty* projects. These projects were ocular rather than participatory, but always concerned with their subject, the knowing contemporary art spectator.

Art, particularly in this highly self-conscious mode, was thus figured as one end of a pairing – with Sutcliffe's audience and authority at the other end. A large number of the *Nought to Sixty* projects, whether in a mode of participation or exhibition, chose to activate the audience or, viewed differently, were motivated by curiosity about the audience and the impulse to identify them. Who are these different groups who comprise the art world? The curation of *Nought to Sixty* implied a mapping of the art world, with emphasis both on the different nodes of production and on the links between them.

I have argued that mapping is something that a number of the works do themselves – that is, position themselves within a chartable field – and though not all the works fit into this model, the general placement of artwork on a flat plane with 'living reality' suggests a move among young artists to replace allegorical frameworks with concretist ones, restricting the work's purview to a portion of the actual that can be vouched for by the artist. In the kind of delegated authorship by and large seen here, connections are transparent, and where the message is deferred it leaves a traceable path. In such a way *Nought to Sixty* moved away from the idea of the faceless public, and investigated different possibilities for community: not of individuals formed into a single thing, or even holding something in common; but of an audience found in a sense of recognition, and in specific terms, and that was invited to realise and expand the possibilities of the artworks on display.

Nought to Sixty in pictures

1
Nina Canell and Robin Watkins

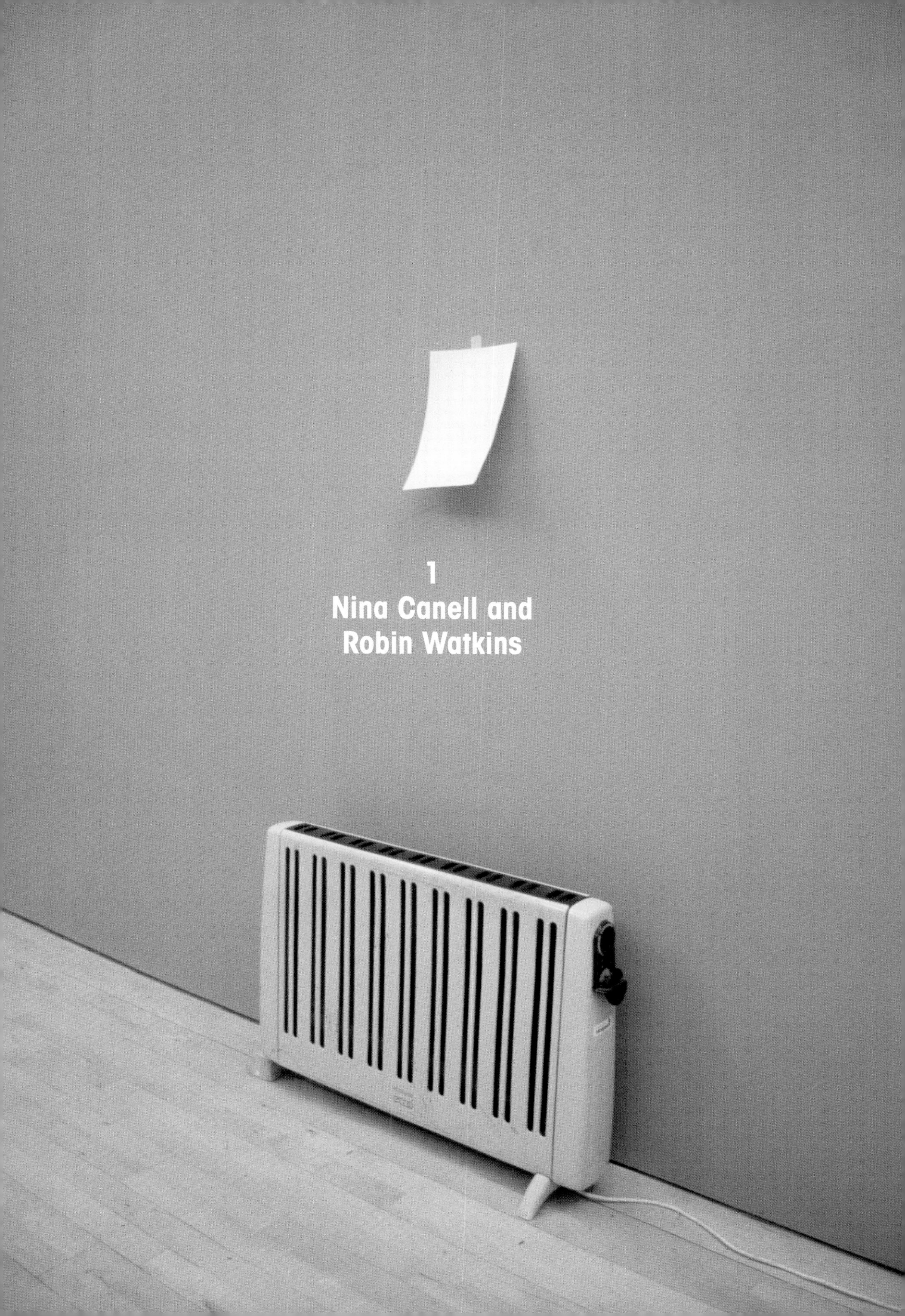

2
Babak Ghazi

3
Matthew Darbyshire

4
Hardcore Is More Than Music

5
Kim Coleman and Jenny Hogarth

6
Aileen Campbell

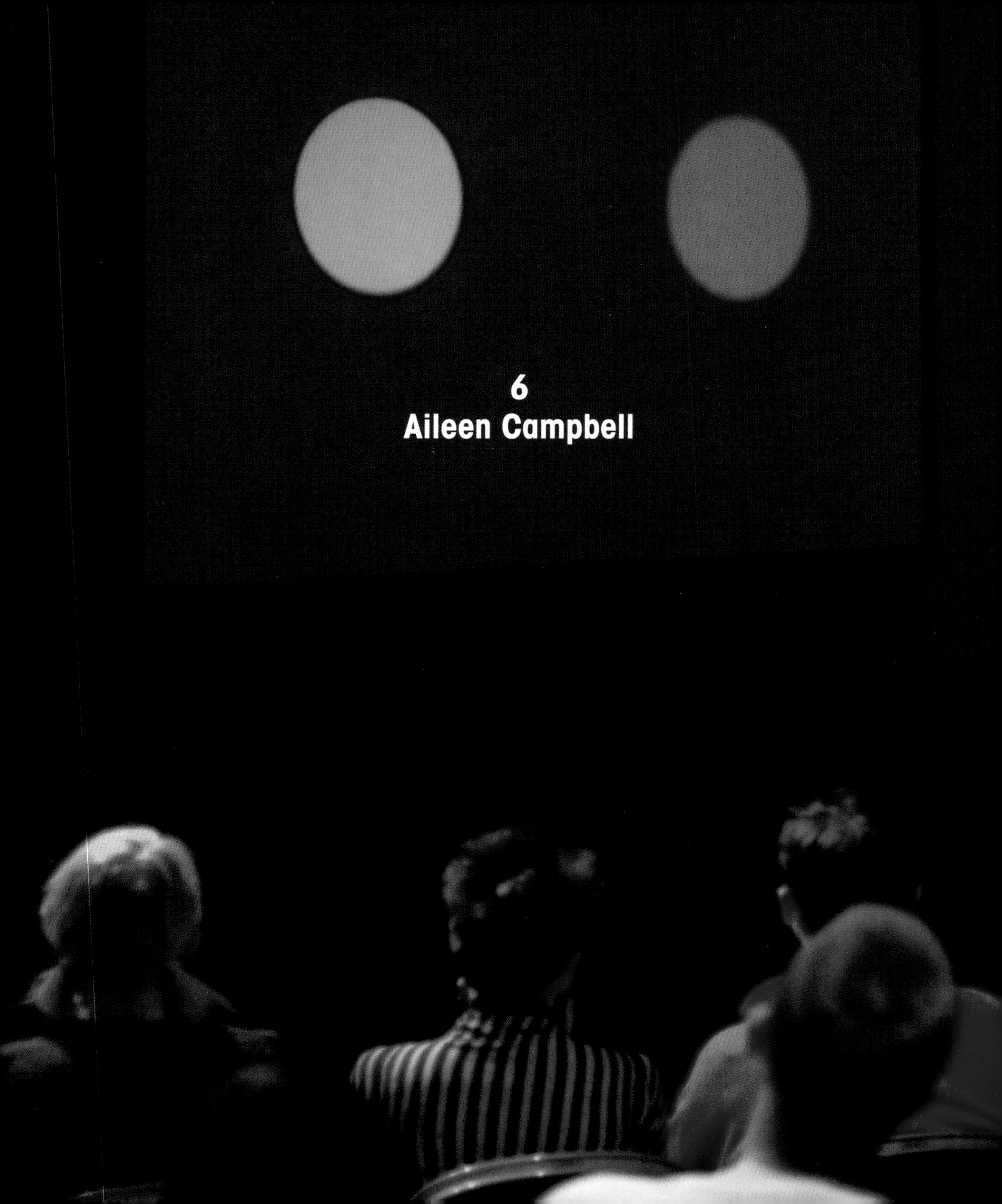

7

Seamus Harahan

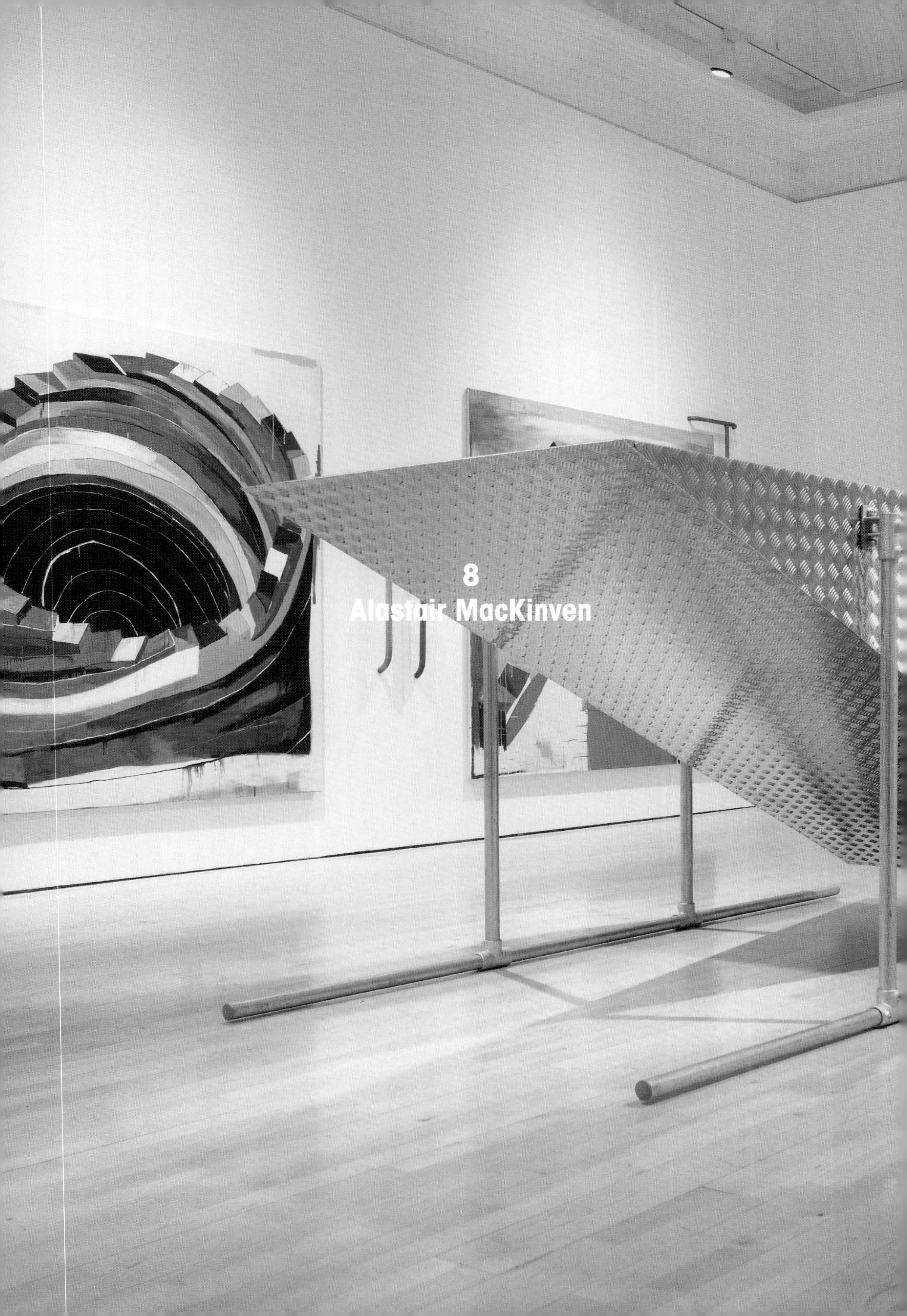

8
Alastair MacKinven

9
Freee

10
‘Independent publishing and critical discourse’

With Matthew Arnatt, Melissa Gronlund, Daniel Jewesbury, Pablo Lafuente, Olivia Plender

11
Guestroom

12
Anja Kirschner and David Panos

13
Clunie Reid

14
Jesse Jones

15
Emma Hart and Benedict Drew

16
Mike Cooter

17
Alexander Heim

18
Juliette Blightman

19
Andrea Büttner

A stone Schwitters painted in the Lake District

20
Thomas Kratz

21
'Independent spaces and emerging forms of connectivity'

Devised by Anna Colin, chaired by Alessio Antoniolli, with Francesco Pedraglio and Pieternel Vermoortel, Emily Pethick, Alex Sainsbury, Joe Scotland and Sarah McCrory, Maria Zahle and Jason Dungan

22
Redmond Entwistle

23
Andrew Hunt

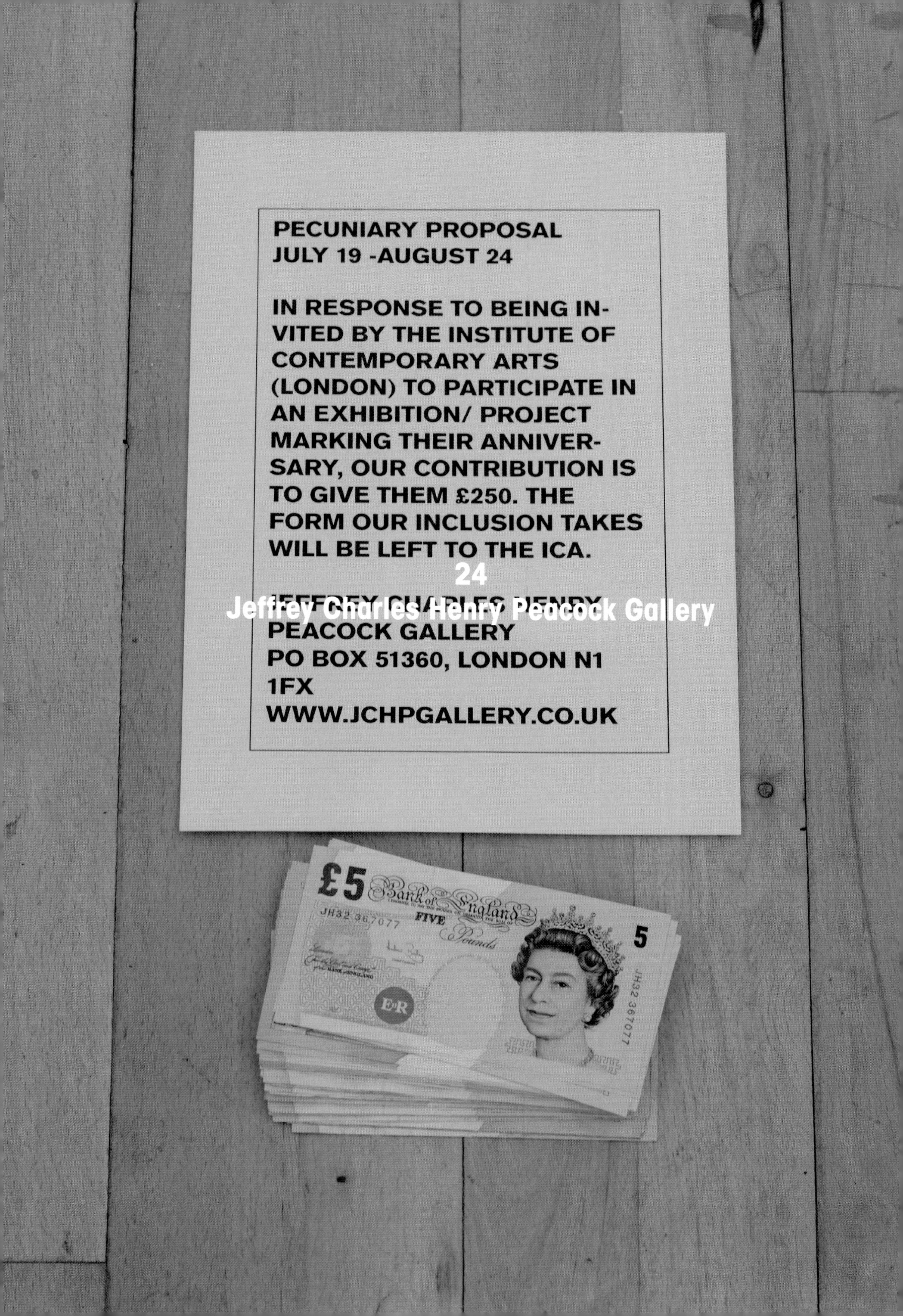
PECUNIARY PROPOSAL
JULY 19 -AUGUST 24
IN RESPONSE TO BEING INVITED BY THE INSTITUTE OF CONTEMPORARY ARTS (LONDON) TO PARTICIPATE IN AN EXHIBITION/ PROJECT MARKING THEIR ANNIVERSARY, OUR CONTRIBUTION IS TO GIVE THEM £250. THE FORM OUR INCLUSION TAKES WILL BE LEFT TO THE ICA.
PEACOCK GALLERY
PO BOX 51360, LONDON N1 1FX
WWW.JCHPGALLERY.CO.UK
£5
Bank of England
FIVE
Pounds
5
JH32 367077

24
Jeffrey Charles Henry Peacock Gallery

25
Nina Beier and Marie Lund

26
Andy Wake

27
Sean Edwards

28
The Hut Project

29
Will Holder

30

Hannah Rickards

He was trying to sp

of painting air.

31
'You talkin' to me? Why art is turning to education'

Organised by Dr Paul O'Neill and Mick Wilson, with Dave Beech, Liam Gillick, Dr Andrea Phillips, Sarah Pierce, Professor Adrian Rifkin

32
Iain Hetherington

33

James Richards

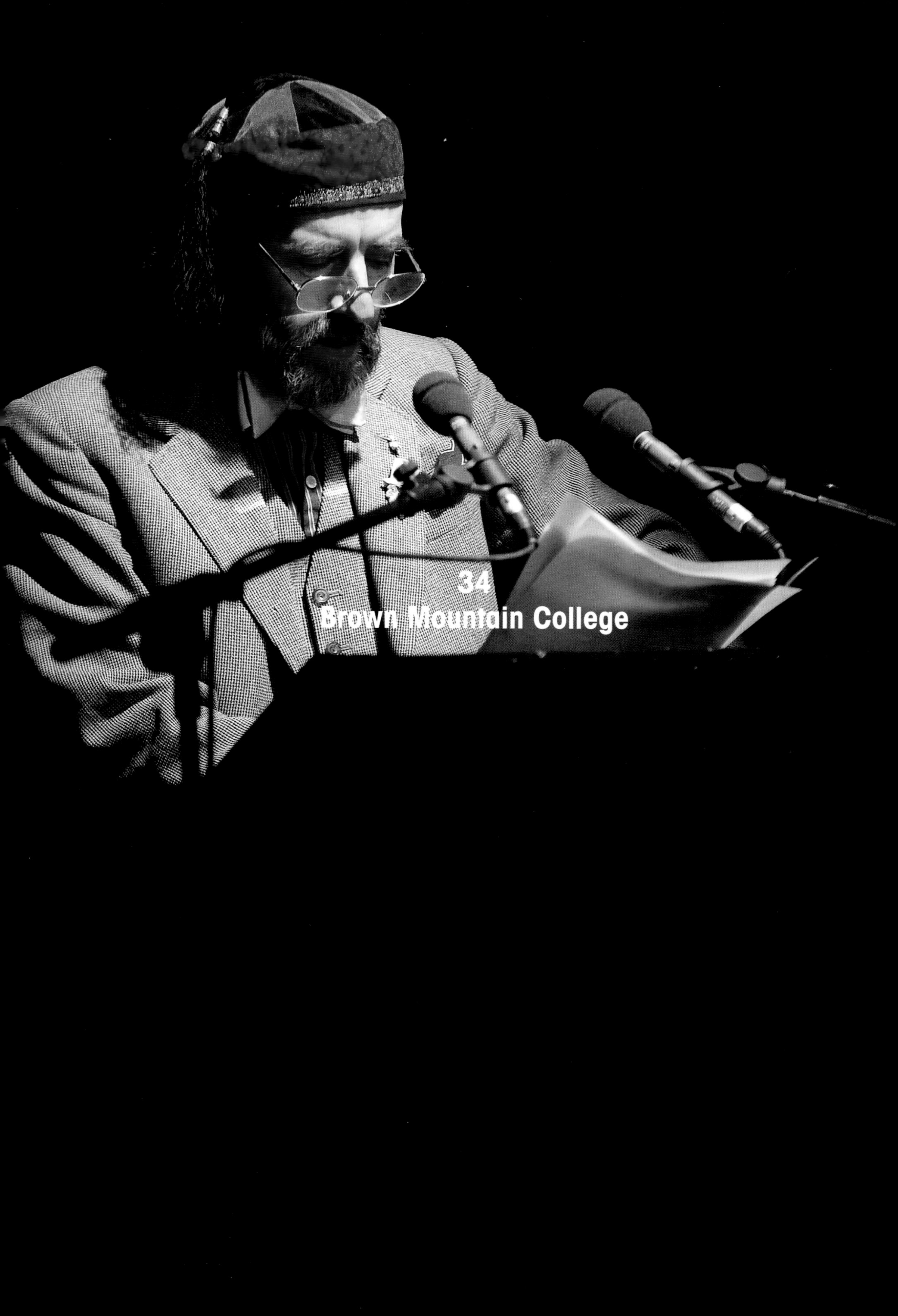

34

Brown Mountain College

35
Tris Vonna-Michell

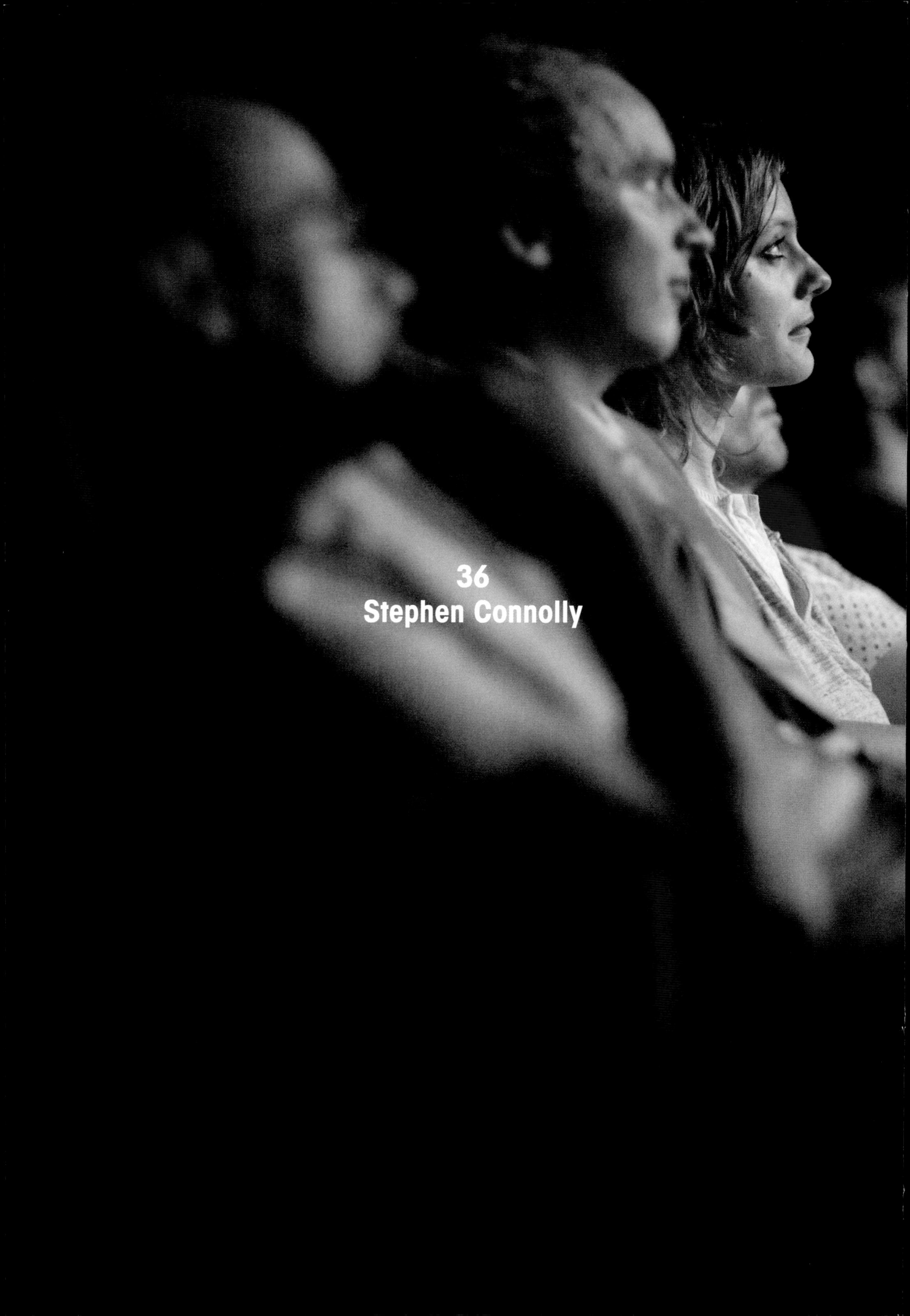

36
Stephen Connolly

37
Lorna Macintyre

38
Ursula Mayer

39
'Salon of salons'

Chaired by Miss B,
with Sebastian Craig, Russell Martin, Bettina Pousttchi, Jen Thatcher

40
Junior Aspirin Records

41
Sarah Pierce

42
Giles Round

43
Ben Rivers

44
Maria Fusco

45
David Osbaldeston

46

Stephen Sutcliffe

47
Ruth Ewan

48

Garrett Phelan

49
Open Music Archive

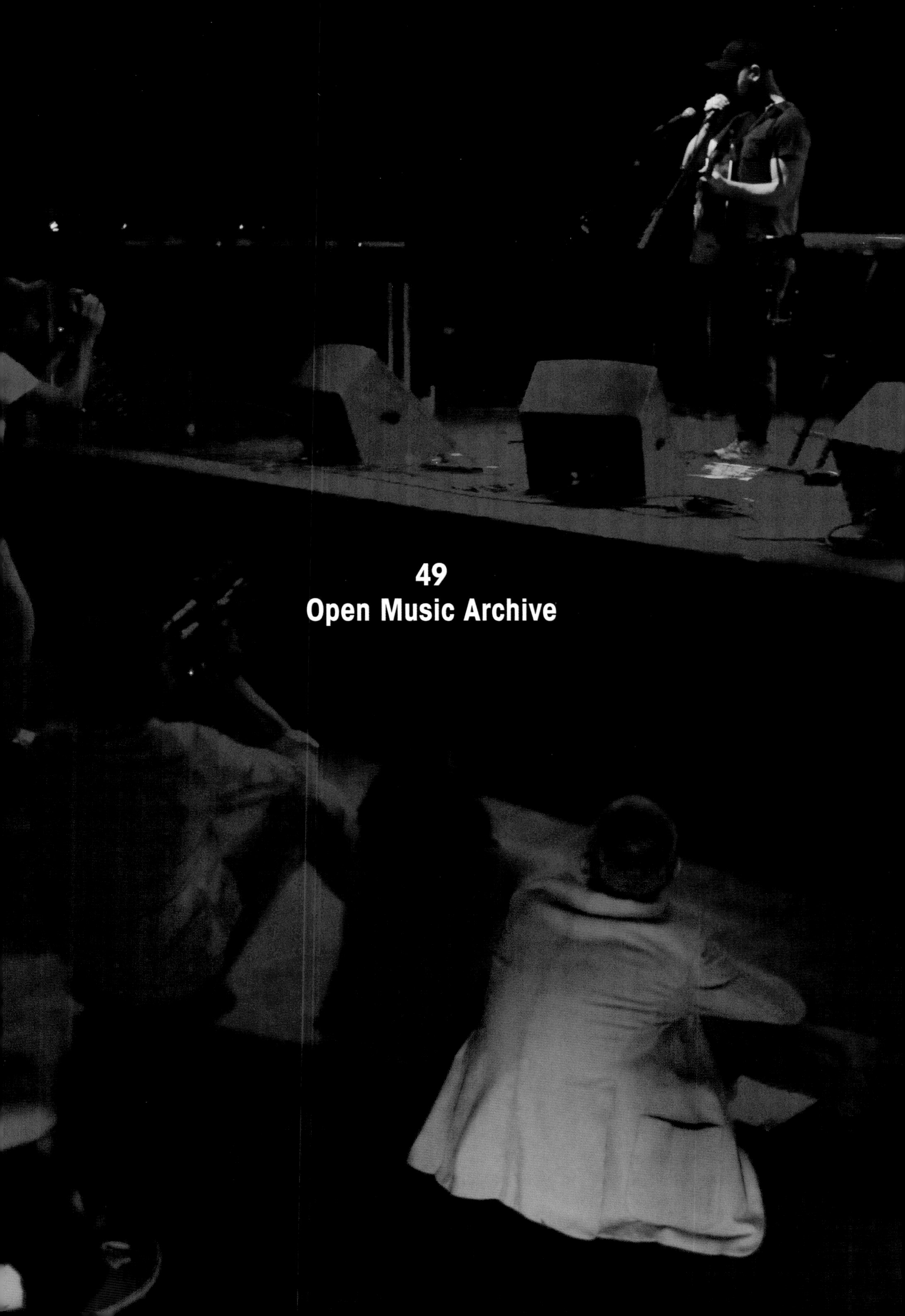

50
'Contemporary art, music and fashion'

With Francesca Gavin, Craig McCarthy, Nina Manandhar, Christabel Stewart, Matthew Stone

51
Alun Rowlands

52
Matthew Noel-Tod

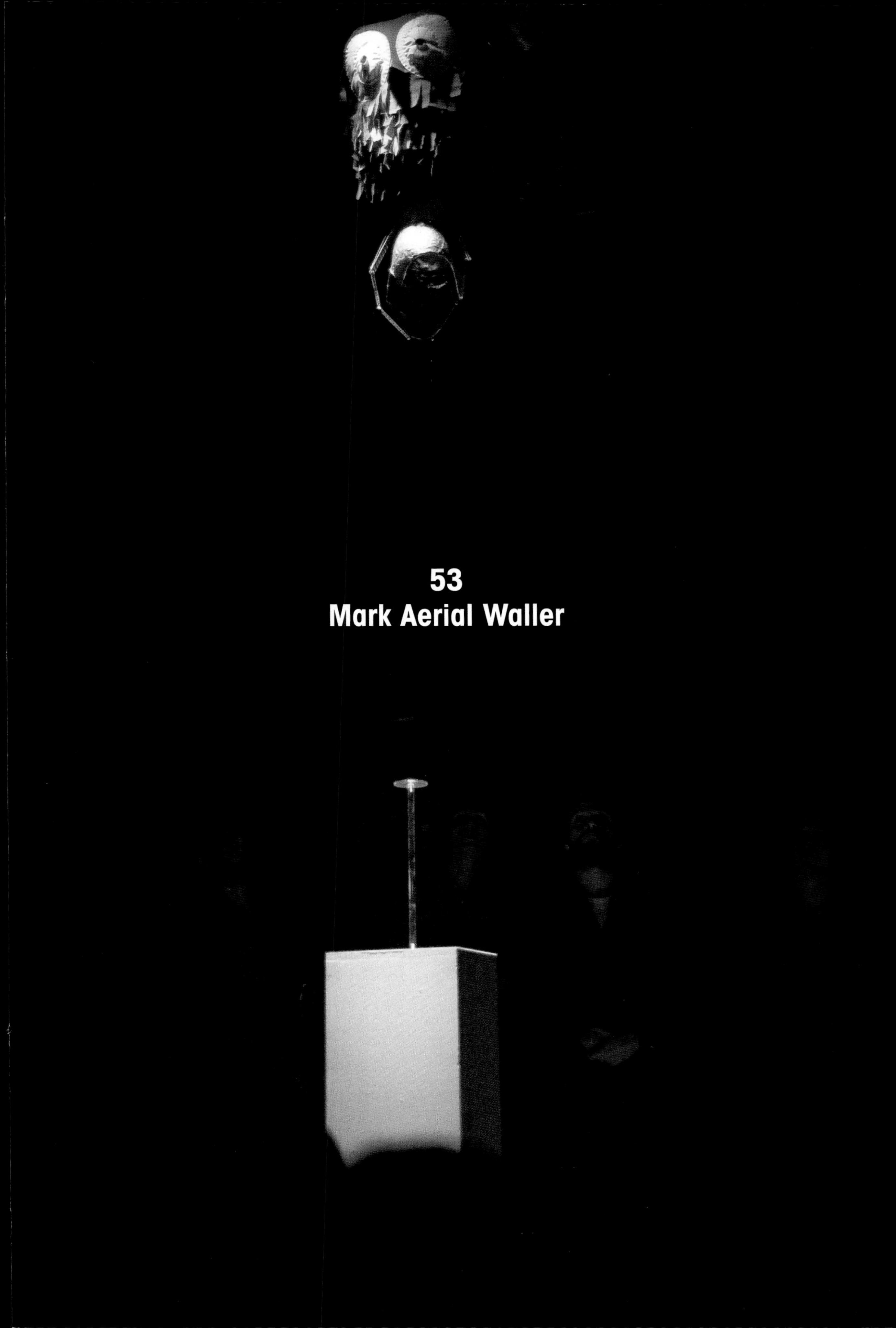

53
Mark Aerial Waller

54
Torsten Lauschmann

55 Gail Pickering

56
Duncan Campbell

57
Fiona Jardine

58
Macroprosopus Dancehall Band / ELECTRA

59
'Feminism is on the agenda'

With Kathrin Böhm, Toby Carr, Amy Feneck, Torange Khonsari, Nathalie Magnan, Ruth Morrow, Doina Petrescu, Jane Rendell, Rebecca Ross, taking place collective, Jeremy Till, Maria Walsh

60
Support Structure

1

Nina Canell and Robin Watkins

Exhibition, 5–12 May 2008
ICA Upper Galleries

Nina Canell (born Växjö, Sweden, 1979, lives in Dublin) and Robin Watkins (born Stockholm, Sweden, 1980, lives in Dublin) are long-term collaborators. Canell creates sculpture in the most expanded sense, assemblages that fuse matter, light and sound to create surreal testing grounds. Working together, Canell and Watkins have previously realised several film works and musical recordings as well as numerous live performances and events. For *Nought to Sixty* the artists made a new gallery-specific installation, one which brought together a number of recent works to form a sculptural whole. The film work shown was *Digging a Hole* (2008), which portrays a man in his overalls digging in a bog. The sculptures included *A Meditation on Minerals and Bats* (2007), *Heat Sculpture* (2007) and *Score for Two Lungs* (2008).

Nina Canell and Robin Watkins / *Digging a Hole* / 2008

Nina Canell and Robin Watkins / *Heat Sculpture* / 2007

For her most recent solo exhibition, *Slight Heat of the Eyelid*, mother's tankstation, Dublin (2008), Canell created an installation of seven sculptures, independent yet complementary. The works seemed like elements in a periodic table that had been energetically shaken, leaving them re-ordered and re-charged. The title of the show goes some way to indicating the interests of the artist, who explores what Samuel Beckett called "all that inner space one never sees." In Beckett's *Molloy* (1955), the character 'C' decides one day to climb a hill rather than simply peer at it from afar, and moves from observed to physically-learned experience and on towards a third, more intuited realm. Similarly, the flickering sights and sounds of Canell and Watkins' ICA installation – the first solo presentation of their work in London – were best navigated by the incalculable, intuited or imagined.

One central characteristic of the works of Canell and Watkins is their use of unorthodox sculptural materials and combinations – including found debris as well as precise custom-fabricated objects. *Heat Sculpture* (2007), for example, comprises a leafless branch, trapped or cradled in the fingers of four neon lights, the whole composition tied together with cables. Another characteristic of the duo's work – and one which emphasises its extra-linguistic properties – is its use of music. In a recent interview Canell and Watkins said that, "in contrast to audio-art which foregrounds perceptual effects,

Nina Canell and Robin Watkins / *A Meditation on Minerals and Bats* / 2007

technological progression, and self-referentiality, [we are] interested in engaging with acoustic phenomena as a catalyst for collective imagination, the construction of a magical image [...]". Music, whether played live, pre-recorded or merely signified by the presence of instruments, is a key mechanism within their work, and always an agent of transformation.

Isobel Harbison

2 Babak Ghazi

Exhibition, 5–12 May 2008
ICA Upper Galleries

Babak Ghazi (born London, 1976, lives in London) is the mastermind of an irregularly published magazine called *Not Yet* – a title that hints at what his overall practice proposes: the idea of things existing in a temporal narrative that is available to him to re-order and re-present. Ghazi's practice draws on notions of appropriation and history; he dips back and reframes past works of art and cultural imagery, presenting them as new, unfamiliar and changed – or simply suddenly remembered – in the present.

For a work shown in 2007 at the Chelsea Space of the Chelsea College of Art and Design (where Ghazi teaches), the artist bought a 1975 issue of *Data Arte* magazine that had been missing from the school's library, put it on display and donated it to the institution after the exhibition was finished, literally recuperating the contents of the publication. The 1970s and 80s are key to his practice: for other works he has mined photo spreads, album covers and 'designer' objects from these periods, including Perspex cubes and glam-dripping sunglass advertisements.

Ghazi's work owes a great deal to Pop Art and the latter's inclusion of popular material as both affirmation and critique; like that movement's best-known star, Andy Warhol, he also pushes such material close to abstraction. A series of altered images of David Bowie, entitled *ShapeShifter* (2004), depicts the singer with his face swollen and stretched as if in a funhouse mirror. Another series, *Untitled* (2004), overlays a magazine photo of sunglasses with kaleidoscopelike fragments of broken CDs. Finally, in the work shown at the ICA, *Model* (2008), Ghazi pays homage to Warhol's exceptional series of paintings, *Shadows* (1978). Warhol's paintings are made from silk-screened images of shadows, used in both negative and positive form, and perhaps surprisingly summon up the Abstract Expressionist style that he had earlier helped to displace. Ghazi's work, in turn, employs an image of a model wearing a Katherine Hamnett slogan T-shirt from a 1984 issue of *Vogue* – a pouty image very much of its time – and reproduces it in a number of negative and solarised versions, hung around the room in a manner which mimics the serial installation of the Warhol original.

Ghazi's *Model* evokes Pop, abstraction and the will towards trauma within Warholian repetition – as well as both 1978 and 1984, and the present moment of encounter with the 'digitised' image. In creating a new inventory made by accumulation and repetition, it frames the strident projection of identity contained within the dated magazine image. And in the gap between Warhol and himself Ghazi invokes the shifting territory of selfhood, and the borderline areas of public imagery that are at once superficial and politicised.

Melissa Gronlund

Babak Ghazi / from the series *Model* / 2008

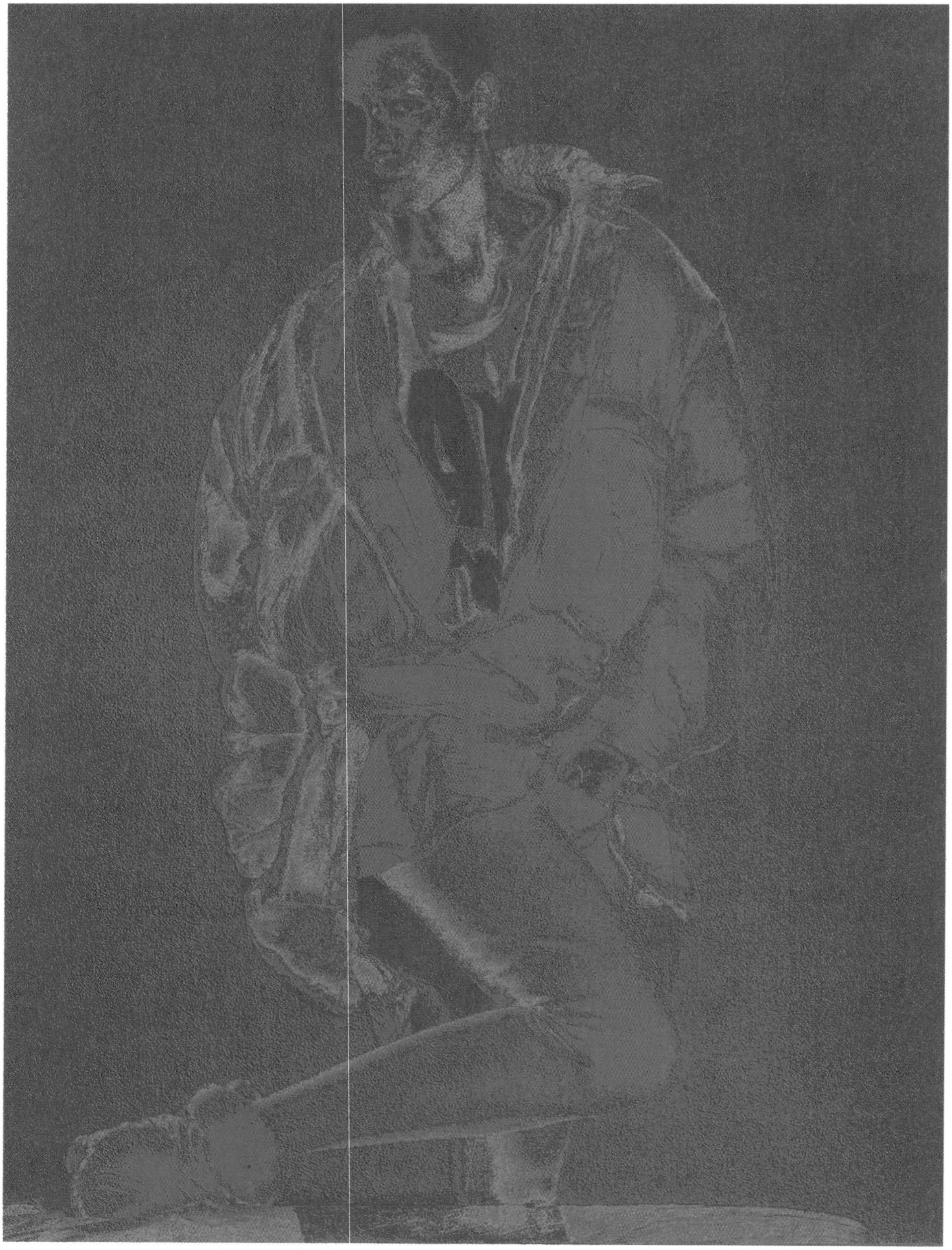

Babak Ghazi / from the series *Model* / 2008

3 **Matthew Darbyshire**

Architectural interventions,
May–September 2008
ICA public spaces

Matthew Darbyshire (born Cambridge, 1977, lives in London) lives in a bubble of deep turquoises, fuchsia pinks and acid yellows – he sees these colours everywhere and so, he points out, do you. Darbyshire is interested in the non-specificity of today's design language: the fact that bright CMYK dots are the logo for an estate agent and a cinema, as well as a NHS walk-in centre; that Arne Jacobsen egg chairs can be found in London's Zetter boutique hotel as well as in recently rebranded McDonald's restaurants. For *Nought to Sixty* his work was not in the ICA gallery spaces but in the publicly available, non-art spaces that are open to being branded, advertised in or hired for functions; as his ICA project these spaces were given the coloured lighting schemes of other public, retail and corporate spaces from across London.

The ICA's windows looking out onto the Mall were illuminated in different colours each month. In May, for instance, they mimicked the yellow lighting of the façade of Selfridges (a department store that has itself used the feminist artist Barbara Kruger's trademark black, white-and-red posters for its advertising campaign; co-opting work that was originally critical of consumerism).

A magenta light strip on the ceiling over the ICA ticketing area alluded to the lighting in the entrance to the Hackney Community College – a far cry from Selfridges, but an organisation that has chosen to express its identity in the same visual vocabulary. A green cast on the desk of the box office evoked the green in the lobby of the British Petroleum headquarters.

One of the most interesting issues raised by Darbyshire's practice is the polymorphous role of the art institution. Whilst Selfridges, Hackney Community College and BP have little in common, one can imagine links between the ICA and each of

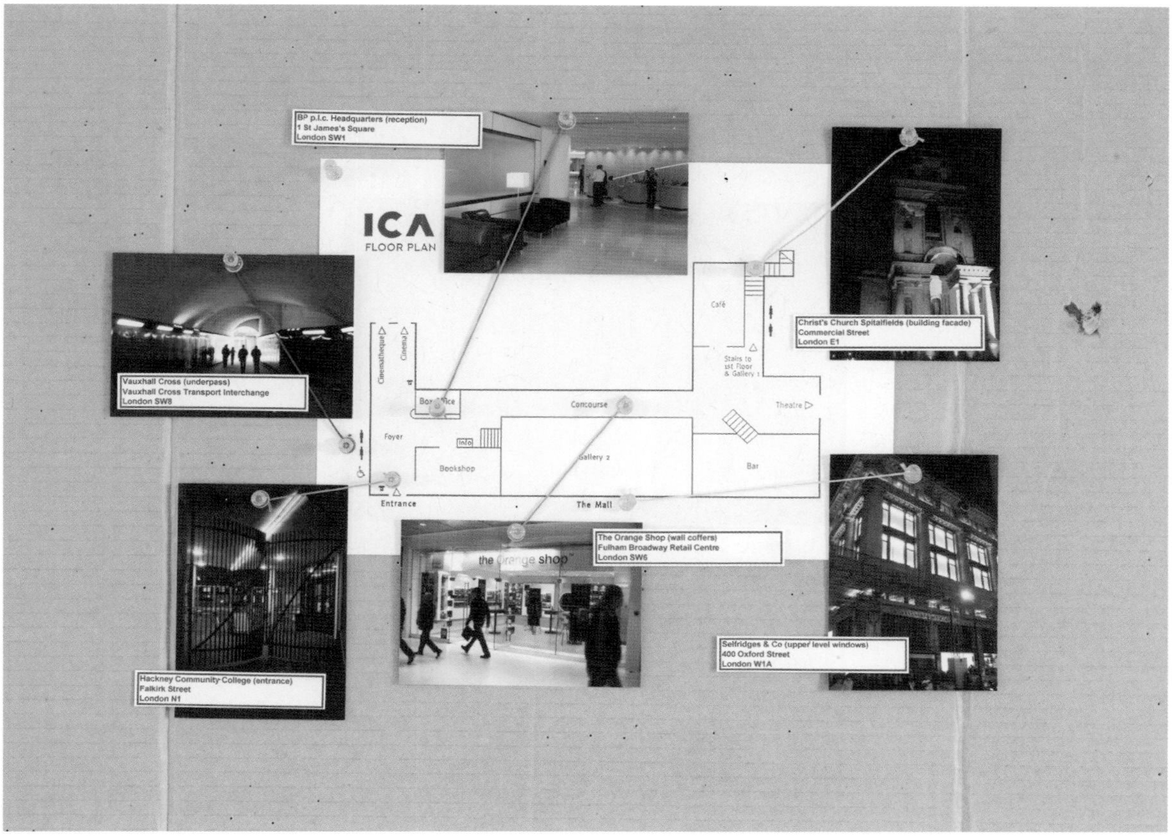

Matthew Darbyshire / Plan for the ICA / 2008

these, whether in terms of leisure activity, audience, education programmes or sponsorship. Perhaps most importantly, the ICA was able to utilise the design language of CMYK nonspecificity while also to critique its ubiquitous presence.

In Darbyshire's recent solo show at Gasworks, a non-profit space in South London, the gallery was used to recreate one of the privatised council flats opposite the venue – the type of property that a young media professional might move into. Darbyshire decorated the transformed gallery fashionably, using a brightly coloured mélange of furniture and accessories – bought and borrowed from interior decoration stores ranging from George at Asda and Tesco Direct to Vitra and Fritz Hansen. The work employed the aspirational aesthetic of this imagined resident but pushed it to satiric excess. In the same way that *Blades House* (2008) analysed contemporary design as well as Gasworks's own role in the process of gentrification, Darbyshire's *Nought to Sixty* work evoked the ICA's use of branding, but also asked the viewer to look outwards, towards the corporate realities of London.

Melissa Gronlund

Matthew Darbyshire / *Vauxhall Cross Underpass, Vauxhall Cross Transport Interchange, London SW8 / 2008*

Matthew Darbyshire / *BP p.l.c. Headquarters (reception), 1 St James's Square, London SW1 / 2008*

4

Hardcore Is More Than Music

Publishing project, May–November 2008
Off-site

Hardcore Is More Than Music is a banner under which artists Nendie Pinto-Duschinsky (born Oxford, 1980, lives in London) and Nina Manandhar (born London, 1981, lives in London) have grouped a series of varied and hybrid collaborative activities since 2002. Founded whilst the pair were students at Chelsea College of Art and Design, the project began with the production of an eponymous fanzine and has developed into what Manandhar and Pinto-Duschinsky describe as a 'social enterprise'.

The initial self-publication of three fanzines sought parallels between a personalised experience of art and the sub-cultures of musical genres such as hardcore punk, techno and grime. HIMTM used interviews, treatise and photography to explicitly develop a 'fan's' response to the creative energy associated with the social spaces of both art and music.

The production of these zines enabled Manandhar and Pinto-Duschinsky to draw connections between established cultural practioners and groups of teenagers whose opinions and activities HIMTM tapped into. Simultaneous to these publications they toured a series of participatory projects around schools and youth groups in London, culminating in a set of workshops at Stowe Youth Centre in Westbourne Green (*Best Body*, 2004), in which influential musicians and producers including Graham Massey (808 State) Jon E Cash (Black Ops) and Alasdair Roberts (Rough Trade) shared expertise with groups of local teenagers.

The subsequent incarnations of HIMTM as an increasingly professional magazine (including a supplement produced for *The Guardian*, and a publication produced with several youth groups over a day-long workshop at Tate Britain) have highlighted a fusion of artistic concerns with the principles of social enterprise. The twin tools of marketing and fundraising have enabled Manandhar and Pinto-Duschinsky not only to pursue and promote their own interests, but also to engage in collaborative activities outside a traditional cultural framework. The language of 'social exclusion' and urban demographics is at once the territory they manipulate and the site for a mode of creativity.

Left: poster for *The Cut* / 2008
Right: *The Cut* / issue 1 / March 2008

As part of *Nought to Sixty*, Hardcore is More Than Music developed a relationship between the ICA and a new newspaper project based at Stowe Youth Centre. This project focuses on providing training opportunities for unemployed and excluded young people in the Borough of Westminster, through the production of *The Cut*, a quarterly newspaper featuring the views and interests of this group. The first issue was launched in March 2008 at the ICA, and in October 2008 *The Cut* launched both a limited edition poster by Will Kay and the third edition of the magazine, which focused on the ICA and the community built around the *Nought to Sixty* programme.

Richard Birkett

5 Kim Coleman and Jenny Hogarth

Event, 12 May 2008
ICA Theatre

Kim Coleman (born Northern Ireland, 1976, lives in London) and Jenny Hogarth (born Glasgow, 1979, lives in Edinburgh) work collaboratively, placing a great deal of emphasis on the participatory and performative aspects of art practice. They describe their approach as a 'discussion about creativity and making art as well as a model of teamwork and friendship', and this dialogue has manifested itself both in their joint practice and in the development of numerous artist-led activities that have been central to the Edinburgh art scene for several years (including Embassy Gallery, founded in 2004). Previous collaborative performance works, including *Raiding the Icebox* at Talbot Rice Gallery, Edinburgh, 2005, and *Fools Mate* at Ross Bandstand, Edinburgh, 2007, have been characterised by a staged and spectacular quality while equally emphasising group participation. Their work often opens up the process of collaboration for dissection – monitoring the mechanisms by which it is produced. While this makes the process transparent, it also provides an overabundance of information and serves to obfuscate the outcome, the focus on the act of representation rendering the practice theatrical. This creates a tension between the spontaneous and the premeditated; a dialectic greatly inspired by the pioneering performance pieces of the Boyle Family, one of whose works was re-interpreted by Coleman and Hogarth as part of *Nought to Sixty*.

In the mid sixties the Scottish artists Mark Boyle and Joan Hills organised a number of important events and performances in London, including several at the ICA. These performances exemplified the emergent psychedelic liberalism of the period, most notably the infamous *Son et Lumiere for Bodily Fluids and Functions* (1967), wherein a couple who had not met before made love on stage whilst wired up to ECG and EEG monitors, their heart beats and brain patterns projected onto the screen above them. In 1965 the Boyles arranged *Oh What a Lovely Whore*, an event not carried out by the artists themselves, but orchestrated by guests invited to the ICA, who were presented with a series of props and invited to make their own happening happen. A DIY affair, it signified a paradigm shift that characterised

Both images: *Kim Coleman and Jenny Hogarth with Boyle Family* / 2008

the art of the sixties: the transferral of responsibility from the artist to the viewer.

The Boyles' happenings are scores that can be replayed and reinterpreted. The audience and its participation is paramount; it makes up each event anew. The happenings are, potentially at least, as much a part of the ICA's present as they are of its past, and this raises questions worth considering in relation to the re-staging that was conducted by Coleman and Hogarth. What happens when a happening happens amidst an audience armed with the hindsight and cynicism of today? Knowledge or experience of the origins of performance might have prevented openness to invitation, and the invitation to play certainly had different connotations. In the current climate – one dominated by the ideology of the artist as facilitator or cultural services provider – the scripting and directing process was more managerial than it once promised. Given this, was today's audience responding with the same degree of enthusiasm and autonomy as their mid sixties equivalent? If it was possible that the free-play and anarchistic spirit of the inaugural happening had been inhibited in these more self-conscious times, then it was just as likely to have proven to be a powder keg for a frustrated fraternity.

In the event, as soon as licence was given, there was no shortage of fervent interactivity. An art school band formed within seconds, making use of the new instruments provided. The piano was played then ceremonially smashed (much as it was the first time around). Drawings were drawn, sculptures sculpted, performances performed. Meanwhile the ICA security did their best to keep the audience healthy and safe by improvising their own arbitrary rules of play. A group of nudists were curtailed from frolicking around in the ball pool ('Pants Must Be Kept On At All Times'). Free alcoholic drinks, once taken out of the space, could not be taken back in again, thus spearheading a booze-induced exodus to the ICA bar. Such impromptu acts of prohibition, coupled with a small fire, helped put out the proceedings. What's certain, is that this was as effective an acid test of the current cultural climate as it was in the mid-sixties.

Neil Mulholland

6

Aileen Campbell

Event, 19 May 2008
ICA Nash/Brandon Rooms

The works of Aileen Campbell (born Greenock, 1968, lives in Glasgow) span performance, sound and video. Central to her practice across these modes of presentation is the human voice – both its live presence and its manipulation through documentation and structured film works.

Campbell is herself an experienced chorister, and her work demonstrates an investigation into the voice's connection to the body, and how this relationship is disrupted through training, experimentation and amplification. Whilst her works can refer to music, the processes of disconnection and manipulation that she uses create a more primordial sound – a sound which originates with the body and is intrinsically linked to its restrictions. Early live performances involved Campbell synchronising and combining her own vocal sounds with those of domestic appliances, such as a popcorn machine and a hairdryer. Performed on a podium, the theatrical manner of these experiments is often humorous, but also suggests a fundamental form of communication through mimicry.

The framing of Campbell's performances, and the importance of their subsequent presentation through video, is indicative of her position between visual art and experimental music. The artist is a member of the Glasgow Improvisers Orchestra, a band of musicians who pursue improvisational techniques via experiments in musical structures within large group contexts. Campbell draws links between her own musical practice and that of the pioneers of vocal techniques from the sixties, including Meredith Monk and Joan La Barbara. Whilst exploring similar territories of sound-making that ground the female voice, she also utilises the structures of performance to play with the visual expectations of an audience.

In her 2005 work *As Jane Edwards and Geoffrey Rush*, Campbell presents a performance that relates to a dramatic section of footage from the 1996 film *Shine*. The sequence shows the character of pianist David Helfgott bouncing on a trampoline whilst listening to a Vivaldi aria, and Campbell replicates this sequence live, herself

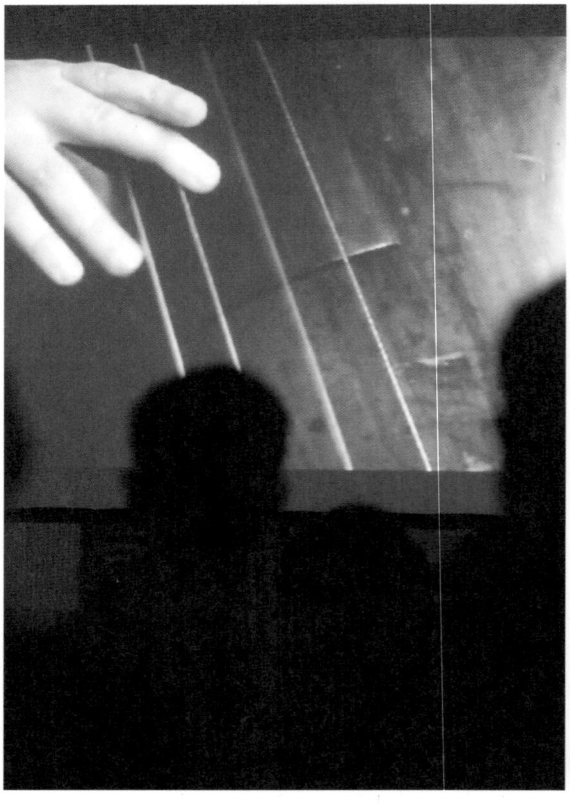

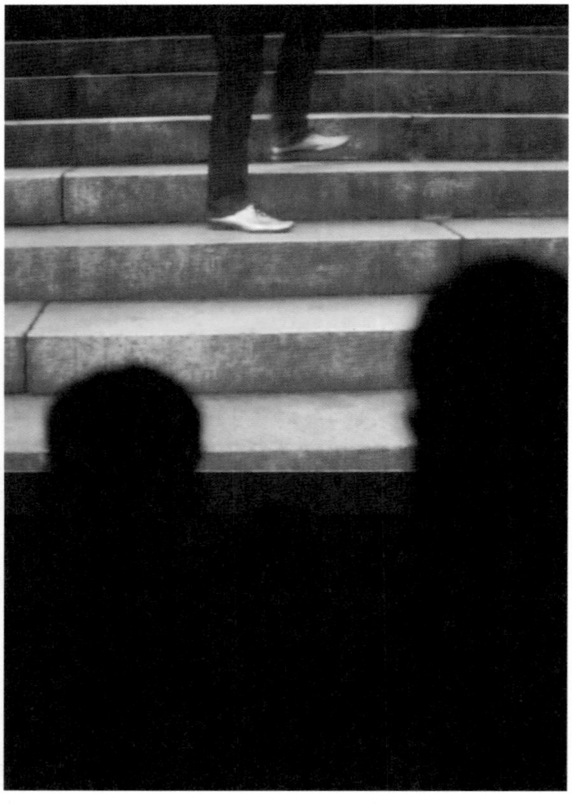

All images: Aileen Campbell / *In the manner of songs and drones* / 2008

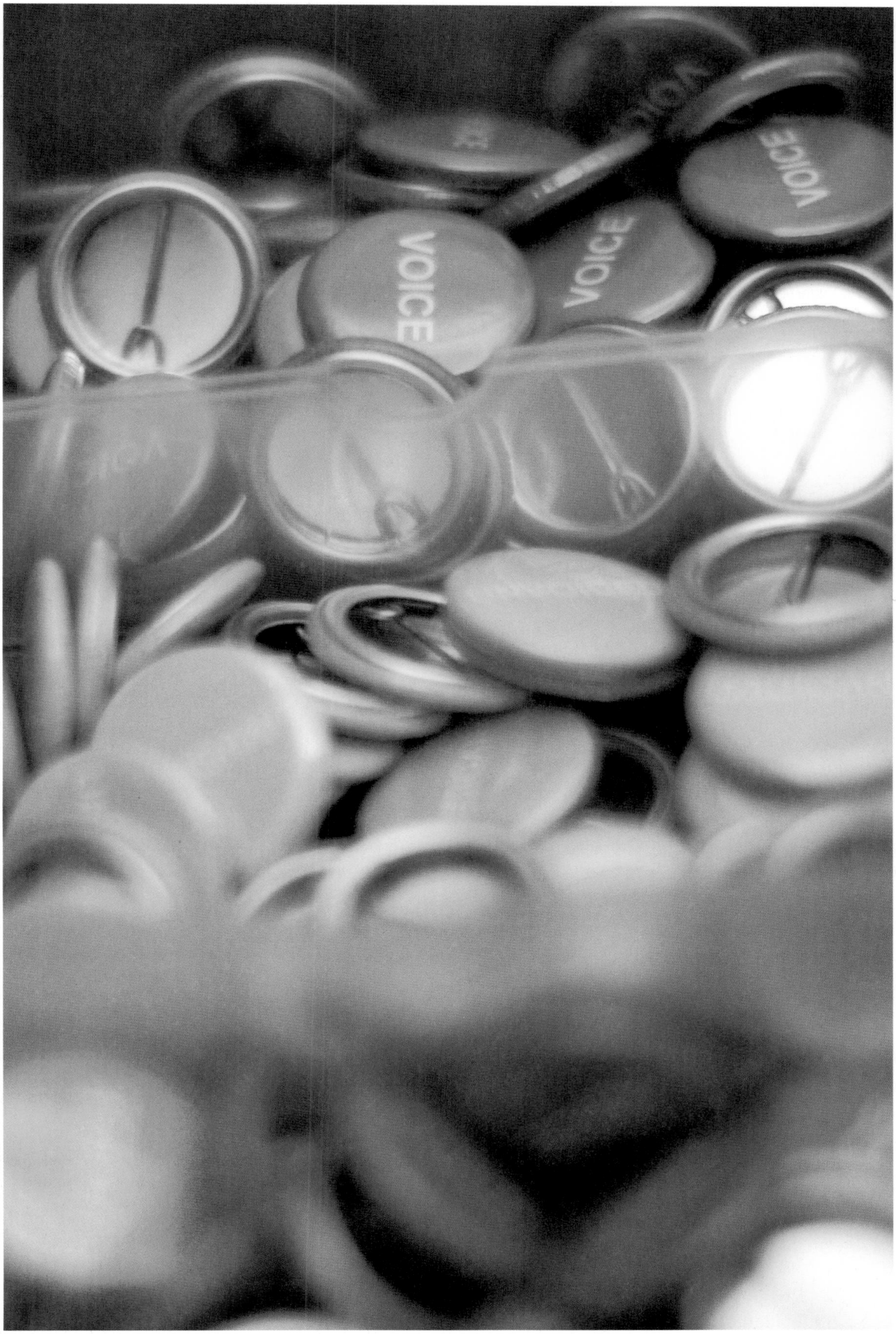
VOICE
VOICE
VOICE

bouncing on a trampoline whilst singing the soprano part. Accompanied by a string quartet, her feat both echoes the conventional arrangement of a classical recital and disturbs it through the absurd and drawn-out endurance exercise. The work plays on a perception of the female voice as transcendental, creating a version of the uplifting soundtrack that is re-formed around guttural and unmanageable bodily sounds.

Campbell's project for *Nought to Sixty,* entitled *In the manner of songs and drones* (2008), developed these concerns around the conventional parameters of a musical performance, and the awareness of physicality within it. Re-working an earlier piece entitled *Rehearsal Room* (2006), the work engaged an audience as a choral mechanism that created a live soundtrack. This element of group participation activated the role of the viewer, yet also reduced it to a common action. This commonality only achieved purpose through the eyes and ears of a second group in an adjoining room (the audience having been divided via the distribution of two sets of coloured badges), and created across the two different spaces a seemingly random noise performance and a simultaneous audio/visual accompaniment.

Richard Birkett

7 Seamus Harahan

Exhibition, 19–26 May 2008
ICA Upper Galleries

Seamus Harahan (born Belfast, 1968, lives in Belfast) uses his video camera – a relatively accessible and moderately affordable technology – to take hand-held, seemingly amateur footage, the contents of this footage locating Harahan through found activity occurring around him. The main subject is the urban environment, its incidental detail and fugitive nature. The light is often unfiltered and the image over-exposed, implying a mode of filmmaking that prioritises recording before thought, the absent-minded gaze.

Music is a vital element in all of Harahan's works, with songs used as soundtracks or informing the composition, title or duration of individual pieces. The artist takes songs from an eclectic range of sources, including reggae and hip-hop as well as traditional English and Irish music. The recording style can be equally telling, from scratchy track-intros (*Picking Up Change in the King Fu Theatre,* 2004) to a John Peel introduction to a live session track (*Free as a Bird*, 2006). These seemingly disparate musical sources are laid over Harahan's urban footage, often coming with references to war and conflict, including lyrics intending to motivate or comfort soldiers and freedom fighters. The marriage of such lyrics to footage of Belfast, but particularly to images that focus on the minutiae of found activity, strike a balance between a sense of political conflict and an intuitive response to individual human concerns.

In *Clonemen* (2004), a track by an American rap group accompanies footage of Northern Ireland's hinterlands, over which the British flag constantly reappears, a journey that detours along the M1 to Belfast. Avoiding dogmatic rhetorical devices, the artist manages to suggest not the eye of surveillance, but instead the viewpoint of a fascinated bystander – one whose environment is in a constant state of unravelling (a position echoed in the artist's choice of music). Harahan's work can be interpreted as an open and sophisticated exploration of the shortcomings of social and political representation in general, rather than a lament or protest concerning Northern Ireland in particular.

At the ICA Seamus Harahan presented a two-screen video installation entitled *Valley of Jehosephat / Version – In Your Mind* (2007). In this work the same footage is projected alternately on two adjoining walls, the two loops accompanied by different songs. One is a roots reggae track by Max Romeo from the late seventies – referring to a biblical valley of judgment. The other is Bryan Ferry's *In Your Mind* (1977), which suggests a philosophical quest for personal resolution. Both songs accompany the same footage of the Bloody Sunday commemoration in Derry, and Harahan's camera captures marchers, uniformed bandsmen, bystanders, commemorative banners, political murals and graffiti – as well as other cameras recording the event. The alternating soundtracks destabilise our reading of the work, which becomes almost meditative in quality.

Isobel Harbison

8

Alastair MacKinven

Exhibition, 19–26 May 2008
ICA Upper Galleries

Alastair MacKinven (born Clatterbridge, UK, 1971, lives in London) has an obsession with the body – its limits, idiosyncrasies and various behaviours. In his 8mm film *All the Things You Could Be By Now If Robert Smithson's Wife Was Your Mother* (2007) he transferred a pile of dirt from one area of a lawn to another, remaking the 1979 work *Star Crossed* by Nancy Holt (who was Robert Smithson's wife). MacKinven embedded a large pipe in the pile, undressed, then passed naked into the pipe and came out, wrapping himself in a silver blanket like a newborn child. Like the title, the work refers to conception, birth and supposed transformation; the artist's bare body becomes a base from which MacKinven questions art's myths, and in particular its associations with the transformative.

MacKinven's exhibition for *Nought to Sixty*, entitled *Et Sic In Infinitum Again*, employed the so-called 'Penrose stairs' – familiar from MC Escher's 1960 lithograph *Ascending and Descending* – which connect into each other in an impossible loop. MacKinven made a series of paintings of the stairs, and surrounded the canvases with the kind of handrails used to help the elderly and infirm. Installed incongruously in the gallery space, these handrails were perhaps guides to viewing: ridiculously corporeal aids for a supposedly intellectual activity.

In these and other projects MacKinven treats the body both as something mystical, to be revered in its complexity, and as something problematic, a site of antagonism that must be regulated either through pseudo-Conceptualist scientific discourse or by adolescent shock tactics. Both these strands are evident, for example, in a soft-focus photograph from 2006: the exoticism of the subject matter (it is an image appropriated from *National Geographic* of a naked girl getting out of the water) and the crudeness of its title *(Default Masturbatory Stimuli).*

Alastair MacKinven / Installation view of *Et Sick In Infinitum Again* / 2008

Similarly, for a recent performance at the Camden Arts Centre MacKinven glued his hand to the floor of one of the galleries. He then sat there waiting to see how long it would take until the institution's attendants offered him help – brought him a glass of water, for example – or tried to unglue him from the floor. This piece, which clearly plays with notions of institutional critique, was given a different spin in its title, *Cut Off My Hand to Spite My Cock* (2008), shifting the emphasis from a public investigation to a private act. Issues such as trust, vulnerability, violation and shame are all relevant to his practice – as they are to many canonical works of art and performance of the 1970s, works which MacKinven often references.

A series entitled *Critical Theory*, shown at the Art Basel fair in 2007, is constituted by a group of paintings in MacKinven's trademark grey palette. The paintings depict different star ratings: from one (poor) to five (excellent). He asked his gallerist to sell them at prices that accorded to the rating, so that a 'one star' painting would cost less than a 'five star' one. Throughout his practice MacKinven's base humour satirises the value systems of the art world, whilst wryly deflecting to a more corporeal practice of involuntary evaluation.

Melissa Gronlund

9

Freee

Billboard project, May–October 2008
ICA Bar and off-site

PROTEST DRIVES HISTORY

Freee is the collective title for London-based artists Dave Beech (born Warrington, 1965), Andy Hewitt (born Hull, 1966) and Mel Jordan (born London, 1966). Collaborating under various guises before beginning to work exclusively as Freee in 2004, Beech, Hewitt and Jordan draw on Jürgen Habermas' model of the public sphere – which looks towards creating space where debate can occur – and are interested in the various modes of public protest.

Freee uses a variety of media – postcards, t-shirts, online videos and billboards to name a few – and invest its chosen medium with polemical slogans and attitudes. While provocative titles and statements underpin the collective's practice – in works such as *The Concept of Public Space, Beloved of Lonely Myopic Law-abiding Right-on Gushing Morons, Can Only Imagine the Public as a Mass of Bodies* (2007) – these slogans plainly state Freee's political motivations with a directness that demands the observer take a critical position in response. Freee has also enlisted other figures in its productions. In one such instance the group approached comedian Norman Collier with a script consisting of a list of slogans, and asked Collier to perform the work in the style of his notorious 'broken microphone' routine – resulting in the short video *Have You Heard About the One About the Public Sphere* (2006).

Since 2004, Freee has been developing a series of billboard and poster works. In pieces such as *The Economic Function of Public Art is to Increase the Value of Private Property* (2004), and *The Neo-Imperialist Function of Public Art is to Clear a Path for Aggressive Economic Expansion* (2005), the group use the visibility of these billboard spaces to critical and often comic effect. The latter work was photographed in its original site, then fly-posted as a new image on another billboard. The process was then repeated, until the image was subsumed within the 'Droste Effect': becoming a billboard within a billboard within a billboard. The design of these billboards employs colours and fonts recommended by 'futures' research, studies which predict future trends.

Beech, Hewitt and Jordan have recently begun to appear in the billboard images, underscoring their collective presence as a means of intervention. And for *Nought To Sixty*, Freee designed a new work in this spirit entitled *Protest Drives History* (2008), which appeared on a wall of the ICA Bar and on a billboard in Hassard Street in Bethnal Green. Using a photograph taken in one of the UK's biggest quarries, the monumental scale of the environment belies the size of Freee's own five-metre-long banner depicting the title statement.

The seemingly simple nature of Freee's slogans, and their reproducibility, allows for a casual and repeated dissemination across various media and sites – from large billboards, to photographic documentation, to ephemeral postcards and magazines. Freee's strategies undermine the uniqueness of the original aesthetic encounter, dispersing the experience of the work across a number of formats, and promoting the message of the collective over the individual, while also retaining the conviction behind each message.

Isla Leaver-Yap

Freee / Protest Drives History / 2008

10

Independent publishing and critical discourse

Salon discussion, May 2008
ICA Nash Room

Participants:
Matthew Arnatt, co-director, Rachmaninoff's
Melissa Gronlund, associate editor *Afterall*
Daniel Jewesbury, artist and co-editor, *Variant*
Pablo Lafuente, managing editor, *Afterall*
Olivia Plender, artist and former editor of *Untitled*

Nought to Sixty was intended as a space where artists and artist-orientated organisations could discuss their work on their own terms, fostering a dialogue among themselves and with a broader public. The series of monthly salon discussions was central to the discursive element of the programme, seeking to address the networks that contribute to an emerging art scene, and edited transcripts of the six discussions are included in this book. The first was organised by the research and publishing organisation *Afterall*, and addressed current models of art publishing, and the role of criticism within them.

MELISSA GRONLUND: We're going to talk about what independent publishing might mean in London, as well as what critical discourse might be. Is it something to do with funding, leadership, art world credibility, or a particular aesthetic? Tonight's speakers include Daniel Jewesbury, who co-edits *Variant*, a free newspaper that looks at culture and cultural policy and tends to be very political. Olivia Plender makes artists books and was an editor of *Untitled*. She also runs Canal, a roving series of talks, exhibitions and film events to produce independent discourse but not necessarily through a text-based format. Matthew Arnatt co-runs Rachmaninoff's, a gallery and publishing house which is loathe to describe the books it creates except for ones that are in tune with their thinking at the time. Pablo Lafuente and I work at *Afterall*, a publishing and research organisation based at Central Saint Martins College of Art and Design. We do small, pocket-sized books and we also publish a journal, which looks at artists in contextual or theoretical essays.

PABLO LAFUENTE: *Afterall* has been publishing a journal of contemporary art since 1998. I've been there for three years. The original remit was to look at art practice that was considered relevant to socio-political and contextual issues, as well as art issues that seem to be playing an important role at that particular moment. The journal initially had five artist profiles and two essays on each. When I came in, we discussed different kinds of writing and whether writing from the perspective of the artist as the individual producer was enough when the market was skyrocketing.

There was concern at seeing the journal on the table at galleries, at art fairs, and a worry about the journal being seen as a marketing tool. We thought of not eliminating the ways of seeing the artist as the producer, but looking at different formats. We came up with *One Works*, a series of books in which we talk about art from the perspective of an artwork. The books deal with an artwork's relation to the artist's production and its context, history and influence.

We are part of the research department of Central St Martins. Our salaries are paid for by the university and our funding comes from the Arts Council from the university. Also it comes from California Institute of the Arts, Los Angeles, and MuHKA in Antwerp. Because of that, we have a research and educational remit. As we are funded by the Arts Council every year we also have to relate loosely to their agendas. Public funding determines your role as a political organisation. The journal is not an artist publication, although some of the people involved are artists. It aims to start from art practice, not from theory. We position ourselves in the opposite spectrum to something like *October*.

We publish three times a year so we are unable to respond quickly to developments. Through the length of the articles and the slow publishing process, we try to digest practice and see what is happening at a particular time. We are not an independent organisation; we are an institutional organisation. We also sell advertising. It's a small part of the revenue but it's important because of the other income. You *could* argue that it affects our decisions. It doesn't. We are not independent in the sense of the critic who is someone acting in a separate realm from the producer who digests practice and passes it on to the public. There is no art practice without discourse. You shape the way art practice is not only received but somehow made.

OLIVIA PLENDER: I'm an artist, but for six years I was involved with *Untitled* magazine and for about five of those as co-editor. *Untitled* was a relatively small art magazine with a pretty small distribution and output, but during my time it would come out three times a year. It was funded by a small grant from Arts Council England and goodwill from contributors. It was running for 15 years, originally set up by Mario Flecha and John Stathatos.

When I arrived, the format was set: a review section, a feature section, and two artist projects per issue. I tried to push for artist voices creating the discourse around the work, so it's not just critics and curators writing about artists. We had interviews with senior artists like John Latham, Andrea Fraser, Mark Dion, Oliver Ressler, and we often had features on much younger artists. My intention was to write about people who weren't getting into the public eye. We published the first text on Matthew Darbyshire, who's currently got a project here at the ICA, and we had an artist project with Pablo Bronstein very early on in his career, and later on he wrote a text about postmodern architecture in London, which is central to his research and practice as an artist. We also published the script from Melanie Gilligan's performance *The Miner's Object*.

I was interested in fiction and different ways of producing discourse around a work. For five years I did a comic book called *The Masterpiece*, a critique of the contemporary art world variously set in the sixties and eighties. It was always meant to be a satirical but critical look at the contemporary art world. The last issue was about corporate sponsorship of the arts. More recently, I did a book with Bookworks called *A Stellar Key to the Summerland*.

DANIEL JEWESBURY: I'm an artist and writer, and I do freelance research. I'm originally from London and studied at the College of Art in Dublin. Afterwards I moved to Belfast and I've been there for 12 years now, mainly because of Catalyst Arts, an artist-run gallery set up in 1993.

Variant is distributed free across the UK and Ireland. Within Ireland there is one visual art magazine [*Circa*], which began in Belfast but slowly migrated south for the last fifteen years and is now temporarily based in Dublin. The existence of this single magazine meant that there was a lack of critical context, venues and spaces in which to discuss art. It's a difficult climate for young writers thinking about how to contextualise art practice. One of the problems with *Circa* is that Ireland is a very small country and if you're writing about somebody who's exhibiting there, you probably know them. There's nothing wrong with that, but *Circa* clings to a pseudo-objective model of art criticism.

I've been involved with *Variant* for about eight years. It began in Glasgow in the early 1980s, edited by Malcolm Dickson who went on to run the Street Level Photoworks Gallery,

Glasgow. Malcolm ran *Variant* for about ten years as an A4-format colour magazine that was funded by the Scottish Arts Council. Around 1994, the SAC pulled the funding and the magazine closed summarily. About two years later, artists Leigh French and Billy Clark approached Malcolm and asked if they could revive the magazine in a newspaper format and distributed it free around the country to galleries, art centres, bookshops and independent organisations. Malcolm had no objections but said he didn't want to be involved.

The magazine was relaunched as an artist-led project. We are often criticised – not least by potential funders – for having a remit that strays too far from a narrow, visual art context. We're interested in the instrumentalisation of culture within the last ten years. We've seen a New Labour agenda to do with culture and that's been developed in various stages. *Variant* has been keen to map that through the magazine. We respond to the criticism that we're writing about politics and not art by saying we're artists writing about whatever we choose and how it impacts, in the broadest sense, the field of cultural production.

We're steadfastly independent in ways we would not have chosen. Sometimes we're independent through imposition. After 20 years of working in a context where we're reasonably well recognised, it is still amazingly difficult to publish our magazine, which we distribute free. If you don't have friends that have an old copy of *Variant* down the back of their sofas, then you need to change your friends.

We have routinely run into difficulties with our funding. We receive the same level of funding from the Scottish Arts Council now as we did about eight years ago. As someone within visual arts has decided that we represent the Antichrist, we've had to go to somebody in the literature department. We also receive little bits of short-term funding from Glasgow City Council, the National Lottery or Arts Council England. It's fairly precarious; sometimes we are able to pay our contributors, sometimes we aren't. Most contributors are surprised and grateful when we present them with a cheque, which makes us feel a bit sordid. We don't have any affiliation with any academic institution. But we have good connections with academics within institutions who are glad of the opportunity to publish in a magazine that is able to look at serious criticism. We tend not to review exhibitions. The scene in Glasgow, which *Variant* grew out of, is self-congratulatory. We didn't really see much point in us adding our plaudit to an already confident and self-aware scene. This is seen as proof that we are not interested in culture per se.

GRONLUND: Matthew, one of the things that I think Olivia and Pablo picked up on was the relation of production to art discourse. I think it would be interesting if you could concentrate on that to lead off the discussion.

ARNATT: I have no idea of what art discourse could possibly be. You seem to be spending a lot of energy on having a relationship with art and then extracting something interesting from it. I don't understand what relationships would be apart from some low-level tedium. I don't conceive of anyone I know having an art practice. I imagine that one would have a more day-to-day relation with oneself, which was quite critical of oneself, but whether that's something you can talk about publicly seems to be another matter. I can't understand why it can't be a private matter.

GRONLUND: But you publish books.

ARNATT: Yes, but I think our motivation for publishing books (that's myself and Maggie Smith, my partner, and we run a small gallery) is that occasionally people introduce ideas to us that we've never quite had. Occasionally we're able to talk to people or produce something that conceivably they might not have been able to do in a different set of circumstances. The situation starts with other people.

GRONLUND: But you set yourself up as a conduit of it.

ARNATT: No, I am not a conduit. I think we were approached by people on occasion. When you listen to the way people describe their ideas it can be an interesting thing for them to talk about in a relatively formal way. We would see ourselves as simply recognising something that's there. It is about our judgment. Having made that judgment, there are other situations that occur where people might be writing something or doing something, which is entirely different. Otherwise I think you're in danger of spiking something and everything becomes quite circular.

GRONLUND: How much do you work with your writers?

ARNATT: Frequently books don't get beyond the first stages. I think sometimes we should do this more because we have half-life books with bits of writing in them. I think they will get together one day and form a book, behind my back and in the dark. They're our failures. Sometimes I can work with other people and they make something really good. That surprises me, but so what? We pay them for the work that they've done when they've done it. What you're all saying sounds totally reasonable. I wonder about the expression 'independent'.

LAFUENTE: The way you were talking about independence seemed to be financial independence.

JEWESBURY: It's not financial independence. It's penury. We produce *Variant* for nothing. We spend as much posting the magazine as we spend printing it. Independence isn't a label we attach to ourselves and strive for and put up as a badge. We produce this thing in the way we do it because it's the only way to do it. By dint of that, we happen to be independent of larger institutions.

LAFUENTE: The premise of the word 'independence' is almost always used as a screen. Independent writers are often freelance; they're not independent unless they have income from somewhere else. Independent from cultural conditions? I'm being a bit Marxist here. There is no independence. You have to deal with certain parameters that are financial and cultural.

PLENDER: I wonder if it's more a question of scale. If you have a large art magazine and a big distribution, producing a lot of copies, that's expensive. If you're working on a smaller scale it's cheaper and you have greater flexibility. But the price of that is the lack of a wide audience.

ARNATT: One of the best defences of *frieze* is that it is commercially responsive. An intelligent reader would inevitably read off the nuances of relationships between galleries and funding organisations very quickly.

PLENDER: I think work often produces discourse on its own. A lot of artists are involved in the process of producing discourse. I'm not interested in separating critic and artist, or discourse and art production.

LAFUENTE: Work is constructed by the discourse and the discourse is produced by the artist, the dealer, the auction house, the critic/cultural commentator/philosopher.

PLENDER: But the work exists 'in the studio' before it hits any of that.

LAFUENTE: The only reading of the work is possible through a theoretical apparatus that allows you to try to look at it. The way that we can look at art today was shaped by a discourse produced around 1800, the German Romantics and Kant. We can choose not to do that and choose other non-dominant discourses, but that frame is there. Discourse exists in ways of making in art as well as in books. The way that artists work and exhibit is looked at and shaped by several kinds of discourses.

GRONLUND: Olivia's work uses a comic book format. She is defining the terms in which her work should be read. I don't need to write a review of Olivia's work to let people know how to read it.

LAFUENTE: She's defined a set of terms that I can choose to follow or not as a reader, but she is working within a framework; the fact that I can call this art is dependent on a tradition. If that didn't exist, which is a history of understanding what art is, she wouldn't be talking here about that as art.

PLENDER: As an artist, you work within the existing set of paradigms, but those aren't static things. Practice is part of what shifts the paradigm and contributes to the flow of discourse.

CLEMENTINE DELISS (audience): We're talking about independent publishing, but actually it's to do with the promotion of self-publishing. We've had a lot of events in the art world recently within contemporary art practice, such as Documenta 12's magazines project, which brought together over 100 magazines. There was a very specific agenda, which was described as islands that would have ships of various sizes that would dock in to Kassel and represent their critical discourses as independent organs. *Afterall* was a participant; I was a participant in terms of *Metronome*.

One of the key issues about independent publishers is that we're independent. We're not particularly interested in translating between the discourses that we create. There is the fairly banal but nevertheless useful Degree Zero, built around the publications of curators. There is Kiosk, built around Christoph Keller, and the now quite tired UK organisation Publish and Be Damned. This has a context. The institutional problem, the issue of independence, is a reference to whoever is creating a roof over your head, be it an educational institution, Arts Council funding or city council funding. They are the least interesting issue about independent publishing.

The most interesting issue is that you do it with a group of people that often include artists and that you have editorial control over it. You don't say to anybody, "and damn Arts Council publishing". You'd rather give the things away. It can fail or it can last two weeks. It's about intellectual emancipation, not about being independent about art practice. You are completely partisan when you're doing publishing; the more independent you are when doing publishing, the more partisan you are.

LAFUENTE: As an editor, you found a magazine to respond to a particular context, and once that context is changed, you have to modify your approach to it. I don't know if inheriting a publication that is not the one you founded is problematic.

JEWESBURY: The reason for reviving the title was because it was felt that *Variant* in its original format had done something that wasn't being done in any other format. There are plenty of magazines that are more directly concerned with talking about art and nothing else. They do what they do very well and that's great. We're interested in a broader question of cultural politics, the conditions of cultural production. We think that other people recognise a demand for us to do this because a lot of people read the magazine and tell us that they appreciate it. In Scotland there is a publication called *MAP*. The Scottish Arts Council spend I don't know how many tens of thousands of pounds on it. If that is what they want to spend their money on, that's fine. We think it's a waste of money, and a bit of a scandal that they waste money in that way. We think the way they went about setting that magazine up, choosing who would run it, was a bit ridiculous. It's got nothing really to do with what we're doing. So all those other things that are going on don't really obviate the need for us to carry on doing what we're doing.

MARK SLADEN (audience): It's interesting to hear the panel talk from institutionalised positions about publications you're involved with or have been in the past. But what intervention would you recommend to make a difference, whether it's taking all public funding away from publishing or tripling it or starting a new magazine?

JEWESBURY: Our biggest source of funding has been Leigh's giro and has been for about ten years. I don't want to prescribe what intervention would necessarily make the most difference. If somebody feels what we're doing is boring, conservative, or not sufficiently responsive to being produced by artists, then let them do what they want to do. I wouldn't want to say funding should go into this type of thing and not that type of thing.

GRONLUND: Intervention towards what end?

ARNATT: Olivia was talking about how paradigms are constantly shifting. Given that, what new interventions would respond to recent shifts in paradigms?

GRONLUND: Do you mean the influx of money in the art world?

SLADEN: That would be one important factor.

PLENDER: I wouldn't want to prescribe an agenda, but one of the reasons I left *Untitled* was that I got tired of the fixed format and doing something three times a year when you don't always feel like it's necessary. The art magazine and self-publishing scene is completely oversaturated. I want to produce occasional publications that are trying to shift the paradigm and produce friction, and not work within bog-standard existing formats.

JENNIFER THATCHER (audience): Pablo writes a useful essay in the June issue of *Nought to Sixty* which defends art criticism against the various critiques of the 'crisis of criticism'. I don't think many of the other people in the panel would describe themselves as art critics. Does independent publishing have a way of defending or promoting different kinds of writing?

PLENDER: One of the things with the division of labour between artists and art critics is an educational difference. Artists are at an educational disadvantage when it comes to writing art criticism because we're not trained art historians. But the two have often blurred and overlapped.

LAFUENTE: I would reject that division of labour. Anybody can produce art criticism in the way I understand it, and producing articulated thought about work, anybody can do that. I don't have any art history background.

PLENDER: But you have got a university education.

LAFUENTE: I was reading *The State of Art Criticism*, by James Elkins. It complains about how nobody reads anymore and people don't know how to write. It relies on the ideas of the division of labour and stuff that is not appropriate today when we talk about art. You cannot decide beforehand who can talk about art and who's allowed to write about it. It's an exercise in exclusion. Documenta's magazine project was full of problems, but one of the nice things about it was that you saw different models for approaching art publishing from different parts of the world. Looking at different models, writing and funding, and also the way things look, was refreshing.

GRONLUND: The role of the art critic has been usurped to an extent by the independent curator. I think there was a time when the critic was aligned with the audience and it shifted. I think that model persisted until art history and contemporary art became specialised disciplines.

LAFUENTE: This idea of the decay of the role of the art critic is not helpful. The idea of power is completely unappealing. If we want to go back to the Greenberg model, this fight between the curator and the critic – this "oh, they're taking our role and we should get it back" – doesn't really go anywhere.

GRONLUND: The better art criticism is, the better the person knows contemporary art, art history, and the philosophy of the history of aesthetics. If that person has that specialised knowledge, they should be accorded some kind of respect.

LAFUENTE: If you want the art historian to talk about art to you, you open up *October* and you have a really nice discussion. They know every single piece by Morris and Duchamp, and that closes down the discourse completely.

ANONYMOUS (audience): Are any of you interested in a wider public beyond the art world?

PLENDER: I'm very interested in a wider audience. *Untitled* was a small art magazine, a limited print run. You can only reach people who are part of your existing network. I started making comics through the desire to talk to different kinds of audiences. Öyvind Fahlström talked about creating an alternative distribution network for artworks so people could have access to or purchase artworks as multiples – I've found this very exciting as an idea. So I started making a comic and attempted to get it into different networks through comic bookstores or art bookstores as well. My desire is to break into other fields and speak to other audiences.

GRONLUND: I don't think *Afterall* is aiming for a wider audience. There's the issue of dumbing down, and who you're writing for should determine your content.

11 **Guestroom**

Event, 2 June 2008
ICA Nash/Brandon Rooms

Top: Guestroom / *The Librarians* / 2008
Bottom: Guestroom / *Reading Room* / 2008

Guestroom is a collaborative project by artists Maria Benjamin (born Broxburn, 1972, lives in London) and Ruth Höflich (born Munich, 1976, lives in London), working out of their shared studio in Dalston, East London. It originated in 2002 as an annual publication, which has contained elements such as CDs, DVDs, posters and stickers, and featured contributions from artists and writers such as Pablo Bronstein, Claire Hooper, Mark Aerial Waller, Anna Colin and Olivia Plender. At the same time Guestroom has expanded to include various other activities, such as an ongoing series of events, entitled *Passerby*, in which artists are invited to present a project in three parts: one in the windows of the Guestroom studio; one on a small disused billboard nearby; and one through a live event or presentation.

The participation of other artists or cultural practitioners in Guestroom's projects is always framed by an emphasis on the creation of communities, whether these are grouped around one-off events or more long-term projects that develop wider relationships.

Benjamin and Höflich are especially interested in self-organisation within groups, and bring other practitioners together so as to document the formation of ideas within such activities as collective reading, live performance and shared correspondence.

Part of Guestroom's identity has been formed through its participation in projects curated by other organisations and institutions, and they have responded to these invitations by developing new means to reflect on the nature of collaboration. A recent residency at Grizedale Arts, in the Lake District, has formed the basis for two ongoing projects entitled *Reading Room* and *The Librarians*. These projects were at the centre of Guestroom's event at the ICA, where the group used the Nash and Brandon Rooms as a site for production, presentation and performance.

The Librarians is a series of eight video portraits of people working in the arts, all people with highly personal libraries or collections. The project looks at how individual selection processes – and by extension the design and organisation of personal environments – reflect and relate to a person's wider practice. *Reading Room* extends the analysis of 'influence' through a series of performances by artists reading from personally selected texts. These events take place within a purpose-built environment, one that is adaptable to the particular performer's needs. For *Nought to Sixty* this setting became a kind of a TV production studio, so that performances could be simultaneously broadcast on agrifashionista.tv – a web-based arts TV station curated by Grizedale Arts for A Foundation.

Richard Birkett

READING ROOM

THE LIBRARIANS

Shaun Pubis, aka DJ Rubbish, London
Michael Leslie, pianist based in Munich
Tom McCarthy, writer, London
Lorenza Boisi, painter, Milan
Pablo Bronstein, artist, London
Isabel Waidner, writer based in London
Rebecca Bligh, writer, London
Adam Sutherland, director Grizedale Arts

originally commissioned by Grizedale Arts for Afoundation
and agrifashionista.tv
edited by Anne Monnehay, Maria Benjamin and Ruth Höflich

THE READERS

Florian Roithmayr and Sam Dowd (I): Lawrence Durrell to Anne Ridler (Blue Star Line, Monte Video, 1947); Charles Darwin to J.S. Henslow (1832); Rupert Brookes from a letter to The Westminster Gazette (New York, 1913); to Mrs Austin (Grand Cairo, 1862); Virginia Woolf to Ethel Smyth (Hotel Majestic, Athens, 1932); the Marquess of Dufferin (Reykjavik, 1856)
Ruth Höflich (I): If on a Winter's Night a Traveller by Italo Calvino and Offending the Audience by Peter Handke
Michael Smythe: K9 Pawmistery
Laura Cull: Programme (relative to Acephale) by Georges Bataille
Peter Donaldson: The Trickster: a study in American Indian Mythology by Paul Radin
Linden St. John: Heart of Darkness by Jospeh Conrad
Hilary Koob-Sassen: Niche Construction: The Neglected Process in Evolution by F. John Odling-Smee, Kevin N.Laland & Marcus W. Feldman
Claire Hooper: Saint Jerome Letter LVII to Pammachius on The Best Method of Translating written from Hippo about the year 394
Eva Stenram (I): The Birds & Night of the Living Dead
Alistair Hudson: The Art Teacher
Maria Benjamin: Long Extract from A Painting by Han Yu (768-824)
Eva Stenram (II):The Birds & Night of the Living Dead
Ruth Höflich (II): If on a Winter's Night a Traveller by Italo Calvino and Rings of Saturn by W.G. Sebald
Florian Roithmayr and Sam Dowd (II): Rudyard Kipling from A Travellers Letters - Egypt of the Magicians (1913); Lady Wortley Montague to Anne Thistlethwayte (1717); Charles-Edouard Jeanneret (Le Corbusier)Recollections of Mount Athos (1914); William Cullen Bryant from a letter to Dionisio da Borga San Sepolcro (1336)
Adam Sutherland: Take Control of The Hole

The programme for this event is available from Guestroom, priced £5.

www.guest-room.net

Guestroom / programme for *Reading Room* / 2008

Anja Kirschner and David Panos / poster for *Trail of the Spider* / 2008

12

Anja Kirschner and David Panos

Exhibition, 2–9 June 2008
ICA Upper Galleries

Anja Kirschner (born Munich, 1977, lives in London) and David Panos (born Athens, 1971, lives in London) collaborate on both moving image and music projects. As part of *Nought to Sixty* they showed a film, *Trail of the Spider* (2008), addressing themes of class conflict and displacement through the transposition of the Western genre onto contemporary London.

Kirschner's work spans a number of disciplines, including film, painting and music. Since 2003 the artist has made a series of films which combine documentary, literary and historical sources and reference popular genres such as sci-fi, soap opera and action adventure. These films' increasingly elaborate production and use of digital effects gesture towards the scope and conventions of mainstream cinema, but subvert them through the use of non-actors and narratives that are rooted in the political conflicts of London today.

A previous work, *Polly II – Plan for a Revolution in Docklands* (2006), portrays the flooded ruins of East London in a fusion of Ballardian sci-fi dystopia and eighteenth-century social satire. Borrowing themes and characters from Hogarth and John Gay – in particular *Polly* (1728), Gay's heavily censored sequel to *The Beggars Opera* (1727) – Kirschner's film shows dispossessed workers, political radicals, whores and pirates negotiating the deliberate flooding of their city by the agents of high finance and property development. The staging of the film in the manner of a Brechtian 'learning play', and the use of vignettes of dissent and debate, highlight the complexities of social and political transformation.

The writers of American history report an
economic boom in the years after 1870,

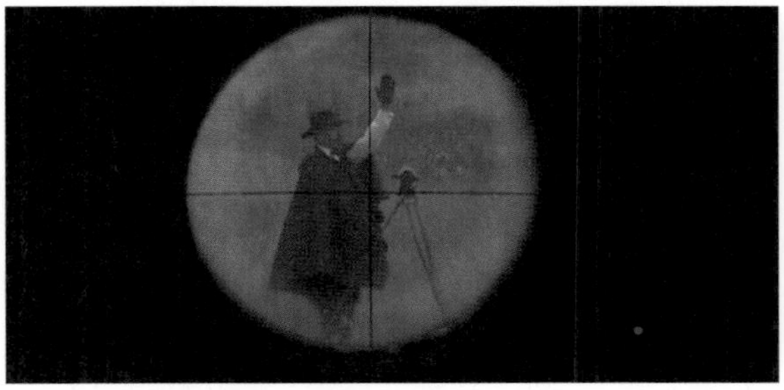

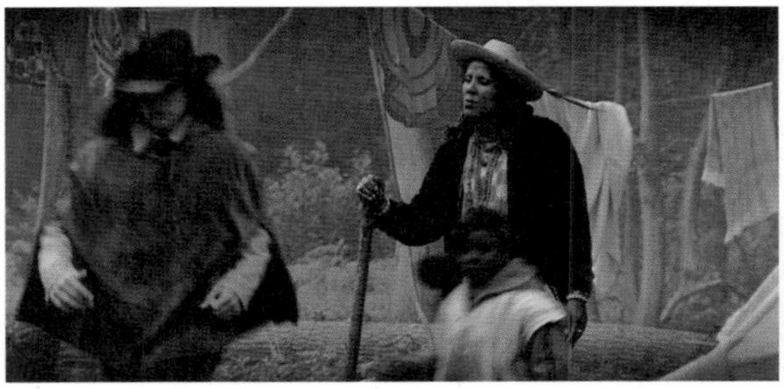

All images: Anja Kirschner and David Panos / *Trail of the Spider* / 2008

Trail of the Spider collides filmic references – such as the stylised violence of the Spaghetti Western and the sentimentality of golden era 'Horse Operas' – with the suppressed history of the multiracial American West, where many cowboys were black, and alliances that crossed racial boundaries were common. Shot in Hackney and Essex, the film recreates the epic panoramas of the Wild West using landfill sites in the Thames Gateway, gravel pits serving the Olympic Park, and the vistas of Hackney Marshes – an area affected by the land grab accompanying the 2012 Olympics.

Using the standard Western plot devices of the 'arrival of the railroad' and the 'end of an era', *Trail of the Spider* explores the compromises and ordeals of a population facing a new order, as a territory once characterised by abandonment – but relative freedom – is brought back into circulation. Many members of the film's cast (themselves residents of East London) are in a sense playing themselves, although speaking through the filter of Western mythology and melodrama. Subtitled *A Passage Through Limbo*, the film creates an allegory of the shrinking space for self-determination and collective agency – in an urban reality increasingly determined by financial speculation and private interests.

Richard Birkett

13 Clunie Reid

Exhibition, 2–9 June 2008
ICA Upper Galleries

Clunie Reid (born Pembury, 1971, lives in London) creates aggressive and rampant photo-collages that question the media they are created from, as well as the integrity of the source images which they employ. The artist uses deliberately cheap material, gaffer-taping her collages to the wall and emphasising the act of composition rather than the final product. In one group of works Reid takes photographs of her studio floor; in others airbrushed images of beautiful women are broken into fragments, scribbled over and adorned with slogans that resound with irony.

Reid's *Beautiful* (2008) shows a majorette, her facial features pixelated. The original poster was found and photographed by the artist in Venice, already defaced with blue biro scribbled over the figure's eyes, nose and mouth. On her legs appear jagged scrawls of pubic hair. The dancer is superimposed over a postcard picture of a Venice sunset, and across the top of the image Reid has written 'beautiful' in childlike lettering. These are the cliches that form one idea of beauty: flat-chested girls in glittery tops performing arabesques, tourist sites at sunset with Prosecco at the ready. Bringing together these overloaded signifiers of beauty compounds the indeterminacy of the original image – and especially of the woman's identity. This message is further complicated in the artist's messy but carefully accomplished installation, in which the work must be seen as one of many conflicting and competing images.

In her work for *Nought to Sixty*, however, Reid moved away from paper collage to create more sculptural juxtapositions, affixing different images and media fragments onto industrial foam board. In the same way that the artist uses standard paper sizes, here she used generic wire picture hangers to suspend the collages, undermining their potential commodity status but also co-opting the same industrial standardisation that she critiques.

While Reid's debased, deskilled aesthetic challenges the ideologies that her source images support, it also enables a mode of performance: the quickness of execution reflecting the swiftness of thought, as well as its potential for change. Misspellings are left in place, or simply blacked out, as the artist carries on. If impermanence is one of the qualities of the fashion and celebrity economy, Reid performs this flux in her foam board collages, sites where information is exchanged and updated. The strength of Reid's works is not manifested in any single piece but in the multifarious accumulation of meaning, quickly tacked to the gallery wall.

Melissa Gronlund

Clunie Reid / *SHE GETS EVEN HAPPIER!* / 2008 / detail

14 # Jesse Jones

Screening, 9 June 2008
ICA Cinema

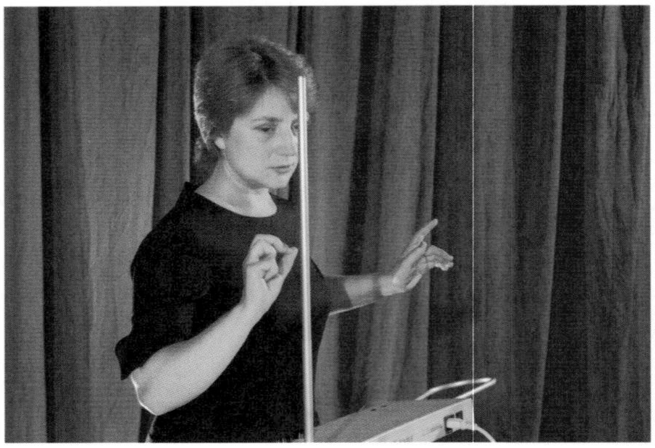

Both images: Jesse Jones / *The Spectre and the Sphere* / 2008

The work of Jesse Jones (born 1978, Dublin, lives in Dublin) primarily takes the form of short films, works which renegotiate the material and ideological structures of cinema. They are concerned with how cultural artefacts can be restaged to reveal embedded histories of dissent – and their contemporary relevance. The artist isolates forms and subjects that can be utilised as tools, both in re-imagining and in directly intervening in the public sphere.

In 2006 Jones initiated *12 Angry Films*. This ambitious collaborative project attempted to recuperate the 'drive-in' cinema – a form of mass entertainment associated with 1950s America – in order to investigate how it might be developed as a collective activity and transformed through radical content. Developed over a nine-month period, the production of the 'drive-in' films started with an invitation sent out to various Dublin trade unions and community groups (including some non-English speaking participants). The project developed around a series of workshops, including screenings and non-verbal drama sessions, and the final films were guided by a number of rules: they should be set in a car, should last three minutes, and should not be in English.

The resulting six short films tackle personal subjects as well as wider concerns about employment, globalisation and human experience. They formed the centre of a film programme, screened in a temporary drive-in cinema constructed by Jones in Dublin's Docklands. The programme also included a series of features themed around radicalism and protest, including *Salt of the Earth* (1954), Herbert J Biberman's film about strike action in a New Mexico mine. As Maeve Connolly remarked, *12 Angry Films* is 'simultaneously a critique of cinema history, a site-specific public artwork and form of political action', and epitomise Jones' interest in the recuperation of theatre and cinema as spaces of popular imagination.

Jones' own short films are largely non-narrative vignettes, and often employ a particular location as an arena for performance. For *On the Waterfront* (2005) the artist invited members of a boys' brass band to perform the score from Elia Kazan's 1954 film of the same name – about trade unionism in America – in an open space between two housing blocks. The resulting film depicts the space as a resonant amphitheatre, the ethereal music helping to create a web of social and political histories.

For *Nought to Sixty* Jones showed a new work, *The Spectre and the Sphere* (2008). The film looks at the history of Marxism, and includes artefacts that trigger a number of ideological echoes. The soundtrack employs a ghostly recording of *The Internationale*, performed by Lydia Kavina on the Theremin, and the film explores Vooruit, a castle in Belgium that was built by socialists in the early twentieth century and is now a flourishing arts centre. Jones chose to accompany her screening at the ICA with a showing of *The New Babylon* (1929), a satirical film by Soviet filmmaker Grigori Kosintsev about the defeat of the Paris Commune in 1871.

Richard Birkett

15

Emma Hart and Benedict Drew

Event, 16 June 2008
ICA Theatre

The collaborative work of Emma Hart (born London, 1974, lives in London) and Benedict Drew (born Kyneton, Australia, 1977, lives in London) returns cinematic experience to its constituent elements of image and sound. Exposing the interdependency of these two elements within a live setting, Hart and Drew orchestrate events informed by their respective expertise. Although both of the artists actively pursue their personal practices – Drew's background of musical composition and experimental sound, and Hart's interrogation of the still and moving image – the pair collaborate without hierarchy or specific roles.

Working together since 2005, the artists' have produced four collaborative performance works to date: *Untitled 1.* (2005) through to *Untitled 4.* (2008). With nods to the history of 'expanded cinema' and artists' film (both Richard Serra's *Hand Catching Lead*, 1968, and David Lamelas' 1960s and '70s films are echoed in their practice), Hart and Drew transform the 'black box' space into a notably mechanical and sculptural environment.

All of the performances take the destabilisation of the moving image as their start and end point. In *Untitled 1.*, for example, loose, white washing powder lies in the cone of a speaker. The sound of the live projector fan plays through the speaker and the powder is moved in time to the audio. This movement is captured on camera and simultaneously projected. This technical process produces an image which is at once hypnotic and epic, while also challenging the usual precedence of cinematic visuals over scored sound.

This Mobius-strip approach applies increasingly to the artists' collaboration itself, and is visibly intensified in their subsequent work, *Untitled 2.* (2006). One artist loops clear-and-black 16mm film leader between a film projector while the other, illuminated in the beam of the projector, extends the same ribbon through the strings of an electric guitar. In an abrasive performance, the guitar is dramatically recast as a mechanical extension of the

Emma Hart and Benedict Drew / *Untitled 5.* / 2008

filmic apparatus. The film strip is drawn across the metal guitar strings like a violin bow, as the projector simultaneously produces a flashing beam. The performance appears as if in a zoetrope or filmic countdown, to the soundtrack of a relentless score. The event becomes a test of endurance as well as a precarious endeavour: a willful misappropriation of tools to the point of their physical destruction, ending with the final snap of the film reel.

While this antagonistic device was extended in *Untitled 4.* (2008) into a physical tug-of-war between two film projectors pulling at a tangled pile of 16mm film on a central table, in *Nought to Sixty* Hart and Drew presented *Untitled 5.* (2008), a series of works which foreground their collaborative process. Using both domestic and industrial equipment, the artists' playful and structural interventions revealed the physical connections between the productions of sound and light – and their mutual reliance.

Isla Leaver-Yap

16 Mike Cooter

Exhibition, 16–23 June 2008
ICA Upper Galleries

The videos and installations of Mike Cooter (born Epsom, 1978, lives in London) bring together any number of apparent and false correlations, his meticulously researched works often beginning by exploiting some found connection. The film *Strangers (as the raven laughs)* (2006), for example, is a kind of self-portrait in which Cooter interviews an actor playing the role of 'Mike Cooter'. The work was inspired by a security poster that the artist found, stole and exhibited, and which features the slogan 'Are You Questioning Strangers?' Within Cooter's practice, in which each incidental detail is potentially significant, the given world is conceived as a film ripe for analysis.

Drawing on a Conceptualist predilection for following rules and reducing the artist's subjective decision-making, Cooter sets out and follows strict premises in the material production of his work. Text piece *Redaction* (2006) is a work that was completed according to the artist's injunctions, and demanded that his gallerist print out the document in full and then, using a black marker, remove all the sources. The instructions concern both the content of the work, as well as its production ('black out... print... fax...'). The document evokes, in its unmoored sketches of cinematic scenarios ('I threw my clothes off and got into the shower. Nothing was strange at all'), the tropes of American film noir. So too does *Redaction*'s form: a declassified testimony, or a letter sent to someone it was not intended for.

This idea of the mismatched recipient or the mistaken identity is key to Cooter's practice. In the video *Diagnosis Murder* (2003) twelve actors (eleven amateurs and one professional) re-enact an implausible resolution from a crime show of the same name, a denouement which circles around the whereabouts of a character called René, and a discussion concerning his likelihood to commit blackmail or murder. Meanwhile, the previously mentioned *Strangers* poses and refuses to answer the question of Mike Cooter's identity, lending the flavour of noir sub-plotting and untrustworthy appearance to an otherwise straightforward interview.

The question of transferred and displaced identity was also present in Cooter's contribution to *Nought to Sixty*, a network of objects, texts and references entitled *Original Intent*. In one element, the typically noirish image of a glass door, represented on the cover of a paperback of Dashiell Hammett's novel *The Maltese Falcon*, was reconstructed in the ICA's exhibition space, as Cooter replaced the gallery windows with panes of reeded glass. This reference was expanded in other elements of the installation, including a series of letters that the artist wrote to the American legal scholar Robert Bork.

Bork was nominated to the US Supreme Court by President Reagan, but was rejected as a result of uproar in the liberal media over his right-wing views. The viciousness of the attack on Bork's politics reached such a level that his name has since become a verb: 'to bork' someone being a usage that found its way into the OED in 2002. Cooter noticed a statue of the Maltese Falcon, from the 1941 film of the same name, in a television interview with Bork, and used this connection to begin a correspondence with the political lawyer, deftly mirroring this man – whose name became a symbol – with the fictional prop that has now become a real objet d'art.

Melissa Gronlund

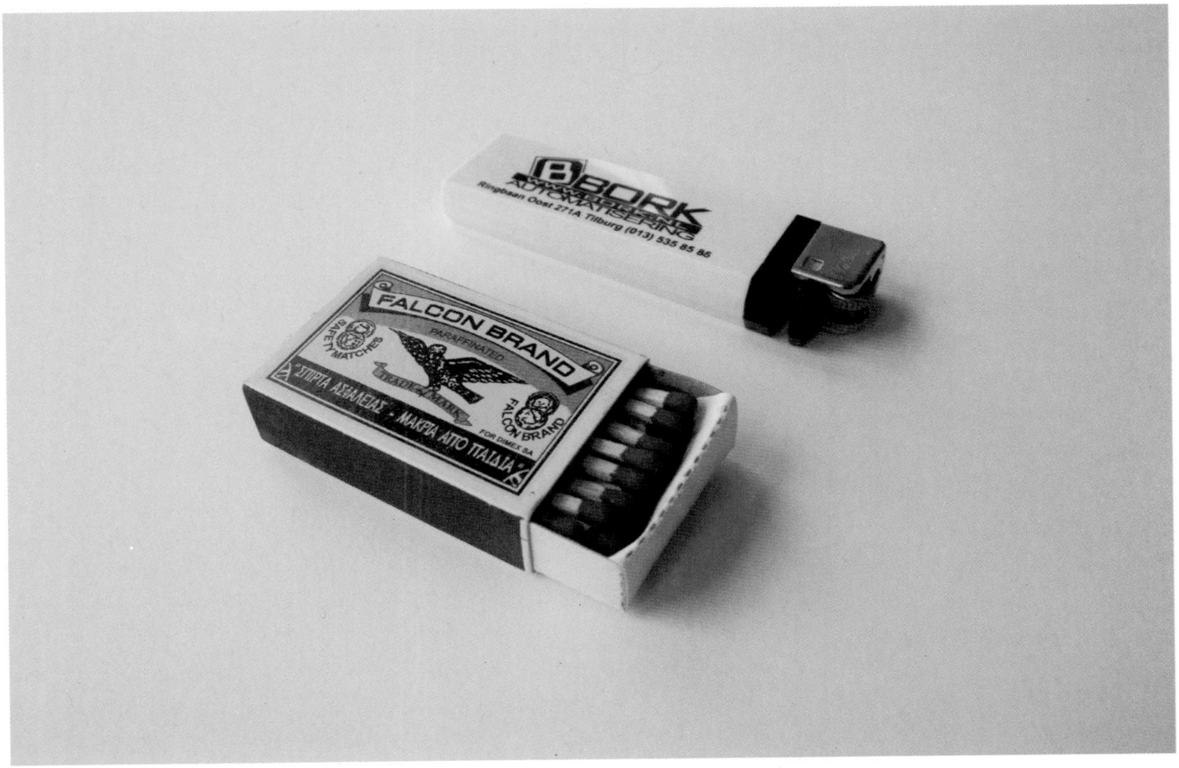

Mike Cooter / *Untitled (Falcon...Bork)* / 2007

17 **Alexander Heim**

Exhibition, 16–23 June 2008
ICA Upper Galleries

In *Untitled (Dog)* (2006), a video by Alexander Heim (born Hamburg, 1977, lives in London), a stray mongrel loiters in the middle of a busy road in China while buses, trucks and motorbikes rush past him. A six-wheeler truck passes within an inch of his ear; cars honk. Heim scores this found choreography with triumphant, even radiant, music – transforming the dog into an anthropomorphised, thinking subject; an enlightened canine monk, both aware of and oblivious to the worldly traffic around him. The self-sufficiency of the dog is almost comic, but Heim also frames it as a genuine example of dissent: this mangy dog ignores the function laid out by the developers and users of the road.

Heim's practice encompasses video, installation and sculpture, and addresses those intrusions into urban life where animals, processes and chance routines create self-sustaining pockets of otherness. The work examines things that happen – despite the planned nature of the urban environment – on their own.

Alexander Heim / installation view / ICA / 2008

In his graduate show at Goldsmiths College, 2006, Heim looked at the Rotherhithe Tunnel in East London. Built in 1908 to accommodate horse-drawn traffic, the tunnel features a zigzagging path designed so that horses would not be tempted to rush towards the light at the other side. Now used by cars, the tunnel is littered with wing mirrors that have been clipped off cars on too-tight corners: battered objects with cracked-glass faces, comparable to detritus such as crisp packets or perhaps even to natural forms such as sea glass. Heim exhibited these items as precious objects placed on a tall plinth that, like the soaring soundtrack in *Untitled (Dog)*, exaggerated the role of artistry in their presentation.

Heim's video *Three Seasons* (2007) continues this juxtaposition of emblematic purity with the urban mundane: dirt-grey snow melting under car wheels; a tubby middle-aged man swimming in an indoor pool. In the film's final segment – the third of the three seasons in this variant calendar – the rhythm of joggers and exercise machines marks the passing of time. This video corresponds to a series of ceramic bowls, with centres made from elements of melted glass, and both works were shown as part of *Nought to Sixty*. When struck, the bowls produce a reverberating tone similar to that of a Buddhist gong. Heim incorporated these sounds into parts of the video's soundtrack. A rhythmic succession of images follows the pace of the musical composition – trees sway in the wind accompanied by random sounds recorded in the corridors outside rehearsal rooms in a music school.

In the altered scheme of nature proffered by Heim, conventional distinctions between 'natural' and 'man-made' are disrupted. Rather than holding up the moral card of environmentalism, the artist's observations appear to provide a view of nature in which everything, even a crisp packet, has its place.

Melissa Gronlund

Alexander Heim / *Three Seasons* / 2007

18 # Juliette Blightman

Exhibition, 30 June–7 July 2008
ICA Upper Galleries

The work of Juliette Blightman (born Farnham, 1980, lives in London) demands that the viewer refocus his or her attention. Using film and slide works, and direct yet subtle interventions in the gallery space, Blightman's work frames and enacts a certain kind of unadorned reality. Within a structure marked out by deliberately simple gestures, the marking of time gradually gives way to a sense of epiphany.

In a series of 16mm films made since 2005, Blightman uses the basic parameters of the medium to emphasise the reality of what is in front of her camera. Each work consists of a single shot, the length of which is dictated by the standard three-minute duration of the film stock. In *as a period in which nothing happens* (2007), the shot frames a domestic living room. Central to the composition is a single armchair directed towards a television, upon which can be made out the flickering image of Agatha Christie's Poirot. The shot lingers, a still composition in which the only evidence of time passing is the movement on the television screen, an occasional car on the road outside, and the pattern of sunlight falling through a pair of French windows. The vignette concludes when the camera pans unexpectedly to the left, coming to rest on a second set of windows.

Blightman's compositions are characterised by an objectivism that is gradually infected with the minute and shifting experience of passing time. The rigid, almost schematic approach to representation is reminiscent of the novels of Alain Robbe-Grillet, in which the perspective is limited to the surface of visual experience, and in which – to use the words of Roland Barthes – the object "never conceals a secret, vulnerable heart beneath its shell". Another characteristic of Blightman's work is the clear ordering of time (the clatter of the film projector serving as an ever-present metronome). In certain exhibitions she has asked that a film be played just once a day, at a designated time. This device perhaps presents a parallel to the 'represented' time in the film, but it also emphasises personal and associative qualities – and the attempt to recapture the lucidity of a certain period. The processes through which time is measured are shown to be fluid, their slippages invested with a sense of memory and loss.

Blightman's work for *Nought to Sixty*, entitled *Please Water the Plant and Feed the Fish* (2008), employed the simple placement of objects and turned the gallery into a live composition. A houseplant and fish bowl, placed in front of the gallery's windows, activated internal frames that echoed the way in which the windows framed the external world. Blightman asked that her brother perform the action requested in the title of the work, and he visited the gallery at 3pm every day, a function which required the restructuring of his daily routine.

This performance created an enforced shift of attention towards the banal and the non-event, and the way in which its repeated structure was used to impose order offered a parallel to the artist's films, although it was also a highly personal intervention. Once again, as in other pieces by Blightman, the world's stubbornly objective quality was balanced by the essentially emotive experience of the passing of time.

Richard Birkett

Juliette Blightman / *Please water the plant and feed the fish* / 2008

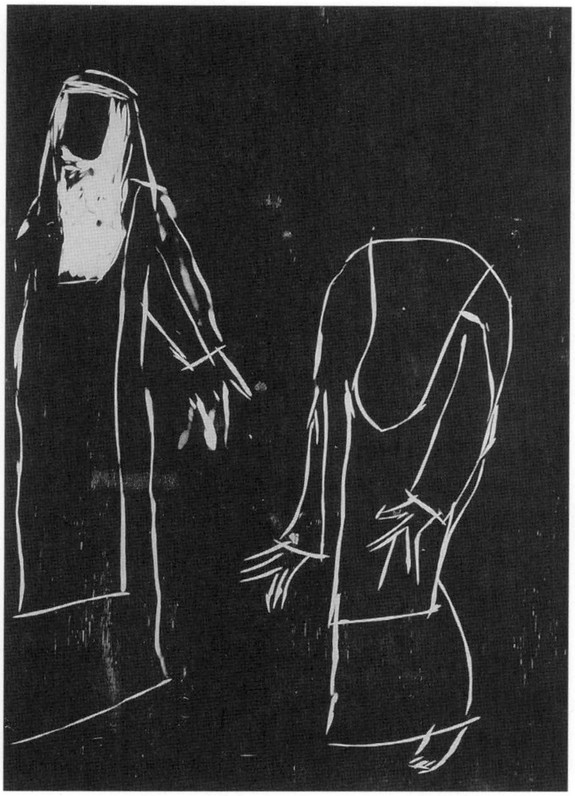

19 **Andrea Büttner**

Exhibition, 30 June–7 July 2008
ICA Upper Galleries

Using outmoded techniques such as woodcut and glass painting, Andrea Büttner (born Stuttgart, 1972, lives in London and Berlin) explores the enduring myths that cloak the figure of the artist. Büttner's prints bear self-deprecating statements – "I want to let the work fall down" or "I don't know what to do". These slogans hold a mirror up to a contemporary culture of 'shamelessness' – epitomised by the painful aspirations of reality television or in 'tell all' tabloid confessionals – and interrogate the potential dilemmas and pitfalls facing the artist in the expectant space of the gallery.

Büttner's interest in woodcut lies in its contradictory status as a medium that is fetishised for its involvement of the artist's hand (particularly in historical works by master craftsmen), but which is also by its nature expedient and democratic (and one of the earliest means developed for creating mass produced images). Büttner exploits the way the medium betrays every inaccuracy, and combines her aphorisms of failure with a technique where craft meets reproduction. The resulting images reflect what one critic described as "the emptiness of the codes by which our lives are defined".

Religion is a recurring subject in Büttner's work, and she is influenced by historical figures such as Sister Corita Kent, whose artwork of the 1960s and '70s brought together both her religious and political beliefs. Büttner uses religious values as a lens through which to examine modern life, and

for several years she has been observing the lives of a closed order of Carmelite nuns in Notting Hill, London. Initially making impromptu pencil sketches of the nuns at prayer, Büttner delved further into the art practice of these women in her short documentary film, *Little Works* (2007), which featured in her *Nought to Sixty* exhibition.

Unable to film within the walls of the convent, Büttner handed the camera to one of the sisters to record the making of 'little works' – small handcrafted offerings made in the nuns' recreational time, ranging from crochet baskets to religious icons. While the nuns' concerns over the manufacture and display of their work are similar to the self-doubts of a professional artist, *Little Works* presents a wistful image of a creative microcosm untouched by the compromises of a secular age.

Büttner's project for *Nought to Sixty* brought together several prints, as well as a new series of photographs that revisit the Carmelite nuns. The documents of the nuns' recent works were displayed in and among Büttner's spatial interventions, while the walls of the gallery were daubed in brown paint as high as the artist could reach unassisted. Fresh clay sculptures nestled in corners of the gallery space, gradually drying out and disintegrating over the course of the exhibition. These bold elemental gestures evoked the physical presence of the artist, framing the project as an endless labour where completion and satisfaction were infinitely deferred.

Andrew Bonacina

Andrea Büttner / installation view / ICA / 2008

20 Thomas Kratz

Event, 30 June 2008
ICA Nash/Brandon Rooms

In many respects, the work of Thomas Kratz (born Waiblingen, 1972, lives in London) defies summation. Kratz operates across a variety of media, and his approaches can appear cyclical – not necessarily generating an ordered structure but one in which reoccurring facets are placed alongside one another across spaces, exhibitions and works.

Kratz has an interest in the early twentieth-century Portuguese poet Fernando Pessoa, who devised a means of writing from multiple points of view. These different identities are heteronyms – rather than simple 'nom de plumes' – as he gave them distinct characters, each with its own biography and physical characteristics. Kratz does not go so far as to nominate plural identities from which his work emanates, yet his approach to making art is founded on a set of positions, each with clear material and conceptual characteristics.

Kratz's performance for the ICA, entitled *Strawberry Camouflage* (2008), contained within it actions, objects and fetishes that have appeared in various incarnations in his previous works. The processes at play linked back to the artist's 2006 performance *How I Explain Pictures to a Dead Hare*, an action reprising Joseph Beuys' iconic 1965 performance *How to Explain Pictures to a Dead Hare*. The piece by Kratz – like that by Beuys – involved the artist moving through a gallery whispering to the eponymous animal, his face plastered in honey and gold leaf.

However, Kratz's version also contained significant departures from the Beuys orginal. The audience watched from behind glass doors, with the artist's whisperings relayed to them via loudspeaker; and the 'pictures' at the centre of narrative were absent (a poster detailed the list of imaginary works to which the artist referred). Joining Kratz were two surreal additions to the Beuysian score – an exercise bike, and a small robot singing *Daisy Daisy*. The artist redefined Beuys' materialbased shamanism through theatre and artifice, using the iconography of the original performance as the basis of a new ritual.

Objects, both constructed and pre-existing, are reincarnated throughout Kratz's work. Bicycles appear frequently: propped against the gallery wall, as if offering a means of escape; or leant against a set of glass doors, preventing entry to the gallery beyond.

The layering of such elements creates a ritualistic amplification, taken to the point of overload, and *Strawberry Camouflage* forms an almost perverse extension of *How I Explain Pictures...*, with Kratz 'in communion' with a hybrid hare/android figure in garish Beuysian garb.

Kratz' action, however, was also a poised, aesthetic composition that reveled in the communicative possibilities of an archive of objects and gestures. This style of identity formation – drawing on sources that range from visceral painting to refined architecture – is recurrent throughout the artist's work, often highlighting the false constructions that commonly occur within art and exhibitions. Kratz creates a language of objects and gestures that is highly diverse, but which in total speaks of the contingencies and rituals of art.

Richard Birkett

21 # Independent spaces and emerging forms of connectivity

Salon discussion, 23 June 2008
ICA Brandon Room

Devised by
Anna Colin, Exhibitions Curator, Gasworks

Chaired by
Alessio Antoniolli, Director, Gasworks and Triangle Arts Trust

Invited speakers
Francesco Pedraglio and Pieternel Vermoortel, FormContent
Emily Pethick, Director, The Showroom
Alex Sainsbury, Founder and Director, Raven Row
Joe Scotland and Sarah McCrory, Curators, Studio Voltaire
Maria Zahle and Jason Dungan, The Hex

Whether public or private, institutional or artist-run, small-scale 'independent' spaces are currently evolving new structures and models for the presentation of emerging practice. Issues pertinent to the sector were addressed in this salon, organised by Gasworks, a non-profit art and studio space in South London. Conducted in a spirit of collaboration, and structured as a public meeting, the discussion explored the potential flexibility within a landscape characterised by financial constraint.

ANNA COLIN: Tonight's discussion is titled 'Independent spaces and emerging forms of connectivity'. We've opted for quite an informal set-up which consists of a core group of speakers representing a range of spaces: public, private, artist-run and studio spaces. Unfortunately only from London, but I can see in the audience that there are people from outside of London, so hopefully they can contribute to the discussion.

The core speakers have been given a few topics to think about. As we've outlined in the communication, we see this event as a public meeting, so participation from the audience is more than key for this discussion to be productive. One of the aims of tonight is to get to know better who we work next to in London and beyond, and to talk about ways of furthering what already exists on an informal basis but only takes place behind closed doors, that is, the idea of communicating one's ideas and future projects as a way of identifying common interests and developing collaborations as opposed to competition. How realistic is this? Who agrees with it and who doesn't? And what are the implications of sharing knowledge when we know that some people make a living out of consultancy work?

Although it is important to acknowledge the economical implications of this optimistic proposal, we're hoping to avoid talking too long about the current and future state of art funding. But the money issue keeps coming back. And, in fact, other than being intellectually fulfilling and often very productive (i.e., two minds are better than one), collaboration can also be pragmatic. It allows two or more spaces or institutions to share funding and audiences.

Collaborating can also imply exchanging ideas and disclosing one's plans and objectives in order to make connections with someone else's plans and objectives. Sharing knowledge to avoid duplicating research and content. But what are the conduits for sharing research between curators and institutions that do not know each other's agendas? What position must collaborators occupy to constitute a trustful network?

The aim is to discuss the viability of a more open approach to curating and perhaps to prepare the foundation for a sustained discussion/communication between curators, programme managers and directors. I will now hand the reins over to Alessio who will chair the discussion.

ALESSIO ANTONIOLLI: We should just briefly introduce ourselves.

JASON DUNGAN: Hello, I'm Jason and this is Maria, and we both run a space called The Hex out of a flat in Clapton. We're both artists and we started the space as a way of showing some solo projects.

JOE SCOTLAND: Joe and Sarah from Studio Voltaire. Studio Voltaire is an artist-led studio complex and gallery in South London.

ANTONIOLLI: Anna and I are from Gasworks, which is perhaps better known as a gallery space, but also houses studios for London-based artists, runs a programme of residencies for artists based outside the UK and is part of Triangle Arts Trust: a network of artists and arts organisations in various countries around the world.

EMILY PETHICK: I'm Emily Pethick. A month ago I started working as the director of the non-profit gallery The Showroom, which in the past has been a space concentrated on producing new work by artists that have not had solo shows in London before.

ALEX SAINSBURY: I'm Alex Sainsbury. I'm setting up a non-profit gallery called Raven Row, which will open next year.

PIETERNEL VERMOORTEL: I'm Pieternel Vermoortel, and together with Francesco we run the curatorial project space FormContent, a very small space in the East of London off Mare Street.

ANTONIOLLI: Ok, the idea is to really bring in the audience from the beginning so there won't be questions at the end, but instead throughout. With Anna we've decided to split the evening into two main topics and some of the speakers here have been introduced to that. The first one is about this idea of connectivity, this idea of creating a network of possible exchanges between non-commercial spaces. And the second main element of the night will be about the idea of identity – who we are and how we define ourselves as non-profit spaces, and whether these definitions or distinctions still make sense.

So to recap a little and to kick off with the discussion, as non-commercial spaces we are often competing for the same audiences and the same funding. And we all know that if you are a publicly funded organisation, the two things go together. This competition seems to be getting more fierce as the number of projects grow and funding – as well as audiences – are becoming thinner and thinner. And I'm not even going to talk about budget cuts or funding bodies' priorities that are forcing us into having a specific inclination for our programme, because I think this is a topic in itself and we could spend a whole evening just on that. Because of this funding situation, which we can take as a given, some of us are considering the option of creating organisations running on mixed-economies and looking at the implications of new forms of sustainability (new at least for galleries of our size, because we know that the Tate has been sponsored by huge corporations for years and some of this is starting to filter through).

Many of us are toying with the idea of moving in that direction. But for most of us this continues to be a fundraising strategy in our plan because it is really very difficult to find commercial sponsorship from large corporations in relation to our programme and our location.

So, the questions:

In this competitive situation – funding, audience and spaces – how controversial is it to talk about collaboration and the possibility of sharing audiences and funding? And I guess what I'm really asking is: what do people intend or understand by collaboration?

EMILY PETHICK: I recently moved back to London from the Netherlands, where I was working at a space called Casco, Office for Art, Design and Theory, in Utrecht. There I initiated a lot of different collaborations in order to re-energize the organisation. From my experience, one of the main difficulties of running a small non-profit space is that you can become very isolated – and because of this I think it's really important to try and connect out on many levels. So one of the things I'm doing with The Showroom is to start collaborating more. For example, we are working with Gasworks on a large presentation of The Otolith Group in 2009.

The Showroom will also work more closely with two other European spaces: Casco in Utrecht and Objectif Exhibitions in Antwerp. These collaborations are just the beginning, as our aim is to build a much stronger network for The Showroom. In this sense I think Gasworks is exemplary, as they have a gigantic global network, which seems somewhat under-recognized in London. When you look at the history of Gasworks you see that an incredible amount of people from all over the world have been coming for residencies, and it has maintained forms of exchange with all sorts of other organisations.

I think that working collaboratively is a way in which many spaces might have to start working, as economically it's a difficult time, and to be competitive is probably the wrong way to address that.

ANONYMOUS (audience): What does it mean when two spaces collaborate?

PETHICK: Well, the first collaboration I mentioned is with Gasworks, with whom we are co-producing a new film by The Otolith Group, as well as organising a joint presentation of this and other works, and a programme of events. Through this we hope to expand the possibilities of what both organisations can do, and we will give the artists an opportunity to do something much more ambitious. The European network that I mentioned will again enable much more ambitious projects to be realised. In this case it's not about just producing a work and sending it round three spaces, but we will use the fact that projects will travel as a way of developing them.

ANTONIOLLI: I think the question "what do we mean by collaboration?" is a good way to continue the discussion. Triangle Arts Trust, the network of which Gasworks is part of, impacts on London through the philosophy under which Gasworks operates, something that is shared by all Triangle's constituents. The main aim of the network is to support artists' mobility, dialogue and the development of new work through processes of collaboration between international artists and hosts. Significantly, the network focuses on artists' exchanges through workshops and residencies, where dialogue and process are favoured over the final product as a means to encourage experimentation. The network is mainly present in countries in Africa, Asia and Latin America, where we, in the UK, have very little connection. As such, Gasworks has quite a unique position in the UK arts scene, as it becomes the gateway for connections with artists and organisations in these parts of the world.

SAINSBURY: I was thinking that the non-profit sector is not just within art but generally government policy and capitalism itself has allowed the non-profit sector to become more efficient – or that's what it reckons. It's driven it to more efficiency and it's in the name of efficiency that a great deal of this competition and notions of individuation has taken place. Any charity now will ring-fence itself, individuate, describe itself as something different, attract different audiences in order to attract funding. So that in a way is a negative aspect of the market system in which we're living at the moment. So the onus is on us to try to undermine that by being collaborative again. That sort of communitarianism could be interpreted as something rather overly idealistic, but it's certainly something, again, as a recourse we perhaps have.

SARAH MCCRORY: It seems that the two sides of this are collaboration or, as it's been mentioned, competition. But there might be some concern – wherein not-for-profit organisations start acting as a kind of group and collaborating – that you might lose some of the individuality of how programmes run. There's that kind of crossover of collaboration or homogeneity.

ANTONIOLLI: What do you mean by 'homogeneity'?

MCCRORY: I'm talking generally about levels of where artists are coming from, how much exposure they've had. When projects come about in certain spaces it is sometimes by accident. Also they might not function in a very typical way. I'm trying to think of something that's based around the idea of Studio Voltaire and some of the projects that have happened there, which were very spontaneous and unsuitable for collaboration. But then it's two-fold. We have also done that.

MARIA ZAHLE: We are a space, we've never got funding for anything. We are running the Hex very much on a shoestring budget – it's out of our own flat. So in that sense we've had total control over everything we've done, we haven't had to fill out any forms or apply for anything or get permission to do anything, which is kind of why we wanted to do it. I've just never thought about any idea of competition in relation to spaces. Maybe in terms of being an artist, but never in terms of running a space. And I don't think that's about turning down the ambition of it. Maybe it's an amateur in relation to a professional – that anything is really possible.

ANTONIOLLI: Then I think the question really stands as to what is a type of collaboration that is comfortable and how many types of collaborations might there be?

POLLY STAPLE (audience): Just to follow on with a practical example, can you say what sharing the project with The Otolith Group will mean for the audience? What will I see at The Showroom and what will I see at Gasworks? Two halves of one show?

COLIN: It's not completely defined yet, but of course it will be a different show, most probably a new work at The Showroom and more of a retrospective at Gasworks; the two together will form a mini-retrospective of what they have been doing over the last few years. It's under development so we're not completely sure what the manifestations will be yet, but we will share a public programme, which will be two energies, two organisations with different histories and with different experiences coming together. The product will be different.

STAPLE: I'm going to press it a little more. Are there any reasons that you chose to work with The Otolith Group on this project? I'll tell you the reasons I'm asking that: often when you work collaboratively you work with another organisation because they have some specialist knowledge that you don't have, and that's brilliant. For example, when I was working at Frieze Art Fair, I worked with LUX because they had specialist knowledge that I didn't have and it was a really happy and equal collaboration. Gasworks, you have these specialist international links with Triangle Arts Trust, and I was just wondering if that helped shape The Otolith project.

PETHICK: The way this collaboration came around is that we both approached The Otolith Group with a similar idea, so we thought why not do it together? I think collaboration doesn't only have to be pragmatic; it can also be about having a conversation.

ANTONIOLLI: And I think with the specific case of The Otolith Group, we are two small organisations giving the artist the opportunity to have more space in which to show their work, and the history of our organisations are also going to be part of this discussion. And of course the international debates are part of what they're interested in.

STAPLE: I've got one more, quick question which relates to that. Is the form of the work determining these kinds of collaborations? Obviously if you're working with people making a film, you're working as commissioners much more in the role of a film production agency. For example, would you collaborate on a painting show? Or to stretch that point, would you then be collaborating possibly with a commercial gallery, and what does that type of collaboration mean? And is that collaboration suddenly on the wrong side of the line?

PETHICK: I'm never closed to any idea that makes sense for a particular reason.

ANTONIOLLI: I think it has to do with who you are and what you want to present as your programme. But then I feel the same; I wouldn't want to feel we are confined only to work in a certain way. There are different ways of engaging with different organisations, and one has to ask what we have to give the other and what the other has to give us.

COLIN: And this is something we will talk about later – the blurring of positions. Take for example the Lisson Gallery doing a show – with Sharon Hayes … This is something we would be interested in working on with the Lisson because it's something that we tend to do and we can relate to it. Artist-run spaces are taking part in art fairs and commercial galleries are doing shows about activism. At this level there is such a blurring of boundaries you can really collaborate pretty much with anyone.

RICHARD BIRKETT (audience): We are also talking about distinct layers. This specific example of a collaboration between Gasworks and The Showroom is about two organisations that are on a similar tier. There are people here who are involved in very hand-to-mouth, small spaces. I'm wondering what collaboration means for smaller spaces? Because what we're talking about is knowledge-sharing in some way as an idea of collaboration beyond just sharing a show. Is it realistic to consider a group forum where smaller spaces can impact on programmes at larger spaces? How can this be realised?

MCCRORY: Studio Voltaire works as a not-for-profit gallery and studio space and is funded on a project basis. We have recently been working to develop a strand that is commercial in some, but not all, ways. We have portfolios and sales of unique works, as well as having a patron scheme. Because of the current funding landscape, we're trying to stick a finger in every pie possible. I think there are quite a lot of spaces that cross over slightly in different ways and in manners that are not obvious.

COLIN: Silvia, would you mind talking about the Lisson Gallery's programme?

SILVIA SGUALDINI (audience): Well, we obviously are a commercial gallery. We represent artists and sell their work and that's where the funding for any side project comes from. I have recently co-curated a project with a colleague of mine; it's a series of events or installations by artists including some who are not represented by the gallery. We're not having a commercial gain from this project, which was mainly born of a curatorial interest, of the will to do a project that went outside the gallery space. We have tried to collaborate with institutions where it made sense, and one example is our partnership with Lux on a series of performances by American artist Sharon Hayes. Because she already had a connection with Lux, it made sense to present the documentation of this work, which is an integral part of the work itself, as an exhibition in their new space. For us it is interesting to mix different audiences and to see what happens when you work with an institution.

SAINSBURY: It's interesting ... It seems the question of audience is huge here. Collectors like artworks to have a sexy audience, and collectors aren't a very sexy audience, so there's a need for commercial galleries to gain critical credibility by attracting an audience beyond the collector.

SGUALDINI: I don't really agree with that.

SAINSBURY: It certainly seems to me that commercial galleries need the credibility of the non-public sector in order to gain a critical mass for their work.

SGUALDINI: I think they need credibility full stop. So obviously you try to produce something that has value, which is not necessarily a commercial value.

ANTONIOLLI: Why do you think a commercial gallery would invest in that? Why not just in something that has commercial value?

SGUALDINI: I don't know, maybe I'm the wrong person to speak because I come from a curatorial background – I don't come from a dealer's background. The fact that the structure of the gallery where I work is divided between a sales and a curatorial team says quite a lot about that.

SAINSBURY: I agree with you. I think it's blurred, again because, partly, you can say commercial galleries are not actually shareholder companies. If it was a shareholder company then the only object of that company would be to increase the value of the art object. Now, you could look at some galleries and see that that's clearly their sole motive. So one's scepticism – cynicism – is to imagine that this is one way to increase value, because curating is so trendy and 'important'. Like in the old days Waddington produced a catalogue, because all a collector needed was to see their artwork in a catalogue. Now they need to see it curated. As a consequence of that, of course, curators are incredibly cheap, because the non-profit sector pays nothing. For someone like Nicholas Logsdail [director, Lisson Gallery], clearly his intention is not just to increase the value of art objects; he has a deep passion for art that is most motivating.

GAVIN WADE (audience): I might be able to give a good example of a strategic attempt to set up a gallery space with a mixed economy. I'm just setting up Eastside Projects in Birmingham at the moment. I don't see why you wouldn't be strategic, in a way. We're Arts Council revenue funded, we're partnering with Birmingham City University who are giving us £200,000 worth of equipment to be able to use in the gallery. There are brilliant things about the commercial art scene, such as the fact that an artist gets to show again in the same space ... So I want to try and see how we can take what's interesting from commercial galleries and what's interesting from public galleries and what's interesting from an artist-run space. So I've proposed a gallery as an artist-run space and as a public gallery, and we want to get bigger. How big can an artist-run space be without just becoming completely an institution and no longer being an artwork or wanting to be part of an artwork production process? You have to look at all the strengths, and I don't really understand why not take all those things and put them together.

ANTONIOLLI: I completely accept that; in fact my question was deliberately contentious. For the sake of the argument, though, does anybody feel compromised by this possibility?

SCOTLAND: For Studio Voltaire, in many ways, by having a mix of different sources of income our actual levels of autonomy can be stronger; because, for example, we're not answerable to the Arts Council or the local council.

ANTONIOLLI: Do you find then that the choices you make in your programme are determined by the venues in which you decide to show the artist? Does having a stand in the Zoo art fair determine which artists you work with and what you commission them to do?

SCOTLAND: No. Well, the relationship with the artist comes first. All the presentations we've made at art fairs have always been reflective of our programme.

ANONYMOUS (audience): I'm just wondering how the spaces we're talking about today are described and considered in terms of the mechanisms of the international art scene: they're always considered as emerging, which is, whatever ... If they are working for more than ten years they are still emerging and alternative. So curators have to present something different than other institutions, and independent, whether or not they are taking public funds. So how do you as spaces feel in terms of these descriptions in the art scene as 'emerging', 'independent' and 'alternative'?

PETHICK: That's actually something I'm working on at the moment, trying to move away from the term 'emerging artist'. To me definitions of early-mid-late career are both institutional and linked to the marketplace. In the past, The Showroom has defined itself as a space specifically focused on showing 'emerging artists'. However, we are now trying to open that up a bit and shift towards talking more about emerging practices and ideas. Thus it's not about what stage of career an artist is in, or what age they are, but about exploring new ways of thinking and doing.

IAN WHITE (audience): I wonder whether it's useful to talk about a cultural economy and other kinds of economy, a financial economy, because it seems to me that it's the relationship between those two things that is defining a lot of what people are talking about. I think what Sarah was talking about in terms of the importance of visibility is precisely about the relationship between a cultural economy and a financial economy, and I think many other people's comments have been based around those things. And it seems everyone is painting quite a rosy picture of an idea of collaboration and working together and knowledge-sharing. And it seems to me that within a cultural economy, right now, there's actually quite a fierce competition – but this is reiterating things that have already been touched upon.

COLIN: I'm aware that what I said at the beginning might sound optimistic and somewhat naïve, but this way of working has proven to be perfectly suitable for an organisation of the scale of Gasworks. I was saying earlier that a few spaces throughout the world may work on the same topic at pretty much the same time. A favourite subject has been spiritualism and ghosts in the last two to three years, for instance. The fact that the takes on these subjects haven't been that different from one place to the other leads one to think the communication between these spaces hasn't been great. With this in mind – the idea of sharing the research we generate here at Gasworks for each project – we have created a second online presence called Pipeline, on which we post articles, texts, bibliographies and other material according to projects. For each project carried out at or by Gasworks in 2008, we have a number of entries that give web users an insight into the research process and into the material we have come across and which may have informed the given project.

MARK SLADEN (audience): To summarise, a lot of the conversation tonight was about survival strategies and these new collaborative approaches as basically a survival strategy. Then we got onto audiences and a question about whether these new practices in the non-profit sector can benefit audiences. But I think how we measure this, as one of the questioners pointed out, is a very slippery thing. So, I suppose I just wanted to bring it back to this idea of what the actual benefit to artists is, and perhaps Anna could comment on this: with this new arena of collaborative practices between different institutions, whether you think that it is following and prompted by new practices among artists, which is surely what should justify any changed institutional model?

COLIN: Perhaps institutions really started to move in this direction in the last five or six years – a phenomenon some have labelled New Institutionalism – or perhaps in the mid-1990s when they started to engage in projects that would challenge them from the inside. In the late 1990s and early 2000s there were countless exhibitions and initiatives that consisted in inviting artist-run spaces to play themselves inside the museum or the gallery. Bringing alternative models inside the art institution shook the institution and introduced it to more fluid and informal ways of operating. For instance, containing very different models and approaches within a fairly rigid structure, operations that can be extremely spontaneous or non-costly or both. This finally became noticeable in London some three or four years ago, although it didn't come as rapidly as in the Netherlands.

PETHICK: This is certainly why I've stuck working with small institutions; they are more flexible and open to change, and they have the potential to be influenced by, and change with, artists and practices.

22

Redmond Entwistle

Screening, 7 July 2008
ICA Cinema

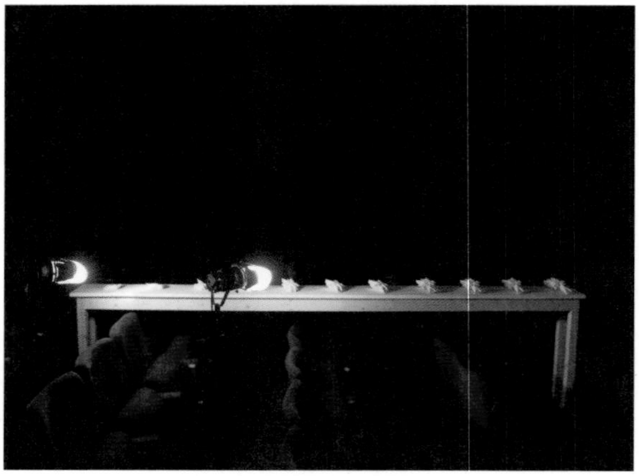

Drawing on the unreliability of the filmic medium and the subjective quality of recollection, the relationship between place and memory is a theme that recurs in moving image practice. Filmmaker Redmond Entwistle (born London, 1977, lives in London and New York) homes in on these properties, demonstrating how they relate to the space of the auditorium, while also illustrating film's historic relationship to the development of cities. Entwistle's films create portraits of cities as both spatial entities and sites for personal testimony, by skirting around their edges or by focusing on the invisible or the implied.

Entwistle's *Paterson – Lódz* (2006), a 16mm film about two towns (Paterson, New Jersey, and Lódz, Poland), is interrupted by audio tracks that simulate these urban spaces within the cinema auditorium. The audio components play in a different order each time the film is screened, making the work a unique encounter – an event experienced at a particular moment in time by a particular group of people. This activation of film's spatial effects on the viewer is central to expanded cinema, a type of experimental film practice that emerged in the 1960s and to which Entwistle's work has been compared. In *Paterson – Lódz*, Entwistle activates 'the space between' – literally, the blank spaces between the two films, in which sounds of public spaces in the two cities are heard – and also the space between Lódz and Paterson, two cities that were the start and end points of emigration for many Jews in the early twentieth century. This transition reflects the production of culture within these populations, and the continuities and discontinuities formed through geographical displacement.

For his *Nought to Sixty* screening programme Entwistle presented *Skein* (2008), a video that he chose to expand in the auditorium with sculpture and performance. In *Skein*, as with *Paterson – Lódz*, the space around a city – the memories of it, journeys from it, obstructions to it – becomes as important as the image of the city itself, and the space occupied by the cinema audience watching the film. Ostensibly a portrait of New York, *Skein* was filmed on the peripheries of the city: along a route through the New Jersey suburbs. An interviewer asks residents how they think of their home district in relation to Manhattan – which they prefer, how they compare – and various visions of the city and sense of distance from it emerge.

In an early version of *Skein*, Entwistle overlaid image of interviewees with abstract white sculptural forms. For the ICA event, however, these small objects were displayed on a long plinth in the cinema's seating area. During a sequence of intermissions the artist displayed these objects before a live camera, cutting from the film to close-ups on a large adjacent monitor. These forms were 3D renderings of the spaces around the bodies that appear in the film's interviews. Their emergence is at once incompatible with the documentary image, while also offering a different means of mapping the movement away from the city that the film describes. Their decontextualised presentation suggests a process of simultaneous accumulation and erasure, of the multiple forces that impact on a form in its development.

Entwistle's presentation of *Skein* activated the site of the ICA (and its role as a bearer of 'radical' histories) through the display of these agglomerates of negative space. The latter physically manifest the metaphorical gaps within the oral histories – both in on-screen interviews and in a live performance reading in the ICA, proposing a template for an expanded notion of social, political and historical portraiture.

Melissa Gronlund

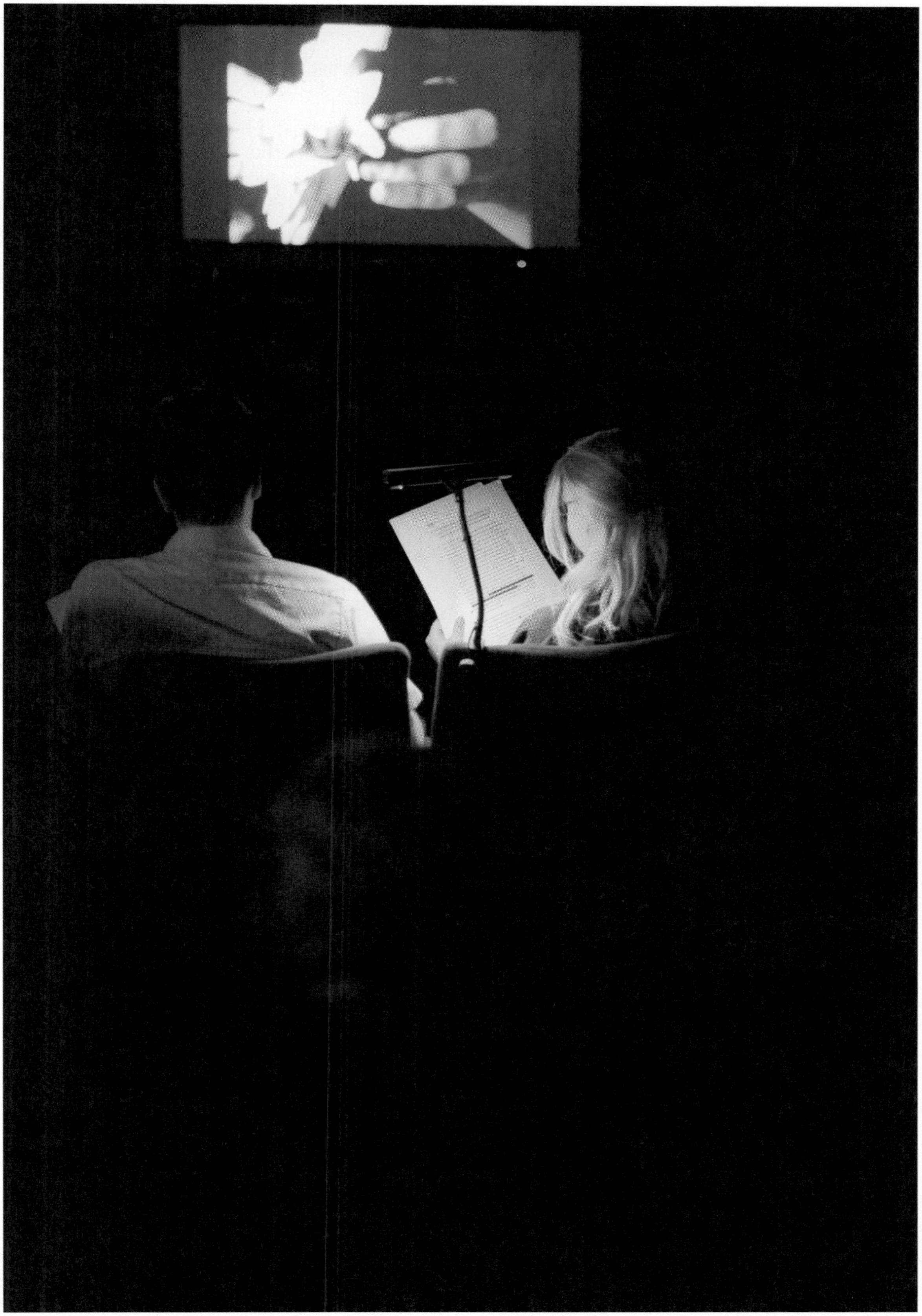

Redmond Entwistle / *Skein* / 2008

23 Andrew Hunt

Event, 12–13 July 2008
ICA Upper Galleries and off-site

Artist, curator, organiser, publisher, critic, collaborator, facilitator, commissioner. Andrew Hunt (born Luton, 1969, lives in London) has embraced these and many other roles within the contemporary art scene over the past ten years. Reflecting the growing diversity of positions available within contemporary art, Hunt's wide-ranging activities traverse and connect distinct disciplines to bring about new possibilities.

Although initially training in fine art, Hunt has taken up curatorial roles at institutions such as Norwich Gallery – where he worked on the annual EAST event – and he is currently the curator of International Project Space (IPS) in Bournville, Birmingham. A significant addition to art in the Midlands, IPS at Birmingham City University stages solo exhibitions and group shows, while also publishing artists' editions and catalogues.

In 2000 Hunt initiated *Slimvolume Poster Publication*, a non-profit annual publication that invites selected artists to produce editioned posters and prints that are compiled into a single 'volume'. Hunt and the contributors distribute copies to a carefully recruited audience – a grouping of friends, musicians, artists, curators and others, which he terms an "extended family tree". By strategically targeting artists and audiences according to the nature of each publication, Hunt constructs new communities united by receivership, although the methodology of the groupings and the social relations that unite them are not necessarily apparent. The individual volumes can be unbound or preserved in their original formats, and the printed matter generated by the project has been exhibited widely.

Slimvolume was founded to allow contributors to expand their practice within a collaborative context, and to date it has involved commissions by over 150 artists.

Although Hunt is the strategist, publisher and distributor of the project, it is because of his multifarious roles – rather than in spite of them – that he can be considered an artist of the most contemporary kind. Echoing Boris Groys' description of the role of the contemporary artist – as simultaneously the analyst, critic and receiver of artwork – Hunt's mutable positions reflect the heterogeneous production and presentation of art today.

For *Nought to Sixty* Hunt created a weekend event that included the work of Jonty Lees, Alastair MacKinven, and Erik Blinderman and Michael Eddy, amalgamating these artists' diverse concerns into an investigation into the nature of performance. The event took place both inside and outside the ICA, placing an emphasis not only on action but on the deferral of action via photographic and video documentation, installation and text. Hunt and Lees held the inaugural meeting of The Artists' Cycling Club, while MacKinven, Eddy and Blinderman staged a series of displaced performance activites, built up over the 48-hour period. Together, the activities questioned a number of issues related to performance – including its live/unique attributes, its sites of occurrence and its modes of reception – as well as the role of live events within projects such as *Nought to Sixty*.

Isla Leaver-Yap

Both: inaugural meeting of The Artists' Cycling Club / July 2008

23 cont'd Erik Blinderman and Michael Eddy, Jonty Lees and Alastair MacKinven

Invited artists Erik Blinderman and Michael Eddy, Jonty Lees, and Alastair MacKinven presented a two-day project centred on the contemporary relationship between performance and photography. While the ICA's Upper Galleries were used primarily as an exhibition space, performances took place off-site throughout the weekend.

In the history of performance art, individual works have traditionally been presented as a mechanical sequence of events: from the site and time of an original action, to its documentation, critical evaluation and – as sometimes happens with seminal works – subsequent re-enactment. This problematic chronology serves to canonise a performance work within the field of historical discourse. For *Nought to Sixty*'s event, however, the selected artists attempted to skew and disrupt the logical progression of performance and time by combining new photographic documentation, props, projections and films with off-site performances and performative installations. The artists aimed to present alternative readings of an 'original' event.

Alastair MacKinven, who had already participated in *Nought to Sixty* with an installation comprising paintings and sculptural objects, this time pursued the performative aspect of his practice. For his performance, *Time Shifter, Sailor Killer, Moth Fucker*, MacKinven visited the Royal Observatory in Greenwich on the evening before the two-day project. The observatory projects a laser at zero degrees longitude, representing the path of the Prime Meridian – the international timeline. MacKinven's action at this site was documented and the resulting footage was shown in the ICA Upper Galleries for the rest of the weekend. Presented alongside the video, an incongruous prop used at Greenwich was wedged into the same space, referring as much to Charlie Chaplin's precarious walking cane, or W.C. Fields' absurd billiard cue, as to Robert Smithson's mirror displacements.

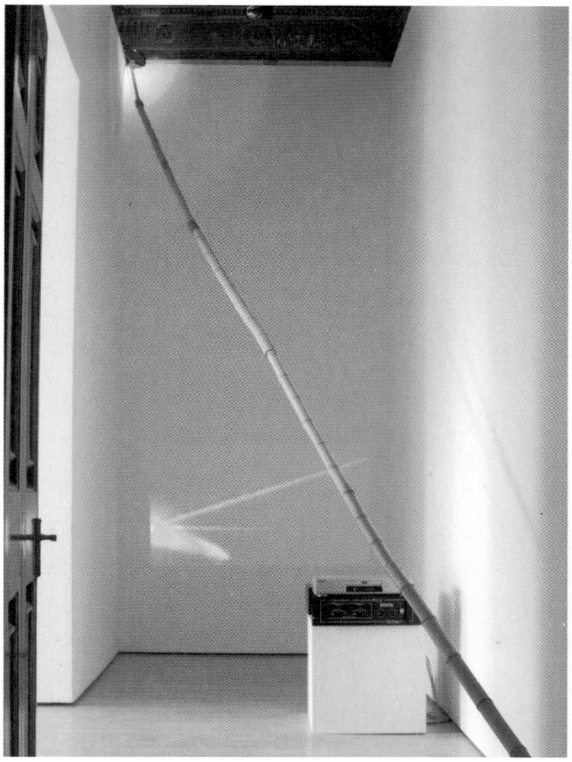

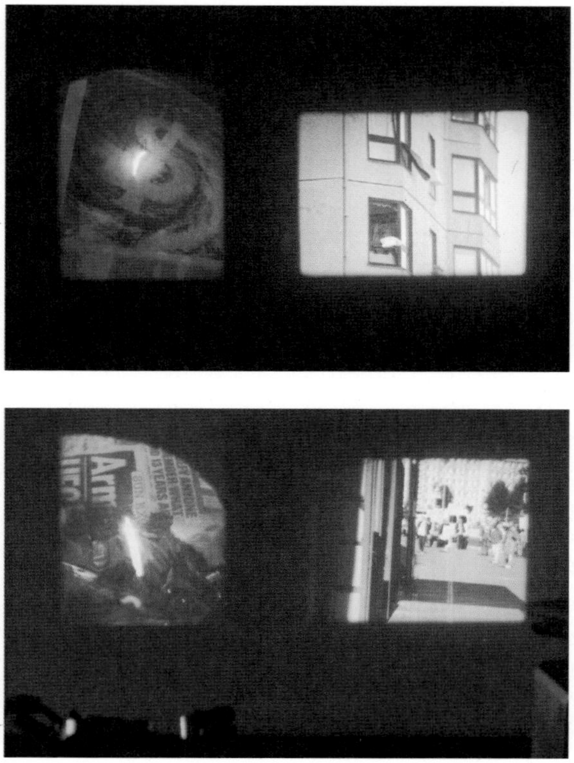

Left: Alastair MacKinven / *Time Shifter, Sailor Killer, Moth Fucker* / 2008
Right: Erik Blinderman and Michael Eddy / *The Tattler and I* / 2008

Artists Erik Blinderman and Michael Eddy, who recently studied at the Städelschule in Frankfurt, create films that deal with mirrors, reflection and refraction through time-based work. For the *Nought to Sixty* weekend, the artists presented a 16mm film installation in which two films they produced independently were projected. Blinderman's film, made using a deceptively angled 'spy camera' built by the artist, engages the history of artists' surveillance – especially the work of Walker Evans, Henri Cartier Bresson and Gordon Matta-Clark – with the goal of constructing an 'indirect cinema'. Eddy's film, made using a camera fitted with a magnifying glass that burns holes through and into its subject, questions the notion that the camera is a neutral gatherer of information.

Jonty Lees produced numerous works for this weekend exhibition. His irreverent array of ideas – which Martin Clark and Michael Archer documented for the artist's 2007 Tate St Ives residency – were pushed forward to include the site of the ICA as their starting point. Lees used one of the Upper Galleries to present an installation of performance and still imagery, which again referred to actions beyond the space. Lees' series of sonic interventions referenced legendary producers such as Joe Meek and Martin Hannet (and their ingenuous experiments with noise), while interfering with the ICA's building in an impish manner. An inaugural meeting of The Artists' Cycling Club also occurred within the ICA, while the area outside the building similarly saw the initiation of playful actions, both visible and veiled.

Andrew Hunt

24

Jeffrey Charles Henry Peacock Gallery

Exhibition, 19 July–24 August 2008
Off-site

While the name Jeffrey Charles Henry Peacock Gallery has a prestigious – if unwieldy – ring to it, the title in fact stems from the amalgamation of two non-profit exhibition spaces: Jeffrey Charles Gallery (founded in 2001 by artists Kev Rice and Dave Smith) and Henry Peacock Gallery (run by artist and gallerist Thom Winterburn). Both spaces closed their doors in the same year, merging in 2005 to form an entity that sits outside conventional gallery structures.

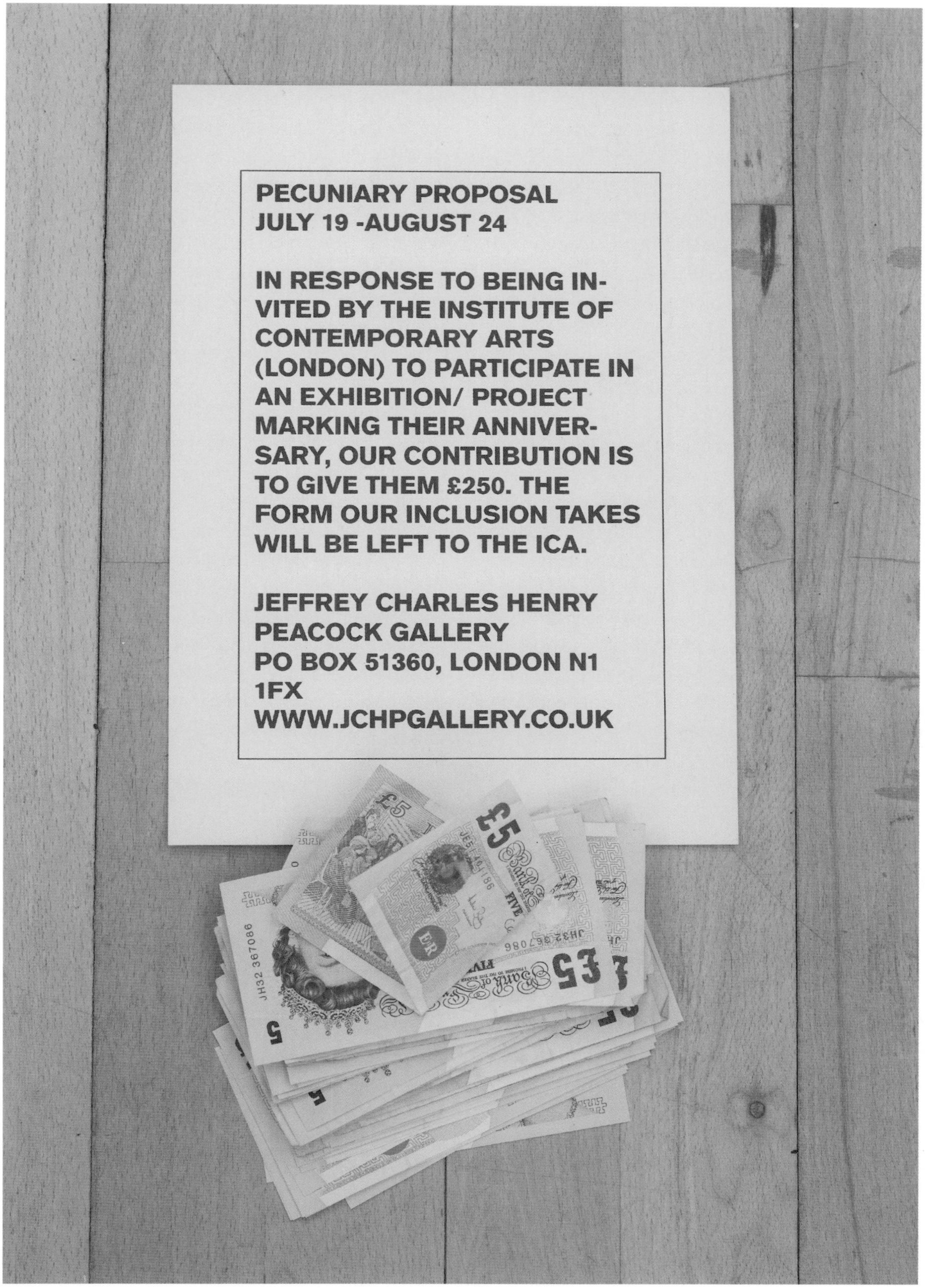
PECUNIARY PROPOSAL
JULY 19 -AUGUST 24

IN RESPONSE TO BEING INVITED BY THE INSTITUTE OF CONTEMPORARY ARTS (LONDON) TO PARTICIPATE IN AN EXHIBITION/ PROJECT MARKING THEIR ANNIVERSARY, OUR CONTRIBUTION IS TO GIVE THEM £250. THE FORM OUR INCLUSION TAKES WILL BE LEFT TO THE ICA.

JEFFREY CHARLES HENRY
PEACOCK GALLERY
PO BOX 51360, LONDON N1
1FX
WWW.JCHPGALLERY.CO.UK

Jeffrey Charles Henry Peacock Gallery / exhibition proposal delivered by hand to ICA / 19 February 2008

JCHP Gallery is based on a denial of the need for physical space as a means of presenting art. The 'gallery' exists without an address, manifested instead through the dissemination of information and the participation of the recipients. Since 2005, JCHP has commissioned artists such as John Miller, Terry Atkinson and Michael Corris to create editions, projects publicised by an invitation card or email and sent out to those who respond. The invitations have also served as announcements for 'exhibitions' that exist purely through instructions, or in an intangible act of exchange. The experimental and declaratory use of language, as well as the importance given to typographic design, offers parallels with a number of avant-garde movements from Dada to Fluxus.

If a conventional gallery implies a generalised, impersonal interaction with art, the requirement for response in a JCHP instruction suggests the personal completion of a contract. For *Do not like do not dislike* (2006), the invitation listed the names of four paintings, the address of Tate Britain and a set of opening times and dates for the exhibition. The implication was that the recipient would fulfil the exhibition by visiting the gallery within the allotted dates and times, engaging wholly and only with a set of designated works. JCHP operates within the contractual mechanisms of cultural appreciation, but its methods, though demanding and exclusive, disavow the value systems that can dictate how art is perceived. To quote from the invitation for the former project, "Do not like, do not dislike, all will then be clear. This does not mean do nothing at all, but only have no deliberate mind. Do not select or reject anything."

The ICA's invitation to JCHP to propose a *Nought to Sixty* project posed the question of how such processes of reassignment could exist within a larger system. The gallery's response to the request was to hold up a mirror, 're-gifting' the invitation by inviting the ICA to complete a JCHP exhibition, entitled *Pecuniary Proposal*. This project entailed the payment of £250 to the ICA in order to facilitate an unprescribed activity. In response to the conundrum of how to complete this 'contract', the ICA resolved to use the funds to reproduce the original invitation card for *Pecuniary Proposal* and to distribute this copy within one of the *Nought to Sixty* mail outs. This unsanctioned act provided a further layer to *Pecuniary Proposal*, creating a parallel exhibition through the recipients of the ICA mailing, one that replicated the 'original' exhibition as manifested through JCHP's own distribution system.

Richard Birkett

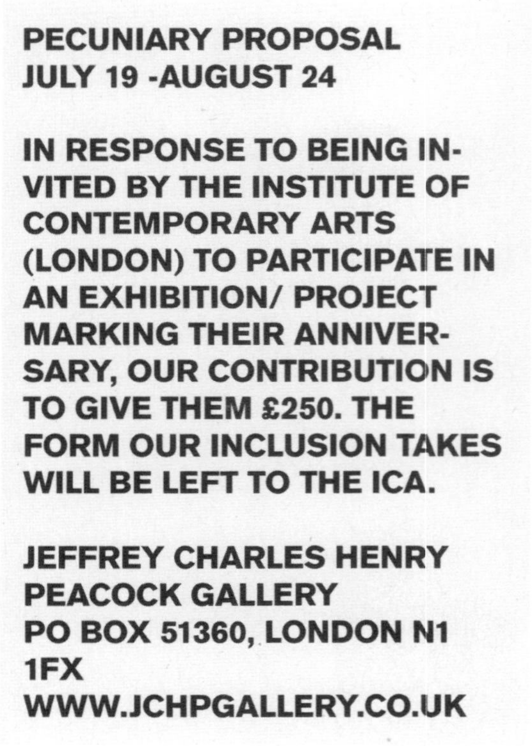

PECUNIARY PROPOSAL
JULY 19 -AUGUST 24

IN RESPONSE TO BEING INVITED BY THE INSTITUTE OF CONTEMPORARY ARTS (LONDON) TO PARTICIPATE IN AN EXHIBITION/ PROJECT MARKING THEIR ANNIVERSARY, OUR CONTRIBUTION IS TO GIVE THEM £250. THE FORM OUR INCLUSION TAKES WILL BE LEFT TO THE ICA.

JEFFREY CHARLES HENRY
PEACOCK GALLERY
PO BOX 51360, LONDON N1
1FX
WWW.JCHPGALLERY.CO.UK

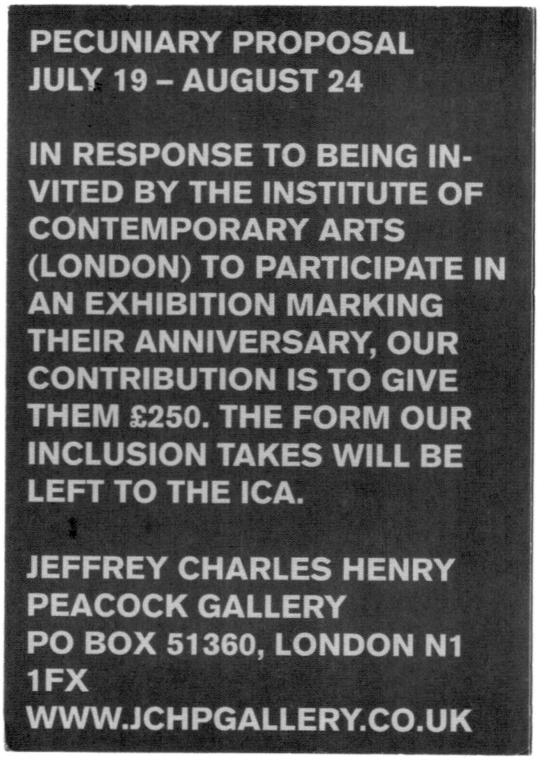

PECUNIARY PROPOSAL
JULY 19 – AUGUST 24

IN RESPONSE TO BEING INVITED BY THE INSTITUTE OF CONTEMPORARY ARTS (LONDON) TO PARTICIPATE IN AN EXHIBITION MARKING THEIR ANNIVERSARY, OUR CONTRIBUTION IS TO GIVE THEM £250. THE FORM OUR INCLUSION TAKES WILL BE LEFT TO THE ICA.

JEFFREY CHARLES HENRY
PEACOCK GALLERY
PO BOX 51360, LONDON N1
1FX
WWW.JCHPGALLERY.CO.UK

Left: Exhibition invitation card printed and distributed by ICA / July 2008
Right: Exhibition invitation card printed and distributed by Jeffrey Charles Henry Peacock Gallery / July 2008

25

Nina Beier and Marie Lund

Events, May–October 2008
Various locations

Nina Beier (born Århus, Denmark, 1976, lives in London) and Marie Lund (born Hundested, Denmark, 1975, lives in London) have been working as a duo since 2003. With staged events as well as videos, photographs and sculptures, Beier and Lund tinker with social hierarchies and group dynamics. They often start by issuing a simple set of instructions that participants – both collaborators and audience members – are free to interpret.

In the recent intervention *All the People at Tate Modern* (2007), Beier and Lund strategically positioned members of Tate staff around the building and asked them to start applauding at a set time. A few posters stuck on the museum's walls also invited visitors to clap. Video documentation of the event shows this clapping, which starts shyly but soon turns into a roaring wave of applause. Mass participation quickly becomes the norm in such a situation, but Beier and Lund's interest lies in when such behavior becomes 'abnormal'. Not only did *All the People at Tate Modern* disturb the religiously silent atmosphere expected in an art gallery, but it also blurred the usual boundaries between the public and museum professionals – all temporarily united in the shared experience of an extraordinary standing ovation.

For *The Division* (2007), a work staged at Tate Britain, Beier and Lund announced that 50 beautiful people had been invited to the event. Without any further information, visitors were left to eye each other up and divine who those fabulous guests might be. Like many of the artists' situations, *The Division* was as much a physical intervention in a group – the audience – as it was the creation of an imaginative space where anyone was a potential participant. However, the work's title also implies that beauty is a divisive force, stigmatising those who may not be deemed conventionally attractive.

The underlying awkwardness of social interactions is a recurring feature in Beier and Lund's production, and the interventions they staged for *Nought to Sixty* extended these concerns. The first of these works, *The Artist* (2008), was announced in issue one of the *Nought to Sixty* magazine. A black-bordered caption simply stated that a previous ICA exhibitor, who had since stopped their professional art practice, would be invited to the *Nought to Sixty* launch. During the opening night, Beier and Lund were frequently approached by people suggesting possible candidates for this mysterious figure. For *The Witness* (2008), meanwhile, a gallery attendant at the ICA agreed to grow his beard and hair for the six-month period of *Nought to Sixty* – personifying the duration of the project as a whole.

The final part of the trilogy was *An Encore*, for which a music act that had recently performed at the ICA was invited to return to the scene and repeat every gesture of the original evening. As a group, the trilogy underlined the importance of context and – by exploring the hierarchical position of participants – Beier and Lund highlighted the institution's own contradictory position as both a risk-taking art laboratory and a supposedly authoritative, 'culture-making' organisation.

Coline Milliard

≥ *The Artist*

A person, who once exhibited at the ICA and no longer calls himself an artist, has been invited for the opening of the exhibition.

Nina Beier and Marie Lund, event, ICA, May 5th, 2008

« *An Encore*

A young singer-songwriter, who recently performed at the ICA, is invited back on the premise that he play, say and act exactly the same as he did the first time around.

Nina Beier and Marie Lund, concert, ICA, July 14th, 2008

Top: Nina Beier and Marie Lund / *The Artist* / 2008 / caption in *Nought to Sixty* magazine
Bottom: Nina Beier and Marie Lund / *An Encore* / 2008 / caption in *Nought to Sixty* magazine

26 **Andy Wake**

Event, 21 July 2008
ICA Nash/Brandon Rooms

Andy Wake (born Dundee, 1978, lives in Dundee and Glasgow) produces videos, drawings, texts and sculptures, for both exhibition and performance formats. Yet Wake's body of work appears to rebel against the confines of these forms of display. Rather, the artist seeks to thwart the observer's ability to experience the work within a finite encounter.

Engaged in the crossover between the categories of artwork, artefact and prop, Wake works with an array of objects which he recasts in constantly changing contexts – props for video occasionally go on to appear in sculptural installations, or video monitors might later integrate with sculptural objects. Building up a series of loose leitmotifs, Wake re-works meanings, titles and media over different displays. Time is conceived as nonlinear; subjected to the mechanics of video technology, it appears scattered, folded, cyclical.

The installation *The Basest Horn of His Hoof is More Musical than the Pipe of Hermes* (2007) is based on one of Wake's recurring objects – a large structure resembling the shape of an old gramophone trumpet, positioned centrally on a

All images: Andy Wake / *The Storming of the Bastille* / 2008

stage. The structure's front face reveals a projection screen with a closed-circuit strobing image showing the internal space of the sealed object. The sporadic image lurches in and out of legibility as the flashing light disrupts the camera's auto-focus. This eye of surveillance – and the implicit sense of mistrust that accompanies it – is turned inwards on itself, yet fails to distinguish anything except a fitfully illuminated void. The moving image is doomed to the continual failure of its own mechanics.

The work's title, taken from Shakespeare's *Henry V*, cites another of Wake's frequent reference points – the Greek god Hermes, a shape-shifter who has the ability to cross the thresholds of the divine and the human, the sacred and profane, under a cloak of invisibility. Wake, fascinated by the mutability of this figure, created *Trickster Cycle* (2007) a video that explores the various legends of the Greek god. In this work and *The Basest Horn*, the artist fuses his interest in quasi-scientific narratives and mythological order with investigations of recorded and real time. Extending the early experiments in closed-circuit televisions, as well as the instant feedback loop employed by artists such as Dan Graham and Vito Acconci, Wake is less interested in the process and materiality of his work than in how objects and technology can be exploited to collapse time-based perception – and activate the Romantic imagination.

For *Nought to Sixty*, Wake presented an event, entitled *The Storming of the Bastille* (2008), that sought to evade the temporal parameters of live performance. Using masked and hidden performers, prerecorded and live video footage, and sculptural interventions that included monumental paper screens and a live pipe organ, Wake looped and condensed both sound and image in an unending Droste effect. The sound of one performer's voice would appear in a neighbouring room, or a video image would present the audience in time delay. Wake's project gestured beyond the single event or presence, pushing the audience's sense of becoming into an experience of belatedness.

Isla Leaver-Yap

All images: Andy Wake / *The Storming of the Bastille* / 2008

27 **Sean Edwards**

Exhibition, 21–28 July 2008
ICA Upper Galleries

Often using remnants of previous activities as base material – found or borrowed objects, bits of other works or studio knickknacks – Sean Edwards (born Cardiff, 1980, lives in Abergavenny) investigates the sculptural potential of the everyday. For his recent solo show at Moot, Nottingham, the artist exhibited two recuperated dowels, one of them elongated to match the length of the other, with a layer cake of cork and felt. The patterned regularity of the resulting assemblage displays a distinct graphic sensibility – one that is common to many of Edwards' sculptures.

Since 2006 the artist has been buying a copy of The Sun newspaper every day, and has integrated the publication into a number of artworks. From this starting point Edwards has created works which exploit the tension between two- and three-dimensions. In K_007 (2007) the artist cut a sheet of dolls house paper into the silhouette of a page 3 glamour model, and twisted the paper into a cylinder. Another ongoing work has involved elegantly cutting and compiling the letters 'U' and 'N' from the mastheads of all the issues that Edwards has bought. However, The Sun project is more than just a formal exercise. By incorporating the purchase of the newspaper into his artistic practice, Edwards pointedly brings together the high and low, the quotidian and the 'timeless'.

Edwards also sees this duality in the works of others. During the 2006 World Snooker Championship the artist filmed the crew responsible for assembling the competition tables (Table, 2006). In this video the overwhelming abundance of raw materials – slate tabletops, swathes of green fabric, tacks – highlights the sculptural core of the craftsmen's activity. 16mm film Lap Steel (2008), presented in Edwards' *Nought to Sixty* exhibition, shows a close-up of an anonymous hand playing lap steel guitar. The wooden fingerboard and the metal slide look like the disembodied elements of a moving

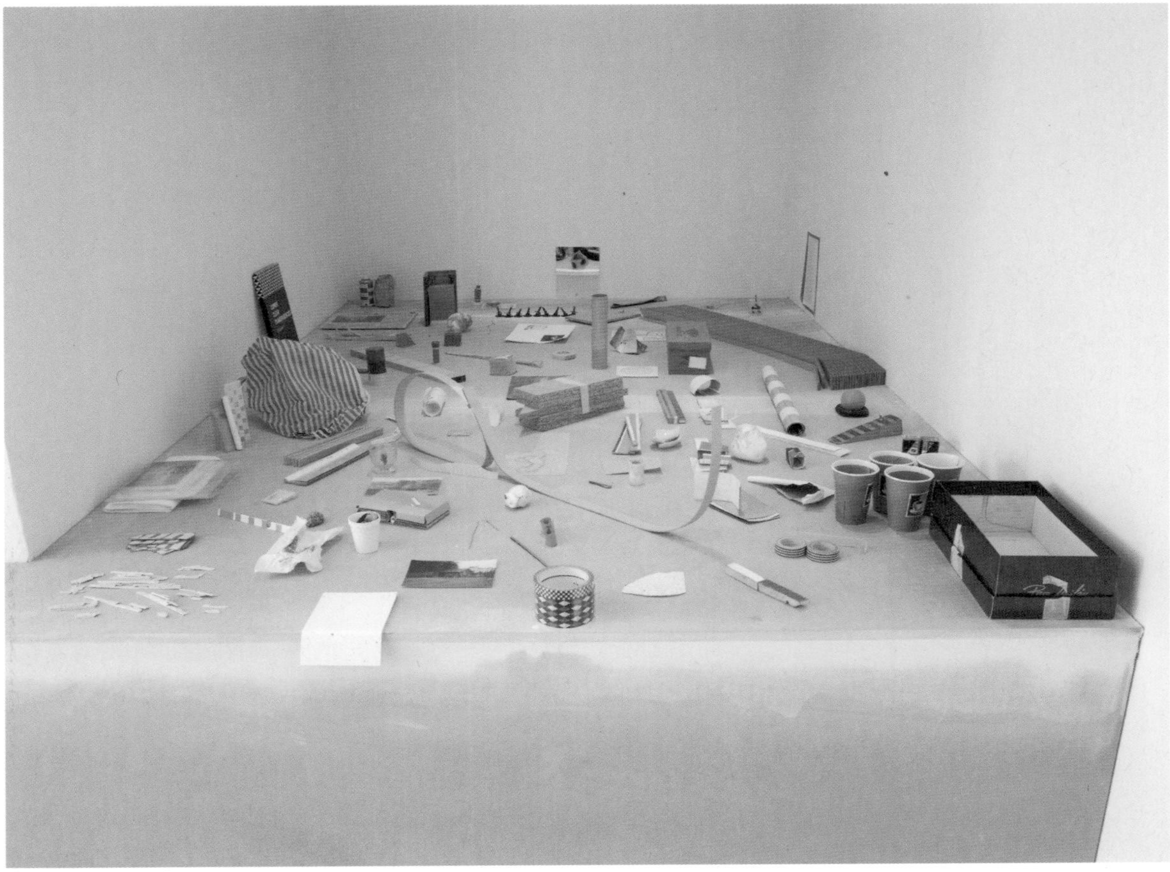

sculpture, brought together only by the skill and energy of the performing musician.

Edwards' choice of materials is highly self-reflexive. Devoid of a studio context, his carefully selected utilitarian equipment embodies a sheer potentiality reminiscent of Giovanni Anselmo's twisted cloth piece *Torsione* (1968). The artist's *Nought to Sixty* project, entitled *turning it around, slowly, in the light*, included a series of assemblages that extended this engagement with objecthood. *Practice Table (ICA)* (2008), for instance, configured an array of detritus accumulated from the artist's studio over a period of time, including paper cups, shoe boxes, gifts from friends and 'unfinished' artworks. Displayed on a wide unpainted plinth, these ephemeral pieces were given sculptural autonomy, incomplete works achieving an unexpected status within the company of other serendipitous objects.

Coline Milliard

28

The Hut Project

Exhibition, 21–28 July 2008
ICA Upper Galleries

The Hut Project is an artists' collective based in London, one that was formed in 2005 by Chris Bird (born Birmingham, 1971), Ian Evans (born Glasgow, 1982) and Alec Steadman (born Sidcup, 1983). The group's collaborative practice took shape through a shared sense of alienation from their studies at Middlesex University, and one of their first acts was to construct a temporary hut within the grounds of the university, from which they could offer an intellectual position from the 'outside'. Since then The Hut Project has been observing the art world with an absurdist eye, pursuing a brand of institutional critique that is invested with humour, but which also reveals the underlying pathos of the desire to make art.

Sean Edwards / *turning it around, slowly, in the light* / 2008

Extracts from correspondence and discussions with the artists' mothers, 2008. With thanks to Ruth Evans, Jan Steadman and Janet Weaver.

If I did something it would just look like something it wouldn't look like anything. At school when you had to draw a bowl of fruit, mine looked like a drawing of a bowl of fruit whereas my sister Sharon, hers would look as though you could literally take the apple and eat it. That's why I don't think I could ever be an artist because I think artists jumble things. They can do little lines and big lines but it all matches, if I tried to do something with littlelines and big lines it would just look like a row of lines. I can't have big and little things together I have to have little things, medium things, big things. Going back to the bowl of fruit, I would have apples on one corner then pears, then bananas, I couldn't have apples, bananas, pears all together and then bananas and apples, it would all have to be in order, do you know what I'm saying?

What do you think about The Hut Project?
I find the idea of collaboration in art difficult because I always think of art as being the product of one imagination and not several. But it's… interesting.

So the problem is it's not imaginative, it's calculated?
What do you mean, 'calculation'? Intelligence? Thinking?

Deciding what art you want to make.
There's obviously some kind of crossover between the imagination and the brain, isn't there? Artists who use their art to progress political ideas - satirists, poets - aren't just using imagination, they're using imagination to progress an intellectual idea.

That's interesting because you're bringing in function.
It's more difficult to imagine for the visual arts - but a poem, for example, is an artistic production which is impelled by intellectual ideas which then stimulate the imagination, in my view…

In the studio I have put the art stuff and memories of your childhood. I was not sure about this idea but as I went through the cases I found myself in tears. I was not sad exactly but felt the poignancy of objects and images from a child, who no longer exists, except in our memory.

I guess I had hoped one day when I am old and forgetful you might come by and we could look at this stuff together so that I could relive what was one of the great happinesses of my life. I am sorry I have not been a better mother. I did my best. I have given you one thing though and that is your art. I remember painting your feet when you were tiny so that you would walk on paper and make marks, showing you how to draw an ellipse on the top of a pot to create the illusion of volume, bringing home a pig's head so that you could draw and then burn it.

I hope you either return the memories or keep them safe so you can show me when I have forgotten.

For *Nought to Sixty* The Hut Project created *Old Kunst*, a retrospective exhibition of their work – both collective and individual – assembled without qualitative judgment. The exhibits included all the creative output that they were able to source, as well as indexes of works that they were not able to display. The project satirised the myth-making tendencies of the art world, while also providing compellingly personal narratives.

The strategy of self-deprecation is just one of the tactics that The Hut Project has used to analyse the base 'equations' through which the art world operates. The group pushes these formulas to an extreme, and there is always the risk that their self-reflexive project could implode, but their work also looks beyond these confines – and is characterised by the desire to understand the sources of a belief in art. The text that accompanied *Old Kunst*, taken from correspondence with the artists' mothers, attempted to ascertain how the members of the group had arrived at this juncture. It is a text with an emotional core, in which the project's conceptual exercise is set within the loaded context of a parent/child relationship.

Other recent works by The Hut Project include *It's Not Me, It's You*, a project exhibited at Limoncello Gallery in 2008. This piece involved a series of formulas and transpositions, designed to ascertain the relationships between the work of The Hut Project and that of artists represented by the gallery – including the conceptual and financial differences – and express these relationships as exhibits. The process managed to combine the most basic art market valuation with a kind of poetic transubstantiation, and was characterised not by finger pointing, but by a delight in the conceptual and theatrical possibilities within the structures of the art world. *Old Kunst* extended these strategies by creating a comprehensive index of artwork produced at every stage of the artists' lives, while also incorporating a number of works related to their own practice, including work by contemporary artist Giorgio Sadotti and William Hogarth's wry *Time Smoking a Picture* (1761).

Old Kunst suggested that the origins of production are located in childhood, and in the opinions and attitudes of parents. This research serves as an example of the wider questions posed by the group. Rooted in both aspiration and a necessary petulance, The Hut Project discovers the poignancy within the desire to produce art and to be included within its communities and value systems.

Richard Birkett

29 Will Holder

Event, 28 July 2008
ICA Nash/Brandon Rooms

Through his multiple roles as artist, writer, editor and designer Will Holder (born Hatfield, 1969, lives in London) explores the transformative processes at play in the act of publishing. Holder's *Nought to Sixty* project took place on Marcel Duchamp's birthday, 28th July. Entitled *Bachelor Party*, this event, which Holder has staged for a number of years, is a celebration encompassing a range of activities, including film screenings, performances and lectures.

Acknowledging Duchamp's belief in the primacy of concept over form, yet choosing to scrutinise the form of concepts, the project foregrounds language (speech) as an adaptive material. *Bachelor Party* becomes an interdisciplinary platform from which to "edit, design and 'publish' material which ordinarily will not allow itself to be represented on paper". For *Nought to Sixty* Holder constructed a programme in two synchronised parts – performance and commentary. Holder curated a film and performance programme in one space, while in the adjacent room a panel of art professionals were tasked with discussing those events simultaneously. Holder's audience were forced to choose between witnessing a performance or listening to its live documentation.

Holder's practice takes many forms, and his work includes printed journals and dialogues with other artists, as well as live readings and social events. In these various formats Holder interrogates the relationship between language and the object, exploring how text in all its forms can manifest in three-dimensions, and how the fixed nature of objects can be destabilised through linguistic interpretation. Holder's biannual journal *F.R. DAVID*, edited with Ann de Meester and Dieter Roelstraete, provides an experimental space in which to discuss these relationships, and in which to explore the use of language in the service of the visual.

The script is a recurrent framework for Holder, providing a structure that presupposes a transition from written text to spoken word through performance. Through such enactment the written text is inevitably opened up to change and adaptation, as well as to the slippages of meaning that occur in the space of translation. In recent performances Holder has appropriated existing texts and used them as scripts for readings, resulting in pieces such as *Indeterminacy* (2008) and *The Making of Americans* (2007), based on eponymous works by John Cage and Gertrude Stein. Holder sets up a mise en abyme whereby texts that examine the materiality and mutability of language are self-reflexively performed.

Holder is also engaged in several ongoing collaborations with artists, projects in which his role approaches that of mediator, and for which he devises performative publishing frameworks that allow for development or ongoing reinterpretation. One such project is a forthcoming publication on Falke Pisano, for which Holder and the artist wrote a dialogue/play as part Manifesta 7 (2008). While the text will explore Pisano's ideas about language and sculpture, it will only ever be 'performed' within the pages of the book.

Reinterpretation is key to Holder's ongoing project *Middle of Nowhere*, a serialised novel in which he is translating William Morris' utopian social fiction *News from Nowhere* (1890) into a fictional guide for design education and practice. Set 130 years in the future (as Morris' text was), *Middle of Nowhere* – a speculative history of the twenty-first century – envisages a society that finally comes to value language and information over objects. *Middle of Nowhere* resonates with *Bachelor Party* – both projects investigate the discrepancy between word and object, and between language as information and as process.

Andrew Bonacina

Will Holder / badge produced on the occasion of *Bachelor Party* / 28 July 2008

NASH room

Programme

8pm * Glenn Gould, "Dialogues on the Prospects of Recording" (excerpt) audio 15 mins

8.20 * Mark Knoop plays Peter Ablinger's "Voices and Piano" (Marcel Duchamp and Gertrude Stein 5 mins / 3 mins30 resp.)

8.30 * Peter Rose, "Secondary Currents" (1982) 15 mins, 16mm

8.50 * Robert Ashley, "Pillars" (2008) 24 mins, audio

9.20 * Mark Knoop plays Rolf Wallin's "Concerning King" (version for piano and tape), (2006) 3 mins

9.25 * Adam Pendleton's "Black Dada", read by Will Holder (2008) 20 mins

9.50 * John Smith, "The Girl Chewing Gum" (1976) 16mm, 12 mins

10.05 * Michael Hiltbrunner, "Singing over a Voice Study (of Palestine Charlemagne)" (2008) performance, 15 mins

10.25 * Rahsaan Roland Kirk & John Cage, "Sound" (1966) video, 12 mins

10.40 * Dexter's Laboratory "A Dog Story" (1998) video, 10 mins

10.50 (end) * The Hut Project, "Epic Stupidity or Epically Stupid"

* confetti, with compliments of Alex Rich, Jürg Lehni, Jon Hares & Richard Hamilton

BRANDON room

Discussion, led by Ian White, with:

8pm Maki Suzuki, Ekow Eshun, Vanessa Desclaux

8.30 Richard Birkett, James Goggin, Bart vd Heide

9.00 Will Bradley, Chris Evans, Lisette Smits

9.30 Dan Kidner, Raimundas Malasauskas, Francesco Manacorda

10.00 Nav Haq, Emily Pethick, Mark Sladen

10.30 Stuart Comer, Cally Spooner, Mike Sperlinger

11pm (end)

Marcel Duchamp's 121st Birthday, ICA London, 28th July 2008

(hosted by Will Holder)

Will Holder / programme for *Bachelor Party* / 2008

30 Hannah Rickards

Textual interventions,
August–October 2008
Nought to Sixty magazine

The work of Hannah Rickards (born London, 1979, lives in London) investigates the translation of naturally occurring phenomena into sounds, texts and installations. For *Birdsong* (2002), the artist took recordings of six different passages of birdsong and lowered their pitch, creating longer musical phrases within her own vocal range. She then sang and recorded these readymade melodies before raising them back to their original speed. The resulting tunes are presented in the exhibition space alongside a typewritten text that described the production process. In reducing the sonic complexity of birdsong to something humanly reproducible, the piece not only negates the sounds' origins, but also suggests a kind of representation somewhere between replica and reinvention.

Thunder (2005) is based on the same mechanism of reproduction. A recording of an eight-second thunderclap was stretched into a seven-minute passage, transcribed and arranged into a score for a sextet by composer David Murphy. The subsequent performance was recorded, and compressed to last eight seconds. In the resulting musical storm, viola and trumpet bursts can still be heard, but like *Birdsong, Thunder* is not concerned with the straight imitation of a source sound but rather with its enrichment through misrepresentation. In the installation, accompanied by a text pinned to the wall, the manufactured thunderclap could be heard an average of 12 times per hour, at intervals ranging from 30 seconds to 11 minutes. *Thunder* can therefore be experienced as one roar, many, or none.

It is this last possibility that sheds light on the importance of textual material in the artist's practice – Rickards' texts encapsulate the essence of the experiment, summing up all the stages involved in the creation of the piece. But despite this informative content, these documents retain a strong degree of autonomy, echoing the use of the written

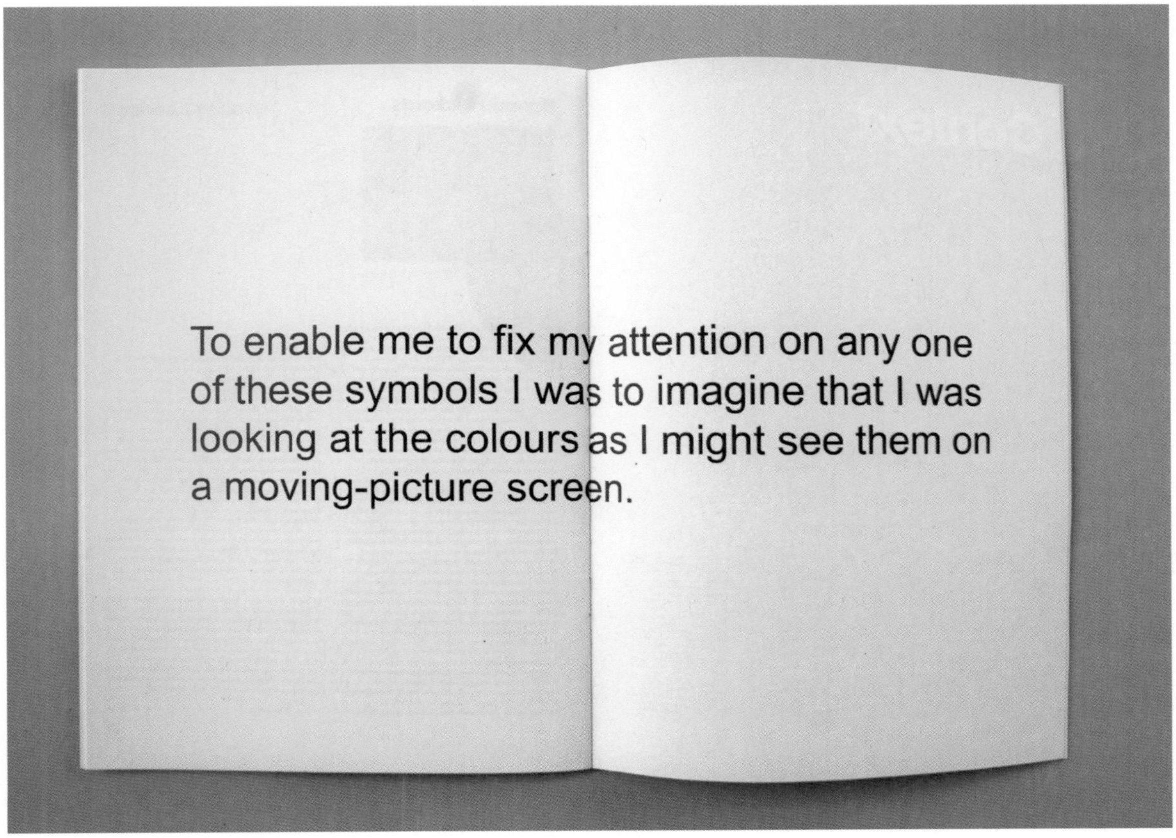
To enable me to fix my attention on any one of these symbols I was to imagine that I was looking at the colours as I might see them on a moving-picture screen.

Hannah Rickards / To enable me to fix my attention on any one of these symbols I was to imagine that I was looking at the colours as I might see them on a moving-picture screen. / 2008

word within Conceptualism and confronting the viewer with the physicality of the artistic process.

In *Birdsong*, as in *Thunder*, there is nothing left of the original sound, as Rickards' method requires the loss of the replicated sources. Such absence is at the very core of the installation *'... a legend, it, it sounds like a legend...'* (2007). For this project, the artist tackled a scientific oddity: the rarely perceived sound that accompanies the Aurora Borealis, the light phenomenon that is regularly observed in circumpolar regions caused by electromagnetic solar winds colliding with the earth's outer atmosphere. Rickards collected accounts from those who perceived the sound in Alaska and Canada.

Three monitors display extracts of the transcripts while the speakers play their recordings at times echoing the text, at others acting as a counterpoint. "It was like a crackling sound," says one witness, while another evokes the humming of a "lightsaber, you know, from Star Wars". Each testimony is a striking example of language's inability to accurately communicate a sensorial experience.

Rickards' project for *Nought to Sixty* was manifested within the pages of three of the season's monthly magazines. Unframed and unexplicated, these non-sequitur additions consider the return of language to the realm of the mythical, and the published document as a means to disseminate a sense of the ineffable. Operating between modes of perception and representation, and a slippage between what is said and what is understood, Rickards highlights the human desire to speak the unspeakable.

Coline Milliard

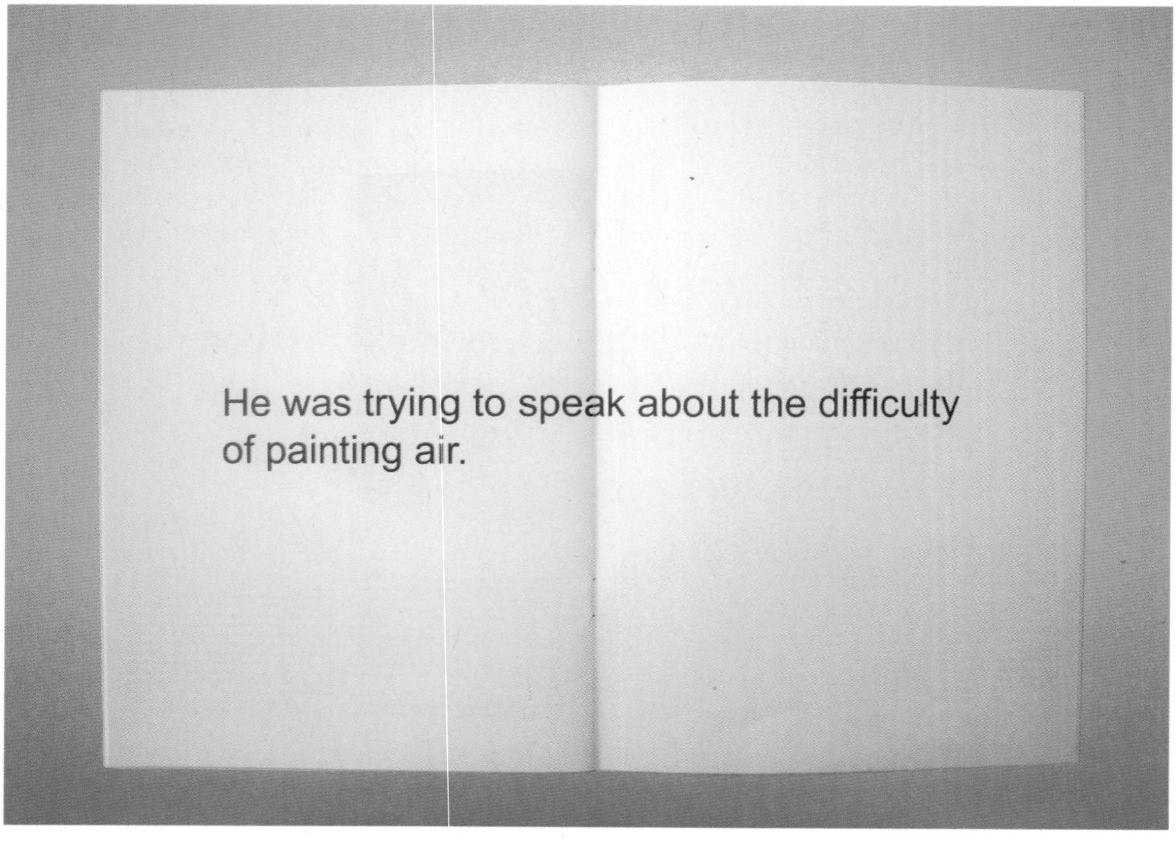
He was trying to speak about the difficulty of painting air.

Hannah Rickards / He was trying to speak about the difficulty of painting air. / 2008

31

You talkin' to me? Why art is turning to education

Salon discussion, 14 July 2008
ICA Theatre

Organisers
Dr Paul O'Neill, artist, curator and writer
Mick Wilson, artist, educator and writer

Participants
Dave Beech, artist, Freee
Liam Gillick, artist
Dr Andrea Phillips, assistant director, MFA Curating, Goldsmiths
Sarah Pierce, artist
Professor Adrian Rifkin, writer and educator

In recent years there has been an emphasis on the pedagogical within both artistic and institutional practice, with a proliferation of talks, panels and other discursive activity. Dr Paul O'Neill and Mick Wilson chaired this debate, inviting panellists to explore the 'educational turn' within the art world, and to examine why artists and curators are looking to education as a space for new critical practice.

DR PAUL O'NEILL: Why are artists turning to education? Why have more discursive events been happening over the past five years, whether as part of a fair, biennale museum or gallery programme?

It is a pleasure to introduce the panel: Mick Wilson is dean of GradCAM, a PhD research program in Dublin. He is an artist, writer and publisher of numerous texts, particularly focused on the crossover between education and the discursive turn in artistic and curatorial practice. Sarah Pierce is an artist, sometimes curator, sometimes educator, sometimes writer, and one of the *Nought to Sixty* artists. Sarah has looked at ways of thinking around discursivity and the informal nature of gathering and discussing. Two of these projects are The Metropolitan Complex and Paraeducation, the latter initiated with curator Annie Fletcher. Dave Beech is also exhibiting in *Nought to Sixty* as part of Freee art collective. Dave teaches at Chelsea, he has published many articles, edited a number of books including *The Philistine Controversy* with John Roberts, and he is a frequent contributor to *Art Monthly*. Dr Andrea Phillips is a writer, educator, assistant director of the MA programme in curating, and director of Curating Architecture at Goldsmiths College. Liam Gillick is an artist and writer who teaches at Columbia University. Liam has participated in the Academy show, a collaboration between the Visual Arts department in Goldsmiths, Kunstverein Hamburg, MuHKA in Antwerp and Van Abbemuseum in Eindhoven. Professor Adrian Rifkin, who I was taught by, is a writer, cultural theorist and thinker who teaches at Goldsmiths College.

Prior to this evening we sent a series of questions to the participants as a way of guiding the discussion. Mick will go through them before we begin.

MICK WILSON: What is at stake in this turn to informal educational practice? Why, in recent years, have we seen a range of projects, exhibitions and ancillary activities around large biennales that take an educational paradigm or model, and use that as a basis for elaborating a cultural practice? Mainstream formal art education is in trouble; it is being made over by a quality management business administration. We want to look to the space within contemporary practice, outside the academy, which appeals to notions of the pedagogical.

Exemplary projects are Manifesta 6's failed project to implement an alternative art school in Cyprus; the United Nations Plaza project that emerged from that earlier history; and Documenta 12 with 'education' as one of its three overarching themes. There are also small-scale, informal projects that don't break through to the mainstream, but are engaged by questions of education and learning. Many of these projects were quite remote from the standard educational outreach agenda that publicly funded institutions tend to adopt. Participants in these projects were not necessarily engaged in a never-ending project of self-improvement, and many of these projects promise an alternative cultural practice, not predicated on the construction of 'the good subject'. There is clearly potential for these projects to be recuperated by a dominant institutional discourse focused on edutainment.

We asked panellists not to prepare scripts but respond to the conversation that might emerge tonight; to gain new ideas or insights flowing out of the interactions of viewpoints, rather than have people rehearse fully resolved positions.

O'NEILL: Homi Bhabha said, "In every emergency there is an emergence." If there is an emergence of a particular type of practice within art, which is turning to education, then why is it happening now?

SARAH PIERCE: I think I can respond with reference to the Paraeducation project that I'm involved in with curator Annie Fletcher (who's based in Eindhoven). In 2004, when she was in Amsterdam, there was a report released called the *Cultura Nota*, which noted that discursive and research-based activity in arts institutions was considered not very practical, not very important, something that shouldn't be taking precedence at that time. The release of the *Cultura Nota* coincided with a show at Witte de With and TENT, where six curators were asked to "take the cultural pulse of the city of Rotterdam". Annie found herself in a position where she had been invited to produce one-sixth of an exhibition while a crisis surrounding the *Cultura Nota* was emerging. She asked herself what is an appropriate response to this as a curator? Is it to produce an exhibition? We talked to friends in Rotterdam about something that is not organised in relation to a critique – not even in relation to 'grassroots', 'high end', 'self-organised' and 'institutional' – but something to dispense with such axioms. We were thinking of the institution as a space where certain discussions can take place, and to assert those discussions instead of doing an exhibition. We borrowed a term that comes out of George Bush's politics: 'paraeducation'. Paraeducators are those who come into a community or school – grandmothers, aunts, mothers – and supplement the lack of education within a particular neighbourhood's schooling institution.

There were three things that I wanted to make sure I mentioned in relation to this talk tonight. Firstly, how to set up in relation to visibility, or to an art world that is fixated on the visible. By 'visibility' I mean among those professionals who stake professional claims – those who show up, who appear on a panel, who appear in exhibitions. In the context of Rotterdam, the art world was fixated on 'spectacle' – literally the display of capital in relation to an exhibition or an artwork. So secondly: how to do something that we started to define as 'minimally articulated', as it were; how to pay attention to those moments that are quieter and, in terms of institutional space, take less space and resources. Coming out of such issues there was another term that emerged for us: 'affinity'. We looked at the use of the word in relation to activism and civil disobedience groups. Act Up usefully defined 'affinity group' as a group of 5–15 people who work together over a durational period of time. Act Up discovered that when you go beyond 15 people, it is difficult to build and sustain affinity. What would it mean if we tried to build affinity within a community of people in Rotterdam (who already gather around exhibitions) and provide space within an institution where people could gather and, importantly, where there'd be no audience present? There would be no representation in terms of "I'm the artist on the panel", but there would be a space where you could do U-turns, where you could take things back, put things out, and you didn't have to remain fixed. The final thing I wanted to touch on is the idea of duration. This theme arose from reading together as a group, and also in relation to Derrida's *Eyes of the University* [Stanford University Press, 2004]. Work done in a group is paradoxically both a point of order and it's a point of pause – a hesitation perhaps.

O'NEILL: Liam – you've participated in quite a few of those educational projects, including the so-called failed Manifesta school, United Nations Plaza and the Academy show. Do you have a particular interest in 'subject forming', or something other than that?

LIAM GILLICK: In my experience of being educated in art schools, there was an assumption that 'horizontality' would be the way to function – that you could make systems of engagement that are horizontal in nature, with borders, barriers and parallels. There was a desire to keep relationships in a horizontal matrix, but also to turn it round in order to reveal that there were implicit hierarchies within the system. A discursive model of practice can generate ideas or reflect on certain things when a matrix is not purely vertical, but when you can see a mesh of situations. In all the projects you mentioned – as well as a project I've been doing in New York called *A Prior* – the key was realising that the horizontal matrix model could not break through to questions of age or self-evident disciplines. Students would apply to Columbia University because they thought it'd be interesting to go to an art school where they could listen to Rosalind Krauss's lectures. This is an example of a horizontality matrix, where you think, "I'm entering into the university system, and I'll be able to access these nodes of productive thinking," but that was difficult to do because you would meet defined horizontal borders that would prevent you from going any further. When talking about drawing new connections, you're already stuck in horrible languages that sound too friendly and positive. Some of these connections are uncomfortable and people don't want them.

One of the other issues is a return to the discursive. A productive aspect of all those projects (and it can only be temporary) was people sitting down and accounting for themselves in front of a new constellation of individuals. At UN Plaza there was a new audience that wasn't a usual audience; it was a strange mixture of young art historians, displaced proto-curators who didn't want to enter the curatorial frame, artists who didn't necessarily want to produce anything; people who wanted to be engaged without the obligation to produce.

O'NEILL: Andrea, you've been involved in a pedagogical context. Much of your work at Goldsmiths is with young curators. Is there a distinction between those discussions happening within postgraduate training courses and those happening in more public contexts?

DR ANDREA PHILLIPS: In the past two years we've spent a lot of time talking about pedagogy in the curatorial programme and, in particular, something I would call an 'aesthetics of the pedagogical'. I'm concerned we're pulling together different practices under the single heading of a pedagogical turn within arts practice.

The second thing is that a lot of this discourse has been generated through people turning to Jacques Rancière's earlier writing. At the moment curators are influenced, if not obsessed, by his writing. A number of good curatorial projects have come out of the Goldsmiths curatorial programme this year, directly taking elements of Rancière's *The Ignorant Schoolmaster*. Interestingly, they have turned to artists who use the notion of a 'gathering space' – an 'equalised' space to use Rancière's terms – as an aesthetic for making work. That's very different than setting up a series of public talks, yet both of these things are lumped together under this concern for pedagogy. Rancière is attractive because he offers a format for equalising democracy, and we all want art to be equalising and democratic, but his ideas become generalised by certain types of curatorial approach.

Of course, education is the cheap option when it comes to making exhibitions. It's cheaper to make discursive work than work that involves putting sculptures in museum spaces. Artists might tell me I'm wrong ... [panel laughs]

What do we want when we want an alternative? What is alternative about pedagogy? Rancière points out the entrenchment within our current democracy, of the master-pupil relationship. His essay *The Emancipated Spectator* (for our subject tonight, tellingly published in *Artforum)* is a critique of a performative avant-garde that is still influential within theatre and returning once again to visual art. In the essay Rancière looks at Brecht and Artaud. In both cases their work demonstrates a desire to encourage participation. That is partly what the pedagogical turn claims to be all about – producing spaces of participation. Rancière argues that the most interesting spectator is a passive one, who sits and watches and thinks. This kind of spectatorship really needs to be thought through as a viable politicality, in opposition to the participatory.

O'NEILL: Linking to the 'alternative' – a term used in relation to *Nought to Sixty* – I turn to Dave, who has developed this in a number of texts and the exhibition: *There is always an alternative*. If artists turn to education through various formats, is it proposing a real political alternative to a pedagogical model within institutions as they currently stand?

DAVE BEECH: When I think of the rise of education in culture, I think of TV programmes like *What Not to Wear, How to Cook, Grand Designs, Gardener's World, Don't Get Done, Get Dumb*. There is a plethora of formats in education-as-entertainment, and education as a form of consumerism. In those programmes, the educational programme is getting you to be a more informed shopper, to be a better consumer. It's genuinely emancipating. Education always has this emancipatory aspect. But to be emancipated as a consumer is a limited way of thinking about emancipation.

While art, artists, museums and galleries are turning to education, they're not doing this alone. They are doing this within a culture that uses educational formats as a semiotic code for talking to experts in amateurism. It's an easy way of addressing somebody if you address them as master in relation to pupil. If you are an expert in relation to their amateurism, then you know how to address them and they know how to address you. This has become a familiar mode of address on all levels of culture. When we look at art in particular, we can see that context more specifically. If we're talking about the educational turn, look at Nicholas Bourriaud's examination of relational art. Bourriaud wants to make a claim for relational art by saying that it has a collective viewer. When you view, when you participate, when you take part in a relational project, you are aware of other people also viewing it and taking part in it. Bourriaud draws a distinction between the experience of relational art and that of Abstract Expressionism, where one is meant to be an individual. Relational art opens you up to collective engagement. For him collectivity is often a convivial one. If we are talking about the educational turn, we are talking about another model of that collective subject, or perhaps a collective viewer of the classroom. Even when you're watching *Don't Get Done, Get Dumb*, you learn something, you are being emancipated.

Are there models other than education that we can use for the potential collective subjects for art? Civil disobedience groups don't work in the same way; they help to maintain, sustain and develop shared beliefs. The pressure group, the subculture, the avant-garde (like Dada and Surrealism), the mass, the workers union, revolutionary patter – these are models of the collective subject not best described by the education model. They're worth thinking about in terms of re-thinking the collective subjective in art, perhaps in the way that Bourriaud inaugurates.

PROF ADRIAN RIFKIN: I'm quite into nostalgia. I want to say this because all the speakers have spoken about the importance of guarding ourselves against slipping into terminologies that might seem satisfying or operative. This makes it terribly difficult for us to speak generally. I missed out on the educational turn, but that's probably because I've been in education all my life and was not in the position to see it happening. [panel laughs]

When I say I'm interested in nostalgia, that's because I can't see how to proceed unless we are working with an abusive discourse. Rancière points this out when he talks about equality and the aesthetics of politics. Without asking us to imitate his discourse, he asks us to think about what differences were generated by the desire for equality; none of which are commensurable with each other. There, in a way, resides Rancière's Kantism. His categorical judgment is that there is no categorical judgment.

What troubles me is that maybe the institutions we most admire, like Okwui Enwezor's Documenta 11, are profoundly conservative. They instate a generalised doxa as a condition for looking at art. For me, Documenta 11 was a Council of Trent of our times. It wasn't a moment of liberation; it was a moment of Counter Reformation. Once you institute a range of theoreticians – Slavoj Žižek, Bhabha, Stuart Hall, whoever – as the means through which you spiritually prepare yourself for art, you're in the Counter Reformation. You're in the Eucharistic education, which ironically Jesus was trying to avoid by telling people to look away; not to look at the law. The history of becoming aware of the limitations in being educated involves some kind of abuse in order to escape from it. I'd rather take the philosophy in the boudoir of Sartre than I would the educationally political structures of our own time. Sartre simply says that you have to break the rhetorical rules, to put things end-to-end in order to formulate the relations between elements of speech that indifferently cuts across discourses and which we try to make commensurable. It is a good place to go in a world dominated by anti-essentialist discourses.

O'NEILL: Are you suggesting that this nostalgic turn is a good thing?

RIFKIN: It's a counter to anti-essentialism. It allows oneself to engage with misrecognition for that which you are nostalgic. When I think of the late 1960s and early 1970s I remember the Marxist part and the hippy part. I think I now prefer the hippy part, which I would not call the accursed share. That's the point where nostalgia shapes itself around misrecognition, which is interesting because it's not what I expect. I don't make a judgment. I don't want to go hippy.

PHILLIPS: I refer to nostalgia very differently from the way you're framing it, as a political nostalgia for educational formats. I'm talking about a misrecognition whereby an essentialist encapsulation of politicality is perceived to have occurred at a time before a clampdown. In Britain that would be the clampdown of Thatcher, which of course we all know wasn't like that (by which I mean it wasn't all brilliant beforehand). But why is now the time of misrecognition, the time to co-opt wholesale the dreams of the past via a shift to education-as-subject? What is this perceived space and time of togetherness, of collaborative participatory fantasies?

BEECH: Nostalgia is a kind of realism. If you understand culture from the perspective of Adorno or Frederick Jameson then nostalgia is a way of recognising what your current culture lacks. Therefore nostalgia shows you what you would rather be. Nostalgia isn't necessarily a misrepresentation.

GILLICK: This is about who possesses the future in the recent past. It's clear even 'progressive' American liberal institutions are often obsessed with possessing the near future. Goldsmiths' mission statement contains a commitment to lifelong learning, so you have a terrible choice between terminal education or being strategic about the near future, recuperating the recent past as a way of restaging things, which can be powerful. People's sense of where nostalgia starts and ends is clearly different. I like listening to Adrian speak, but part of the reason for the education turn is because of what he said and the way he said them, which is not to undermine him. There's an absence in established educational structures that leaves an enormous void. Choosing between being a hippy or being a Marxist does not account for enough multiplicities and urgencies. The problem is when you start talking about education it becomes personal history. It's about where one went to school. On this panel you've got clear differences in terms of the concept of what education means and the experience of it.

ANONYMOUS (audience): Art schools are dominated by a client service provider model. The preponderance of these initiatives outside the art school is only enabled by the idea of education, which now defines the schools themselves. It's easy to have the notion that as a student you are buying a piece of education rather than entering some kind of lifelong commitment. If it's just something you can buy, then why not farm it out to other institutions? Universities are becoming businesses. As Andrea describes, these things enable education to be used as the cheap option for art production, so I don't know why we're discussing the master-pupil relationship.

PHILLIPS: There is a complex and tense relationship, which is psychoanalytically interesting, politically interesting, between an expert and inexpert, and a client and provider. There is currently a tension between those things, which makes it an energetic place to be politically. But I wonder why it's happening in art and not in education.

GILLICK: It's quite clear. People running art schools seem to be incapable of preventing problems from happening, but they're not bad people, so some leave wanting to start another kind of art education. What these people experienced was *not* functioning. This has certainly been my experience at Columbia Graduate School. The model of art teaching and of educational practice within most university art school structures is not relevant to what people do or are interested in, but they have to do it in order to create and have something to discuss within their discursive teaching system. But it doesn't work. The model I've been involved in is about drawing in people who are deeply dissatisfied about their previous educational system or who feel the old assumption (the hippy assumption) that if you put students in an Arcadian situation they will teach each other and themselves. Part of the problem is the hippies won. You've got the Ben and Jerry syndrome, where hippies are running corporations if you look at it that way. The powerful people in these situations have no urgency to do anything about it. They've let it happen over the last 20 years, certainly in Britain. Some people have had enough and they're establishing their own structures because the old ones aren't working.

BEECH: The educational turn could be linked to subject formation and to Terry Atkinson's desubjectivication. There are tensions in this, particularly regarding the first educational turn in British culture – the formation of the Arts Council, and the idea that the masses must be taught how to initiate this culture. A key idea within the emerging Arts Council was that exhibitions have to be brought to people; people should be taught about exhibitions; there must be a meeting between people paying for the Arts Council and the work they're paying for, and that meeting will be brought about through education. The Arts Council put education at the heart of its practice. Arts institutions and the people who work in them have since learnt not to teach art in a top-down way. We've got a more horizontal, open-ended exchange in the educational turn this time round. I'm not sure how much of what we're dealing with is a continuation of policy in a sophisticated guise, or if we are looking at the transformation of the subject.

PHILLIPS: The other key thing in past gallery and educational publicly-funded forms was a paradoxical formulation of the relationship between the master-servant and the client-provider. That formation is happening within galleries and museums too, and even within the private gallery system, which is to do with developing new buyers.

GILLICK: Those at *Frieze* believe that there is enormous demand for their brand, and it would be possible to expand into art schools because those institutions are currently so ineffectual. I've spoken to them about it. Maybe I'm telling things I shouldn't be. *Frieze* were thinking about New York and thought that within a year it would be possible to fill the space of two other art schools that no one would want to go to anymore. I couldn't tell you which ones [panel laughs]. I'm just trying to illustrate what might be at stake. Although those at *Frieze* were being funny – we were supposed to laugh about it – they were also deadly serious.

ANONYMOUS (audience): Artists are habitually poor until they make it big. They live in poor rundown parts of town, and their practices are used largely for regeneration purposes. What about the economics behind the educational turn? The economics of education, of betterment or improvement – the emancipation Dave was talking about.

BEECH: I think there is a relationship between the educational turn and this perception of the demise of the art school. Now that art schools have to broaden their social mix, there is a perception of a loss of quality and value within the art schools. I think this nostalgia is about a narrow version of what art education might be like, which is teaching art to people who already understand this culture. When you're a teacher of art and you're teaching people for whom art is a foreign language, then you have to teach in a different way. Your experience of that educational experience will be different. It will feel more antagonistic. The culture within art schools has changed. It has become more professionalized, more bureaucratic. It's become more institutionalised. I don't subscribe to this nostalgia for an art education that would be free of all of that – that we can practise in the art gallery as artists.

RIFKIN: I'm nostalgic about a relative economy of means compared with now. That's what I refer to with this 'hippy' part. The 'Marxist' part had huge means and thought one knew everything and knew nothing, and in the hippy part one had minimal means and thought one knew nothing, but knew a lot. In that sense one discloses in the past what one knew.

WILSON: What are the consequences for elite formation projects like art schools when you now have mass higher education? How is it that you have the *Harvard Business Review* citing the MFA as the better business qualification than the MBA? Even within the world of business and management science, there is investment in the notion of 'creativity' and 'education for creativity'. Maybe it's not the questionable politics of these scenarios, but rather some other form of time consciousness that might be taken to be at stake in this discussion of potential and emergence. There is another way of thinking agency and positions within history that is not a rehearsal of 1980s postmodernism; it's not a retrenchment of modernism. It's a notion of agency and project that posits openings in the future. I'm not championing this, but is there something here that we can draw out further? Is there 'hope' here?

ANONYMOUS (audience): Could the panel elaborate on the idea of the turn to education as a reintroduction of a passive audience?

PHILLIPS: I mentioned passivity in relation to Rancière's *The Emancipated Spectator*, partly because it is a retort to other forms of Rancièrian thought around equality and the politics of the aesthetics being a force of production and action. It seems as though there is a productive contradiction in Rancière. His understanding of the crucial politicality of looking and being passive is interesting to reintroduce here, in order to question the vague or pseudo politics often posited by discursive frameworks placed around exhibitions by institutions like the ICA and the Tate, for example, and also in relationship to the political ambitions of artists who use the pedagogical as an aesthetic format for their production. Harvard Business School is opening art institutions in Abu Dhabi as a quintessential political-spatial-geographical appropriation and doing so with the clear understanding that to train up a generation of artists is to formulate the future very specifically, but not necessarily along artistic lines. That's a nostalgia for the future.

BEECH: The question of passivity within the educational turn is a red herring. To assume passivity when you appropriate educational models is to have an outmoded idea about education. Maybe it's also an outmoded idea of subjectivity. I don't want to look at the ethics of individual practices within the educational turn. We need to see the educational turn in terms of a broader set of contexts, which is why I mentioned all the education we get on our daytime TV. At the same point as we're talking about the educational turn at the ICA, there's a debate going on in *Art Monthly* about the demise of art education. I think there's a relationship between these things. It's not about individual projects. It's about the cultural turn as a social event that has taken place.

O'NEILL: The educational turn may be a critique of the failure of art education; it may be a contestation of the rising power of the art market; while from another perspective it might be an interest in how knowledge is produced rather than the knowledge produced and absorbed by the art market. The types of projects discussed within an art-worldly context exclude others. The Serpentine Gallery educational programme is completely invisible, but you will acknowledge the fact that when the pavilion opens in a few weeks and Hans Ulrich Obrist does his 24-hour marathon, it will be seen as an educative experience. It has been packaged, framed and formatted in a particular way that submerges another kind of educational programme, which is happening within museums, galleries, etc. Pedagogical models have been curatorialised, particularly within the biennial circle, within the art markets, within museums. There is a submergence created by the visibility of this curatorial gesture, of that structure and principle of organisation that becomes a heavily mediated and individually, curatorially altered space. Why are these discussions happening in an art world context rather and not in educational discourses? Perhaps there is a gap or a fold here that can be productive, as a point of departure for a more informed discourse that must begin by asking why is art turning or returning to education now.

Iain Hetherington / *Composite Picture 1 (Diversified Cultural Worker)* / 2008

32

Iain Hetherington

Exhibition, 4–11 August 2008
ICA Upper Galleries

Iain Hetherington (born Glasgow, 1978, lives in Glasgow) interrogates the crisis of portraiture in both a painterly and cultural context. In his painting practice, as well as in the fanzines he produces with Alex Pollard (*Mainstream* and *Radical Vans and Carriages*), Hetherington uses oblique titles and comic gestures to mount attacks on politically correct or 'focus group' culture. His painting technique, meanwhile, combines a traditional representational approach with the use of collage, and the incorporation of apparent detritus from the studio – newspaper, scraps of canvas – into the surface of the image.

While portrait painting traditionally conveys a subject's likeness or character, in Hetherington's recent works these aspects are significant by their absence. The defining physical features of his subjects remain entirely spectral, as the space where one expects to see the hands or faces of these figures is rendered in a muddied impasto, whereas their tracksuits and hoodies, jewellery and branded baseball caps, are rendered with photorealistic care. For Hetherington, these are the real cultural signifiers of portraiture in our media-obsessed age – the social markers of neds, chavs and football casuals. For *Target Audience* (2005) the artist pasted a pair of plastic googly eyes at the centre of a shapeless form of acrylic paint – a slapstick gesture, but one that in the context of the title creates a hollow laugh.

For *Nought to Sixty* the artist presented work from his recent series of oils, *Diversified Cultural Workers* (2007–08). Hetherington has his own definition of 'cultural workers', encompassing symbolic figures used to make art more appealing to wider audiences. Recurring motifs, such as Burberry baseball caps and gold chains, are depicted with seductive painterly finesse; while, in a couple of paintings, Swarovski diamonds are embedded in the surface of the canvas. Yet these fashion accessories are at odds with the portraits' satirical titles, such as *Studio Delinquents shield themselves from attack using the international language of confusion* (2007), and *Privileged Mis-representer subconsciously attempts a quasi-corporeal merger with the market research project worked upon, resulting in the flattening of difference* (2007).

Hetherington was initially attracted to the portrait format because of its problematic and unfashionable status within contemporary painting, but his explorations also point to wider issues. Undermining glib notions of multiculturalism and 'diversity' within the cultural sector, Hetherington re-expresses the portrait in the language of market research and social types, challenging conceptions of audiences and society not simply within his paintings, but in the space beyond the frame.

Isla Leaver-Yap

33 James Richards

Exhibition, 4 August–11 October 2008
ICA Upper Galleries

The presentation of film and video within art is often highly conventional: the short, looped, monitor-based video and the black box of the longer film projection. The practice of James Richards (born Cardiff, 1983, lives in London), which has the moving image at its core, transcends these constraints by accumulating imagery in a manner that resists completion. Rather, the material of video is treated as a resource for constant manipulation, and the 'work' emerges through the act of continual reconstitution.

Richards also shifts the form of presentation of his work, moving between formats associated with the public realm – the screening, or the live VJ mix – and the suggestively private and devotional form of the mixtape.

This approach derives from the processes of archiving and of 'scratch' video. The practice of re-editing VHS footage gained prominence in the 1980s through artists such as George Barber and Gorilla Tapes, whose overtly politicised work was presented as inserts on TV channels, or as an accompaniment to nightclub performances by experimental bands such as Cabaret Voltaire. Re-mixing can explore the possibility of repetition and distortion, and can also respond to external factors such as the beat of music or the rhythm of a superimposed narrative. The archive is constituted by a wealth of media imagery, and can speak of multiple possibilities, but also of the obsessive impulse to collate.

James Richards / installation view / ICA / 2008

James Richards
List of works sampled and compiled for *Active Negative Programme*, exhibited 4 August–11 October 2008

- *Eye windows. Using eye-controlled zooming windows for focus selection* (intro)
- Bruce Parry, *The Frozen Lens Cap*
- *Poetry interpretation*
- *Portrait lighting techniques no.1*
- *Portrait lighting techniques no.2*
- Patsy Rodenburg, *Free the Voice*
- *Antigua Passa Passa (part 2)*
- Chris Saunders, *Untitled* (1993)
- *Why you are watching this tape*
- *Portrait lighting techniques no.3*
- Chris Saunders, *The Revolutionary Cleaner* (1995)
- *Practice Theory*
- Paul Bush, *Lost Images* (1990)
- *Jumpen Video* (outro)

Lost Images by Paul Bush was commissioned as part of the Arts Council of England and BBC Two season One Minute Television.
The work appears courtesy of LUX. *Untitled* and *The Revolutionary Cleaner* by Chris Saunders both appear courtesy of LUX. Special thanks to Benjamin Cook and Ian White.

Richards' interest lies in the possibility of the personal amidst this media morass, as well as in the scratch form as a means of layering previous intentions, narratives and recordings, and of returning images to the world. For the viewer the sources – which span the internet, appropriated video archives and original footage – are buried and obscure, but the continually reassembled sequences build on themes of desire and obsession, using the friction between the deconstructed image and untouched footage. *Voice Hits and Near Misses Compilation* (2007) cuts from a montage of gay porn, theoretical texts and collaged hand gestures, to slowed sequences of hazing frat boys and unconscious children, trancelike loops of TV entertainer Michael Barrymore and night vision footage of a rave or protest. Coupled with prolonged silences and repetitious house music, the work touches on the formation of identity through communality, as well as on the vagaries of personal desire.

For his exhibition at the ICA, Richards presented *Active Negative Programme* (2008), a work that heightened the conflict between video as a mass medium and as a bearer of transgressive messages. Shown alongside this work was a series of commemorative blankets, bearing photographic images and simple emblems. This latter group of works, *Untitled Merchandise (Lovers and Dealers)* (2007), depicts lovers and gallerists of the artist Keith Haring, the images cropped to edit out the presence of Haring himself. Commissioned from an American company that produces blankets for families of soldiers, the work is charged not only with the history of the AIDS epidemic of the 1980s, but with private and marginal narratives of love and ambition.

Richards uses the accumulation and reassembly of imagery as a devotional and elegiac process; the archetypes of the mixtape and of the souvenir create and demonstrate the obsession of the fan, the transformation of the mass archive into a personal one. He proposes an arena of subjectivity distinct from the one bounded by commerce and the media, and in so doing redefines processes of making and showing.

Richard Birkett

34 Brown Mountain College

Performance, 4 August 2008
ICA Theatre

Brown Mountain College of the Performing Arts was founded to encourage interdisciplinary collaboration within the context of performance. It boasts the most departments of any art college, including both traditional and non-traditional disciplines, the latter featuring circus skills, magic, activism, bar tending, sports, dating and creative accounting. As the College is without permanent premises, staff or students, it invents new scenarios for each project, proposing formats and engaging practitioners.
For *Nought to Sixty* the College staged *Those That Can…*, a cabaret-style showcase of skills, including stage fighting, giant origami, dog-paw reading and a scientific demonstration, all by experts from the faculty. Sir Gideon Vein, Professor of Re-skilling, presented this esoteric display to an audience that, by implication, became prospective students.

Both images: Brown Mountain College / *Those That Can…* / 2008

Brown Mountain College considers Black Mountain College (1933–67, North Carolina) to be its staid younger sister. Brown Mountain relishes scatological humour, metafictional nuisance and general absurdity, while also honouring the integrity of the work it facilitates. Like its sibling institution, the College champions experience as education, regarding the invigoration of curiosity as paramount and aiming to construct situations in which historical and theoretical insight and ribald humour can coexist. With its metafictional approach, Brown Mountain College produces multiple implicit and explicit jokes about performance and its frame – a comedic strategy that has been employed throughout the twentieth century by the likes of the Theatre of the Absurd, Monty Python and Fluxus.

The ultimate aim of the College is to revisit and reconfigure, through explosive laughter and the keener tools of comprehension, the overlooked roots and offshoots of performative genres and critical discourse. As the late, great anthropologist Mary Douglas suggests, "Aesthetic pleasure [has] something in common with the joy of a joke; something which might have been repressed has been allowed to appear, a new improbable form of life has been glimpsed."

Brown Mountain College was founded in 1906 and claims such influential faculty and alumni as Paul Robeson, John Cage and Lamb Chop. The current Deans of College were appointed in 2006 and aim to revive an avant-garde ethos of collaboration between artists, dancers, actors, filmmakers, political activists and comedians. The Deans are Mel Brimfield (born Oxford 1976, lives in London), Sally O'Reilly (born Portsmouth 1971, lives in London) and Ben Roberts (born London 1976, lives in London). Previous Brown Mountain College events include an ongoing series of thematic screenings, *The Erratic Film Club* (2006–ongoing), the celebratory *Centenary Cabaret* (Bethnal Green Working Men's Club, London, 2006) and *Cabaret of Curiosities* (Royal Academy Life Room, 2008), while a recent *Brown Mountain Festival of the Performing Arts* took place in the Slade Research Centre, Woburn Square, London, during Frieze Art Fair, 2008.

Emma Ridgway

Tris Vonna-Michell / *hahn/huhn* / cinema projection room / ICA / 2008

35

Tris Vonna-Michell

Event, 11 August 2008
ICA Cinema

The performances of Tris Vonna-Michell (born Rochford, 1982, lives in Southend On Sea) are fluent, astoundingly rapid monologues that weave together histories and fictions tangentially related to the artist's own past. Vonna-Michell's delivery has been compared to the seductive, cajoling patter of a market trader, and the incongruity of this comparison is apt – the artist takes as his subject the translation of meaning from one era to the next, and the changing significance of place.

Vonna-Michell's ongoing performance *hahn/huhn* (2004-), extended as part of his *Nought to Sixty* project, focuses on the Anhalter Bahnhof in Berlin, a disused train station that was the headquarters of first the Nazis, then the Allies and, finally, the Stasi. At the end of their tenure the Stasi engaged in an intensive destruction of documents, the scraps of which are now being obsessively reconstituted by 'puzzlers' employed by the German government. Suggesting the power of rumour and our inability to really 'know' history, Vonna-Michell's quick-fire delivery is too fast to be fully apprehended, while his stream-ofconsciousness mimics a journey through the Berlin streets.

Vonna-Michell's style is both physical and intimate, and he uses ephemeral objects both as markers within his narratives, and to highlight his proximity to the audience. The artist often uses an egg timer to determine the duration of his monologue, sometimes asking his viewers to dictate this time frame. Consequently, his monologues are both dramatic performances and exercises dictated by self-limitation and external constraints. Props and images used in the performance space – 35mm slides, documents, photographs, found objects – form a web of personal and historical associations, ghosts of previous works and places.

For the sprawling installation *Studio A* (2008), created for the attic space of Berlin's Kunst-Werke, Vonna-Michell worked once again with the fragmentary nature of historical memory. The installation comprised rooms constructed from remnants of stage sets, employed audio and video clips from the *RoboCop* series, and was set in the depressed city of Detroit. Turning his focus on the latter city, the

artist explored the ways in which its history overlaps with that of Berlin – a place characterised by a flux of wealth, delinquency and regeneration. The space of the installation became an analogy for such fleeting histories: the pre-fab walls could be moved to form various enclosures, fluctuating between non-sites and spaces for performance and interaction.

Vonna-Michell's work enlivens popular history in an explicitly cinematic manner, shifting the register from a generalised history available to the many, to a subjective rendering accessible only in real time. The artist's *Nought to Sixty* event expanded these concerns. Staged in the ICA Cinema, the performance space was a readymade *mise en scène* for the projected image. Divided into groups of three, audience members were led through the cinema to view a series of black and white 35mm slides projected on the screen. After a few minutes the group were guided to the projection room where the seated artist delivered a short, rapid-fire monologue fragment for those individuals alone. This atomised performance, only experienced in fragments, used the restraints of its context to constitute an incomplete and ongoing narrative.

Melissa Gronlund

36 Stephen Connolly

Event, 18 August 2008
ICA Cinema

Some of the strongest cultural responses to the shifts in the political and social landscape that followed 9/11 have come through film, and particularly through the mode of documentary. Stephen Connolly (born Montreal, 1964, lives in London) is an artist-filmmaker who employs the investigative and reconstructive aspects of documentary, exploring how its formal conditions can reflect on both individual and social agency. Shown at film festivals as well as in gallery contexts, Connolly's work uses various practices associated with conceptual film, including atemporality and montage, while always emphasising a central motif or subject. The artist does not foreground his own presence, but employs a multitude of voices and modes that include direct commentary, reportage and reconstructed speech.

Connolly's *Film for Tom* (2005) attempts to piece together elements of a deceased friend's life. It is a portrait, yet one that is necessarily fragmented – in response to a personality that was not

straightforward, and that was not comfortable within 'conventional' society. The artist's own audio recordings of Tom, conversing on politics and on his place in the world, are coupled with images and sounds that operate as traces of the man: an answer-phone message from his old school, reporting an entry in the school records; images from an archive of his photographs. *Film for Tom* is a searing and poignant act of remembrance, but also a rounded expression of the difficulty of understanding an individual's position in the world.

Connolly's earlier film *The Whale* (2003) is described by the artist as "an oblique meditation on safety, fear and notions of faraway places". Here the fleeting image and voice of Ulrike Meinhof, who was one of the leading members of Germany's Red Army Faction, is intertwined with footage of people in an urban park and of a walk through Cairo's City of the Dead. A dialogue between mother and child unites these disparate elements.

In Connolly's hands the documentary is a nonjudgmental form, undogmatic about its status as historical document or mode of investigation. *Great American Desert* (2008) moves from contemporary footage of recreational vehicles in the Arizona desert, to images of a re-staging of the Hiroshima bomb as propagandistic entertainment within the Los Angeles Coliseum in 1945. Through a mode of filmmaking rooted in the personal and quotidian, Connolly highlights the origins of our culture of spectacle and leisure – a culture that can obfuscate both history and truth.

Connolly's *Nought to Sixty* presentation included screenings of *The Whale* and *Great American Desert*, along with a discussion relating to a third work in production, *Más Se Perdió* (2008), that forms the final part of a series entitled *Afflicted States*. The artist embarked upon this group of works in 2001, and it is at once a response to global events and an extension of his exploration – also evident in *Film for Tom* – of individual subjectivity and of the individual's relationship to society and the state.

The two existing works combine archive footage, textual quotations, interviews and semi-scripted recordings, drawing links between nature, our relationship with space and the restrictions on liberty that have unfolded in the twenty-first century.

Richard Birkett

All images: Stephen Connolly / *Más Se Perdió (scratch)* / 2008

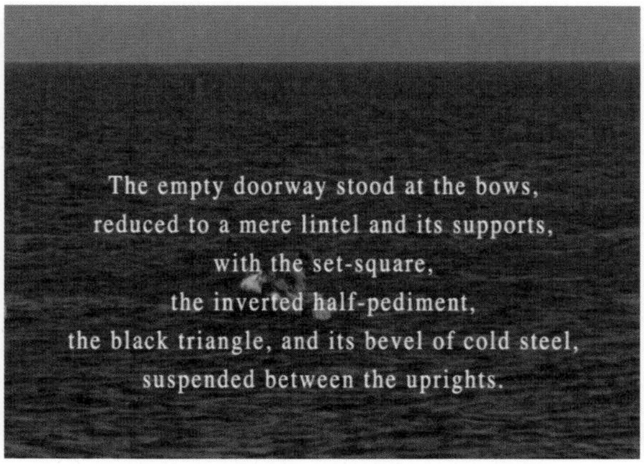
The empty doorway stood at the bows,
reduced to a mere lintel and its supports,
with the set-square,
the inverted half-pediment,
the black triangle, and its bevel of cold steel,
suspended between the uprights.

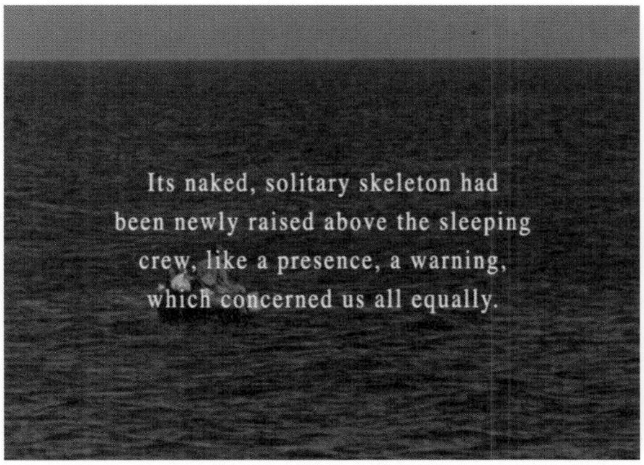
Its naked, solitary skeleton had
been newly raised above the sleeping
crew, like a presence, a warning,
which concerned us all equally.

Suddenly, the blade fell with a hiss,
and the cross piece stood out clearly,
like a real lintel above two jambs.

The Plenipotentiary, whose hand
had activated the mechanism, muttered,
"We must protect it against the saltpetre".

And he closed the Door,
by throwing a huge tarpaulin over it.

From time to time the water
grew bright with the flash of scales,
or with the passage of some
floating wreath of sargasso.

37

Lorna Macintyre

Exhibition, 18–25 August 2008
ICA Upper Galleries

Lorna Macintyre (born Glasgow, 1977, lives in Glasgow) creates sculptural and photographic installations, marrying discrete objects into tableaux replete with personal and mythological associations. Using a diverse range of materials – such as wood, copper, mirror and string – her studied compositions are always more than the sum of their parts, while also retaining the air of vulnerability inherent to assemblage.

Works often appear fragile, poised and – due to an incongruous combination of components – highly surreal. *Aeolian Sculpture* (2007) is one such fantastical sculptural object. A dried-out hunk of driftwood appears lifted from the floor by a row of guitar strings. This weathered assemblage invokes notions of music, as well as the idea of time as a process in which things are both created and destroyed.

Such combinations of the organic and man-made are characteristic of Macintyre's work, and so too is the use of literary sources. As part of her ongoing exploration of literary figures, titles and tropes, the artist titled one recent installation *Hekate* (2008), invoking the Greek goddess associated with thresholds and boundaries. The installation is a display of slippery doubles and ciphers – Macintyre's photographs and sculptural objects are characterised by reflection, duplication or mimicry. One of the installation's components, *Serpent*, is a rusted piece of piping that appears to crawl from underneath a mirror, rearing up to meet its own reflection. Its real and mirror image appear like a Rorschach test, tipping the mundane into the surreal.

Macintyre often seeks to give concrete form to literary images, and in her earlier works the artist can be found invoking an original text within the title of a work.

Surprise is the greatest new spring (2008) and *Sign of Four* (2007), for instance, relate to works by Apollinaire and Conan Doyle respectively, while the sculptural installation *Say All the Poets* (2006) quotes Fernando Pessoa's poem *The Keeper*

of Sheep. The latter work comprises a stepped wooden pyramid, its shelves displaying small objects whose configuration mirrors the elegant structure of Pessoa's original poem. This mode of display – the shelf as plinth – is a recurring feature throughout the artist's work, which foregrounds the act of display, while also demanding an intimate engagement.

For her *Nought to Sixty* exhibition Macintyre presented a new installation that drew on the genre of still life, reflecting on her ongoing fascination with a number of artists who have explored this genre in unexpected ways. Expanding on recent researches into the photographs of Paul Nash, and the paintings of Juan Sanchez-Cotan and De Chirico, Macintyre's installation employed a diverse range of objects and exploited the gap between the quotidian and the fantastical.

Isla Leaver-Yap

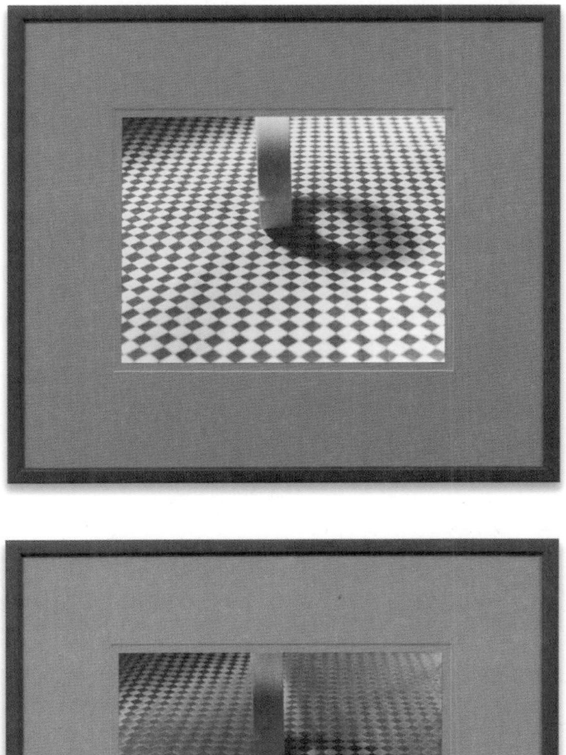

Top: Lorna Macintyre / *In the morning there is meaning* / 2008
Bottom: Lorna Macintyre / *In the evening there is feeling* / 2008

38 Ursula Mayer

Exhibition, 18–25 August 2008
ICA Upper Galleries

The films of Ursula Mayer (born Ried im Innkreis, Austria, 1970, lives in London) reflect upon and dismantle elements of cinematic narrative. Referencing architecture, the Modernist avant garde and the beginnings of Hollywood's Golden Age, Mayer's loosely constructed fictions engage in a dialogue with the conventions of the moving image.

Mayer's trilogy of films, *33 Portland Place*, *Keeling House* and *Villa Mairea* (2005–6), centre on the image of a female performer moving slowly around an architecturally significant interior (a Victorian house, a modern cluster building and an Alvar Aalto house respectively). Without scripted dialogue, the trilogy unravels in a dreamlike exploration of the relationship between the living and the built. This connection is central to much of the artist's work. The film *Interiors* (2006), for example, portrays two women wandering through the London home of architect Ernö Goldfinger and his wife Ursula, a house which was a meeting point for the 1930s intelligentsia.

Mayer extends these issues of identity and architecture in *The Crystal Gaze* (2007), the work she screened as part of *Nought to Sixty*. In this eight-minute film, three female actors languorously move through the grand interior of Eltham Palace in South London. Their luxurious 1920s dresses – a shimmering sequined bodysuit, a satin cocktail gown and an ethereal negligee – compete with the splendour of the stunning art deco surroundings. The alluring textures and figures, the slow movements of the camera and the soft piano music – an extract from Peggy Lee's tragi-comic song *Is That All There Is* – create a cinematic image that is at once seductive and strangely familiar.

However, *The Crystal Gaze* uses this opulence as a background for a dislocated and complex script. As the first character walks down the stairs – with an ease reminiscent of Rita Hayworth – a voiceover announces, "the first time I saw you I began to fantasise about you and I coexisting". This statement sounds like the start of a standard flashback, but Mayer (using a written script for the first time in her film career) defies such a conventional narrative. Instead, the voluptuous characters recite quotations on desire, fame, possession and abandon. They could be talking to each other, but the answers don't match. Phrases are superimposed and looped, their utterances teeter and occasionally collapse into a murmur of sensuous repetition.

Like much of Mayer's work, *The Crystal Gaze* challenges the temporal linearity of the filmic medium. The actors' lines alternate between past and present tense, and the film, shot primarily in colour, is regularly interrupted by short sequences in black-and-white. These disturbances jumble the contemporary and the historic, the 'now' of colour with the 'long ago' of black-and-white. The frequent shifts in the dialogue from 'I' to 'us' accentuate these gaps and hint at a shared history that binds Mayer's elusive characters together.

The stranger-companions of *The Crystal Gaze* seem to exist both for, and in total opposition to, each other. They are brought together and pulled apart in stagy, subtly homoerotic choreography, highlighting their conflicting desires for independence and for a validating gaze. Prisoners of a titillating scenario reminiscent of Sartre's *Huis Clos*, the protagonists of this filmic ballad are, in the end, their own captors.

Coline Milliard

All images: Ursula Mayer / *The Crystal Gaze* / 2007

39 Salon of salons

Salon discussion, 25 August 2008
ICA Theatre

Chaired by
Miss B, founder of Miss B's Salons

Participants
Sebastian Craig, i-cabin
Russell Martin, artist and Artquest programme coordinator
Bettina Pousttchi, artist
Jennifer Thatcher, curator, writer and ICA Director of Talks

Closed forums, or 'salons', can offer a sympathetic and responsive space for emerging artists, creating discourse around a practice before it reaches a broader public, and fostering the social networks essential for the development of emerging scenes. This debate was chaired by Miss B, who asked the panel and audience to reflect upon the resurgence of the salon within the contemporary art world.

MISS B: Tonight we might want to think about why salons exist – what's important about them, their format and their relationship to art practice. I run Miss B's Salons, which has been meeting since February – now about once a month. It started off with about twelve members who would try to come every week for six weeks and we'd talk about each other's work, show films and just share things we were interested in. That's developed now to include different topics. The last one was in Liverpool and was about cycling as a radical act. We also had one about the bucolic, in which Andrew Tullis showed films; and one about the artisan and the everyday, where we made beer and Matthew Harrison talked about his work. There are many other salons currently running in London, including Comment, an international artists' salon/discussion group run by Karen Mirza. Mirza is also involved in no.w.here's Light Readings, which are neither wholly public, nor entirely private opportunities to talk about films. Public works runs Friday sessions. There is the Manifesto Club and many artist-run film clubs. Also I recently heard of Session, in New York, where each participant is required to come alone and a new set of rules are applied each time, which shape one's actions and interactions. So there are a lot of salons that set about creating rules for their discourse. On that note I'd like to introduce the panel.

SEBASTIAN CRAIG: I'm an artist and I run i-cabin, a gallery, publishing house and artist in its own right. I-cabin makes work and takes part in exhibitions. Its practice crosses over with my practice. I have an interest in artists' private practice and why and how they choose to make that public, or how artists make their private thoughts public. That's where i-cabin ties into the idea of the salon, although I don't think of i-cabin as such. Exhibitions are residency-based, and I think of them as a discourse between me and an artist, which could be viewed as a private mini-micro salon situation that becomes public through the exhibition. I'm interested in promoting the idea that everything should be public rather than take place in a private space. I brought along a few published texts here as proofs of my commitment to that. These are public manifestations of private conversations I've had recently. One is a discussion I had while working in collaboration with Barry Sykes while he was in Finland. It was a published version of every word that was exchanged between us in the manufacture of a work. The second is *Mythologies*, a published version of a discussion that was had between me and a few other people. As an artist, I believe it's an important thing to show the workings that manifest themselves in your artwork; it's a commitment to honesty.

RUSSELL MARTIN: I'm also a practicing artist and for the past ten years I've been working without making any objects. I use dialogue as a medium, so holding salons and doing collaborative dialogue-based works is a significant part of my practice. My work is less a salon in the traditional sense, but rather it's the process of my work. One project I was involved with was called Speakeasy, which ran for about three years and which was like a salon. Eight permanent members (just like the Security Council, as someone pointed out to me) came along every month and could invite guests along as well if they wanted them to be a part of a dialogue. We spoke about works in progress, about exhibitions that we'd seen, and about currents in the art world. This morphed into what became the forum project Artquest, which initiated four groups to meet six times within six months, supported them, gave them money and access to resources and conceptual assistance if required. I'm interested in collaborative activity, and I want to draw attention to that activity rather than necessarily the content of whatever people happen to say to me. None of the dialogues that I run have any audience.

JENNIFER THATCHER: I've been asked along to this panel because I'm quite schizophrenic. On the one hand I run the talks department at the ICA, and on the other I'm involved in some private conversations, so I'm a private/public partnership in one person. The public talks I organise have advantages and disadvantages, but ultimately they are entertainment. People pay to come and see these events. Perhaps sometimes they're rehearsing existing arguments, which a private salon won't be doing.

Private debates don't necessarily have these elements. They're more hospitable than entertaining. Maybe this is why the private conversation that I'm part of is nominally a Critics' Curry Club. This private debate is about something that already exists in public about being honest. This is the only chance that we have to be private and to re-group and reassess what we do. Art writing is a very solitary activity by nature. We don't meet that often and so it's a social event. There are no other associations of art writers of our generation that I know of. Within the group some just want to meet and have a curry once a month, while others want to discuss which magazines pay and don't pay, what influence we can have here, and what press cards we can use there. There are professional issues as well as social issues.

BETTINA POUSTTCHI: My name is Bettina Pousttchi. I'm an artist from Berlin. I came to London in January for a six-month residency in London from the Research Centre for Transnational Art Identity and Nation. So when I came here I had a particular interest in conversations, not only because it's an important part of my artistic practice, but also because it's a good way to engage with the London art world. I am the first female member of the Brutally Early Club. I'm going to read out a statement from Markus Miessen, one of the founding members of the club. These are not my words but his, but it gives you an idea of what the Brutally Early Club is, and how it happened:

"While London is one of the most global cities, its actual spaces for real social debate are limited. As opposed to most global cities, the temporal structure of London remains that of the city in the 60s. If one wants to meet early in the morning or late at night the only possibilities there are consist of crowded nightclubs or private homes. Not even the train stations are open. In a city that for a decade has been the stem cell of New Labour, most of its structures are still based on Romantic notions of untroubled solidarity, social inclusion and philanthropy. Participation is often understood as a means of opening up, empowering and shared authorship. But does reality match this institutional ambition? New Labour's legacy, that of the politically correct nirvana, presents us with more participatory frameworks than ever before, while the country is now at a historic low of people actually willing to get involved. Hans Ulrich Obrist and I created a small club without mandate: a miniature discussion group that meets on a weekly basis at a time when everyone can meet without being distracted by work, phone calls or people yelling through corridors. Instead of being the next generation of facilitators and mediators, we attempt to promote the role of the uninvited outsider crossbench practitioner independent of prerequisites and existing protocols. We do not attempt to serve a community but to produce it. On a snowy winter morning of 2006, the Brutally Early Club assembled for the first time. The Starbucks branch squeezed between the legendary Sylvia Naylor and Urban Turban in Notting Hill was declared our new base soon after. Since then the club assembled 35 times. It is my sincere pleasure to witness that finally the club's picking up, as always intended by Hans Ulrich and I. Unfortunately this happens at precisely the moment when I am leaving London for Berlin. Nevertheless, it still makes me incredibly happy that the club's now gaining momentum. As intended, it is not a local but a global phenomenon. Wherever we are, travel or happen to be, the club surfaces and sets up new relationships. The Brutally Early Club currently exists in three cities: London, Paris and New York. The next branch has just been founded in Berlin. The saga continues.

MISS B: The irony of this public discussion as a salon hasn't escaped us this evening. We've told you who we are and now we're going to mingle. We've got some things to get people moving a bit. [Shows two cards on which 'PRIVATE' and 'PUBLIC' are written] This is to write your private thoughts on and this is to write your public thoughts.

(Audience broken into groups for 10 minutes, then re-grouped)

MISS B: Is a social environment conducive to a critical conversation?

MARTIN: Yes. It's easier to be honest with people you know a little bit, and easier to be critical of someone's position – I mean 'critical' in the normally used sense of having a bash at it.

MISS B: I had a discussion with Markus about his statement. I should have said that the Brutally Early Club meets very early in the morning. I think the earliest has been 5:30 am. Is that right, Bettina?

POUSTTCHI: No, it's at 6:30 am.

MISS B: 6:30 am? That's more relaxed – everyone has a lie-in. I asked Markus if that means everyone's more brutal.

POUSTTCHI: I don't think we're more brutal, but the fact that it's so early sets up your mind in different ways. The first thing that you do if you meet at 8:30 am is to check your emails and then go to the meeting, but the 6:30 club is really the first thing that you do. You feed your brain from the beginning of the day with important questions. The rest of the day is very different when you've started like this. It was a convenient time to meet because everybody was free. But it's not just practical, it's also a different way to use your hours of the day.

CRAIG: Jen mentioned that the Curry Club can talk about what magazines pay more than others, and it's about creating a space where you can say things that aren't generally accepted for people to say in the public sphere. You don't often come across people who are really being brutal in public. When you do, it's refreshing.

MISS B: So, to what extent does context influence the outcome?

MARTIN: If someone creates a salon then the first thing you're doing is inviting people. You're automatically putting yourself in a position of authority or responsibility over the group and what's going to happen.

MISS B: That might be what differentiates it from peer critiques like artists showing their work, talking about their work. That's not the same as a salon that is sort of hosted by someone.

CRAIG: At art school there was hardly any brutal honesty going on between peers, and I don't think there is now. Running i-cabin, inviting artists to show there and then having a discourse with them – that is a setup where there's scope for that. Whether that's because I feel compelled to push artists or they feel compelled to push the gallery. We work together to end up with something that we both consider to be important. Is that because we're not two artists in that scenario? The only time you have really critical discussion is in a professional scenario rather than a friendship one. I think that's true in my peer group anyway.

POUSTTCHI: Concerning Brutally Early Club, the point is we're not all from the same field. It's architects, visual artists, a novelist, a graphic artist, a graphic designer. We try to share ideas that link our practices and to have an interdisciplinary exchange of ideas. So I think it is probably a different situation...

MISS B: Sebastian, a lot of your projects orchestrate rules and inflict them on people very deliberately.

CRAIG: The purpose of i-cabin and the purpose of my artistic practice is about defining intention really. I am often mistrustful of the way there are certain codes that define what artworks look like, and how artists feel compelled to talk in a semi-abstracted language about what they are trying to do. I think that generates a scenario whereby artists use that as an excuse to not really have an agenda – because you can hint at different things in an artwork without actually putting your neck on the line. When we started running the space there were rules. I don't really enforce them anymore, but the only rule is that there is a resonance and a discourse that takes place. Each artist that I work with at i-cabin – in terms of it being a gallery – is invited to show in a different way because we want to work towards this and we want you to collaborate with us on achieving this.

MISS B: So conversations should be public for everybody's benefit because that makes people justify the things that they do?

CRAIG: Yes. Artists should be forced to justify what they do.

THATCHER: Why? Who is it interesting to? I don't need to know how everyone works.

CRAIG: Not *how* they work but *why* they work.

THATCHER: It would be really boring for art critics: "I had a cup of tea ... stared out the window ... wrote another couple of words ... stared out the window."

CRAIG: It's not critics. I think that in general artists have an easy time.

ANONYMOUS (audience): What?!

POUSTTCHI: That's bullshit.

MARTIN: Do you mean intellectually, where the process isn't necessarily exposed in the final artwork? That it's an intellectual journey that they should be explicating a bit more?

CRAIG: Absolutely. I'm an artist – not just a gallerist or someone just saying artists have an easy time. I think that a lot of artists don't ask themselves forceful enough questions about why they're asking us as a viewing public or as other artists to interact with them. I try to expose everything that I do in terms of leaving open all the flaws in the practice; making it all visible and confessing things which I might be quite worried about.

ANONYMOUS (audience): As you were saying that artists don't really talk about their work much, I was thinking historically why that has actually happened. If you think about manifestos, you can think of the Futurist manifestos or the Surrealist manifestos. Those were eras when people actually believed in some kind of group authority. I think we've reached a point where, with feminism, with the civil rights movement and so on, we've challenged authority or power. And with French critical theory, deconstruction... We haven't found a way to replace that kind of social need for a forum in which to come together. I think artists are suspicious of authority. In London there are lots of little movements or no movements or the individual. We've fragmented out rather than come together to create grand narratives.

CRAIG: Manifestos are about setting forth an intention and, as you say, they are not something you hear of anymore, and nor is artistic intention as such. It's naïve that artists should expect something of themselves and set their sights on creating something that aims to do something quantifiable. I jotted down this little quote – you mentioned French philosophy – this is Foucault's definition of what a work is, "that which is susceptible of introducing a significant difference in the field of knowledge, at the cost of a certain difficulty for the author and the reader, with, however, the eventual recompense of a certain pleasure, that is to say of access to another figure of truth". A work is something which is susceptible of introducing a significant difference in the field of knowledge. That's a fucking tall order, but that's the kind of scale we should expect from art. I think we should expect a hell of a lot more from it than I feel we're getting, as an artist and as a gallerist and as everything else.

THATCHER: So do you see yourself as an educationalist? Is it as important for you to educate other artists in learning about French philosophy or ways of being?

CRAIG: God, no.

THATCHER: I'm just responding to one of your questions, which is whether or not salons should be educational.

MISS B: Does anyone think salons are about self-education? They could be said to be mimicking the seminar structure that's very common in higher education.

CRAIG: It's not educational. I'm just talking about people pushing themselves or questioning or being questioned.

ANONYMOUS (audience): Collaboration and equality is difficult to achieve and often unachievable because egos are there. I was wondering how much self-interest is in salons? What's the difference between the self-interest in private conversations and self-interest in public conversations?

MARTIN: Artquest wanted to make something that was a bit more controlled by artists rather than facilitated by organisations. Given that I'd run Speakeasy at the time for about three years, I knew that it worked as a model and I knew that you could give artists a chunk of money and you could trust them to do their thing. We didn't ask for an evaluation or report at the end. It was the activity that was important, where people were meeting regularly and creating their own support. I mean 'support' in terms of being critical about exposing that process that usually isn't exposed, and questioning that and making sure that it's as strong as it could be.

CRAIG: Collaboration is inextricably linked with self-interest because it is on one level networking par excellence. Artists that build a career out of collaborating with different people is like picking up friends. You get self-promotion and a cross-promotional game whereby you also get their contacts.

MISS B: Why is there an expectation that there's collaboration in a private conversation or that there's a production when you don't have that expectation of a public debate?

THATCHER: In public debates here at the ICA, I might have an agenda whereby in September I'm organising a debate on the future of art education. Now I do actually have an agenda for making sure that public policy makers are there and that in some way perhaps we can contribute to public policy.

MISS B: Are these public debates more important?

THATCHER: No. The debates we're having are preparing the ground for many public debates that maybe we will have later as art critics. To be honest, the public debates around art criticism at the moment are so boring that there's no point anymore being involved unless you want the money. If we're going to do anything interesting we may as well meet privately and then come back with something interesting later. It's also about the maturity of the debate and what you feel you want to happen. If private debates were really pressing then maybe somebody in your group would take that onto a public level.

ANONYMOUS (audience): Most of my practice is socially – or politically – based, and I find that the dialogue with the audience is essential. In some circles, where art doesn't have political or social agendas, dialogue is not necessary or is not perceived as necessary. As a result, from the artist's perspective there isn't much need to define what they want to do. But it is extremely important and sometimes this intention is actually withdrawn by the artist so that the audience can form an opinion or even sometimes for political reasons. For example, they may want the message to be somewhat fuzzy so that the market can attach their own labels to the work and they can sell it better. I think this happens in lots of places like London where there's a division between art market movement and artists who intend to say something with their work.

ANONYMOUS (audience): A lot of the developments in the context of the salon relate to society historically. If you can imagine artists at the time of the Second World War when artists got together and they had their salons – the Surrealist movement being one. Political context is absolutely essential to the mood of what artists or critics talk about. If the zeitgeist is one of irony then that's what you will get. If the zeitgeist is cynicism, then I guess that's what you get being reflected in the salons. The salon itself can be a snapshot of the historical mood of the time.

MARTIN: I don't think salons will fill any one particular function in relation to the rest of society, but there will always be a number of salons that will fulfil a lot of those different roles.

POUSTTCHI: Returning to Markus's statement, as an architect he understands this notion of participation also in the context of otherism: how to use a city, what are your possibilities there? Markus and Hans Ulrich were trying to find a space open at 6:30 am and it wasn't that easy – that's why it happens at Starbucks. It's now questioning how a city is built and how infrastructure is built according to your needs. I guess this is also the idea behind participation in relation to your city and your built spatial surroundings.

CRAIG: That statement is a mini-architectural manifesto for a city.

ANONYMOUS (audience): Maybe salons are inherently urban.

MISS B: These salons are microcosms of self-organisation. It is the grassroots activity where people can reinvent and question, but it's also not necessarily any more effective than the institution. These things exist in tandem, but there are means of questioning an activity and being active within it.

40

Junior Aspirin Records

Event, 1 September 2008
ICA Theatre

If counter-cultural icon Don Van Vliet – aka Captain Beefheart – were ever to abandon painting and come out of musical retirement, then he truly couldn't find a more appropriate recording home than Junior Aspirin Records (formed in 2002, based in London).

For one, the label is highly sympathetic to visual artists: Skill 7 Stamina 12, one of Junior Aspirin's bands, includes artists Maaike Schoorel and Nathaniel Mellors, along with writer Dan Fox; while both Polly Braden and David Noonan have contributed artwork to the label. Moreover, The Captain would need look no further than Junior Aspirin musicians for recruits for a re-formed Magic Band: Skill 7 Stamina 12's Ashley Marlowe is one of the few living drummers who can rightfully claim rhythmic lineage from the Magic Band's John French. Even if Junior Aspirin don't manage to sign Beefheart, they needn't worry. The label works with London's own genius avant-garde redneck bluesman, The Rebel – BR Waller of the Country Teasers.

The music of Skill 7 Stamina 12 is in part a continuation of 1970s experimentalism, the elliptical groove on tracks such as '80 Metres' from the album *Skill 7 Stamina Dead* (2007), for instance, revisiting German rock innovators CAN in 1969. Meanwhile, Maaike Schoorel's vocals, positioned somewhere between Ari Up of The Slits and Stereolab's Laetitia Sadler, link the band's music to New York's downtown scene of the early 1980s. Similarly, *Spritza Boy* (2005), by Junior Aspirin stalwarts Socrates That Practices Music (Andy Cooke, Alex Ellerington, Jared Fisher and Grigoris Leontiades), sounds like the ethnic punk-funk of Eric Random and the Bedlamites, obscure early 1980s Cabaret Voltaire associates for all we know, the record could be a dance-floor bomb in the small clubs of hipster Williamsburg, where such African hi-life inspired no wave is all the rage again).

But Junior Aspirin is not mired in replicating music of past eras. Emphasising the artful eclecticism of the label, Junior Aspirin's first compilation, *Remove Celebrity Centre* (2006), featured such diverse sounds as the visceral hardcore of Charlottefield; the toy-town Krautrock of Imitation Electric Piano; DJ Scotch Egg's frenetic

Bob Parks performance / ICA / 2008

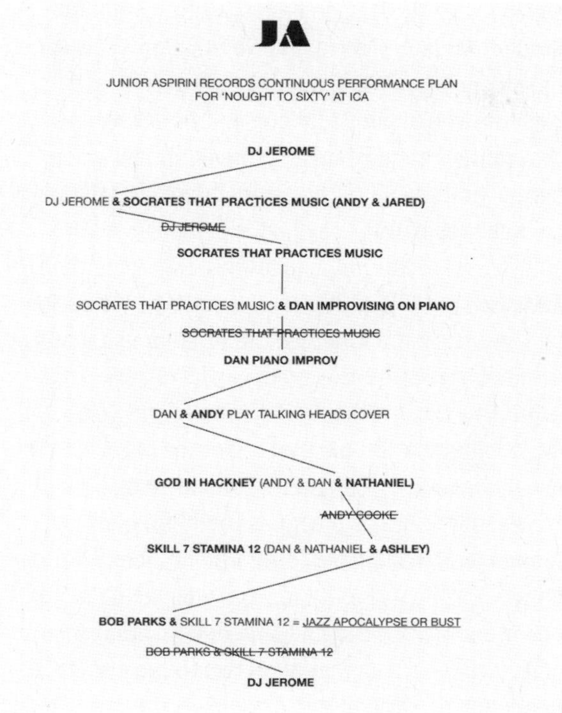

JA
JUNIOR ASPIRIN RECORDS CONTINUOUS PERFORMANCE PLAN
FOR 'NOUGHT TO SIXTY' AT ICA
DJ JEROME
DJ JEROME & SOCRATES THAT PRACTICES MUSIC (ANDY & JARED)
DJ JEROME
SOCRATES THAT PRACTICES MUSIC
SOCRATES THAT PRACTICES MUSIC & DAN IMPROVISING ON PIANO
SOCRATES THAT PRACTICES MUSIC
DAN PIANO IMPROV
DAN & ANDY PLAY TALKING HEADS COVER
GOD IN HACKNEY (ANDY & DAN & NATHANIEL)
ANDY COOKE
SKILL 7 STAMINA 12 (DAN & NATHANIEL & ASHLEY)
BOB PARKS & SKILL 7 STAMINA 12 = JAZZ APOCALYPSE OR BUST
BOB PARKS & SKILL 7 STAMINA 12
DJ JEROME

Game-boy techno; and contributions from moonlighting artists Jack Too Jack (Mark Leckey, Steven Claydon, Ed Liq and Kieron Livingstone), Emily Wardill and Sue Tompkins. As a loose identity for a network of bands and performers, and with a spasmodic series of releases, Junior Aspirin Records exists in an ambiguous and shifting territory between the art world and the music industry.

Just as the influence of experimental bands from the 1970s and 1980s is visible in the counter-cultural sensibility and look of contemporary visual art, so too has recording and playing live become integral to many artist's practices; the playfulness of performance and musical abstraction providing critical tools for considering the 'avant' instincts of experimentalism. Junior Aspirin epitomises this approach, fusing the artistic and the extrovert. The label's *Nought to Sixty* event drew together live performances in a non-stop performance that highlighted its interconnected output. Featuring live sets by DJ Jerome, Socrates That Practices Music, God in Hackney, Skill 7 Stamina 12 and Bob Parks, performers were often joined onstage by other musicians. This united line-up of bands and shared musicians hinted at the tangents and associations that make up the social fabric of Junior Aspirin Records.

Tony F Wilson

41

Sarah Pierce

Exhibition, 1–8 September 2008
ICA Upper Galleries

Since 2003 Sarah Pierce (born Conneticut, USA, 1968, lives in Dublin) has used an umbrella term – The Metropolitan Complex – to describe her art practice. Despite its institutional resonance, this title does not signify an organisation. Instead, it covers various discursive working methods, involving papers, interviews, archives, talks and exhibitions.

Pierce characterises The Metropolitan Complex as "a way to play with the hang-ups (read 'complex' in the Freudian sense) that surround cultural work". Her project demonstrates a broad understanding of cultural work, one that is articulated through both institutional and personal patterns of organisation, and which includes the incidental and coincidental. The processes of research and presentation that the artist undertakes are designed to highlight the potential for dissent and self-determination within such structures.

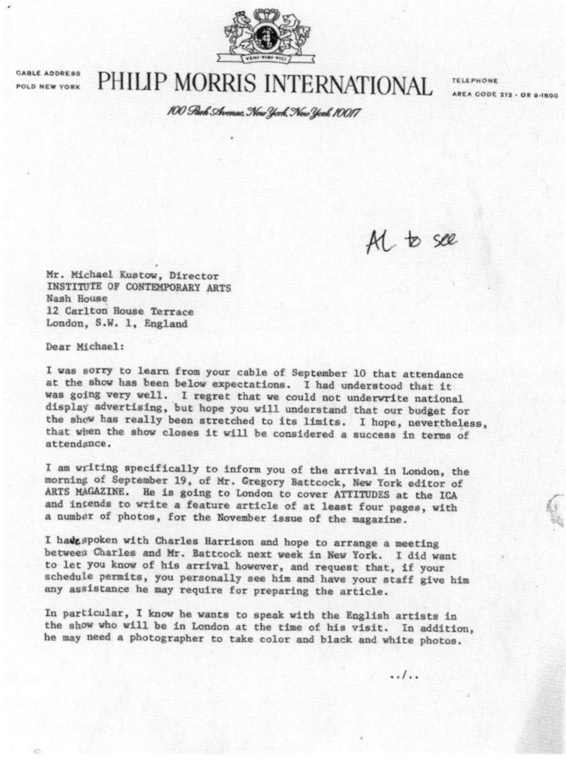
VENI · VIDI · VICI

CABLE ADDRESS POLO NEW YORK

PHILIP MORRIS INTERNATIONAL

TELEPHONE AREA CODE 212 · OR 9-1800

100 Park Avenue, New York, New York 10017

Al to see

Mr. Michael Kustow, Director
INSTITUTE OF CONTEMPORARY ARTS
Nash House
12 Carlton House Terrace
London, S.W. 1, England

Dear Michael:

I was sorry to learn from your cable of September 10 that attendance at the show has been below expectations. I had understood that it was going very well. I regret that we could not underwrite national display advertising, but hope you will understand that our budget for the show has really been stretched to its limits. I hope, nevertheless, that when the show closes it will be considered a success in terms of attendance.

I am writing specifically to inform you of the arrival in London, the morning of September 19, of Mr. Gregory Battcock, New York editor of ARTS MAGAZINE. He is going to London to cover ATTITUDES at the ICA and intends to write a feature article of at least four pages, with a number of photos, for the November issue of the magazine.

I have spoken with Charles Harrison and hope to arrange a meeting between Charles and Mr. Battcock next week in New York. I did want to let you know of his arrival however, and request that, if your schedule permits, you personally see him and have your staff give him any assistance he may require for preparing the article.

In particular, I know he wants to speak with the English artists in the show who will be in London at the time of his visit. In addition, he may need a photographer to take color and black and white photos.

../..

One of the artist's emphases is on a "shared neuroses of place", whether a specific locality or a wider set of circumstances that frame interaction, and central to her activity is the consideration of forms of gathering, both historical examples and discussions that she initiates and transcribes. Another arena for Pierce's exploration of privacy and openness is the archive, both personal and institutional, and the artist refers to the work of sociologist C. Wright Mills as a model for the "interdisciplinary aspects of intellectualism, and the practice of keeping a file, or set of files, that contains all the ideas or materials that compel one's research". Mills advocated generating the archive, not through a static ordering, but through a constant reassessment and rearrangement of elements, where spontaneous proximity leads to unpredictable connections.

Pierce's project *The Meaning of Greatness* (2006) demonstrates her approach to both the gathering and the archive. Through the recreation of artworks and the presentation of archival artifacts, the artist considers the influence of Eva Hesse, the incidental similarities between the lives of Hesse and Pierce's own mother, and the significance of periods of student protest in both the US and in Yugoslavia – Pierce conducted research into the Student Cultural Centre archive in Belgrade. Such projects explore the slippages between individual work and the institutional context, providing a telling assessment of how the structures through which people gather and organise are connected to political gestures in art.

For her project, entitled *"It's time, man. It feels imminent"* (2008), Pierce undertook a period of research in the ICA's own archive, focusing on two seminal events in the organisation's history – the exhibition *When Attitudes Become Form* (1969) and the conference *The State of British Art* (1978). Each event connects to debates around art-making and organisation: Pierce presented both the practical remnants of institutional organisation, including redundant plinths and vitrines and archival documents; and the broader concerns of political organisation, protest and teaching, through interviews and documentation, and video of a closed workshop in which participants acted out gestures and recited quotes from bystanders at various political demonstrations.

Richard Birkett

PHILIP MORRIS INTERNATIONAL

Mr. Michael Kustow
September 12, 1969
-2-

By copy of this letter I am asking Margot Slater if she will also kindly meet Mr. Battcock and give him any assistance he may need, specifically with the photographer. I highly reccommend Sidney Harris who took photos at the opening. I will give Mr. Battcock Margot's phone number.

Since Mr. Battcock does not yet know where he will be staying, I will ask him to get in touch with you. He will be in London about four or five days.

I hope that, in spite of your cable, the show is going well. It certainly was a pleasure, and lots of fun too, working with you and your staff.

We are interested in taking out a corporate membership in the ICA, and I would appreciate it if you could send me pertinent information.

Many thanks and warmest regards.

Yours sincerely,

Mary

Mary W. Covington

MWC:mt
cc: Messrs. I. C. Ludwig
C. Harrison
Mrs. M. Slater

All images: Sarah Pierce / *"It's time, man. It feels imminent"* / 2008

42 **Giles Round**

Exhibition, 1–8 September 2008
ICA Upper Galleries

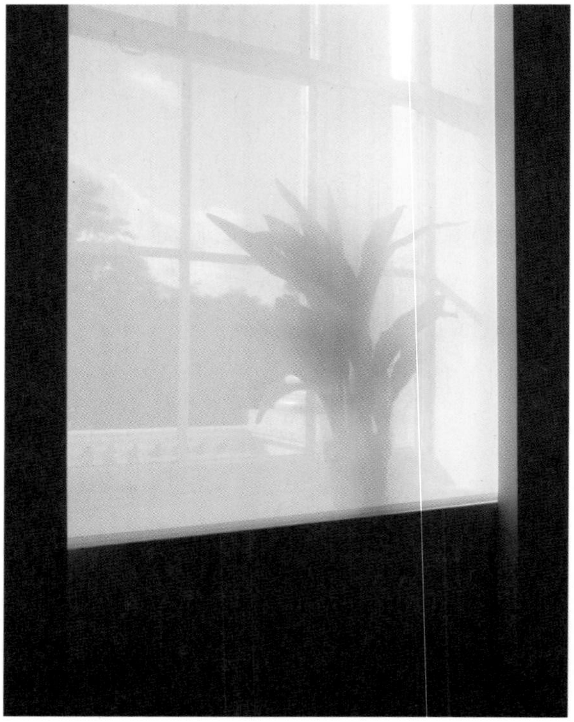

Both images: Giles Round / *Strange days and nights of mystery and fear mixed with excitement and wonder strange days and nights strange months and years* / 2008

Giles Round (born London, 1976, lives in London) creates sculptures and assemblages that employ geometric structures, monochromatic panels, lights and typographic schemes. His works utilise the formal language of modernist and minimalist art and design, and explore a synthesis between material and shape. But these balanced 'displays' also address the cooption of such conventions within decor, and the use of modular elements within high-end living spaces. Moreover, Round's works are highly ritualistic, employing the repetition of purposeless form to invoke the romantic hedonism of a hallucinatory state.

Linear structures of mahogany or brass are often a central feature of Round's sculptures, formed into the angular shapes of frames, supports and grids. These planar shapes and modular units make up improvised stage sets, upon which are hung or placed secondary elements, an interaction of structure and ornament that references the homemaking of such pioneers of art and architecture as Donald Judd and Ernö Goldfinger. In *Time Just Falls Away* (2006), a triangular wooden frame supports a series of hanging neon shapes, while a canvas becomes the projection screen for pulsating coloured text.

The relationship between line and volume that is explored by Round in these structures is also found in his typographic work. The artist has created a series of fonts that mimic this formal balance, and which he uses on the posters, hangings and animations that feature within his installations. These 'signs' contain texts that fluctuate in their legibility, overwhelmed by the structure of the font and its gridlike presentation. Containing phrases of romantic excess, their semantic collapse evokes an altered state of perception; the bourgeois refinement of forms and arrangements shifting towards a giddy, transgressive lyricism.

Round's *Nought to Sixty* project made reference to the British sculptor and printmaker Eric Gill (1882–1940), through a phrase lifted from the latter's diaries: "Strange days and nights of mystery and fear mixed with excitement and wonder strange days and nights strange months and years". Round's use of the text – which operated as a leitmotif throughout the exhibition – evoked Gill's influential work as a typographer, but also the latter's complex persona. During his lifetime Gill presented himself as a deeply religious man, publishing numerous essays on the relationship between art and religion, and encouraging the formation of arts and crafts communities. This worthy image was shaken when the artist's diaries were published in the late 1980s, documenting his adulteries, incestuous liaisons and experiments with bestiality.

The confrontation between noble aspirations and transgressive desires that is apparent in Gill's diaries was mirrored in Round's exhibition. The poised arrangement of frames, lights and cut-outs – the latter featuring an aspidistra, the Orwellian symbol of bourgeois existence – formed a stage set in which an image of order was overlaid by the shadows of Gill's "strange days and nights". The rhythm of the phrase echoed throughout the show, both as a formal structure (echoing Gill's stone-carved memorials) and as a pulsating lyric. Round's three-dimensional compositions are totems of authority, but also reveal the tendency to excess within the heart of idealism.

Nicola Lees

43 Ben Rivers

Event, 8 September 2008
ICA Cinema

The films of Ben Rivers (born Somerset, 1972, lives in London) are rich, cinematic portraits that explore wilderness environments and self-contained worlds, representing memory through visual fragments.

Primarily shot on 16mm black-and-white film, sometimes on out-of-date stock, Rivers' work has the appearance of ageing, archival footage. The artist shoots on an old Bolex wind-up camera, and works creatively within its limitations – including contraints of duration, since the longest continuous shot is 30 seconds. The aged appearance of the film is also partly a consequence of Rivers hand-processing each film in his own kitchen sink. He compares the creation of his films to assembling a collage, and although he places great emphasis on the editing process, he is in fact strongly involved in all stage of his films' creation, through his roles as cameraman, developer, editor and director.

The distanced quality of Rivers work – albeit a knowing construction – extends to the spaces and subjects that the films focus on. Whether exposing desolate and crumbling interiors in works like *Old Dark House* (2003) and its sequel *House* (2005), or portraying the hermetic world of the 'outsider' figure Jake Williams in the much acclaimed *This is My Land* (2006), Rivers' work is engaged with zones at the edges of contemporary life. Other works, such as *Ah Liberty!* (2008) which depicts a community inhabiting a rural and seemingly sublime landscape, appear to exist outside modern living altogether, signifying less alienation from the mainstream than liberation from it.

Although they depict real-life subjects, Rivers' films are not primarily documentary or ethnographic in style, despite drawing heavily on these genres. Rather, his work is personal and fragmented, reminiscent of the idiosyncratic styles of Scottish filmmaker and poet Margaret Tait and American director George Kuchar. Other influences – perhaps less apparent in Rivers' imagery than in his soundtracks – are as wide-ranging as thriller, film noir and horror. This range of sources reflects Rivers' work at Brighton Cinematheque, where he has helped run a regular screening programme since 1996, one that includes both recent and historical work.

Top: Ben Rivers / *The Coming Race* / 2006
Bottom: Ben Rivers / *We The People* / 2006

Rivers presented a special screening programme for *Nought to Sixty* that drew on his experience at Brighton Cinematheque. The artist showed his own work alongside that of other filmmakers, in an attempt to highlight different strategies for dealing with the histories of documentary and ethnographic film. Emphasising diverse and creative approaches to history was fundamental to the project, as was an attempt to establish a common language lying between the confines of these problematic genres.

Isla Leaver-Yap

Ben Rivers curated screening programme
8 September 2008

- Jean Rouch, *Tourou et Bitti*, 1967, 12m
- Steve Reinke, *The Mendi*, 2006, 9m
- Barry Kimm, *Measurements of Oxford*, 1989, 9m
- Rosalind Nashashibi, *Midwest*, 2002, 12m
- Ben Rivers, *The Coming Race*, 2006, 5m
- Karl Kels, *Prince Hotel*, 1987/2003, 8m
- Ben Rivers, *We The People*, 2004, 1m
- Ben Russell, *Trypps Number Three*, 2007, 12m

Films appear courtesy of the artists and as listed hereafter.
Jean Rouch: CNRS, Paris. Steve Reinke: Video Data Bank, Chicago.
Rosalind Nashashibi: doggerfisher, Edinburgh.

44 Maria Fusco

Event, 15 September 2008
ICA Nash/Brandon Rooms

Maria Fusco (born Belfast, 1972, lives in London) interrogates the phenomenon of writing about art, writing about writing and art about writing, but primarily she is interested in is what she describes as "writing with art". In her roles as art critic, editor, lecturer, fiction writer and Director of Writing at Goldsmiths College, Fusco has searched out diverse styles of writing, not simply for their literary value but as part of an ongoing fascination with the slippery nature of writing, and its intimate relationship to contemporary art practice.

With *The Happy Hypocrite*, launched in spring 2008, Fusco has generated a periodical that nods to the history of avant-garde writing, reproducing the pages of seminal publications, such as the experimental journal *Bananas*, within each issue. *The Happy Hypocrite* is also committed to new forms of experimental writing, and central to its remit is Fusco's desire to make the journal a triangular conversation between writer, subject and reader. Taking its title from a Max Beerbohm's short story, the publication began as a book, but soon outgrew this format, transforming instead into a bi-annual journal. *The Happy Hypocrite* is published by Bookworks, and to date has featured contributions from artists such as Gerard Byrne, Cosey Fanni Tutti and Farhad Ahrahnia.

The Happy Hypocrite was also the focus of a discussion which formed one of the artist's contributions to *Nought to Sixty*. Drawing on Fusco's wide-ranging interests in fiction, analysis, criticism and conversation, the event included a reading by writer Steve Beard and a special screening of the Maysles Brothers' *Meet Marlon Brando* (1965), a 16mm film that has influenced Fusco's understanding of oral culture and literacy. The short portrait – in part created by Albert Maysles, who went on to shoot the seminal documentary *Grey Gardens* (1976) – candidly shows Brando toying with the format of the Hollywood interview, while on a press junket for the film *Morituri* (1966). Sitting in his

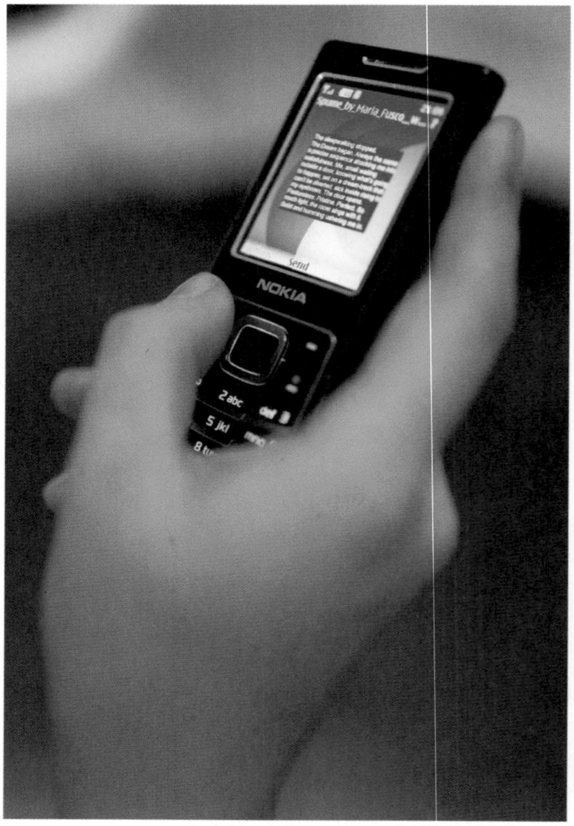

Left: Maria Fusco / *Spume* / 2008
Right: Steve Beard reading from *The Happy Hyprocrite* / ICA / 2008

Maria Fusco, *Spume*
Texts broadcast by Bluetooth from ICA, 15 September–2 November 2008

Week 1
I sleep for an hour or two at most. I can't distinguish my dreams from my thoughts.

Have I been asleep? How long have I been asleep? I struggle, watching you snoozing soundly, thin eyelids gently undulating your eyeballs watching your dreams. I grasp you even tighter, hoping to squeeze out some sleep.

Week 2
I pinch your shoulder, hot and hard, spurred on by my fury, my distress at losing you for the night. You wake up and swear at me. I am pleased. I repent. I deny I've done it. I feel smug all the same, knowing I can still exercise control over you as you sleep, nipping you into consciousness.

Week 3
When I learnt to walk, I learnt to sleepwalk too. My fatigue followed me around the house like a security blanket. As I got older, my nocturnal actions became more accomplished: tender rosebuds picked carefully from their stems and arranged in a semicircle in front of the television, squares cut from the hems of clothes then secreted in school shoes.

Week 4
The sleepwalking stopped. The Dream began. Always the same: a precise sequence shocking me into wakefulness. Me, small waiting outside a door, knowing what's going to happen, set on a dream-track that can't be diverted, sick inside rising to my eyebrows. The door opens. Featureless. Pristine. Perfect. So much light, the room sings with it. Solid and humming ushering me in.

Week 5
Are they in the room already? No. They are made from its glare. I'm terrified. I don't move. I wait. They glide toward me. I recognise their step, their stealth, their advancing speed. I know what's going to happen. I'm only nine in dream-time. I'm four stone. I'm as light as a kitten. They toss me out the window.

Week 6
I hit the ground. No pain just relief, accompanied by a readjustment of the pavement around me. Content, I lie sniffing it. What does it smell of? Petrichor: sunny rain. I cherish these secret steps my brain makes when it thinks I'm beginning to fall asleep, the confidential connections. My generative dream-tissue: it fuses, it fizzes, it endures. It makes sense.

Week 7
My mind burrows for alleviation. Confounded until at last I recall the polished surface of Sizewell's dome. A giant white ceramic egg near the beach. Featureless. Pristine. Perfect. The blankness soothes me, I imagine myself floating inside it. Did I sleep right through, uninterrupted until the morning? You know, I think I did.

New York hotel room, the film star deftly dodges the journalists' often banal questions and exposes their fawning attitudes.

In addition to the latter event, however, Fusco also presented a longer work, entitled *Spume*, that spanned the last two months of *Nought to Sixty*. Building on a previous piece, *Doom Knots* (2006), the artist generated a barrage of texts that were broadcast daily, by Bluetooth, to mobile phones passing within range of her transmitter. The piece, which was based at the ICA, was characterised by a fragmentation of narrative, and it would have been very hard for any one individual to experience the entirety of the work. However, its engagement with narrative as a physical but metamorphic object is typical of Fusco – and one of the things that has lent her work to an art context.

Isla Leaver-Yap

Left: Maria Fusco / Screening of *Meet Marlon Brando* / 2008

45 David Osbaldeston

Exhibition, 15–22 September 2008
ICA Upper Galleries

Right: David Osbaldeston / *The Pleasure of Your Company* / 2008

The work of David Osbaldeston (born Middlesbrough, 1968, lives in Manchester and Glasgow) has a seductive air of familiarity. His subject matter not only slips neatly into the space between art and life, but also articulates the strangeness of reconstructing the past through the eyes of the present, which will itself inevitably slip away. Using drawing, woodcut and etching – an anachronistic, perhaps redundant, method of production – Osbaldeston produces work that resists assimilation, and which instead explores the creative space between original and copy. His practice appears to draw on his audience's nostalgia for certain phenomena, including the rationalist aesthetics of modernism.

Osbaldeston's projects interrogate the galleries in which they are situated, and the support structures that surround such cultural sites. For his Matt's Gallery exhibition, *Your Answer Is Mine* (2006), the artist created a billboard-sized etching that resembled a giant photocopy, and which was meticulously constructed from an absurd array of self-penned ideological pronouncements. His exhibition *Another Shadow Fight* (2008), at International Project Space, involved posters influenced by an eclectic range of sources, including the polemical writings of Wyndham Lewis and a series of works by artist Sidney Nolan. The posters were used to construct a dilapidated version of a newspaper kiosk, one originally designed by Bauhaus pioneer Herbert Bayer.

For *Nought to Sixty* Osbaldeston presented *The Pleasure of Your Company* (2008), which consists of a series of 57 etchings. The different works reproduce invitation cards for projects at ICA, dating from the year of its first solo show in 1950 to 2007. The events range from a James Joyce poetry recital in 1950, to exhibitions by artists such as Francis Bacon, Pablo Picasso, Barbara Kruger, Mike Kelley and Cerith Wyn Evans. Osbaldeston's works are reconstructed 'ghosts' of the originals, and were produced in an edition of one (plus one artist's proof), thus negating the commodification usually inherent within editioned work. Such works expose the labouriousness of his endeavour and what Osbaldeston describes as an absurd counter to the logic of the globalised economy.

Osbaldeston's decision to research the archive of the ICA, and to re-work old preview cards, enabled him to present a visual commentary on the organisation's history – and to comment, in part, on the anniversary celebrations of which *Nought to Sixty* was a feature.

Osbaldeston charts the evolution of the invitations, items which are complex signifiers of their time, and which raise issues such as the elitist nature of the art community. What also becomes apparent within his critique is the often conservative and generic design of the cards, which – together with the ICA's shifting corporate identity – bring into question the assumed 'progressive' nature of the institution. Finally, there was a subtle humour present in the week-long exhibition that encapsulated and recirculated the images accumulated over 57 years.

Matthew Williams

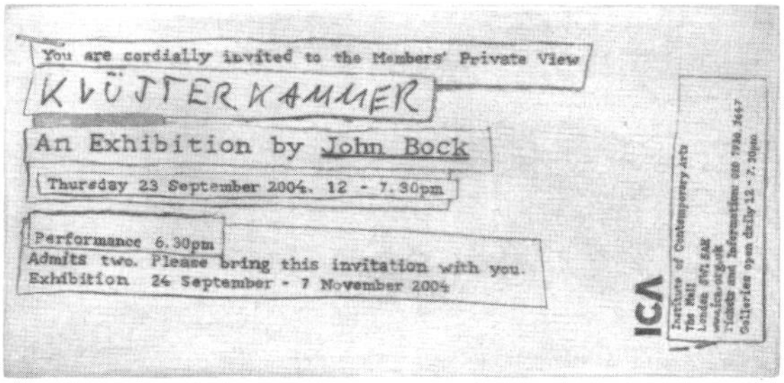

All images this page and following spread: David Osbaldeston / *The Pleasure of Your Company* / 2008

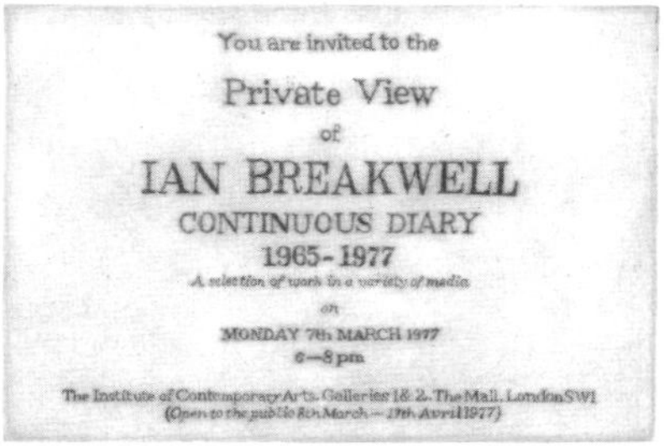
You are invited to the
Private View
of
IAN BREAKWELL
CONTINUOUS DIARY
1965-1977
A selection of work in a variety of media
on
MONDAY 7th MARCH 1977
6—8pm
The Institute of Contemporary Arts, Galleries 1 & 2, The Mall, London SW1

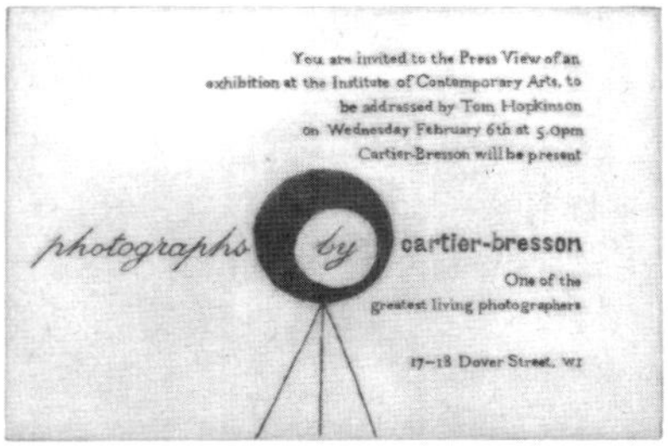
You are invited to the Press View of an
exhibition at the Institute of Contemporary Arts, to
be addressed by Tom Hopkinson
on Wednesday February 6th at 5.0pm
Cartier-Bresson will be present
photographs
by
cartier-bresson
One of the
greatest living photographers
17–18 Dover Street, W1

Calder
The Painter
Institute of Contemporary Arts
17-18 Dover Street, W1
Private View for Members & Guests
Wednesday 28th September 6pm

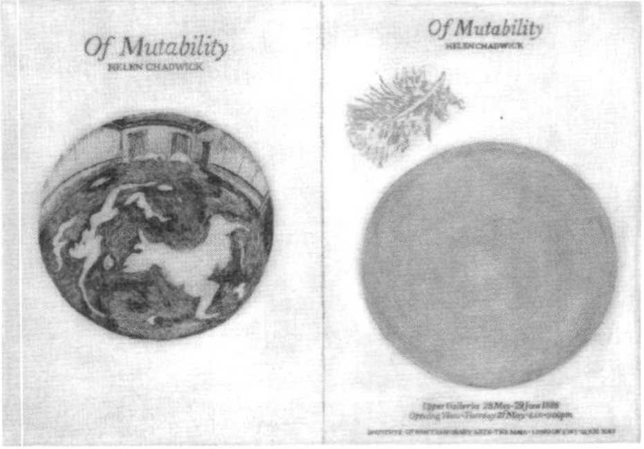
Of Mutability
HELEN CHADWICK
Of Mutability
HELEN CHADWICK

JEAN LUC VILMOUTH
LOCAL TIME
ICA
THE MALL LONDON SW1 01-930 3647

CPLY

JEFF WALL
TRANSPARENCIES
ICA

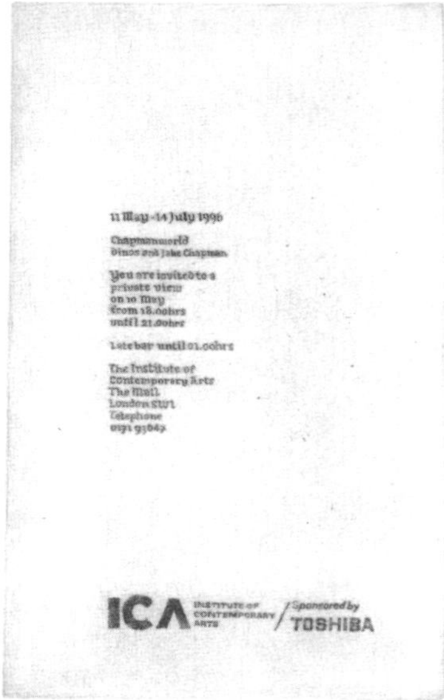
11 May-14 July 1996
Chapmanworld
Dinos and Jake Chapman
You are invited to a
private view
on 10 May
from 18.00hrs
until 21.00hrs
The Institute of
Contemporary Arts
The Mall
London SW1
ICA
TOSHIBA

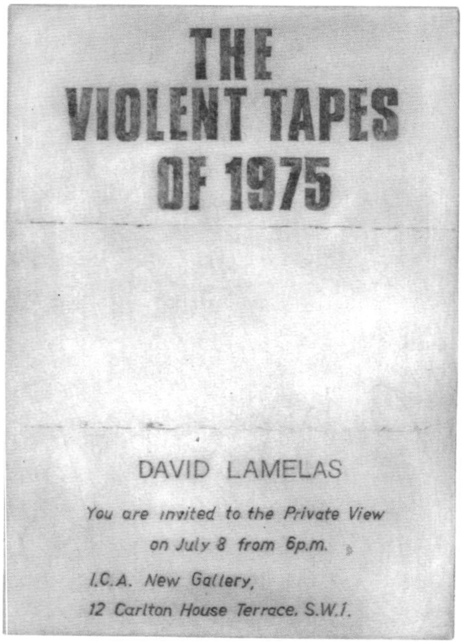
THE
VIOLENT TAPES
OF 1975
DAVID LAMELAS
You are invited to the Private View
on July 8 from 6p.m.
I.C.A. New Gallery,
12 Carlton House Terrace, S.W.1.

GOING BYE-BYES
THE LIVING FURNITURE
STEPHEN TAYLOR WOODROW
OPENING VIEW TUESDAY 19 6-8.00 PM
TUESDAY 19 JULY TO SUNDAY 24 JULY
ICA
INSTITUTE OF CONTEMPORARY ARTS
THE MALL LONDON SW1
SPONSORED BY BECK'S BIER

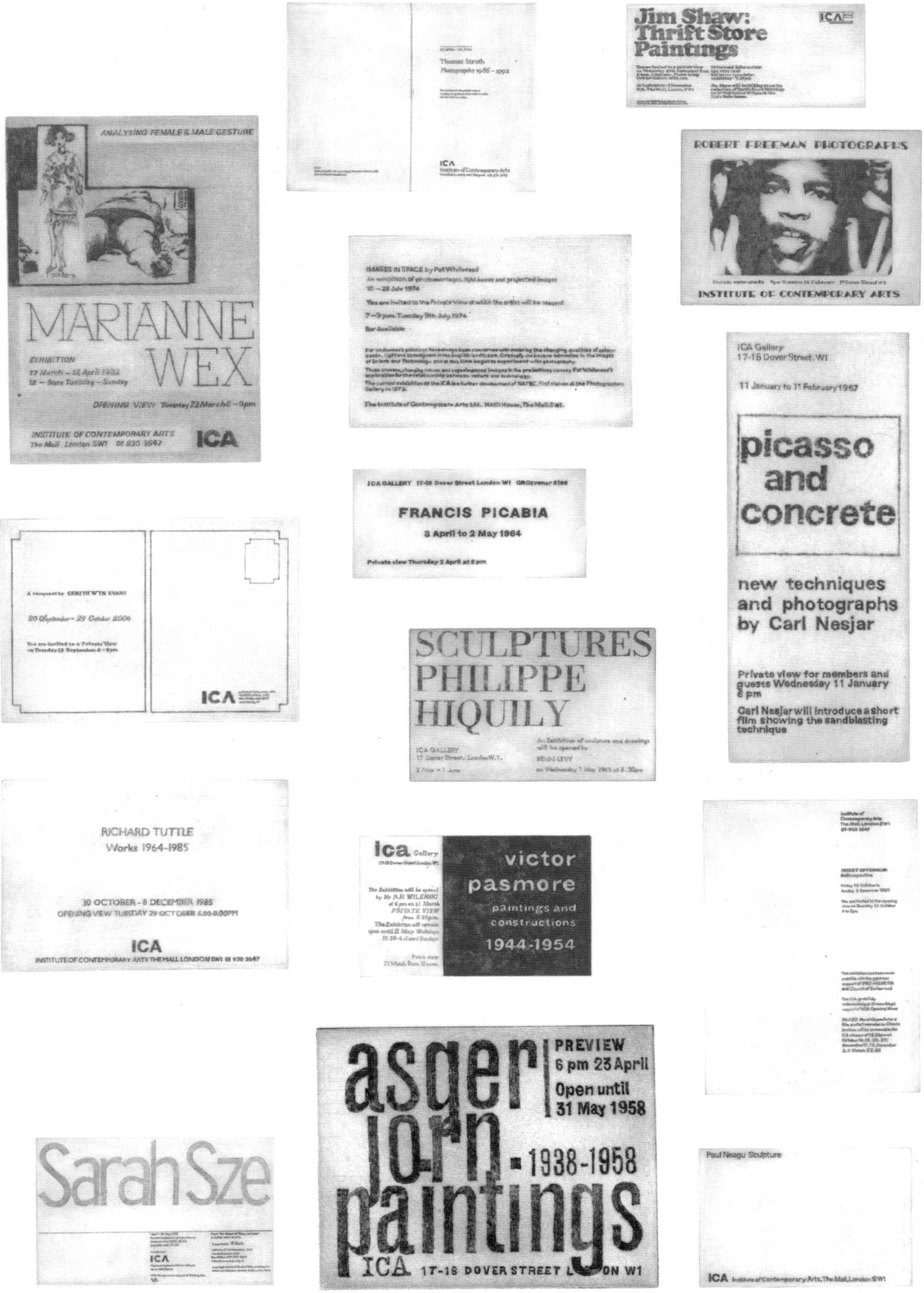
Thomas Struth
Photographs 1986–1992
ICA
Institute of Contemporary Arts
Jim Shaw:
Thrift Store
Paintings
ICA
ANALYSING FEMALE & MALE GESTURE
MARIANNE
WEX
EXHIBITION
17 March – 18 April 1982
12 – 9pm Tuesday – Sunday
OPENING VIEW Tuesday 23 March 6 – 9pm
INSTITUTE OF CONTEMPORARY ARTS
The Mall London SW1 01 930 3647
ICA
ROBERT FREEMAN PHOTOGRAPHS
INSTITUTE OF CONTEMPORARY ARTS
IMAGES IN SPACE by Pat Whiteread
An exhibition of photomontages, light boxes and projected images
10 – 28 July 1974
You are invited to the Private View at which the artist will be present
7 – 9 p.m. Tuesday 9th July 1974
Bar Available
The Institute of Contemporary Arts Ltd., Nash House, The Mall S.W1.
ICA Gallery
17-18 Dover Street. W1
11 January to 11 February 1967
picasso
and
concrete
new techniques
and photographs
by Carl Nesjar
Private view for members and guests Wednesday 11 January 6 pm
Carl Nesjar will introduce a short film showing the sandblasting technique
ICA GALLERY 17-18 Dover Street London W1 GROsvenor 6186
FRANCIS PICABIA
3 April to 2 May 1964
Private view Thursday 2 April at 6 pm
20 September – 29 October 2006
ICA
SCULPTURES
PHILIPPE
HIQUILY
ICA GALLERY
17 Dover Street, London W.1.
2 May – 1 June
An Exhibition of sculpture and drawings will be opened by
BENN LEVY
on Wednesday 1 May 1963 at 6.30pm
RICHARD TUTTLE
Works 1964–1985
30 OCTOBER – 8 DECEMBER 1985
OPENING VIEW TUESDAY 29 OCTOBER 6.00-8.00PM
ICA
INSTITUTE OF CONTEMPORARY ARTS THE MALL LONDON SW1 01 930 3647
ica Gallery
17-18 Dover Street London W1
victor
pasmore
paintings and
constructions
1944-1954
asger
jorn
1938-1958
paintings
PREVIEW
6 pm 23 April
Open until
31 May 1958
ICA 17-18 DOVER STREET LONDON W1
Sarah Sze
ICA
Paul Neagu Sculpture
ICA Institute of Contemporary Arts, The Mall, London SW1

Stephen Sutcliffe

Exhibition, 15–22 September 2008
ICA Upper Galleries

There is something predatory about the use of the moving image in the work of Stephen Sutcliffe (born Harrogate, 1968, lives in Glasgow) – it is both determined and persistent. Gestures and movements, cultural legacies and histories are carefully observed, identified and cut-up. Severing with surgical precision, and splicing words and images together to present a mood or attitude, Sutcliffe reaches into the archive and pulls out his version of its heart.

Writer Jean Genet describes cinema as basically immodest, observing that "the cinema can open a fly and search out its secret" – a function evident in Sutcliffe's short film *Come to the Edge* (2003). This work was generated from his archive of found footage, and appears like a recording from the dawn of the 'home video' age. It opens with a video camera lazily panning across a crowded sixth form common room: a pool table, 1980s wedge haircuts and charcoal blazers. A young man, with an ill-fitting jacket and a spidery suggestion of a moustache, enters the room with an air of imagined sophistication. In all his awkward glory, this lanky figure is something to behold, and the camera takes in the mood of the room – a smirk, a faux kiss blown, a knowing wink. With the speed of schooling sharks the students attack him, pinning him down, yanking down his trousers and pulling his underwear up into the crack of his arse. This figure, reminiscent of Piggy in William Golding's *Lord of the Flies* (1954), has to pay for his difference, for breaking unwritten rules. *Come to the Edge* reveals Sutcliffe's worldview to be exacting, satiric, dark, morbid and peculiarly melancholic.

As part of *Nought to Sixty*, Sutcliffe presented a wall drawing based on a cartoon, a photographic portrait of Richard Warwick in Lindsay Anderson's *If...* (1968), as well as several synched videos by Sutcliffe, including his film *We'll Let You Know* (2008). The piece opens on a young Ian McKellen, sat centre stage and waxing lyrical on the correct approach to the presentation of Shakespeare.

Top: Stephen Sutcliffe / No good on Sundays / 2008

McKellen's mannered platitudes are skewered by a hectoring voice off screen: "Begin as soon as you like, would you?" Oblivious, the actor slides into yet another anecdote, while the off screen voice jabs, "Be as quick as you can would you please?" Sutcliffe questions a culture of class aspiration and intellectual complacency, undermining the apparent self-confidence of the ambitious young actor.

Sutcliffe's films speak of a history of British satire – including Monty Python, *Private Eye* and figures such as Alan Bennett, Peter Cook and Tony Hancock – which is based on a critical class-consciousness. Invariably short in length, and frequently employing borrowed texts, his films also share something of William Burroughs' and Brion Gysin's 'cut-up' approach, even though Sutcliffe's combinations of sound and vision are far from random, and instead purposefully re-articulate the world, revealing the insidious relations between the individual and society. For Sutcliffe – as with a former generations of British artists which included figures such as Art & Language and Sarah Lucas – the personal is political. He is a product of a certain time in Britain, a time when Morrissey had something to say, when the unions held sway and when working class meant more than 'chavs' and the condescending images of *Little Britain*. Sutcliffe provides a critical and witty dissection of a nation haunted by this lingering class hangover.

Mark Beasley

47 Ruth Ewan

Exhibition, 29 September–6 October 2008
ICA Upper Galleries

In 2007 Ruth Ewan (born Aberdeen, 1980, lives in London) commissioned over 100 buskers, placed at different areas around London, to sing *The Ballad of Accounting*. The song was written in 1964 by Ewan MacColl, a leading figure in the folk revival, who was closely monitored by MI5 because of his communist beliefs. Concentrating particularly in the City, for one week the buskers sang MacColl's *Ballad*, posing passers by the questions contained in the lyrics: *Did they shuffle off the pavement to let their betters pass? Did they care if they made a difference? Did they kiss the foot that kicked them?* The work, commissioned by Artangel and titled *Did You Kiss the Foot that Kicked You?* (2007), was as much a celebration of MacColl's political conviction as it was a staging of the mode by which beliefs circulate – a non-hierarchical communication that passes, at times imperceptibly, from person to person.

Protestors, socialists, Anabaptists, rebels, children, the socially-marginalised – these are the figures that populate Ewan's varied projects. Her work often addresses esoteric histories, particularly those of movements that emerge from a groundswell of discontent, nurtured among the people rather than handed down officially. As such the histories of these events remain accessible only to those 'in the know', as memories rather than proper documentation; Ewan's project is partly activist in that it seeks to recuperate these histories by placing them in the public sphere. In *Psittaciformes Trying to Change the World* (2005–06), for example, which was staged at The Embassy Gallery in Edinburgh and Studio Voltaire in London, Ewan attempted to teach parrots protest slogans – recorded at the G8 demonstrations at Gleneagles in 2005.

Ewan's *Nought to Sixty* project grew out of *Did You Kiss the Foot...*, concentrating on one of

the buskers – a poet, musician and bird-lover named Fang. In collecting and recording Fang's ideas and memories (lyrics from the band Arkwright's Ferret, which he fronted in the 1970s; a Conceptual art advertisement for a floor-painting service; and a song he learnt from his father) Ewan created a public archive of a life whose extraordinary creativity has gone largely unseen. The project, entitled *Fang Sang* (2008), is composed of a booklet and CD (while Ewan's video, entitled *Six Feet of Earth*, featuring Fang, was screened at the ICA), and is the result of long discussions between Fang and the artist – conversations in which he told Ewan of his various public art proposals (to make the Archway tower seem to disappear, for instance), of his snow paintings and his interest in magic.

Fang's memories, meanwhile, are inflected by the social history through which he has lived. A lullaby his father sang to him at bedtime – of which, at the start of the discussions, Fang remembered only a few lines – turned out to be *Six Feet of Earth*, a dark song that extols death for levelling the difference between rich and poor. *Six Feet of Earth* grew to represent not only a sentimental memory, but also an encapsulation of his family history and of his father's political beliefs. Rather than a portrait of Fang, *Fang Sang* is an attempt to bring his ideas into circulation.

Melissa Gronlund

ITS JUST LOVE

You pull the curtains,
I'll douse the light,
Pull back the covers,
We'll make love tonight.
You wear the mackintosh,
I'll be the nun,
You be the rapist
We'll have some fun.
There's nothing perverted,
There's nothing strange
Just because I like bondage,
It dont mean I'm deranged.
Its just love.

You bite my buttocks,
And I'll lose my grip,
I'll lay in chains,
While you use the whip.
We'll go to a place
Where nobody goes,
You sit on the bidet
While I suck your toes.
I'll paint all of my private parts red
While you pull my underwear
Over your head.
Its just love.

There's nothing perverted
There's nothing wierd,
I got this way
Through being hand reared.
Its just love.
You pull the curtains,
And I'll douse the light,
Pull back the covers,
We'll make love tonight.

As performed by Arkwright's Ferret, lyrics by Fang, illustration by Chris Dring, 1981

Snow Paintings

Finsbury Park
February 1987

This work was created using as a medium, fresh fallen snow, airborne pollution & treated inks.

It depicts the encroachment of pollution into an urban environment over a period of seven days.

At the onset of snowfall ten grounds were laid out to gather snow and pollution.

18 hours after initial snowfall prepared inks were applied to the surface of the snow, over a number of grounds, & left to filter onto the paper.

These grounds were then retrieved & thawed out.

This procedure was subsequently repeated with the remaining grounds after 72 hour, 128 hour & 168 hour periods had elapsed.

By using this method, a unique visual statement of Nature as the Artist has been made.

Fang

Both images: Ruth Ewan / *Fang Sang* / 2008 / booklet

48 # Garrett Phelan

Exhibition, 29 September–6 October 2008
ICA Upper Galleries

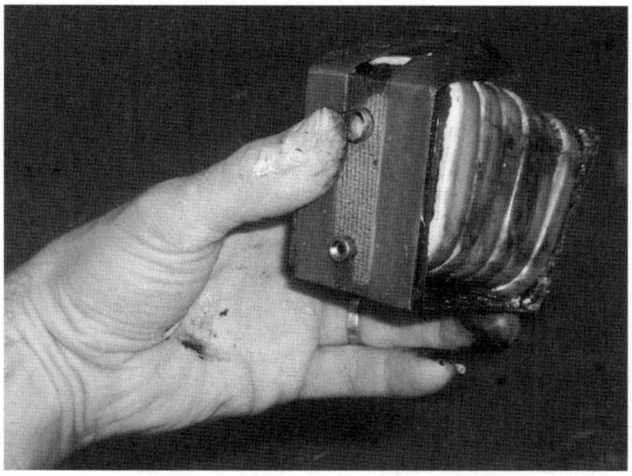

Top: Garrett Phelan / *IT is dead* / 2008
Bottom: Garrett Phelan / *IT will bring you light* / 2008

Artist Garrett Phelan (born Dublin, 1965, lives in Dublin) often acts as an antagonist or anti-editor, combining disparate information together while refusing to draw distinctions or provide perspective. Phelan uses found objects, wall drawings, sculptural installations and broadcast radio to create expansive works that he titles in series according to both subject and mode of enquiry.

Phelan developed *Reception of Information* (2003–07) as one phase of a wider ongoing project entitled *Formation of Opinion. Reception of Information* explores the notion of 'expert' testimony as it is presented in the media. After meticulously collating articles and transcripts, Phelan reorganised and redistributed them, stripped of their context, in public forms such as radio broadcasts, large-scale offsite drawing projects and an online project.

Part of this series is *NOW:HERE* (2003), a collection of erratically executed wall drawings sited in a derelict Dublin flat. *NOW:HERE* mapped rationalist philosophy and experimental science, hermeneutic theories and anti-rationalist belief systems. *Black Brain Radio* (2006), meanwhile, consisted of 24-hour independent FM broadcasts around Dublin. These broadcasts, transmitted over a one-month period, covered a range of randomly selected subjects. Instead of creating seamless links between sound bites or diagrams, these works make evident discrepancies between them and expose the disjointedness of Phelan's compilation, refusing to provide or perpetuate the 'expert' content of the original source material.

For *Nought to Sixty* Phelan addressed the complexity of what he calls "the absolute present", constituted by "real experience and real relationships". Phelan presented a series of works collectively titled *IT, is not IT* (2008). One work, *Interruption, Between Two ITs (part 2)*, comprises a sculptural form made from wood and fabric, covered by a deluge of black spray paint. The work is symbolic of a confrontation, an interruption. Another work, *IT will bring you light*, contains an active radio encased within a black concrete cast. Despite its entombment, the radio continues to play. *IT is dead*, meanwhile, is assembled from dead radio batteries, now superfluous and oozing their chemical contents. Formerly fuelling the word, spoken or sung, as it passed invisibly from studio to speaker, their sticky materiality now charges silence but still refuses to be ignored.

From their production by submersion, decomposition or entombment, to the artist's interest in reversing the transmission of information and formation of opinion, Phelan's work straddles both sculpture and performance. Whether in the gallery, on the radio or in an offsite location, Phelan's obfuscations demand a personal response from the viewer – rather than a reliance on received opinion.

Isobel Harbison

49 Open Music Archive

Event, 29 September 2008
ICA Theatre

Open Music Archive / *Free-to-Air* performance by Serafina Steer / ICA / 2008

Appropriation and re-interpretation have been central strategies in music production across the genres, from blues and jazz to folk and hip-hop. And while the rapid development of online peer-to-peer file sharing networks has provided millions with new ways to access musical material, this technology has also had direct consequences on music making, and has often led musicians and DJs into problematic legal territory.

Open Music Archive, initiated by artists Eileen Simpson (born Manchester, 1977, lives in London) and Ben White (born Manchester, 1977, lives in London), employs such strategies of appropriation, but uses music that has entered into the public domain. It functions as a platform for musical exchange, exploring the possibilities of collaborative creation.

Open Music Archive digitises out-of-copyright recordings – mainly 1920s and 30s blues, jazz, folk and music hall – and distributes the tracks via its website. It also stages live events, and produces and distributes CDs. Most recently it created a 'battle record', a vinyl compilation of samples, loops and sound effects for use by DJs (created for *Discloures*, Gasworks, London, 2008).

For *Clips, Blips & Loops* (2007), meanwhile, Open Music Archive recorded out-of-copyright music from a public collection of music boxes in Stockholm, and invited members of the Swedish collective Fylkingen to rework the recordings. The result was a performance and a free 'copyleft' licensed CD (a copyright-free recording, which also requires all subsequent modifications of the original material to be free). The recorded tracks – combining anachronistic tinkles with the abrupt cuts of breakbeat – are also available for free unlimited download. For such projects musicians are encouraged to release their material under a Creative Commons license, allowing others to use the music freely – a request which has at times sparked debates among the collaborators.

The focus on the production of usable source material is perhaps what sets Open Music Archive apart from other artist-led enterprises that redistribute historical material (such as the American collective Continuous Project). Each project is potentially only the first step in a long chain of reworking, sampling and looping that could reach far beyond the limits of the archive. Applying the principles of peer-based collaboration to wider fields of creative production, Open Music Archive is situated in the debate around Free/Libre and Open Source Software (FLOSS). It promotes an alternative form of creative economy and attempts to challenge the conventional mechanisms of music authorship, ownership, production and distribution.

For *Nought to Sixty*, Open Music Archive presented *Free-to-Air*, a project started in 2007 at Cornerhouse in Manchester. *Free-to-Air* involved an invitation to musicians and DJs to produce cover versions of material drawn from the archive. This process, putting long-forgotten lyrics and rhythms at the centre of contemporary creation, was renewed at the ICA, where a range of musicians performed new cover versions in short sets during a night of performances. The evening also marked the launch of the *Free-to-Air* CD – gathering together a selection of the cover versions created for the project – which was distributed in exchange for a donation.

Coline Milliard

Open Music Archive presents
Free-to-air
Monday 29 September 2008 | 8—10pm | Free entry
a project by
Eileen Simpson & Ben White
out-of-copyright archive jazz / blues / music hall & folk covered / reworked and remixed with support from DJ Dysu and more...
live sets from:
Magic Arm
Serafina Steer
Hest
www.openmusicarchive.org/noughttosixty
CREATIVE COMMONS ATTRIBUTION-SHARE ALIKE 3.0
Free-to-air opens up a temporary channel for music that operates beyond individual, proprietary and commercial interests
ICA
The Mall, London SW1Y 5AH
020 7930 3647
www.ica.org.uk
UK REGISTERED CHARITY 236848
ARTS COUNCIL ENGLAND

Open Music Archive / *Free-to-Air* flyer / 2008

50

Contemporary art, music and fashion

Salon discussion, 22 September 2008
ICA Brandon Room

Participants

Francesca Gavin, writer and arts editor of *Dazed and Confused*
Craig McCarthy, artist and author of *Fly By Night: The New Art of the Club Flyer*
Nina Manandhar, co-director of social enterprise Hardcore Is More Than Music
Christabel Stewart, co-director of HOTEL Gallery
Matthew Stone, artist and founding member of !WOWOW! collective

Art practice often overlaps with other forms of culture, such as music and fashion, and such overlaps have been encouraged by the recent explosion within social networking. This salon discussion, organised by Francesca Gavin, asked if these intersecting networks offer new spaces of production, and the means to move beyond the exclusivity of the art world.

FRANCESCA GAVIN: I write about art. I do a lot of books. I am art editor at *Dazed and Confused*. I am also interested in networking in terms of social networks in art. I'll start with Christabel and she'll say who she is.

CHRISTABEL STEWART: Hello. I'm Christabel Stewart. I'm co-director of Hotel Gallery in London. For seven years I was arts editor of *SHOWstudio*, which I think is the reason I was invited here. It was a multidisciplinary website, started by Mick Knight and Peter Saville. *SHOWstudio* aimed to do something beyond the pages of magazines; look at different things that you could do on the Internet, with the moving image, and look behind the scenes, look at process. On the back of that I conceived of projects that would look at contemporary art but that would make sense on the Internet, often using film. I ran a project called Transmissions, which looked at the growth of performance and performance practice in contemporary art, which sometimes encapsulated music or theatre, but often had relevance to contemporary art practice. I'm also arts editor of *Tank* magazine.

NINA MANANDHAR: I run an organisation called Hardcore Is More Than Music, which started four years ago as a fanzine. I come from a self-published fanzine background. Since then it has become a multidisciplinary arts organisation and we do collaborative projects in the form of events, publications, short films, and I work on that with my colleague Nendie [Pinto-Duschinsky]. We're also in *Nought to Sixty*, with a magazine launch event at the end of October.

CRAIG MCCARTHY: I was the designer for *Dazed and·Confused* for several years. I've just written a book called *Fly by Night*, which is a visual diary that presents 300 or so flyers from this decade of parties, club nights, happenings, performances and devilish parades. It presents a kind of alternative London and it's interested in celebrating the DIY homemade party and the graphic artist whose work shapes the surface of these flyers.

MATTHEW STONE: I work as an artist and also a DJ. I make music. One friend of mine is the fashion designer, Gareth Pugh, and I do all of his soundtracks and so there's a music and fashion crossover there. I organise weekly artist salons that are not quite as formal as this – but I hope that might break down as the evening goes on – so there is this emphasis on creative people coming together and finding a space where things overlap.

GAVIN: You're also a founding member of the !WOWOW! collective – a multidisciplinary collective that moved between fashion and art.

STONE: !WOWOW! is a very loosely defined group of people/period of time, which has a relation to an alternative party scene. We squatted a big department store for about six months in 2004 and had a series of exhibitions and ambitious art after-parties featuring performances. There was an emphasis on dressing up and music as well.

GAVIN: How did you consider those other elements that weren't art-based – those networks with a more social aspect? Do you think that crossover created opportunities?

STONE: Scenes can add momentum and be inspiring for those people involved, but also for others who have romantic notions of them. The idea that things are happening brings authenticity to other people's efforts. A lot of people who were involved in such scenes don't consider themselves artists, and certainly don't show in gallery spaces. But I don't think anyone was particularly worried about whether it was perceived as art or not. It was quite utopian. Although I'm interested in specific ways that can be translated to art.

MCCARTHY: I agree with you. In my experience, there doesn't seem to be a division of labour as such. The artist is the DJ, the artist is the person working the door. Everyone hooks in. That is the spirit of the collective.

GAVIN: In your book, Craig, some of the club night flyers are made by Wolfgang Tillmans, Donald Urquhart and people with an art background, but they're all working, creating things for the pleasure of it. Would you say that the flyers count as artworks?

STEWART: I've actually got a quote I really love from Wolfgang. He wrote a very angry email to *Artforum* because one of their writers had accused him of being a fashion photographer-turned-art photographer. Wolfgang took issue with the notion of crossover, saying, "At no point did I intend to say that magazines and fashion *per se* are art. To me, art and fashion are fields of great excellence and few good results have come from the act of crossing over for its own sake". I think to recognise that these disciplines have their boundaries is a good thing, but that doesn't mean there can't be good conversations between them. Even Matthew saying that people didn't do what they were doing to be able to say, "Oh, I'm an artist". Why is art better than any other discipline? It's nice to have conversations based on their own expertise.

GAVIN: I recently interviewed Wolfgang. He said that he had been creating art for a lot longer than he did fashion photography. He said he intentionally approached fashion magazines as a way to create work for a wider audience. And that's where I think this becomes really interesting – when people look at music, or fashion, or underground culture, and using that as an opportunity to get their work seen by a different audience.

STONE: The work doesn't have to change; the context does, obviously. An artwork doesn't stop being an artwork just because you put it in a different environment.

MCCARTHY: The connections between photography, media and reproduction are quite empowering. Bringing people's work together through different media can liberate them from their usual recesses.

GAVIN: Nina, you've done a lot of mediums: gigs, zines, film projects – a wide variety of projects. Do you think that approaching different mediums from a creative standpoint means there's more opportunity to get work out there? And how do these collaborations work?

MANANDHAR: It's about building a brand identity. In today's creative culture, you either have to niche yourself or become a multitasker. We've gone with the multitasker option.

MCCARTHY: The media of music and fashion has tactical constraints on what they do together though. Going back to flyers and clubs, I think there are parallels. If you've got no money you can put on your own night if you all get together. If you've got no money, you can put on your own show. I think there are parallels between the two. The media has tried to play up this idea of lots of people working together by glamorising it.

STONE: I think there's a difference between the various industries. You can be a struggling artist or band and people are still going to be interested in you and what you're doing. There's a myth you can build on. The ideas surrounding glamour in fashion is more difficult. You can't be an unsuccessful fashion designer for ten years – then you're just unsuccessful. Whereas there is still this myth in art that it doesn't have to be commercially successful to be truly successful.

GAVIN: Do you think that old-fashioned idea of the starving artist persists? It was interesting watching the Robert Hughes piece last night on Channel Four. He was looking at contemporary art in the past 50 years along with the rise of the art market. Is it all about money?

STONE: The artist brings authenticity to fashion brands that commercially want to build on the mythology of their brand.

MCCARTHY: And vice-versa. Donald Urquhart is someone included in my book. He's been around for years. He was born in the 1960s and was a friend and contemporary of Leigh Bowery, the performer. Urquhart founded the 1990s club The Beautiful Bend along with Sheila Tequila. For one of The Beautiful Bend nights Urquhart made a series of images titled *Peroxides on Parade*, which served as flyers, posters and wall decorations. Drawn in black ink on pages of A3, they were images of Diana Dors, Jayne Mansfield, Dusty Springfield and Bette Davis (Davis was scowling of course). They were photocopied, pasted up around the club's interior and free for anyone to take home at the end of the night. That's why I love Urquhart. For me, that's a brilliant example of what I was saying about being able to put on your own show and your own night. There are parallels to be drawn between the two. That's why they co-exist.

GAVIN: For me that is politically really interesting. It's much more about the collective side, the club side, the music side, the not-straight art side that allows you to be less about the money and the value and the objects, and more about the collaborative experience. Playfulness can be involved in the art.

STONE: But there is an exclusivity angle that fashion needs in order to survive commercially. And this exclusivity exists in the art market as well.

GAVIN: There was an interesting piece in today's *Herald Tribune* by Suzy Menkes about 'fast fashion', which describes collaborations between high profile designers and the High Street. For example, you've got Comme des Garçons about to do something with H&M. This is art for the people if you think of fashion as art for the world. Are there things that art can learn from the dissemination of club culture, music culture, fashion, and other ways of getting your work out there?

STONE: I don't see them as separate. But I think there are industries that are separate from the widely held definitions of what are art and fashion. When you start discussing the industries it's difficult not to be discussing politics or anti-capitalism. For me the reason why I'm a photographer but I don't want to do fashion photography is because I don't want to sell clothes. Or certainly I don't want my work to exist to inflate the value of one piece of clothing over another, and I think that is a key issue.

STEWART: Or you might get an artist like Lucy McKenzie. McKenzie's last major UK exhibition demonstrated how she disseminates work in different ways – through fanzines, through record covers, through collaboration with a fashion designer. She is absolutely 100% an artist. Her critical practice is to take it outside of exhibition spaces even though she ultimately presents this in a gallery. Now she has gone to a school in Belgium to become an interior designer. She is always playing with that. It needs her to have been recognised in one form before she could play with those mediums so much.

STONE: That implies an artist would always exist outside the scene. You referred to the idea of these scenes or these activities as being only the potential for subject matter.

STEWART: Well, subject matter and a medium through which to represent yourself.

STONE: How would that be different from someone who doesn't present the end work in a gallery? At what point does it change into art, and how? Is that it? You just put it in a gallery and that's art?

STEWART: I think each of these worlds have ways in which they're read. The fashion world doesn't have *Artforum*. It's got different ways. The club world is a live world, it's about where you are on any night. It's a network of people. The art world does function differently.

STONE: But equally, there are performances that happen in galleries that could happen quite easily in a nightclub as well.

GAVIN: Performance is maybe the ideal fusion of those things. Club culture and the event of a club is almost a performance in its own right. Would you agree?

STONE: When you have an expanded definition of what art is, it's difficult to trace where one artwork begins and another one ends, and a nightclub in itself could be seen as an end artwork of the promoter who's made it. The people who attend and their outfits and the way they conduct themselves can be seen as performances. And it's easier to identify those as art performances when someone says that they are.

MCCARTHY: It's about the intention, isn't it? This is where it gets confusing. The intention has to be there for it to be a dress. People intend for it to be worn. It's a garment. If a club's a club, it's a club.

STONE: Intention is important. The great thing about the art world is that it gives some individuals who are able to work within it an opportunity to contextualise their intentions with the work. The reason I think art galleries exist is because they provide a useful context to understand the work. The salon that I started came out of amazing conversations that had started in nightclubs. There is no record of them. There are all these ideas and passionate individuals, but it's not becoming something that enters culture properly. The people that I meet in nightclubs now can continue those conversations – we meet on a Saturday afternoon. People aren't drunk. We're recording them. We're trying to write manifestos to create texts and work that comes out of that space.

GAVIN: Do you think we're very used to the media deciding art for us?

STONE: There's a commodification of those processes, where you can get a quick buck in associating things, widening the market, getting two big names in.

MANANDHAR: I think people talk about art as if it exists outside the world of money and commerce. It doesn't. If you want to do projects, you have to get money into them, whether it's through brands or through public funding. I don't know how you can get art without money. A lot of money we get is through public funding, but there is a lot of bureaucracy and a lot of boxes to tick. If we're artists and we want to make a living out of what we do there is going to be an element of business. What I'd say now is that we run a non-profit business.

MCCARTHY: Does money in music and fashion means that they can't operate critically?

STONE: I don't think anything is without compromise, but I think that within fashion the compromise is larger. That's the nature of the industry.

ANONYMOUS (audience): In terms of statement of intent, as the organisers of club nights, do you have different layers between you and the music that gets played, then the artists who create all the music, and the DJ who then chooses the music? I don't really see how that's art. How does that relate to a promoter at a club night?

MCCARTHY: I think they're all in on it and everyone understands that that's the intention.

ANONYMOUS (audience): If you have a curator at a gallery getting someone to make art for a gallery, why present the promoter of the situation to be more of the creator of the artwork?

STONE: I think a lot of curators are frustrated artists anyway.

MANANDHAR: You know when you edit something or curate something, there is an element of art in there as well, because you're bringing those people together and you're saying something in the people you choose to put within the show.

ANONYMOUS (audience): I'd like to get back to what Craig's talking about – Donald Urquhart and the democratisation of the artwork that could be taken home at the end of the evening. How do you read integrity as part of the collaborative?

STONE: With objects like paintings, which can't be mass-produced, there is less of a culture of ownership of art than there is with fashion. But it's also possible to be part of the art world by reading about it, looking at it online, and going to galleries.

51 **Alun Rowlands**

Pamphlet, produced October 2008
Distributed in *Nought to Sixty* magazine

Alun Rowlands (born Merthyr Tydfil, 1972 lives in London) researches failed utopian projects and minor revolutions, particularly those deemed too inconsequential to be remembered by mainstream history. Piecing together archival material, and filling in the gaps with his own speculations, Rowlands has developed an unusual form of writing that might be described as 'political fiction'. The artist's publication *3 Communiqués* (2007) collects his observations on three case studies: a man who preached against eating too much protein; a radical artistic commune; and a self-declared nation state precariously perched on an abandoned naval defence platform. For *Nought to Sixty*, Rowlands continued his investigations with *Communiqué § 4* (2008), which delves into the history of the Angry Brigade – the London-based, anarchist-socialist group responsible for a bombing campaign in early 1970s, one whose targets included an MP's kitchen and London's BIBA boutique. More angry than deadly, they never seriously hurt anyone.

As a compact series of black-and-white pamphlets that fold out neatly from their pocket-size cardboard cover, *3 Communiqués* lovingly echoes the homespun literature of revolutionary groups, as well as the underground publications of the avant garde. But if the term 'communiqué' reminds us of the urgency of the missives once issued by these radicals, it now carries a gently ironic, nostalgic tone to match the elegant design of the limited-edition artist's book. As Rowlands clearly appreciates, even the most inflammatory propaganda cannot escape commodification. Nonetheless, the fourth communiqué, surreptitiously inserted inside the final *Nought to Sixty* magazine, mimics the genre's typically

articulation is a montage of various elements – voices, colours, passions and dogmas – within a given period of time. The darker the news, the grander the narrative. News is the last addiction before... what? We don't know. There is life and there is the consumer event. Everything around us tends to habitually conduct our lives toward some final reality in print or film. Everything seeks its own heightened adaptation. Or put it this way, nothing happens until it is consumed. All material is channelled into the glow. Our task here is to drift across the wreckage, engaging an act of interpretation. We will not explain events. Explanation reduces history to information that can be verified or not. Information severs the link between the reader and communal memory, by recasting experience into discrete moments, stultifying sensation. Isolated events explained are lost to the present. We are not concerned with an accurate concatenation of definite affairs, but with the way these are embedded in the inscrutable course of events. Speculation allows new amalgams of the story, provoking changes in perspectives and sensations. It produces knowledge through a subjunctive addition, associating one thing with another. Does the imagination act as a lamp? Thinking ceases to be a marginal affair in political matters. When everyone is swept away unthinkingly by what everyone else does and believes in, those who think are drawn out of hiding. Their refusal to participate is conspicuous and becomes a form of action. This purging element destroys values, theories and convictions that are political by implication. We read somewhere this destruction has a liberating effect on another faculty, namely judgement – the most political of abilities. Thinking deals with invisibles, with the formation of things that are absent. Judgement always concerns particulars and things close to hand – a soundless dialogue. But we are losing focus. Our writing tools are working on our thoughts, no recording technology is neutral. We need to return to our group, to navigate their movement.

The initial actions were unmarked. They existed without any time frame. No set beginning or end. No audience to speak of. Outcomes were unpredictable. An ominous repeat in return. The early communications through newspapers do not register; there is no evidence in our archive. Persistence and an awareness of what is at stake fuel our protagonists. Adventurist attacks against the monadic state are claimed under the name of Butch Cassidy and the Sundance Kid. A further missive remains in the Hollywood genre signed in the name of the Wild Bunch. In addition there are incendiary devices aimed directly at the repressive apparatus of the State. Those long hazy days in Paris are forgotten but colour an expression of a new libertarian movement. There is no middle ground. No liberal indignation. Now they are angry. Having identified an opaque agenda, they must push

Communiqué § 4 ~ Page 8

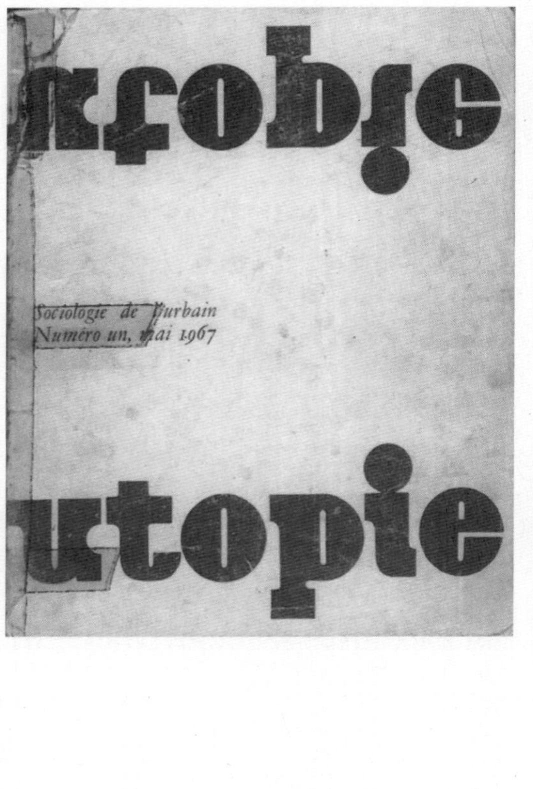

Both images: Alun Rowlands / *Communiqué § 4* / 2008

opportunistic means of distribution. Moreover, Rowlands' compulsion to add further communiqués recalls his first protagonist, Stanley Green, whose days were split between preaching on Oxford Street and revising his cryptically titled, self-printed pamphlet, *Eight Passion Proteins With Care.*

Rowlands' case studies may vary in their duration and geographical reach, and may range in focus from eccentric loners to international campaigns, but a pattern gradually emerges. The experiments all coalesce around 1968 and relate, self-consciously or not, to the Situationist-inspired student revolts of that year. Furthermore, each cause models its ideology on that of earlier theorists, creating strange hybrids and mutations of Aristotle's ethics, William Morris' anti-urbanism, and Wilhelm Reich's and Charles Fourier's Freudian Marxist blueprints for communal living. But it is the shared characteristics of their demise to which Rowlands draws special attention: the burden of their ideological demands; the tedium of an over-determined routine; the seduction of spectacle and consumer capitalism.

Unusually for documentary writing, the reader is continuously made aware of the idiosyncratic, physical nature of the source material itself, including microfiches, home videos and court documents. Far from the dry, neutral tone expected of the historian, Rowlands' atmospheric descriptions and snippets of conversation seem to take us straight to the heart of the action, while at other times the writing shifts tense and voice to reflect a tentative, hypothetical account of events. Rowlands denies the reader key facts and a clear linear narrative, focusing instead on the imaginative and generative possibilities of uncovering recent history. In doing so, he allows radical ideas from the past an ongoing potential.

Jennifer Thatcher

'What matter who is speaking?' someone said, a question of comic potential. The problems of speaking for others are great in detail. The problems reside in the relaying of truth in the desires of others. Those who can be taken account of in a political community are always already those who can be counted, those who make up some recognisable part. Why write? 'Words can do political work; words no longer prescribe a story or what images should be'. They make themselves images. Perhaps, it is to abolish the boundaries between reality and imagination. Imagination is the mode by which we reach out. Arranging montages based on affinities and correspondences. All visions become plural. It is instead a diversion where truth and desire fall together into a deep spiral. Multiply without limits, in the foaming, in the flicker, in desire's immeasurable extension. We need a book to untether political action from paranoia, for developing an understanding of motive and purpose. It would be a book to use politics to intensify thought. Thought and desire use techniques of proliferation, juxtaposition and disjunction. Proceeding from a fiction, a ghost, we reside somewhere between transgressing the divide between text and action. But, as we are all too aware from previous exertions, this can lead to utopia or sheer anxiety. The moment politics becomes possible is distinct from the moment politics erupts.

A succession of images follows. Building and cutting close to the bone. The facades of authoritative government buildings, army barracks and a politician's kitchen all bear the scars of the struggle. The police computer database, records, files and institutional annals feel the heat. These images flare across tabloids and broadsheets alike, acting as kindling to the cause. They are motifs rather than fuel for political militancy. Symbolic commitment to politics corresponds with casuistic emphasis on the political power of symbols – a hunger strike without demands. Amidst the terse brevity of the Brigade's communiqués, condensed like poorly kept minutes of exhaustive meetings, we discern a script. They announce new storms of thought, or perhaps not so much thinking anymore, as theatre. The cast of this theatre will invent their own lines. People will emerge and demand a role and a part in a reconfigured community. People will begin to speak on their own behalf. And, in speaking, will assume the right to occupy public space. Co-ordinates will have to shift to take account of these new voices. Inclusion and exclusion vie in our montage. According to whose rules is this picture organised? Who does it organise and how is this political domain edited? Empty voices cover a lacuna, a gap behind the measures instigated in

Communiqué § 4 ~ Page 12

Resignation is only abdi-
nation and flight, ther is
no other way out for wom
than to work for her lib-
eration.
– Simone de Beauvoir
The Second Sex.
30

Communiqué § 4 ~ Page 13

52

Matthew Noel-Tod

Event, 6 October 2008
ICA Cinema

The videos of Matthew Noel-Tod (born Stoke-on-Trent, 1978, lives in London) emerge from diverse traditions. They draw on conceptual strategies, but also often find inspiration in other artists working in different media. Noel-Tod's impressionistic and abstracted diary video, *Nausea* (2005), for example, makes links to On Kawara's insistent but minimalist date paintings. The execution of Noel-Tod's videos, meanwhile, is informed by cinema history and an intuitive cinematic sensibility. *Obcy Aktorzy / Foreign Actors* (2006) is essentially an ethnography of Polish cinema, articulated in the same medium as its subject and crafted through quotation and montage.

Noel-Tod straddles two giant bodies of reference – art and cinema – through his interest in and application of technology. He explores the particularities of his chosen medium, whether it be a cathode ray tube camera (used in *Obcy Aktorzy / Foreign Actors*) or a mobile-phone camera (*Nausea*). *Atomic* (2003) presents his remake of the Blondie pop video, looped and accompanied by music written for F.W. Murnau's *Nosferatu* (1922). *Atomic* emerged from Noel-Tod's interest in exploring the origins of new technologies – such as early cinema and video – but also his more reflexive interest in the nature and end points of different forms of mediation.

These videos always employ some kind of pre-existing element. The quotes – always referencing form as well as content – cleverly retain an element of their original emotional impact while pointing to evidence of deconstruction. Through their combinations of sequences, and often with superimposed text, the videos also take on enumerable new poetic nuances. Consequently, Noel-Tod's videos exist in a kind of entropic state. There is at once absolute break down, but through the agency of the viewer there is also the potential for a radical new unity. Significantly, the work lies on this threshold, incomplete without such intervention but always pointing to it.

For *Nought to Sixty*, Noel-Tod presented a new work made during his Film London Artists' Moving Image Network (FLAMIN) and Picture This Bristol Mean Time residency in 2008. *Blind Carbon Copy* (2008) primarily focuses on a performance which uses email texts as dialogue. This exemplifies Noel-Tod's application of deconstruction and points to the underlying questions behind it – what does it mean for us to live in a globalised world where we interact with our localities through the mediation of technology? And how does this affect our experience of the world and ourselves? The fractured email phrases sent from different locales refer to different places and states of mind. In this context, slippery detached terms like 'here' and 'there' suggest both metaphysical states and, through performance, are embodied in space (the screening at the ICA incorporated a live performance by dancer and choreographer Saju Hari). In this work, the phenomenological is made material.

William Fowler

All images: Matthew Noel-Tod / *Blind Carbon Copy* / 2008

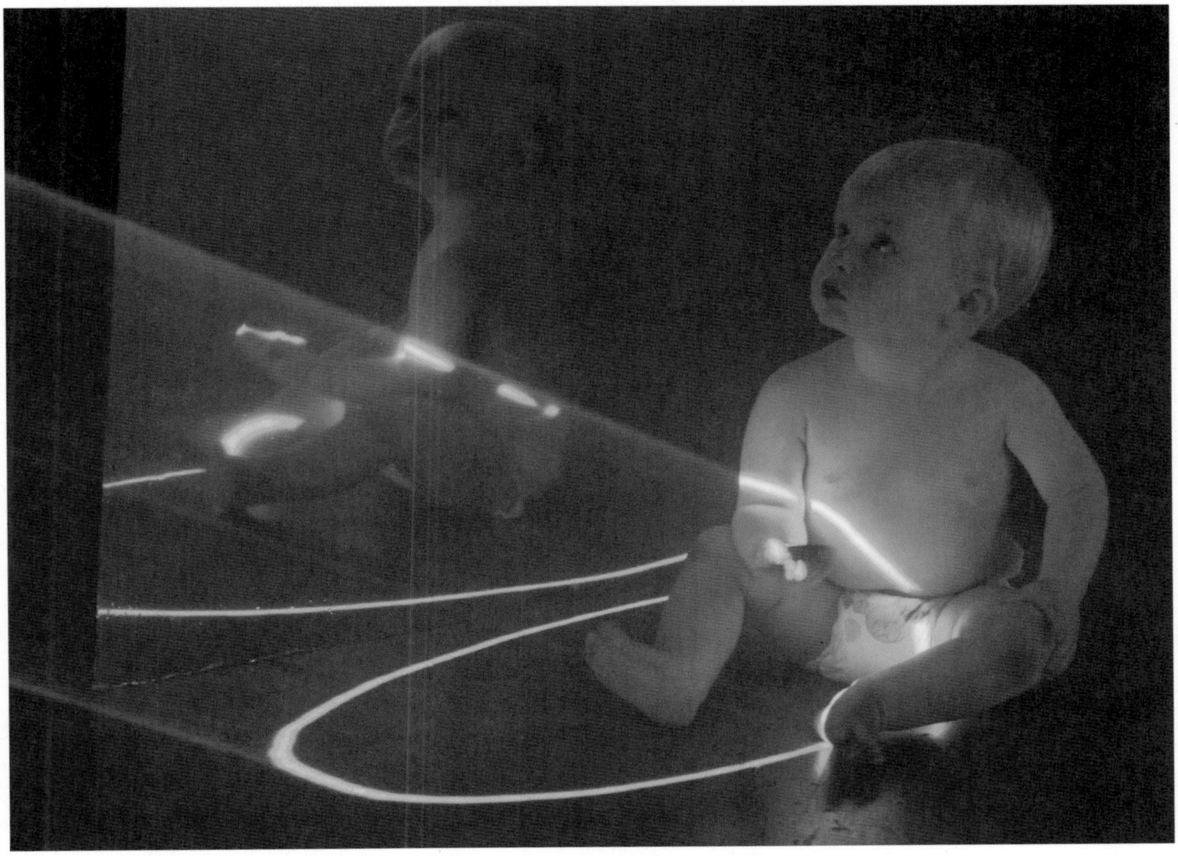

Matthew Noel-Tod
Script excerpt from *Blind Carbon Copy*, 2008

DIALOGUE
Here it is again.

DIALOGUE
Is there anything else you need from me?

DIALOGUE
Tell me what you are thinking.
DIALOGUE
I wanted to tell you that I am disappointed.

DIALOGUE
Love from.

DIALOGUE
I'd like the reading of this email to leave you with the impression that you have traversed a sensual nightmare.
What used to be moral is aesthetic for us.
What was social is now individual.

DIALOGUE
Hope you are well and decide to keep on being an artist.

DIALOGUE
Maybe you are somewhere else!

DIALOGUE
I'm sure it's her, not you.

DIALOGUE
I'll certainly mention you to her if I ever see her again.

DIALOGUE
Her personal spiritual belief included constant communication between the living and the dead.

DIALOGUE
Life is easy!

DIALOGUE
That's rubbish, that's just all to do with ego, you shouldn't even be thinking about that!

DIALOGUE
Life is very civilised here.

DIALOGUE
Tell me more?

DIALOGUE
Definitely tell me more.

DIALOGUE
Fucked up, that shit is.
DIALOGUE
That's the first and last time you can use that joke.

DIALOGUE
I could try harder.

DIALOGUE
Intrigued that you are thinking this… maybe we should talk?

DIALOGUE
I know the massive grey area that exists.

DIALOGUE
What do you think?

DIALOGUE
I have one. Ok!

DIALOGUE
The agony.

DIALOGUE
And how's baby!?

DIALOGUE
I'm already here!

DIALOGUE
The time is now.

DIALOGUE
I wonder if you would be interesting in meeting at any time?

DIALOGUE
Was wondering whether you'd gone mad.

DIALOGUE
That shouldn't really include God.

DIALOGUE
I can imagine that it would be a weird experience. It has been lingering in my memory ever since.

DIALOGUE
The centre of the universe. Maybe I dreamt it.

DIALOGUE
I'm on a train.

53

Mark Aerial Waller

Event, 13 October 2008
ICA Theatre

Mark Aerial Waller (born High Wycombe, 1969, lives in London) makes videos and installations that pay homage to the experimental techniques of the avant-garde – from Surrealism to New German Cinema – within his idiosyncratic narrative frameworks. Indeed, Waller shows a cheerful disregard for linearity, leaping across time zones and genres from classical mythology to science fiction, and collaging sequences from forgotten films and classical plays with his own footage. In addition to his art practice, he uses his film salon The Wayward Canon – and Taverna Especial, a sister salon set up with Giles Round – to provide a platform for 'wayward' re-presentations of little-screened films. For *Nought to Sixty*, Waller gave his recently completed film cycle, *Resistance Domination Secret* (2007–08), the 'wayward' treatment, presenting a special screening with live action.

Waller's trilogy is based loosely on the *Oresteia*, Aeschylus's trilogy of Greek tragedies centring on the murder of Trojan war hero Agamemnon by his wife Clytemnestra. The first film, also called *Resistance Domination Secret* (2007), visualises the murdered Agamemnon as a disembodied golden mask hovering ominously over hellish flames and chastising his wife from beyond the grave: "You treat me like a woman ... ". Waller's homemade mythological drama is spliced with clips from *Les Visiteurs du Soir* (1942), a film made by Marcel Carné during the

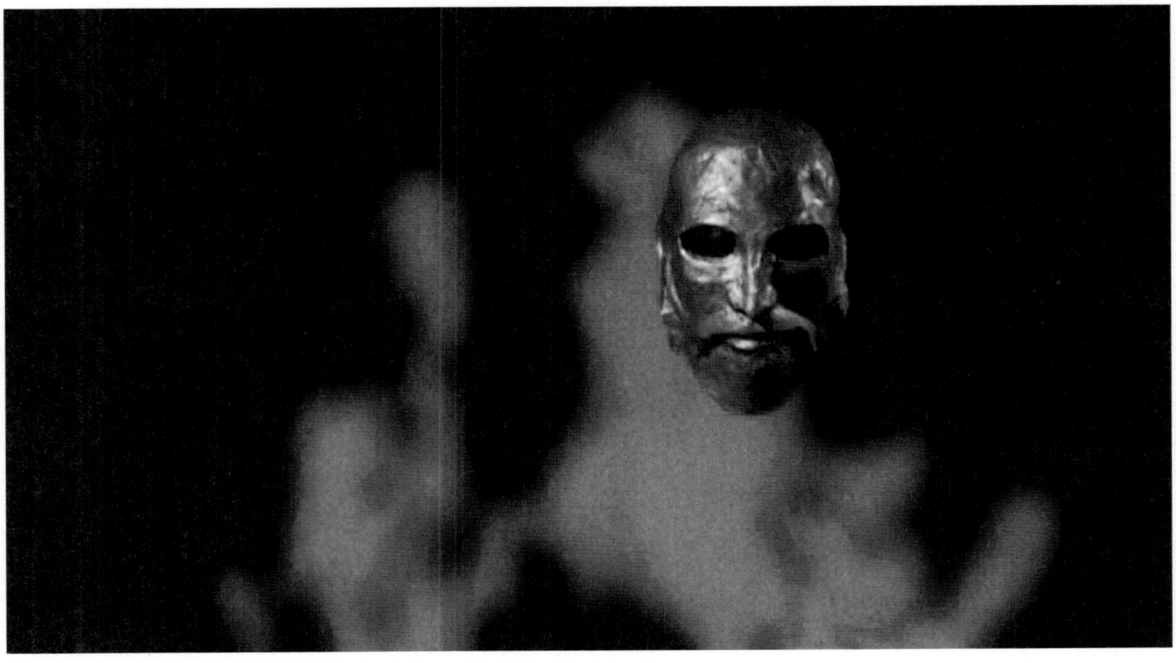

Both images: Mark Aerial Waller / *Resistance Domination Secret* / 2007-2008

French occupation, about a pair of fifteenth-century envoys sent by the devil to disrupt a wedding feast by seducing the bride and groom. Their evil plan goes wrong when one falls in love with his prey, prompting the heroine to muse on the irony of two torturers with no one left to torture. Some 2,000 years divide these two wartime dramas, but both seek to allegorise the violent rupture of a moral order, whether by bloodthirsty ancient warriors or the Nazis.

Waller's second film, *The Flipside of Darkness* (2007), roughly corresponds to *The Libation Bearers*, the second of Aeschylus's plays. The setting has shifted to Warsaw's Palace of Culture and Science, creating a link between the brutality of the Stalinist regime and that of ancient Greece. As with all Waller's videos, the actors could be considered woefully ill-suited to their roles, but paradoxically come across as charmingly sincere: Clytemnestra's thick Polish accent seems to contradict her claims to be a BBC actress; while her murderous son, Orestes, speaks with Michael Caine–style intonation. Waller strips out all the gore from the original play and focuses on the psychological drama of incestuous scheming and paranoia, which he represents symbolically by kaleidoscopic visuals set to a disorientating, sci-fi soundtrack by the band Romvelope.

Waller's final film, entitled *The Children of the Night* (2008), premiered at *Nought to Sixty*. The work mirrors *The Eumenides*, the third play of the *Oresteia*, where darkness is turned into light, physical conflict becomes religious combat and primitive ritual evolves into civilised institution. The screening of the trilogy was set to live military drumming by virtuoso percussionist " "[sic] TIM GOLDIE; and featured a striking finale in which Athena, in the form of an owl, swooped down to capture Agamemnon's golden mask.

Jennifer Thatcher

54 Torsten Lauschmann

Exhibition, 13–20 October 2008
ICA Upper Galleries

Whether manifested through photography, video, sound, online work, drawing or installation, the work of Torsten Lauschmann (born Bad Soden, 1970, lives in Glasgow) is characterised by a thoroughly twenty-first-century approach to art-making. Lauschmann's eclectic, idiosyncratic and multifarious practice is not led by the desire to produce a single object or image, but by the artist's interconnected interests in the theoretical, the personal and the absurd.

Works by Lauschmann can appear to be the anomalous products of particular knowledge systems or technologies. One example is *Fear Among Scientists* (2008), in which the simple equation 3 – 1 = 2 is spelt out in roughly-hewn wooden numbers, but in which the shadows these objects cast – which the artist extends in matching grey paint – misbehave to produce impossible arithmetic. For sculptural installation *Self-Portrait as a Pataphysical Object* (2006), meanwhile, Lauschmann wryly presents himself as a suspended chandelier of sprawling coloured cables and audio adapters. The object's configuration, its mess of wires and connectors, is in excess of its functionality – although it does manage to produce a single shining bulb.

Both images: Torsten Lauschmann / *Feral* / 2008

A similarly eccentric take on portraiture is offered by *The Mathematician* (2006). For this video Lauschmann spliced together audio interviews of Hungarian maths prodigy Pál Erdös, synching the sound with an animated face constructed entirely from numbers (evoking the work of *New Yorker* cartoonist Saul Steinberg). In the voiceover Erdös relates details from his life story – memories of nursery rhymes, of his social clumsiness, of his budding mathematical skills. Meanwhile his facial features – an 8 for his eyes and brow, a plus and minus sign for his pupils – nod, wink and frown in comic yet entirely human ways. The mathematician's quizzical and slightly dumbfounded attitude towards life is in contrast to his ease with maths and philosophy; a dynamic echoed in Lauschmann's own practice, in which the artist often inverts theory and reality – making the former concrete while fictionalising the latter.

For *Nought to Sixty* the artist showed two film-based works, including one in which he intervened within the rigid parameters of display. Toying with the oppositional black box/white cube status of exhibition presentation, *Dead Man's Switch* is a looped projection work that was hardwired into the electrical system of the gallery. The unexpectedly empty but brightly-lit exhibition space was intermittently reduced to darkness, revealing a luminous wall projection of a flickering candle reminiscent of Richter's *Kerze* (1988). During its short sequence the candle is extinguished, suddenly triggering the gallery lights to illuminate the space and empty it once more.

Lauschmann's works may appear counter-intuitive and wayward, but they are also surprisingly humane. Whether orchestrating *World Jump Day* (2005) – in which participants were asked to jump simultaneously in order to alter the Earth's orbit, and therefore halt global warming – or conducting a European tour as solarpowered busker 'Slender Whiteman', The artist's array of ideas transforms the exhibition site into a laboratory of unpredictable objects and visions.

Isla Leaver-Yap

55 Gail Pickering

Exhibition, 13–20 October 2008
ICA Upper Galleries

The performances and films of Gail Pickering (lives in London) often feature abstracted physical movement, a choreography around which the artist layers historical, political and aesthetic associations. Working with professional and non-professional actors and performers, Pickering frames *tableaux vivants* wherein

action occurs not to produce a closed narrative but as part of a social ritual without climax.

In earlier work such as *PRADAL* (2004), the artist's performances – set amid simplified architectural structures and semi-fantastical landscapes – occurred within a gallery during the course of an exhibition. The repeated and somewhat demoralised physical gestures, undertaken by solitary performers, emphasised a contract of daily labour struck with the artist; a labour that often hinted at radical actions such as bomb making and trade-union protest. Pickering has likened these performance works to "open film sets where the viewer experiences the scene in its entirety". Yet her recent use of film and video enables both a restriction on what is viewed, and the revelation of a wider context beyond the single scene.

Hungary! And Other Economies (2006) is a film composed of scenes played out by four porn actors, primarily in the crumbling ruins of the Marquis de Sade's former chateau in the south of France, which is now owned by Pierre Cardin. The actors – dressed in Cardin-inspired retro-futuristic costumes – read sections of Peter Weiss' play *Marat/Sade* (1963). While some sequences in the film are directed with a cinematic eye for composition and melodrama, Pickering also documents the read-throughs of the actors as they travel to the site, blending the play's grisly descriptions of the French Revolution with a playful eroticism. She also depicts the players' boredom as they wait around at the end of the shoot, moments wherein their 'true' personalities might be supposed to emerge – but in which their actions revert to a porn lexicon.

In *Hungary!* Pickering elaborates on the different layers of agency through which the contract between her and her performers is fulfilled. The artist creates a structural and contextual framework around her actors, but the latter also create their own fusion of performance, posture and parody. The extreme and occasionally humorous confusion of positions in this piece, which originates from the overlaying of site and texts, create a new set of relations. The latter are fixed in a physical economy of performance and sexuality, one reduced to a state of latency and manifesting unconsummated radical potential.

The use of site as an associative junction was key to Pickering's *Nought to Sixty* project, at the core of which was a video work titled *Brutalist Premolition* (2008). The latter was shot in Robin Hood Gardens, an East London housing estate designed in the late 1960s by the New Brutalist architects Alison and Peter Smithson. Pickering worked with a group of tenants within their homes, asking them to cast professional actors to play the residents in a folk play. *Brutalist Premolition* addresses the dream and reality of an architectural movement, weaving lived experience into the language of a socio-political essay, and utilising the artist's characteristic layers of scripting, casting and performing (at the ICA the video was also presented within a quasi-architectural framework that served both as a projection screen and physical manifestation of the space caught on camera). It is the ultimate ambiguity of this approach that allows for a sense of unresolved representation, and the formation of new social narratives through the processes of performance.

Richard Birkett

56 Duncan Campbell

Exhibition, 27 October–2 November 2008
ICA Upper Galleries

"Who remembers all that?", the narrator asks in Chris Marker's film *Sans Soleil* (1983), "History throws its empty bottles out the window." The 16mm film works of Duncan Campbell (born Belfast, 1972, lives in Glasgow), and in particular his quasi-documentaries, delve into the question of how to represent history, and how to sift through, recoup or discard the manifold images that history leaves behind.

In *Falls Burns Malone Fiddles* (2003) Campbell looks at the era of the Troubles in Northern Ireland. The film addresses the sheer number of images of the period and the impossibility of synthesising them into any coherent narrative. It is composed of footage taken by Belfast community photography groups, Republican organisations who sought to assiduously document their side of the struggle; and has as its narrator a man with a thick Scottish accent, who, struggling to make sense of the pictures before him, distances and confuses the history at hand.

Campbell's film *Bernadette* (2007), portrays Bernadette Devlin, a Northern Irish Republican who

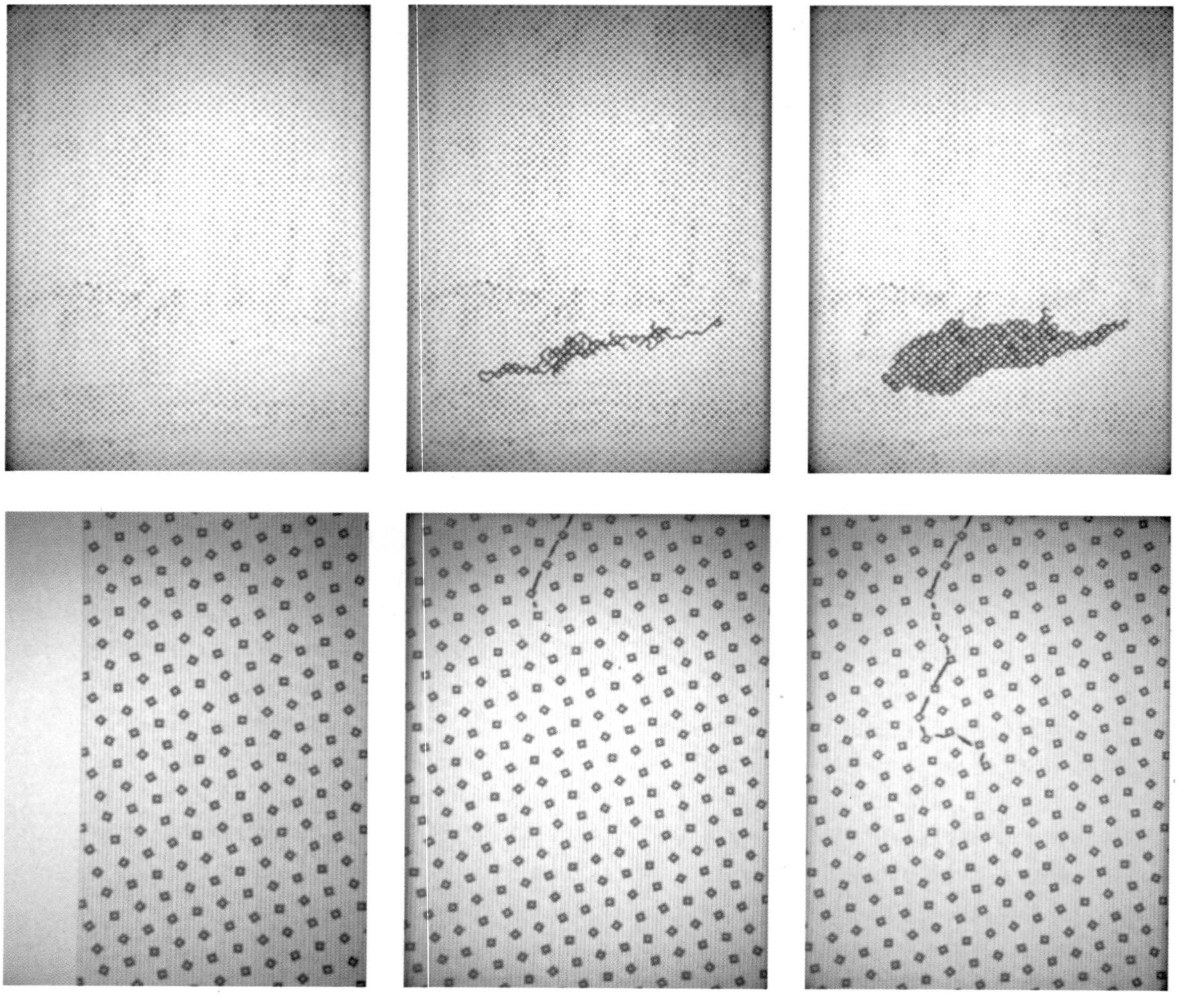

All images: Duncan Campbell / *Sigmar* / 2008

became a street activist in the late 1960s, helped to organise the Battle of the Bogside, and who subsequently, at the age of 21, became the youngest woman elected to the House of Commons in Westminster. Bernadette builds on the sense of disorientation glimpsed in both *Falls Burns* and Campbell's *o, Joan, no…* (2006) – a film comprising alternating bursts of light and sound. Yet *Bernadette* is more precise about where such disorientation is located: here, it is seen originating with the filmmaker himself. *Bernadette*, which is composed entirely of found footage, is presented without commentary or context. It links the state of being lost among representations of the past to one of obsessive – even sexual – enthralment. The film opens with black and white footage of Bernadette's bare skin: her toes, her feet, her arms, her eyes. This extolling of the parts of the body is a cinematic version of the *blason*, an adoration of 'the beloved' which has migrated from its origins in French poetry to film (Jean Luc Godard's *Le Mépris* also opens with a scene of this sort, dedicated to Brigitte Bardot). This portrayal of the beloved is subsequently overturned and then almost forgotten in the rest of the film, which shows a firebrand of a woman, one who, after being prohibited from speaking in Parliament after Bloody Sunday, punched the Home Secretary (and later said her only regret was that she "didn't get him by the throat").

These excerpts are not being given to the viewer in order that a story might be learnt in the manner of a historical documentary. Rather, the viewer is confronted with simply more and more representations of Bernadette, as the film's object of irrational attention. Campbell's film exposes the limitations of historical memory.

For *Nought to Sixty*, Campbell extended *Bernadette*'s motif of the failing testimonial in a new 16mm film, *Sigmar* (2008). Resurrecting an animated sequence created during the making of *Bernadette*, yet closer in character to *o, Joan, no…*, *Sigmar* is a short suggestive portrait that provides the observer with a series of spatial clues to the work's title. Rudimentary drawings, anthropomorphic objects and photographs are presented to the camera as a dense collage, while a nonsensical spoken soundtrack embodies frustration, inquistiveness and humour.

Melissa Gronlund

57 Fiona Jardine

Exhibition, 27 October–2 November 2008
ICA Upper Galleries

Galvanised by a constellation of literary influences – Rabelais, TS Eliot and Bret Easton Ellis to name a few – Fiona Jardine (born Galashiels, 1970, lives in Glasgow) creates work engaged in crossovers between pre-Enlightenment and contemporary cultural conditions. Such intersections are evident both in the artist's holistic approach to her craft – Jardine commits to the production of the work herself rather than using external or specialist processes – and also in the diversity of the materials Jardine employs.

Using polystyrene, wallpaper, papier-mâché and wax, as well as more conventional media including photography and collage, the artist constructs decidedly sensual experiences. Jardine is interested primarily in collage, however, which serves as a practical working method and as a process which seeks not so much to juxtapose images or phrases in order to generate new meanings, but rather attempts to amalgamate discrete objects and images and ideas into a seamless whole. And while distinct interpretations vary from one object to the next, Jardine connects individual works through ambient associations in order to generate alternative and divergent narratives.

April is the Cruellest Month, Jardine's exhibition at Transmission, Glasgow, in 2006, included a work entitled *Pillar* (2006). A freestanding expanded polystyrene column coated in a slick high-gloss paint, Jardine's totemic object is reminiscent of American artist Paul McCarthy's scatological aesthetic. This folly is neither ossified enough to become a monument, nor natural enough to seem biological. Instead it appears to occupy a liminal space between these two conflicting states, aping the form of the classical column with its fantastical and sickly architecture.

In stark contrast to the artificial putrescence of *April is the Cruellest Month*, meanwhile, was Jardine's *Moltke's Eye* (2007) – an exhibition which assumed the cool and stylised sheen of a monochromatic 80s interior. Having papered the whitewashed walls of Sorcha Dallas in Glasgow with intermittent columns of black and white, to create a pattern reminiscent of television static, Jardine then preceeded to hang a series of black-and-white figurative photographs. Presenting a suited male in various poses – seated, or else crumpled on a bare mattress – the figure's face is obscured by a bulbous, glossy black mask, which serves as a comic void or orifice. The motif of the ball-headed figure in *Moltke's Eye* – also present in photograph series *They Became What They Beheld* (2007) – makes a suggestive link with Eliot and Absurdist theatre, most notably Alfred Jarry and Samuel Beckett in particular. Additionally, the work seeks to harness the formal aspects of protagonist Patrick Bateman's apartment in Ellis' novel *American Psycho*.

For *Nought to Sixty* Jardine extended the collage element of her practice, viscerally connecting it with an interest in the human body as raw material. Using images primarily torn from women's fashion magazines, Jardine has reconfigured body parts into a grotesque design of skin and limbs. In two collages Jardine has pasted disembodied hands into the shape of a sphere, which recalls the map of Dante's Inferno – where the levels of underworld are presented as concentric circles – and also as a sphincter – an image that the artist describes as an "ingesting, consuming" rather than an excreting hole.

Jardine's work deploys bodies with a brutal visionary approach reminiscent of arcane or medieval religious imagery. The primary source for Jardine in this instance is the writhing mass of bodies in Luca Signorelli's fresco *The Damned Cast Into Hell* (1499–1503). With a gothic sensibility and dark humour, the artist uses the seemingly innocuous space of the white cube to support a symbolic realm.

Isla Leaver-Yap

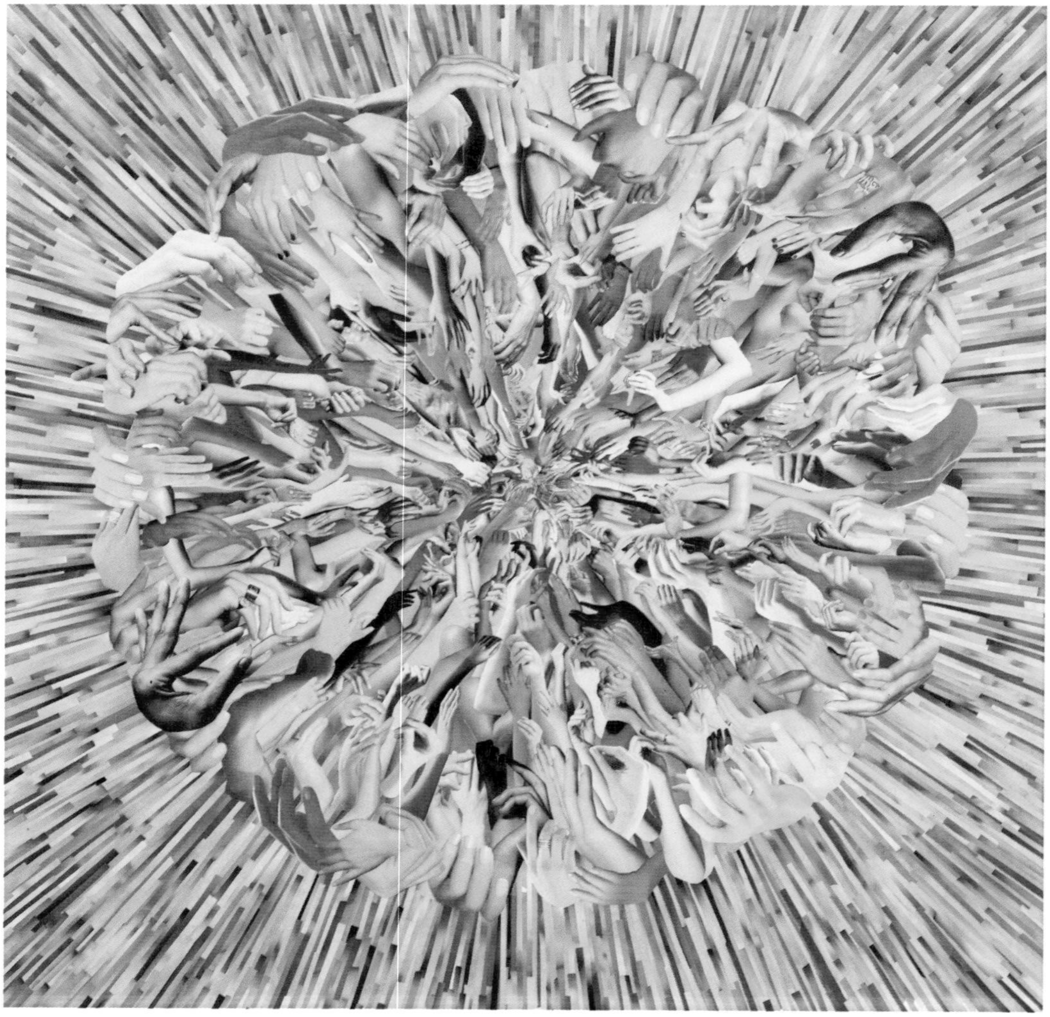

Fiona Jardine / *(For Patrick)* / 2008

58 **Macroprosopus Dancehall Band**

Maya-Victoria Kjellstrand joined the all-female improvised noise ensemble Polly Shang Kuan Band at the age of 20, only a few weeks after her initial exposure to the UK noise scene. Simultaneously working on personal projects, Kjellstrand hatched the idea of forming her own band. The result was Leopard Leg (2005–2006), a large, percussion-driven, all-female ensemble that included over 20 musicians during its existence.

Each of Leopard Leg's performances and recordings was based on a new visual narrative explored by the musicians, who played stripped-down drum kits as well as the occasional bass, guitar or synthesiser. The band produced many tape and CD-R recordings, as well as a 12" EP recorded during a night-time session in the South Downs. Leopard Leg – who were part of an evening organised by ELECTRA at the Whitechapel Art Gallery, London, in 2006 – mixed some of the most interesting elements of noise, DIY punk and improvisation, and such a large group of women and instruments also imbued their performances with a strong visual power.

Since Leopard Leg ceased to exist Kjellstrand has continued to work on musical projects, including her tape label, Hex Out Tapes, through which she releases her own recordings and those of others. Kjellstrand's other activities include *Sound of the Exquisite Corpse*, a project staged by ELECTRA in 2007 as part of *The Wire 25* season, and which involved inviting members of the public to create their own mixes from pre-recorded tapes by some of the most eminent noise musicians – including John Weise, C Spencer Yeh and Dylan Nyoukis.

Kjellstrand has also continued her involvement in bands, including Vard Ov Ard, in which she collaborates with Frances May Morgan. Kjellstrand and Morgan share a fascination with the mathematics of insect formations, and the latter have influenced the band's musical scoring. Recently the two musicians have created the Macroprosopus Dancehall Band, a larger ensemble able to realise more ambitious scores (the group is named after a form of magic that employs the elements of earth, wind, fire and water, and which Kjellstrand and Morgan also draw on for their scoring).

For their *Nought to Sixty* collaboration ELECTRA invited Kjellstrand and Morgan to perform with the Macroprosopus Dancehall Band, which had its debut at the ICA. The performance involved thirty participants: ten in a stringed bass section; ten in an "electronic manipulation section" which included cassette walkman, radio and synth; and ten in a vocal section. The musicians were volunteers from across the UK noise music community, expanding Leopard Leg's network (and including men as well as women). These three sections assembled concentrically to form a semi-circular arc that enveloped the audience both sonically and spatially.

ELECTRA

58 cont'd **ELECTRA**

Event, 2 November 2008
Theatre

ELECTRA develops projects that look to artistic and cultural networks and concerns beyond the restrictions of disciplines and venues. It operates as a contemporary art agency whose wide-ranging activities span commissions, facilitations and production in addition to its curatorial and educational roles.

ELECTRA's approach is collaborative and adaptive, combining the interdisciplinary and open approach of self-organised activities with an international ambition. The London-based organisation was founded in 2003 by curator Lina Dzuverovic and Anne Hilde Neset, deputy editor of modern music magazine *The Wire*, who were joined in 2004 by Irene Revel.

Dzuverovic and Neset first began working together in the late 1990s, with a series of events, entitled *Interference*, that moved between art, avant-music and performance, and that responded to the need for forums other than the exhibition context. *Interference* also revealed a gender imbalance within the sound art and the experimental music community, and in 2001 the two organisers initiated a project entitled *Her Noise*, which aimed to uncover lesser-known female artists from within this lineage. The project began with the collation of an archive of video interviews with practitioners of sound and performance, including figures from punk, noise, electronica and the riot grrrl movement. Subsequently it became a platform from which to commission new artworks and performances, resulting in the formation of ELECTRA.

As a network of people from different disciplines, and as a network of ideological concerns, *Her Noise* has continued to operate at the core of ELECTRA. The project formed the basis, for instance, of an exhibition and event programme in 2005, held jointly by the South London Gallery and Tate Modern; which included commissions by Kim Gordon and Jutta Koether, Kaffe Matthews, Hayley Newman, Emma Hedditch, and Marina Rosenfeld; and which generated an archive that has since toured internationally. The use of sound and performance to investigate social relations, and as inspirations for action and participation, runs through several of ELECTRA's subsequent projects, themes that are developed in the organisation's commitment to certain practitioners and through ongoing research.

ELECTRA's *Nought to Sixty* project featured the Macroprosopus Dance Hall Band, founded by noise musicians Maya-Victoria Kjellstrand and Frances May Morgan. The project highlights ELECTRA's strategy of facilitation and collaboration, and forms part of a wider narrative around the presence of sound and experimental music within an art environment.

Richard Birkett

Performance by Macroprosopus Dancehall Band / ICA / 2008

59 **Feminism is on the agenda**

Salon discussion, 20 October 2008
ICA Brandon Room

Some of the many participants included:

Kathrin Böhm
Toby Carr
Amy Feneck
Torange Khonsari
Nathalie Magnan (by Skype)
Ruth Morrow
Doina Petrescu
Jane Rendell
Rebecca Ross
taking place collective
Jeremy Till
Maria Walsh

The discourse of feminism – or 'feminisms' – has affected every aspect of art practice. This discussion was organised by public works, and followed a previous event of the same name that focused on feminist agendas within architectural practice. The informally moderated and highly participatory debate asked whether feminism should be kept distinct, or seen within a wider context of emancipation movements.

KATHRIN BÖHM: I'm going to give a brief introduction to how this evening came about and explain the format a little bit before we start. We had a Friday Session in May 2008 that was called 'Feminism is on the agenda', so I just wanted to recall the whole history of Friday Sessions.

Friday Sessions started three years ago. We came across them through 26' 10 South Architects, friends and practitioners in Johannesburg – one of the most physically inaccessible cities I've ever seen. They organised Friday Sessions for practitioners to meet each other and open up networks very quickly and informally. We did a Friday Session there and met lots of interesting colleagues and contacts, and got to know the city much faster and better than we would have done otherwise. So we decided to run them in London. Friday Sessions are random in topic – whoever is in town and has something interesting to say is very welcome to suggest a subject for the Friday Session. And so it happened that Helen met Andreas [Lang] from public works, at a conference organised by Jeremy in Sheffield, and there was the idea to run a Friday Session about a project that taking place collective is doing at Homerton Hospital. Out of this idea came the format for the first Friday Session, where we invited five different practitioners to talk about feminist issues that directly inform their practice. For the first session, presentations were given by Liza Fior and Katherine Clarke from Muf Architects, Doina Petrescu from aaa, Femke Snelting from De Geuzen in Brussels, Emily Pethick, Celine Condorelli and taking place collective.

After this evening, which was very presentation-based, there was a strong wish to continue a discussion about feminism, so for this event we invited every person from the mailing list from the first session to suggest issues and questions that they wanted to see addressed tonight, which makes this evening's agenda. There is no agenda set by one person.

The format for tonight is that we have sixty participants. Thirty questions have been submitted beforehand and we want to enter a public conversation. There's a few of us who will feel obliged to chair it if it goes flat, but hopefully not. It's also an experiment in self-organised public realm. The first Friday Session was captured in a fanzine, which was a non-edited, fast publication. We want to produce one tonight mainly using all the questions and issues we are collecting.

RUTH MORROW: One of the dilemmas I had coming today was that I realised I was going to be in a room of people who really know more about feminism and are probably more eloquent in explaining it, or whatever feminisms are, than I am. I wondered: what am I going to say? Is there a place where I can set out what I do in my life, the things that I'm interested in, the work that I do?

If I had a preferred platform, it would be an inclusive one rather than a feminist one, but I can't access this because inclusion is populated by groups who are what I call 'fucking include me' groups. They're very aggressive. I think feminism has once been at that point, but I'd like to think it had gone further. In a way, feminism is a 'fall back platform'. It's an odd thing to say but it is because I think feminism has gone beyond 'fucking include me' to 'I don't know whether I want to be included'. Feminism is probably more theory than practice, but at least that means there's still debate. Within that thought process is space for aesthetics and creativity – the things that I am interested in as an architect. One of the things that came up in the questions is: what does feminist architecture really look like? I really struggle with that question because I think we're so far off that.

DOINA PETRESCU: One of the recurrent questions is what is 'feminist' for you, and how does feminism help you in your current work and life?

MORROW: The one thing that feminism has allowed me to do is to not feel isolated. I don't think this is just a 'woman thing' either. I know I am peripheral, but I really do want to be mainstream.

TESSA: Hello, I'm Tessa. In the context of looking at how one relates to feminism, we could start to make some distinctions between feminine and masculine, female and male, and whether one understands this as an individual action within a bigger system or a collective action that addresses inequality. In what ways can we look beyond our own personal experience and understand this as something that may have an aesthetic? In what ways does the personal become political, to use that classic phrase? To test a few assumptions, do we assume feminine is equated with female? Therefore making certain things in a certain way is necessarily a feminist way of doing things?

ANONYMOUS (audience): I think for a lot of us, feminism is it about multiplicity generally. The women's movement came out of a lot of racial awareness movements. In terms of Ruth's desire to become mainstream, there's the question of whether the mainstream can incorporate lots of different voices – pluralism. I'd like to open that up if anyone wants to say what their idea of feminism is, that isn't just about the women's movement.

ROSS: My interest in feminism has very little to do with women's issues. I'm interested in what it adds to epistemology, and interested in the feminist critique of positivity – the fact-oriented, fixed version of knowing a knowledge. From the 70s and 80s feminism opens that positivity to culture by saying that knowledge needs to be partially attached to some kind of positionality. Where does it come from? I'm interested in how that applies to visual knowledge in particular, and knowledge of space and place. To me that's the most awesome moment in feminist history – the way I take that forward in my thinking through queer studies. It's not just gay or lesbian issues – queer knowledge goes beyond that to contemporary discussions of hybridity, networks and notions of representation that don't separate one representation from the network that gives rise to it.

ANONYMOUS (audience): It's helpful to make a distinction between two different agendas or two different goals. There seems to be a discussion about personal uses of feminism inside the workplace – getting a quota of women up in the top percentile of earners, while not necessarily being part of the bigger emancipatory movement. This is not the kind of feminism I'm interested in. Feminism will always be deeply political, and part of an emancipatory movement, until such a time as people who are at the lowest income level of the world are not mostly women. Feminism is something that could be an agenda to change lives for most people, and therefore part of a bigger egalitarian movement. Those two goals are not necessarily compatible. It's interesting in terms of architects and people who are working for developers funded by women, but funded by wealthy women, not necessarily representative women. Perhaps it is fair to say that there are two agendas.

ANONYMOUS (audience): My name is Jane. I've always felt very torn about another kind of split in feminism, which is the need to address women's issues and the fact that feminism has been able to contribute to discussions on ontology, epistemology and really important philosophical issues. When feminism has contributed to debates that aren't specifically about women, they can become appropriated by others who don't have a woman's agenda. Does that matter to feminists or not? I find this a tricky issue, but feminism needs to retain its specificity and its attention to women's issues. It depends very much on where you are, what kind of feminism has shown us that situated knowledge is really important. It's about the need for feminism to intersect with other kinds of critique, be they critiques of capitalism or neo-colonialism. Feminism has energy and importance in conducting transformation.

TAKING PLACE: A question that was asked of the taking place collective – during our work with a Mother and Baby Unit in Hampton Hospital – arose from the production of a series of works created in dialogue using both the staff and patients: was the work therapy? We discussed it as a group, asking where the politics of a feminist project are located. I think that it came from the idea that a feminist agenda is something that has to be difficult. It's a direct attack at something, whereas we were looking at something that was perhaps much more to do with the feminist approach that starts to unpick the processes and practices. One of the issues we were looking at was privacy around curtain use. It's thinking about something that affects women in that environment, but also thinking about the whole hospital environment as a series of processes that come together to produce certain subjectivities in that specific environment. Does feminism have to be difficult? Is there something more positive we can work with?

MARIA WALSH: I have something to say about situated knowledge and also a response to what you've just said about feminism being difficult or not. I think there is no singular feminism. I'm part of a group at Chelsea College of Art and Design. We deliberately call ourselves Subjectivity and Feminisms because people come at feminism from different points of view, so there can only be different perspectives rather than feminism. I refuse the term feminist because it falls into the problem of being identified as a category with a whole load of assumptions. There are also problems with the ideas about dispersed practices. A lot of ideas that do circulate in terms of different kinds of practices – I mostly know about art practices rather than architectural ones – come out of ideas that have been dealt with in historical feminism. Feminist critiques have influenced culture generally. These things have been then appropriated and they circulate without the affiliation with any kind of feminism. It is perhaps important to resituate those, but not within a singular feminist agenda or identity.

ANONYMOUS (audience): The most important thing that strikes me, as a bit of an outsider here, is where it starts to become practical. Unless you can include people by involving them in practical ways in whatever platform or area that might be, then it becomes a very small group and it is not a way of moving things outward.

MORROW: I take on board the idea that there are many multiple feminisms, and I think that's also inherently the problem. One of the questions I raised is "do you do it in theory?" or "do you put it into practice?" Do people believe that you develop it as a skill? Is there a skill to being a feminist? How would someone looking at your life see that you're influenced by feminism?

AMY FENECK: On a more practical level, I'm talking from an experience I had working with a group of women who belong to a running club. It was a women-only club, but this was about women who wanted to take control of a part of their life when they went for a run. It's about meeting up and a level of sociability. I never directly asked them whether they were feminists or not. It seemed to me that in what they were doing there was some kind of feminist action happening there. They ran at nights, it fitted in with their lives. It was about feeling safe on the streets at night, so there are parallels to Reclaim the Streets, but also it's an everyday thing. They did it two or three times a week. For me, that's a kind of practical, feminist action in a way.

ANONYMOUS (audience): Could I ask one of the five men present if they consider themselves feminists?

ANONYMOUS (audience): I think it is a difficult question, not least for the issues you've just raised. You're exposing a debate where there are multiple feminisms, and so to ask 'are you a feminist' seems like a coded question. I'm really interested in the debate about what feminism means in terms of practice and through some of the work that I try and instigate. I'd like to think that it's an involving process and I'm interested in entering a level of discursive debate. Whether that defines me as a 'feminist man', I'm not sure.

TAKING PLACE: What I find interesting about the work we do together is that we're quite comfortable in describing what we do in terms of theory or in terms of a feminist practice, but not very comfortable in saying why we've chosen to work as women. There are a number of other practices that make that choice. There are people who work in women-only practices here in the audience. I'm interested in that desire to work with women that somehow gets lost when you try to explain your feminism only through feminist theory rather than the fact that it has something to do with women. I don't know whether anyone wants to pick that up.

ROSS: I don't think there's as much of a schism as people are concerned about necessarily. This theory is all about paying attention to specific contexts. I don't think it's that divergent from what you're suggesting.

I'm reasonably well-studied in the history of cartography and I'm interested in its visual form. The association between spatial knowledge and power runs through history. I think that the challenges that feminism brings to knowledge production are great to bring to a practice such as cartography. I am constantly wondering what a more feminist version of cartography would look like, where it would be situated, how it would be produced. I think about cartography having certain visual tropes. It's got very discrete lines, it's got very hard lines. A map is meant to stand alone separately from a place. It's meant to refer to a place from a distance and some of the things that feminism teaches me contradict what a traditional map is. How might a feminist map be used to widen participation in spatial data and therefore decisions about policy and decisions about planning? How could a map, which is such a positivistic form that summarises knowledge about space and place, be less positivistic and a site for increased participation? I don't have an example of a feminist map, though, to show you right now.

BÖHM: Nathalie has Skyped in, "It is remarkable to see the refusal of younger women to embrace feminism until they really start to be active, practising in the working world. And then it goes from 'I'm not a feminist' to being very angry." That's an observation she shoots in from Paris. That was probably an important point from the first Friday's Session. It felt like there was a big audience who came to just listen, seeing and listening to others. They quite comfortably and confidentially talked feminism in a public situation – to pick up on the different '-isms' and forms of making it with your own language and your own issue and your own agenda, and to make it public again. That was one of the reasons for continuing the discussion tonight; not with a specific agenda, but having a platform for practising the public speak of feminism.

ANONYMOUS (audience): If women do become equal to men, then what is feminism? We've really been involved in the social construction of place, and about how we can take place – by the way we behave, the way we move furniture, by the way we can create or our own sense of place... How can these ideas get embedded?

MORROW: When you're a young feminist it doesn't really matter. It's a disappointment for older feminists to expect younger people to be engaged with feminism. It's the natural stance of younger people to be flexible and cope and have a pace that takes them through their life without having really a regard for the context they're in. Feminism only matters when you engage directly with the establishment, and I suppose this is why it often is a middle-class experience. As I get older, the more I have to engage with the establishment, the more angry and frustrated I get, and the more I start to question my own position and my stance toward the establishment: do I stand outside and throw stones? What happens if you take the buck from a certain institution that has a certain set of priorities that you don't align yourself to? I'm really interested to hear from people who are further down the line in their life experiences – what are your strategies for dealing with the establishment? Do you pull away? Do you do it subversively?

ANONYMOUS (audience): But then it's not just about middle-class women; it's about other marginal groups as well. For me, feminism is about starting from the margin, which then also goes back to the idea of "can men be feminists?" If you choose the marginal position then anyone could be feminist. And there's that idea of giving you empowerment from a small position that I like about feminism.

MORROW: I don't want it to be about just middle-class women because I don't think it is. But I think in the main that's what has driven it.

JANE RENDELL: Ruth, in your earlier question you asked, "Is there a skill to being a feminist?" I read this as a critique of practicality or [of the] normative notions of what it means to be practical. One of the skills that feminism has developed over time is a very different way of relating ideas and things or theory in practice in some way. I think it's become quite sophisticated in that discourse, but I think one of the real difficult areas is how feminists relate to the establishment, at whatever age. I find that quite problematic in my life because it doesn't just impact in material ways. My role within UCL in The Bartlett as director of research has meant that I've not been able to simply do a feminist rant or a Marxist rant or whatever it would be. I try to deal with this problem by being inclusive and trying not to repeat patterns of behaviour I would associate with patriarchy. There are brilliant people writing on this, like Chantal Mouffe about "agonism," and a very dear friend of mine once had a phrase: "altruism: what's in it for me?" I think when we're being generous, we're being slightly egotistical, but the important thing I'd like to point to is that it operates on a psychic dimension and that can be a cause for difficulty. I don't think there's an easy way out, and that's why feminism is still on the agenda because that issue isn't resolved.

ANONYMOUS (audience): I work at the moment for a women's organisation. My interest is how we create women's spaces of architecture or create our own space to discuss and maybe explore rather than having to gather in, sporadically, to give more thought, to give more energy. I also understand how to strategically operate, to not compromise on wanting to be a women's-only space, and have a dialogue with the council on that basis. I do get really fed up with theory because it doesn't help me in my day-to-day life, or in trying to keep a women's project going since 1979. I have come with an agenda – it's about that fact that we can talk as much as we want, but what are we going to do about the crumbling, little building down the road? I really love the idea of feminisms because you then cut through that whole dialogue and you don't have to waste time because everyone actually knows that people here are coming from different perspectives and have different experiences.

TESSA: Can I put a slightly defensive theory in? I appreciate the point that action is what we're concerned with, but theory is also the people writing it. Good theory is people discussing ideas in a rigorous, peer-reviewed, academic way. It's a place where people can go to judge their action against or to see where that fits in. Everyone has brought up different viewpoints as being very important in this discussion, but is having different viewpoints therefore fragmentary? Rather than as part of a healthy self-critical process, it seems that many people are suggesting we have different viewpoints and therefore, 'oh well, let's have different viewpoints' rather than generating discussion of how we move forward, how we look at the situation beyond ourselves. Surely we're talking about inclusion of different viewpoints in order to pin something down or discover what is important.

ANONYMOUS (audience): I find a lot of viewpoints, perhaps not articulated this evening, but definitely referred to, as something I don't want to agree with. There was Ruth's comment about young people not wanting to have anything to do with feminism. But those in this room that are younger have been vocal.

60 **Support Structure**

Institutional intervention,
October 2008 onwards
ICA

section of mosque / Yazd / Iran / 2003

Support Structure is a collaborative project initiated in 2003 by architect Celine Condorelli and artist-curator Gavin Wade, a project conceived as an "architectural interface". Support Structure develops relationships with people and organisations, and is engaged with the spatial experimentation and research that underlie the processes of art and architecture, while also resisting accepted definitions of production within each field.

The situational and responsive nature of this practice is inherent in the use of the term 'support'. Avoiding a conventional sense of production, the act of support directs attention away from Condorelli and Wade and towards individual projects and their users. It is an act of generosity that, in the words of art historian Andrea Phillips, stakes a "[direct] political claim: let us help you make something new occur: we will support you. Our role is not to make the new, it is to support the new being made by you". Support Structure takes on board an existing set of relations within an organisational or spatial context, and enhances or reframes these relations, in order to allow a form of 'political imagination' to take place.

Support Structure's various projects have investigated how 'support' can read across power structures, social realities and institutional forms. For the project *What is Multicultural?* (2004), which occurred under the auspices of the Portsmouth Multicultural Group, Wade and Condorelli proposed the formation of a library of resources devoted to expanding and defining the eponymous term. This process addressed the Portsmouth community, encouraging an ongoing archive of books and responses, yet reflected back onto the Multicultural Group by addressing the core tenets of the organisation and its function within the community. Tensions can occur between 'supporting' an organisation's activities and navigating its bureaucracy, and in this case the project exposed rifts between the mission and reality of the Portsmouth Multicultural Group, leading two of its members to resign.

Nought to Sixty – as a feature of the ICA's 60th anniversary year and as an articulation of the institution's relationship to emerging practice – is the most recent context within which Wade and Condorelli have applied Support Structure. Their proposal, *Curtain as declaration of desire for change of function* (2008), asked the institution to make a list of both artists and employees who have been part of the ICA during its 60 years, and to maintain this list in the future. One intention of the list is to draw attention to differing roles and differing levels of influence within the institution, and the metaphor of the curtain is pertinent here: at once a continuous surface and a form of divide.

However, another intention is that the list might function as an equalising system, drawing on a huge legacy of individual experiences and interpretations of the institution, and acting as a pool of participants for dialogues that would address the past and future policies of the organisation. *Curtain as declaration of desire for change of function* might be hampered by the past, including the vagaries of record-keeping and archiving; while its future might be subject to institutional developments, and to shifts in commitment. However, Support Structure's proposal exists as an invitation to consider the ICA as an accumulation of potential, and to provide a collective form of re-imagining that would access this potential.

Richard Birkett

Curtain as declaration of desire for change of function, 2008, by Support Structure (Celine Condorelli and Gavin Wade)

BRIEF
Compile a list of names of every artist or other person who has worked for the ICA since it was founded. The list is to be available to the public both in the institution building and website, and to be updated continually for as long as the Institution can manage. Develop a random system for selecting people from the list to be invited to discuss policy change within ICA.

PRODUCTION
Materials variable. Form to be decided through negotiation with ICA and artists.

FURTHER OUTCOMES
Policy discussion outcomes to be announced and presented publicly at ICA for consideration.

1948
Sir Herbert Read
Jankel Adler
Peter Watson
Jean Arp
Francis Bacon
Balthus
John Banting
Eugene Berman
Pierre Bonnard
Constantin Brancusi
Georges Braque
Edward Burra
Alexander Calder
Marc Chagall
Giorgio de Chirico
Robert Colquhoun
John Craxton
Salvador Dali
Paul Delvaux
Andre Derain
Charles Despiau
Frank Dobson
Raoul Dufy
Jacob Epstein
Max Ernst
Lyonel Feininger
Lucian Freud
Naum Gabo
Henri Gaudier-Brzeska
Alberto Giacometti
Duncan Grant
Juan Gris
Barbara Hepworth
Ivon Hitchens
Frances Hodgkins
Edgar Hubert
Augustus John
Wassily Kandinsky
Paul Klee
Oskar Kokoschka
John Lake
Wilhelm Lehmbruck
Wyndham Lewis
Jean Lurcat
Rene Magritte
Aristide Maillol
Franz Marc
Louis Marcoussis
Andre Masson
Henri Matisse
Robert McBride
F E McWilliam
Joan Miro
Amedeo Modigliani
Piet Mondrian
Henry Moore
Paul Nash
Ben Nicholson
Eduardo Paolozzi
Victor Pasmore
Pablo Picasso
John Piper
May Ray
Ceri Richards
William Roberts
Peter Rose Pulham
Georges Rouault
William Scott
Walter Sickert
Matthew Smith
Stanley Spencer
Graham Sutherland
Chaim Soutine
Yves Tanguy
Pavel Tchelitchew
John Tunnard
Maurice Utrillo
Edouard Vuillard
Edward Wadsworth
Christopher Wood
Jack Yeats
Ossip Zadkine
Giorgio de Chirico
Paul Gauguin
Julio Gonzalez
Wifredo Lam
Henri Laurens
Jacques Lipchitz
Roberto Matta
Karl Schmidt

1949
Frederick Law Olmstead
Eduard Bargheer
G M Hoellering
Ernst Barlach
Roland Penrose
Willi Baumeister
Edward Clark
Max Beckmann
Ewan Phillips
Hermann Blumenthal
E C Gregory
Otto Dix
Josef Fassbender
Franz Xaver Fuhr
Werner Gilles
Willem Grimm
George Grosz
Erich Heckel
Josef Hegenbarth
Bernhard Heiliger
Adolf Hoelzel
Ernst Ludwig Kirchner
Karl Kluth
Georg Kolbe
Kathe Kollwitz
Fritz Kronenberg
Wilhelm Lehmbruck
August Macke
Alfred Mahlau
Gerhard Marcks
Ewald Matare
Georg Meistermann
Otto Mueller
Ernst Wilhelm Nay
Rolf Nesch
Emil Nolde
Max Pechstein
Karl Rodel
Christian Rohlfs
Hans Ruwoldt
Edwin Scharff
Oskar Schlemmer
Karl Schmidt-Rottluff
Werner Scholz
Will Sohl
Fritz Wrampe
Kurt Zimmermann
Mac Zimmermann

1950
Maxwell Fry
Jean Bazaine
Jane Drew
Hans Hartung
Lucian Freud
Andre Bloc
Isabel Lambert
Peter Lanyon
Robert Adams
Reg Butler
F E McWilliam
James Joyce
Peter Blume
Paul Cadmus
Julio Castellanos
Kenneth Davies
Jared French
Henry Koerner
Daniel Mulowney
Walter Murch
Bernard Perlin
Alton Pickens
Charles Rain
Honore Sharrer
George Tooker
Pavel Tchlitchew
Andrew Wyeth
Michael Ayerton
Sandra Blow
Lynn Chadwick
Prunella Clough
Alan Davie
Richard Hamilton
Patrick Heron
Anthony Hill
William Turnbull

1951
Richard Lannoy
Roberto Matta
Ann Balmforth
Humphrey Jennings
A D Sylvester
Gesner Abelard
Miss Edwards
Toussaint Auguste
Miss Acheson
Castera Bazile
Rigaud Benoit
Wilson Bigaud
Dieudonne Cedor
A Chapelet
Prefete Duffaut
Rene Exhume
Jacques Enguerrand Gourgue
Hector Hyppolite
Joseph Jacobs
Adam Leontus
Philome Obin
Fernand Pierre
Louverture Poisson
Robert St Brice
Micius Stephane
Edith Sitwell
Michael Meyer
Le Corbusier
Geoffrey Grigson
Basil Taylor
Sir Lawrence Alma-Tadema
Mark Anthony
Edward Armitage
Francis Barraud
Frederick Bacon Barwell
Aubrey Beardsley
Sir Max Beerbohm
Beggarstaff Brothers
Graham Bell
Robert Anning Bell
Vanessa Bell
Jack Bilbo
S J Lamorna Birch
Ernest Board
Hercules Brabazon Brabazon
Sir Frank Brangwyn
Frederick Lee Bridell
Gerald Brockhurst
Ford Maddoz Brown
Edgar Bundy
Sir Edward Burne-Jones
William Shakespeare Burton
Lady Butler
Sir Reginald Butler
Randolph Caldecott
Sir George Clausen
William Coldstream
James Collinson
W R Colton
Charles Condor
Phillip Connard
Frank Cadogan Cowper
Walter Crane
Joseph Crawhall
Charles Cundall
Richard Dadd
Anthony Devas
Walter Howell Deverall
Sir William Reid Dick
Sir Frank Dicksee
Sir William Fettes Douglas
Richard Doyle
William Dyce
Augustus Leopold Egg
Jacob Epstein
Frederick Etchells
Joseph Farquharson
Bernard Fleetwood-Walker
Sir William Russell Flint
Miles Birket Foster
William Frith
Roger Fry
Louis Richard Garbe
William Gear
Mark Gertler
Sir Alfred Gilbert
Eric Gill
Harold Gilman
Frederick Goodall
Spencer Frederick Gore
Lawrence Gowing
Peter Graham
Walter Greaves
Kate Greenaway
Maurice Greiffenhagen
W O Grey
Charles Napier Hemy
George Elgar Hicks
William Holman-Hunt
James Clarke Hook
Arthur Boyd Houghton
William Huggins
Arthur Hughes
William Henry Hunt
James Dickson Innes
Gwen John
David Jones
E McKnight Kauffer
Charles Keene
Sir Gerald Kelly
Eric Kennington
Dame Laura Knight
Henry Lamb
Sir Edwin Landseer
Phillip A Laszlo deo Lombos
Sir John Lavery
Alfred Kingsley Lawrence
Cecil Gordon Lawson
Benjamin Williams Leader
Alphonse Legros
Frederick Lord Leighton
Charles Dunlop Leslie
John Frederick Lewis
Thomas Lowinsky
Ambrose McEvoy
Sir Bertram Mackennal
Daniel Maclise
Arthur Melville
Sir John Everett Millais
Albert Moore
Henry Spencer Moore
Frederick Morgan
William de Morgan
Robert Morley
Rodrigo Moynhian
Sir Alfred Munnings
Alexander Munro
John Privett Nettleship
C RW Nevinson
Algernon Newton
Sir William Orchardson
Sir William Orpen
John Pettie
John Phillip
Glyn Philpot
Evelyne Pickering (de Morgan)
John Pinwell
Lucien Pissaro
Beatrix Potter
Sir Edward Poynter
Valentine Cameron Prinsep
Dod Procter
Ernest Procter
James Pryde
Arthur Rackham
Herbert Davis Richter
Briton Riviere
Sir Francis Cyril Rose
Dante Gabriel Rosetti
Sir Walter W Russell
Walter Dendy Sadler
Frederick Sandys
John Singer Sargent
Peter Scott
Charles Shannon
Byam Shaw
George Sheringham
Frederick Shields
William George Simminds
Charles Sims
James Smetham
Simeon Solomon
Charles Spencelayh
J R Spencer Stanhope
Philip Watson Steer
Adrian Stokes
Marcus Stone
William Strang
Arthur Studd
Campbell Taylor
James Harvard Thomas
Sir William Hamo Thorneycroft
Feliks Topolski
Julian Trevelyan
Henry Tuke

Keith Vaughan
Edward Wadsworth
Dame Ethel Walker
Frederick Walter
Edward Matthew Ward
John William Waterhouse
George Frederick Watts
J A M Whistler
Rex Whistler
Stephen M Wiens
Scottie Wilson
William Lindsay Windus
Thomas Wollner
Charles William Wyllie
Doris Zinkeisen
W K Smigielski

1952
A J T Kloman
Bernard Meadows
Dorothy Morland
Kenneth Armitage
Brenda Pool
John Hayward
Elizabeth Frink
J P Hodin
Geoff Lawson
Henri Cartier-Bresson
Wilfredo Lam
Saul Steinberg
Bernard Buffet
Feliks Topolski
Derek Knight
Oskar Kokoschka
Michael Andrews
Harold Cohen
Alfred Daniels
Victor Willing
Alan Reynolds
Barbara Braithwaite
Edward Middleditch
John Berger
Toni del Renzio
David Sylvester

1953
Kathleen Raine
Sam Francis
Julie Lawson
Georges Mathieu
Henri Michaux
Alfonso Osorio
Jackson Pollock
Jean-Paul Riopelle
Iaroslav Serpan
Martin Froy
Joseph Herman
William Turnbull
Gerald Wilde
Denis Williams
Nigel Henderson
Ronald Jenkins
Alison Smithson
Peter Smithson
A/ARIBA and ACGI
John Catleugh
Lucienne Day
Humphrey Spender
Marianne Mahler
Mary Oliver
Bernard Poinssot

1954
David Ashley
George Keyt
Stephen Spender
Leonie Cohn
Reyner Banham
Lawrence Alloway
Beryl Coles
Stephen Russ
Edward Wright
Fahr El Nissa Zeid
Robert Melville
Camille Bombois
E Box
Andre Bauchant
Colette Beleys
Mr Bucket of Battersea
Margaret Lefranc
Jean Lucas
Andre Demonchy
Jack Taylor
Alfred Wallis
Gertrude O'Brady
Henri Rousseau
Louis Vivin

1955
Dennis Lennon
Walter Gropius
Troughton & Young
E Maxwell Fry
Sir William Glock
Nikolaus Pevsner
John Amis
John McHale
Felix Aprahamian
Arnold Cooke
Werner Bischof
Jean Dubuffet
Vic Bellerby
Laurence Alloway
Charles Fox
Mark Tobey
Maurice Broomfield
Robert Clatworthy
Peter King
Rosemary Young
Janet Barrett
Kit Barker
Barry Daniels
Jean Duncan
Eric Finlay
Wally Poole
Peter Snow
Carl Fredrik Reutersward
John Bratby
Derek Cawthorne
Sheila Fell
Anthony Fry
Patrick George
David Houghton
Peter Kinley
Norman Town
Phillip Sutton

1956
M G Bendon
Roloff St Beny
Colin St John Wilson
Roberto Burle Marx
Claude Vincent
Gottfried Honegger
Virgilio Guidi
Armando Pizzinato
Bruno Saetti
Giuseppe Santomaso
Romulado Scarpo
Emilio Vedova
Alberto Viani
George Mathieu
Roger Mayne
Charles Addams
Peter Arno
Abe Birnbaum
Sam Cobean
Whitney Darrow Jr
Alan Dunn
Robert Osborn
Mary Petty
George Price
Mischa Richter
Otto Soglow
William Steig
Richard Taylor
James Thurber
Pablo Picasso
Amedeo Modigliani
Man Ray
Brassai
John Hultberg
William Turnbull
John Coplans
Frank Wilson
Dennis Bowen

1957
G S Fraser
Ian McCallum
Roger Coleman
Mike Cordell
Theo Crosby
Paul Feiler
John Forrester
John Wain
Terry Frost
Adrian Heath
Roger Hilton
James Hull
Kenneth Martin
Mary Martin
Rodrigo Moynihan
Bryan Wynter
Margaret Webster Plass
Karel Appel
Asger Jorn
Enrico Baj
Guiseppe Capogrossi
Zoran Matic
Wols
Leon Golub
Charles P Mountford
D'Angelo
Mimmo Rotella
Guy Anderson
Kenneth Callahan
Rhys Capran
Morris Graves
David Hare
Seymour Lipton
Ezio Martinelli
Richard E Fuller
Lucien Clergue

1958
Ian Hamilton
John Barnicoat
Joan Musgrave
Peter Blake
Peter Coviello
William Green
Richard Smith
Nina Tryggvadottir
Anil Gamini Jayasuriya
Jean Fautrier
Hubert Dalwood
Pierre Alechinsky
E L T Mesens
Gwyther Irwin
Lin Show Yu
Henry Mundy
Gillian Ayres
Austin Cooper
William Copley
Robyn Denny
Mrs Charles Damiano
Mr Charles Damiano
Max Bruening
Winfred Gaul
Karl Otto Goetz
Gerhard Hoehme
Karl Fred Dahmen
Bernard Schultze
Emil Schumacher
Hans Platschek

1959
Sir Phillip Hendy
Gordon Fazakerley
Man Ray
Victor Passmore
Harry Thubron
Adolph Gottlieb
E C Gregory
Lund Humpries
Edward McKnight Kauffer
Ettore Colla
Ralph Rumney
Nguyen Manh Doc Ducman
Mario Amaya
Colin Self

1960
Judith Jackson
John Latham
F K Henri Henrion
Karl Benjamin
Lorser Feitelson
Frederick Hammersley
John McLaughlin
Mattia Moreni
Ralph Clements
Morris Louis
Nicolas Schoeffer
Peter Hobbs
Robert Laws
Richard Bogart
Modesto Cuixart
Nicholas De Stael
Lucio Fontana
Antoni Tapies
Vladimir Malevich
Chris Tomlin
Jules Feiffer

1961
July Lawson
Vera Haller
M G Bendon
Wolfgang Hollegha
Peter Stroud
John Bodley
Peter Clough
Jeffrey Steele
Howard Hartog
Gabriel White
Milka Kukoc
Alexander Liberman
Ivor Abramovitch
David Annesley
Keith Arnatt
Peter Atkins
Judith Barclay
Robert Carruthers
Christopher Davison
Franck Demoncheaux
Charles Hatwell
Christopher Lane
Kim Lim
Bryan MacDonald
Francis Morland
John Robson
Dorothy Ruddick
Harold Rugg
Ulrico Schettini
Tim Scott
Joseph Sheppard
Eric Stanford
Neil Stocker
William Tucker
George Ward
Corrine Webb
Helen Yamey
John Youngman
Maurice Jadot
Sonia Delauney

1962
Laurie Fricker
John Harvey
Euston Bishop
Howard Hodgkins
James Meller
Allen Jones
Maria Brockstedt
Stapleton
John Ernest
Andrew Forge
John Plumb
Louis le Brocquy
Sidney Nolan
Madeleine Pearson
Mohsen Vasiri
Pierre Alechinsky
Alberto Giacometti
Hans Hartung
Henri Helion
Andre Masson
Roberto Matta Echauren
Maria Helena Vieira da Silva
Peter Phillips
David Hockney
John Bowstead
Maurice Agis
John McHale
Magda Cordell
Valerio Adami
Maria Romagnoli

1963
Malangatana Ngwenya
Ibrahim El Salahi
Gillian Wise
Arnold Van Praag
Philippe Hiquily
Valentine Dobree
ZVIA
Magdalena Mugdan
Patricia Meyrowitz
Warren Chalk
Peter Cook
Dennis Crompton
Ben Fetter
David Greene
Ron Herron
Peter Taylor
Michael Webb
Wendy Yeo
Peter Startup
Ashu Roy
Jann Haworth
John Howin
Brian Mills
John Pearson
Allan D'Arcangelo
Jim Dine
Robert Indiana
Jasper Johns
Roy Lichtenstein
Claes Oldenburg
Robert Rauschenberg
Mel Ramos
James Rosenquist
Wayne Thibaud
Andy Warhol
John Weskey
Tom Wesselman
F E Mac

1964
Jasia Reichardt
Kenneth Coutts-Smith
Michael Chow
Ken Turner
John Tandy
Gerald Laing
Bernard Bertschinger
Douglas Binder
Mary Rose Ford
R Westwood
D Hall
Francis Picabia
Ronald Hunt
Nicholas Knowland
Henrietta Garland
Ad Reinhardt
Christopher Pratt
Derek Boshier
Patrick Caulfield
Bernard Cohen
Howard Hodgkin
Gordon House
Patrick Hughes
R B Kitaj
Bridget Riley
Joe Tilson
William Turnbull
Trevor Coleman
Barbara de Orfe
Alexander Weatherson
Bill Butler
Anthea Alley
Gwen Barnard
Denis Bowen
Avinash Chandra
Bob Gill
Gerald Gladstone
Roger Leigh
Dante Leonelli
Richard Lin
Halima Nalecz
Kate Nicholson
Helen Phillips
Marcello Salvadori
Judy Stapleton
Roger Westwood
Frank Avray Wilson
Domingo de la Cueva
Manina
Frida Blumenberg

1965
Mary Llewellyn
Arshile Gorky
Leslie Stack
Gerard Franceschi
Stanley Pelc
Robert Freeman
L C McQueen
Julian Beinart
Royston Harper
John Berry
David Thompson
Mauro Kunst
Katharine Colt
Brian Yale
Richard Humphrey
Edward Piper
Paula Rego
Anna Teasdale
Jocelyn Chewett
Bernard Schottlander
Lorri
Antonio Tapies
Rick Ulman
Bernd Berner
Rolf-Gunter Dienst
Raimer Jochims
Klaus Jurgen-Fischer
Eduard Micus
Lother Quinte
Rolf Brandt
Malcolm Hughes
Michael Pennie
Bernard Gay
Victor Burgin
Roger Dade
Peter Millband
David Wise
Radovan Kragulj
Guillaume Apollinaire
Claus Bremer
Thomas Bayrle
Nanni Balestrini
Pierre Albert-Birot
Lewis Carroll
Henri Chopin
Bob Cobbing
Kenelm Cox
Theo van Doesburg
Reinhard Doehl
Tom Edmonds
Ian Hamilton Finlay
Heinz Gappmayr
John Furnival
P A Gette
Pierre Garnier
Eugen Gomringer
Raoul Hausmann
Josef Hirsal
Bernard Heidsieck
Sylvester Houedard
Ernst Jandl
Thomas Kabdebo
Ferdinand Kriwet
Jiri Kolar
Roberto Altmann
Isidore Isou
Aude Jessemin
Maurice Lemaitre
Roland Sabatier
Jacques Spacagna
Filippo Tommaso Marinetti
Hansjorg Mayer
Franz Mon
Edwin Morgan
Christian Morgenstern
Rolando Azeredo
Augusto de Campos
Decio Pignatari
Pedro Xisto
Ladislav Novak
Antonio Porta
Francis Picabia
Josua Reichart
Gerhard Ruhm
Kurt Schwitters
John Sharkey
Ardengo Soffici
Hans Staudacher
Stafan Themerson
Victor Vasarely
Stanley William Hayter
Eugenio Carmi
Lucio Fontana
R B Kitaj

1966
Margaret Luke
Winifred Gaul
Patrick Woodroffe
Yvonne Davies
Ernst Benkert
Francis R Hewitt
Edwin Mieczkowski
Antoni Miraldi
Jean Madison
Katie Lebens
Antonio Saura
Eric Gibson
Colin Jones
Peter Lowe
Andrew Tilberis
Anthony Benjamin
Moy Keightley
Ann Clark
Barry Martin
Bruce McLean
John Whittaker
Pravoslav Sovak
Norman Reid
Bryan Robertson

1967
Desmond Morris
Richard Hawkins
Carl Nesjar
Stephen Plaistow
Joan Rabascall
Sally Downing
Patricia Douthwaite
William Kempner Ltd
Ian Dury
William Ballany
Herbert Kitchen
Michael White
G S Ovenden
Stass Paraskos
Helen Piddington
Jimo Akolo
Michael Bendele
Yemi Bisiri
Adebisi Fabunmi
Rufus Ogundele
Asiru Olatunde
Muraina Oyelami
Twins Seven-Seven
Ibrahim El Salahi
Barry Cook
Edwina Leapman
David Troostwyk
Walter Feldman
Marc Riboud
Robert Howe
John Willett
John Gibson
Stuart Sutclffe
Dolf Rieser
Peter Green
Laurence Whitfield
Glynn Williams
Maria Simon
Simone Beaulieu
Keith Albarn
Hazel Albarn
Chris Coles
John Sampson
Ben Vautier
George Maciunas
Cavan McCarthy
George Brecht
Henry Flynt
Gianni Sassi
Gruppo Falcmartello
Enrico Filippini
Arturo Schwartz
Dick Higgins
Magdalo Mussio
Julien Blaine
Gianni-Emilio Simonetti
A G Fronzoni
Pino Tovaglia
Eugenio Carmi
Arrigo Lora Totino
Seiichi Niikuni
Franz Man
Mario Diacono
Bruno Murani
Till Neuburg
Enzo Mari
Marcello Morandini
Giancarlo Illoprandi
Flavio Luccini
Salvatore Gregorietti
Gerard Hemsworth
Mak Kum Siew
Heather Lavis
Richard Longcraine
Janet Spiller
Graham Tazzyman
Dorothy Carr
Ray Wilson

1968
Michael Kustow
Sue Davies
William Balleny
Roger Hugget
Mike Bygrave
Cesar
Yves Klein
Martial Raysse
Bruce Conner
Guillame Apollinaire
Simon Watson Taylor
Adrian Henri
Gerald Scarfe
Christopher Logue
Michael Vaughan
Marie Laurencin
Maurice de Vlaminck

1969
John Claxton
Kohei Sugiura
Ann Lauterbach
Christopher Jones
Miriam Hackenbrock
Gordon Richardson
Alexander Thomson
Bob Evans
Trevor Jones
Gerald Hurrell
David McClements
Archie Young
Karel Cebula
David Croftsmith
Michael Docherty
John Kraska
Victor Vasarely
Roy Lichtenstein
Jeffrey Shaw
Theo Botschuijver
Sean Wellesley-Miller
Stuart Brisley
Peter Dockley
Carlyle Reedy
Cornelius Cardew
Mark Boyle
Joan Hills
Suzi Gablik
E C Plunkett
Norman Stevens
Glyn Williams
Clive Barker
Phillip Morris
Carl Andre
Joseph Albers
Leonard Baskin
Warrington Colescott
Willem De Kooning
Phillip Guston
Ellsworth Kelly
Robert Motherwell
Louise Nevelson
Claes Oldenberg
Jack Sonnenberg
John Heartfield

1970
Robert Loder
Victor Anton
Clive Barker
Lise Bayer
Norman Baker
Bernard Bertschinger
Oliver Bevan
Tony Bindloss
Michael Bull
Mike Chilton
Ron Dutton
H Eastwood
Alun Evans
Elizabeth Evans
Mary Elphick
Garth Evans
Mary Fedden
Barry Flanagan
Charles Fisher
Don Foster
Tom Frame
Jacqueline Garratt
Roy Grayson
Stephen Gilbert
David Grice
James Griffiths
Joanna Griffiths
Vivien Halas
David Hall
Jay Hammer
Michael Harvey
Dennis Hawkins
Mary Hill
Philip Hodgettes
Richard Horden
Tom Hudson
Diane Ismay
John Jackson
Jasper Hewitt
Robert Johnson
Anthony King
David Leverett
Liliane Lijn
Jeffrey Lloyd
Bill Major
Eric Mason
Mike Moore
Victor Newsome
Peter Nicholas
Simon Nicholson
Billie Old
David Petersen
Bart Phillips
Tom Phillips
J E Pipkin
Phillip Preston
Michael Punt
Jean Reynolds
David Roditi
Matt Rugg
Meg Rutherford
Terry Setch
Dianne Setch
Xavier de la Salle
Christopher Shurrock
Sam Smith
Yolanda Sonnabend
Gillian Southgate
Tom Thurston
Susan Sterne
Marjorie Timmins
Norman Toynton
James Turner
Phillip Turner
Paule Vezelay
Jack Waldon
Islwyn Watkins

Greta Williams
Gjon Mili
Umberto Boccioni
Marcel Duchamp
Ferdinand Leger
Yves Klein
Willem de Kooning
Mark Rothko
Clifford Still
Richard Anuszkiewicz
Oyvind Fahlstrom
Tom Wesselmann
Marisol Escobar
George Segal
Morris Hirshfield
Sonia Kane
Louis Eilshemius
William Doriani
Francoise Sullivan
Dr Hans Jenny
Marios Loizides
Ella Winter
Gene Baro
Roland Brener
Anthony Caro
Phillip King
Roelof Louw
Roland Piche
David Tremlett
Brian Wall
Isaac Witkin
Derrick Woodham
Vaughan Grylls
Elizabeth Harrison
Simon Hayes
Carol Joseph
Bruce Lacey
Diane Livey
Andrew Logan
Marlene Raybould
Gerard Wilson
Alex Issigonis

1971
Jonathan Benthall
Ralph Steadman
Michael English
Keith Milow
Nigel Edwards
Dieter Roth
Michael Leonard
Michael Hughes
Mike Booth
Valerios Caloutsis
Roger Chapman
Roger Dainton
Neil Davies
Gerry Duff
Electronic Music Studios Ltd
Philip Hodgetts
Ambrose Lloyd
Barry Lowe
Don Mason
Erwin Meirhofer
Linda Ness
Christopher Pearce
Alexander Robertson
Steven Willats
Gillian Wise
Gerry Whybrow
Edward Meneeley
Larry Herman
Harvey Daniels
Edward Kienholz
Anthony Whishaw
Group One Four
Conroy Maddox
Derek Southall
Benjamin Stone
Homer Sykes
Paul Keeler
Leonard Freed
Eugene Atget

1972
Giles Marking
John Copnall
Peter Byrne
William Messer
Stacey Marking
Andrew Lanyon
Martine Franck
Nabeel Hamdi
Nic Wilkinson
John Evans
Nicholas Salt
John Russell
John Kasmin
Mark Glazebrook
Max Bill
Josef Albers
R B Kitaj
Oskar Kokoschka
Tom Wesselmann
Peter Stuyvesant
Stewart Mason
Jeremy Rees
Mark Edwards
Chris Steele-Perkins
Richard Wood
Christine Pearce
David Dye
Conrad Atkinson
Ata Kando
Graham Metson
Hazel Fennell
Simon Dring
Frederic Ohringer
Frank McEwan
Anthony Crickman
Duncan Cameron
John Kent
David Medalla
John Dugger
Gustav Metzger
Geoff Teasdale
Mike Webb

1973
Mrs Goldwater
Brenda Thomas
Len Gittleman
Felicitas Vogler
Bernard Lassus
Christian Jaccard
Paul-Armand Gette
Georges Badin
Gerard Duchene
Gervais Jassaud
Jean Mazeufroid
Louis Cane
Marc Devade
Ernst Neizvestny
AA
Ian Breakwell
Kevin Coyne
Cecilia Vicuna
Ben Johnson
Essendine Group
Guillem Ramos-Poqui
John Heap
Peter Yamaoka
Pauline Webber
Derek Boshier
John Hoyland
Stephen Buckley
Pamela Clarkson
Peter Hide
Roelof Loew
Michael Michaeledes
Peter Kalkhof
Alan Green
Antonio Sena
Robin Klassnik
Geoff Reeve
Harriet Freedman
Wilfred Scott
Peter Burrows
Kenneth Martin
Antanas Brazdys
James Stirling
Peter Smithson
Alison Smithson
Cedric Price
Tim Street-Porter
Archigram
Rogers and Piano
Foster Association
Piers Gough
Farrell and Grimshaw
Alan Aldridge
Philip Castle
Patricia Byrne
Michael Farrell
Tony Meeuwissen
Bob Lawrie
Roger Law
Mike Foreman
Peter Flock
Richard Escasany
Peter Bently
Julian Allen
Alan Cracknell
Tony Matthews
Terry Fincher
Eric Lockrane
Jon Gardey
Robert Adams
Geoff Howard
Bob Aylott
Jessie Matthews
William Wilkins
Richard Demarco
Anton Christian
Hermann Nitsch
Gunter Brus
Arnulf Rainer
Walter Pichler
Karl Prantl
Peinter
Haus Rucker Co
Coop Himmelblau
Missing Link
Hans Hollein
Friedrich St Florian
Turi Werkner
Heinz Gappymayr
Erwin Bechtold
Franz Lettner
Oswald Oberhuber
Richard Gregory
Ernst Gombrich
Howard Hinton
Colin Blakemore
Jeffrey Edwards
Maurice de Sausmarez
John Ravilious

1974
David Vaughan
Richard Anaszkiewicz
Theodoros Stamos
Pierre Soulages
Li Show Yu
Niki de Saint-Phalle
Yvaral
Hans Doerflinger
Ivor Abrahams
Joe Goode
Ed Ruscha
John Walker
Lucy Milton
Donald Taylor
Michael Rothenstein
Michael Werner
Artur Laskus
Charles Wilp
Elaine Reinhold
Richard Balzer
Peter W Rea
Joseph Beuys
Mal Dean
Pat Whiteread
Icke Winzer
Richard Bloomfield
Bill Richmond
Brian Shaffer
Eino Ahonen
Mikko Jalavisto
Leo Jokinen
Tapio Junno
Kimmo Kaivanto
Harro Koskinen
Inari Krohn
Matti Kulmala
Rauni Liukko
Ulla Rantanen
Arvo Sikamaki
Esko Tirronen
Sven-Olof Westerlund
Fernando del Paso
Albrecht D
K P Brehmer
Hans Haacke
Dieter Hacker
Klaus Staeck

1975
William Packer
Bernd and Hilla Becher
Caroline Mackechnie
Ted Little
Jo Feiler
Bob Linney
Richard Allen
Ken Meharg
Ulrich Weisner
Marcel Broodthaers
Jimmy Boyle
William Tillyer
David Lamelas
John Bull
Rob Con
Keith & Marie
Mario Merz
Angelo Bozzola
Ben Cabrera
Daniel Meadows
Greg Bright
Bruce Robbins
Bernar Venet
Sal Buscema
Herb Trimpe
Barry Smith
Robert Maguire
Keith Murray
Theophilos
Photios Kontoglou
Nicolas Ghika
Yannis Tsarouchis

1976
Rosalind Dodd
Jan Lenica
Barry Barker
Franciszek Starowieyski
Linda Lloyd Jones
Walerian Borowczyk
Maty Grunberg
Bill Meyer
Roger Dean
Al Capp
Gilbert & George
Andre Cadere
Gavin Jantjes
Dr Warwick Bray
Prof A Thom
Chris Jennings
Fay Godwin
Rhonda Whitehead
Jean-Michel Folon
Francis Ward
Tim Mara
Jean Toppazzini
Lawrence Weiner
John Murphy
Douglas Huebler
Joan M Key
P Levine
Polly Hope
Andrew Watson
Derek Birdsall
Margaret Cogswell
John Garrigan
Tomi Ungerer
Ben Shahn
Richard Avedon
Georgia O'Keefe
Marisol
Michael Craig-Martin
Dan Graham
Mary Kelly
Romulus Linney
K Meharg
Riccardo Zipoli
Cosey Fanni Tutti
Tyson
Edward Ardizzone
C Walter Hodges
Harold Jones
Victor Ambrus
Anthony Maitland
Rowland Hilder
John Burmingham
Helen Oxenbury
Quentin Blake
William Stobbs
Harry Baines
Terence O'Malley
Daniel Buren
Alessandro Manzoni
Stanley Browne
Jan Dibbets

1977
Bill McAlister
Kasimir Malevich
Eva Vine
Tony Elliott
Darcy Lange
Paul Hamlyn
Leslie Waddington
Jane King-Spooner
Ellen Kuhn
Annette Bradshaw
Robert Judges
Pip Paton-Walker
Paddy Summerfield
Embassy Press Ltd
Kate Walker
Cob Stenham
Catherine Nicholson
Bill Gaskill
Phil Goodall
Sally Gallop
John Heartfield
Kathe Kollwitz
Jorgen Bechmann
Frans Masereel
Ludwig Meidner
Margarete von Kurowski
Ernst Volland

Holtfreter
Anton Rausch
Jotter
Christian Schaffernicht
Richard Grubling
Reiner Diederich
Ajit Mookerjee
Mark Houlding
John Davies
David Lach
Domokos Moldovan
Jean-Michel Folon
Chloe Sayer
Marcos Ortiz
Ruth Lechuga
Lawrence Hope
Nick Cudworth
Arman
Fernando Botero
Roman Cieslewicz
Piero Dorazio
Elisabeth Frink
Juan Miro
Michelangelo Pistoletto
Francisco Toledo
Roland Topor
Tadanori Yokoo
Jack Youngerman
Peter Strevens
Stephen Neale
Peter Kennard
Ann Cole Phillips
Christian Vogt
Jeanloup Sieff
Ulrich Mack
Paul Huf
Marie Cosindas
Brian Duffy
Angus Forbes
Ivor Lewis
Bob Cramp
Peter Carey
Edward Booth-Clibborn
John Bigg
Gilles de Bure
Clive Crook
Gert Dumbar
Maciej Karpinkski
Bruno Suter
Christer Svenson
Jean-Paul Bacquer

1978

Justin de Blank
Graham Lyons
Simon Garbutt
Patrick Taggart
Sir Benjamin Stone
Richard Ihnatowicz
Chris Wellsby
Anthony Green
Richard James
Katherine Gili
Carl Plackman
Kevin Atherton
James Collins
Rowan Bulmer
Alexis Hunter
Robert Mason
Clive Garland
Bruce Rae
Michael Druks
Bobby Baker
Laurie Rae Chamberlain
Daniela Mrazkova
John McEwan
Craigie Aitchison
Thomas Joshua Cooper
Hamish Fulton
John Hoyland
William Johnstone
Rory McEwan
John McLean
Martin Naylor
John Panting
Nicholas Pope
Lawrence Preece
Michael Sandie
Eileen Lawrence
Glen Onwin
Hermann Alpert
Ulrich Baehr
Hans Jurgen Diehl
Johnannes Gruetske
Maina-Miriam Munsky
Wolfgang Petrick
Peter Sorge
Klaus Vogelgesang

1979

Archie Tait
Bernd and Hilla Becker
Chris Rodley
Jane Pearce
Dieter Hacker
Paul Hill
John Hilliard
Gabriele and Dieter Nothhelfer
Helmut Nothhelfer
Herbert Distel
Agnes Denes
Alan Green
Ben Jones
Nick Pope
Brian Young
Peter Cannon
Amikam Toren
Shelagh Wakely
Jeanne Masoero
Christo
Adolf Wolfli
Tom Wolfe
Ed Koren
Alexander Hollweg
Denis Masi
Viivi Oulasvirta
Paul Neagu
William Betsch
Lorenzo Merlo
Bernd Naber
Kit Callahan
Nigel Gill
Larry Knee
Michael Kilraine
Philip Hardacre
David Gordon
Ian Middleton
Eamonn McGovern
Braco Dimitrievic
Donald McCullin
Michelle Stuart
Timothy Hyman
Peter de Francia
Jeffrey Camp
Joris Ivens
Tim Page
Johnny Stalin
Anya Teixeira
Leonard Kartstein
Wieslaw Borowski
Andrzèj Turowski
Tadeusz Kantor
Henry Stazewski
Robert Barry
Zbigniew Gostowski
Druga Grupa
Joel Fischer
Ian McKeever
David Maclagan

1980

Sandy Broughton
Lazlo Moholy-Nagy
Dorothy Walker
Sir Hugh Casson
John Aiken
Lord Goodman
James Coleman
Alanna O'Kelly
Lord Reilly
Michael O'Sullivan
Nigel Rolfe
Noel Sheridan
G Lawrence Harbottle
Charles Meecham
Simon Jenkins
Paul Beauchamp
Pat Gilmour
Bill Henderson
Roger Graef
Norman Stephens
Ken Draper
Martin Landau
Dave King
Robert Loder
Jeff Lowe
Hilary Rubenstein
Genesis P-Orridge
Luke Randolph
Anne Rees-Mogg
John Ashford
Susan Richards
John Blake
Adrian Jack
Robert Frank
Chris Newell
Marc Camille Chaimowicz
Simon Emberton
Charles Hewlings
Sandy Nairn
Patrick Jones
Raymond Head
Brendan Prendeville
Rick Rayner-Canham
Helen Sear
Sarah Charlesworth
Douglas Huebler
Joseph Kosuth
Jannis Kounellis
Joan La Barbara
Lea Lublin
Duane Michals
Giulio Paolini
Eve Sonneman
Cy Twombly
Michele Zaza
Yvon Lambert
Jenny Okun
Penny Smith
Ray Smith
Cioni Carpi
Luke Holland
Joyce Agee
Catherine Elwes
Jacqueline Morreau
Lisa Tickner
Sandy Nairne
Glenys Barton
Philipa Beale
Jo Brocklehurst
Lill-Ann Chepstow-Lusty
Helen Cherry
Sue Coe
Eileen Cooper
Erica Daborn
Gertrude Elias
Sally Greenhill
Mandy Havers
Roberta Juzefa
Mouse Katz
Deborah Law
Jane Lewis
Barbara Loftus
Mayotte Magnus
Suzi Malin
Ana Maria Pacheco
Robin Richard
Carole Robb
Anne Ross
Marisa Rueda
Elena Samperi
Tessa Schneidermann
Christine Voge
Joan Wakelin
Helen White
Evelyn Williams
Jenni Wittman
Rose Garrard
John Crossley
Christopher Hamer
Janet Nathan
Michael Porter
Harry Snook
Ed Whitaker
Lucy R Lippard
May Stevens
Margaret Harrison
Suzanne Lacy
Leslie Labowitz
Candace Hill-Montgomery
Jenny Holzer
Maria Karras
Margia Kramer
Loraine Lesson
Beverly Naidus
Adrian Piper
Martha Rosler
Miriam Sharon
Bonnie Sherk
Nancy Spero
Mierle Laderman Ukeles
Sue Richardson
Monica Ross
Nicole Croiset
Nil Yalter
Marie Yates
Glen Baxter

1981

Hannah Collins
Ron Haselden
Gerald Newman
Andrew Cameron
Karen Knorr
Mark Lewis
Olivier Richon
Mitra Tarbizan
Shelagh Cluett
Malcolm Poynter
Richard Wilson
Simon Read
Liz Rhodes
S Garrett
Iain Robertson
Catherine Seely
Julie Stephenson
Ceri Dingle
Anne Lydiate
Maureen Connolly
Sarah Brown
Mona Hatoum
Carolyn Sandys
Nicholas Stuart
Laurie Swarbrick
Michael Johnson
Fiona Wire
Martin Cronin
Josette Brunet
Martin Gallina-Jones
Alison Urqhart
Jefford Horrigan
Norman Ackroyd
Trevor Allen
Lynne Moore
Glynn Boyd Harte
Brendan Neiland
Ellen Kuhn
Gerd Winner
Suzanne Davies
Harry Thubron
Peter Berg
Richard Deacon
Anthony Gormley
Anish Kapoor
Peter Randall-Page
Graham Cowley
Chris Kennedy
Bryan Biggs
Malcolm Garrett
Peter Saville
Bob Last
Al McDowell
Nicholas Albery
Harold Lane
Dave Morgan
Steve Moseley
Roger Westman
Andrew Page
David Brown
Tim Head
Paul Huxley
Bridget Riley
Adrian Berg
John Carter
Brian Falconbridge
Andrej Jackowski
Patrick Symons
Richard Wentworth
Edward Allington
Margaret Organ
Jean-Luc Vilmouth
Bill Woodrow
Sandy Skoglund
Susan Felter
Douglas Baz
John Divola
Mitch Epstein
Jack Fulton
Jan Groover
Len Jenshel
John Pfahl
Leo Rubinfien
Tim Hunkin
Jonathan Borofsky
Nathaniel Tileston
Ralph Turner
Koichi Tanikawa

1982

James Allen
John Austin
Kevin Baird
Jane Barnes
Michael Banks
Corinne D'Cruz
Tessa Beaver
Yolande Beer
John Bellany
Dave Brandon
John Brown
C R Brownridge
David Buckland
Robert Callender
John Carson
Brian Catling
Cozette de Charmoy
William Chattaway
Annette Chevalier
Maria Chevska
The Phantom Captain
Bert Smart's Theatre of Jellyfish

Paul Burwell
Jan Mladovsky
Marty St James
Tina Keane
James Fulkerson
Chris Welsby
Jane Clark
Doug Cocker
Robert Conybeare
Alistair Crawford
Michael Cullimore
Erica Daborn
Anthony Davies
Ivor Davies
Meg Davis
Sidney Day
Graham Dean
Jane McAllister
Eugene d'Espremenil
D'Espremenil
Clare Dove
Richard Eurich
Patrick Eyres
Ian Gardiner
Anthony Eyton
Anthony Farrell
Ken Ferguson
Pete Ferret
Simon Fraser
Jack Garrow
Eric Geddes
Arthur Giardelli
John Glover
Malcolm Glover
Sarah Greengrass
Greenpeace
Stephen Gregory
Keith Griffith
Christopher Hall
Jenny Hann
Kenneth Hickson
Denis Higbee
Judith Higginbottom
Susan Hiller
Barry Hirst
Carole Hodgson
Nick Holmes
Howard Hull
Peter Jamieson
Caroline Kardia
Anastasios George Leventis
Gina Litherland
Ian MacDonald
Clement McAleer
Will Maclean
Denis Masi
Garry G Miller
Bill Mitchell
Lewis Mitchell
Martin Mitchell
David Nash
Elizabeth Ogilvie
Terrence O'Malley
Jacki Parry
Vicken Parsons
Melinda Perham
Deanna Petherbridge
Charlie Pig
Charles Hustwick
Cressida Pemberton-Piggott
Francesca Pratt
Peter Prendergast
Dick Rainer
Robin Croizer
William Richardson
John Rogers
Michael Sinclair
Birgit Skiold
David Panton
Sam Sutcliffe
Len Tabner
John Taylor
Edmund Tillotson
Dick Ward
Boyd Webb
Marilyn Weber
Susan Wells
Victoria Wignall
David Wilkinson
Lois Williams
Arthur Wilson
Richard Wiltshire
Claire Winteringham
Paul Wright
George Wylie
Laetitia Yhan
Anna Amore
Judy Harrison
Nick Hedges
David Hoffman
Mike Goldwater
Ray Morris
Tony Sleep
Dave Walking
William Wise
Jenny Matthews
Raissa Page
Tony Cragg
Piers Gough
Ed Jones
Richard MacCormac
Toni Robertson
Peter Kennedy
Mike Parr
John Lethbridge
Kevin Mortensen
Vivienne Binns
Virginia Coventry
Jill Orr
Robert Randall
Frank Bendinelli
Marianne Wex
Gilles Aillaud
Kerry Trengrove
John Stalin
Duncan Smith
Rosie Thomas
Chema Cobo
Juan Carrero
Enrique Naya
Luis Gordillo
Guillermo Perez Villalta
Jeremy Lewison
Steve Bell
Mel Calman
Ray Lowry
Paula Youens
Glenn Sujo
John Ahearn
Mike Glier
Ken Goodman
Keith Haring
Robert Longo
Judy Rifka
Cindy Sherman
Laurie Anderson
Mark Beyer
Bill Griffith
Hunt Emerson
Joost Swarte
Mongo Baby
King of France
Eric Bainbridge
Tony Bevan
Glenys Johnson
Derek Marks

1983
Martin Lazenby
Mario Botta
Michael Newman
Henri Ciriani
Lluis Clotet
Oscar Tusquet
Frank Gehry
Arata Isozaki
Joseph Paul Kleihues
Charles Moore
Alvaro Siza
Aldo Rossi
Tim Jones
Diana Agrest
Mario Gandelsonas
Alessandro Anselmi
Coy Howard
Robert Krier
Rodolfo Machado
Jorge Silvetti
Franco Purini
Morphosis
OMA
Laura Thermes
Bruno Reichlin
Fabio Reinhart
Massimo Scolari
Mike Fearey
Paul Graham
Sharon Kivland
Maureen O Paley
Bob Phillips
Jan Turvey
Jeremy Dixon
John Outram
Ralph Lerner
Richard Reid
Alan Stanton
Peter Wadley
Bob Allies
Mary Miss
Richard Prince
Carol Conde and Carl Beveridge
Kate Whiteford
John Cooper Clarke
The Pollysnappers: Mary Anne Kennedy, Jane Munroe, Charlotte Pemburg, Jo Spence
Harrison McCann
Franco Rosso
Farrukh Dhondy
Judith Williamson
Tony Wilson
James Faure Walker
Ian Caldwell
Julia Farrer
Guy Brett
Judith Cowan
Howard Rogers
Alison Wilding
Rose Garrard
Caroline Tisdall
Richard Layzell
Patrick Keiller
Michael Eldridge
Barbara Kruger
Robert Mapplethorpe

1984
Anthony McNeill
Hans Peter Adamski
Peter Bommeis
Walter Dahn
Jiri Georg Dokoupil
Gerard Kever
Gerhard Naschberger
Terry Morden
Derek Jarman
Bill Culbert
William Morris
Julian Opie
Rita Donagh
Jeff Wall
John Maybury
Graham Crowley
Harry Hammond
Bill Watmough
Tony Mottram
Steve Rapport
Mike Owen
Derek Ridges
Helen Chadwick
Terry Atkinson
Lubaina Himid
Faith Gillespie
Terry Shave
Zoe Redman
Steve Hawley
Trevor Matthieson
Julia Wood
Jean Michel-Basquiat
Flick Allen

1985
Roberta Graham
Sonia Knox
Shinro Ohtake
Duane Michels
Svend Bayer
Alison Britton
Elizabeth Fritsch
Wally Keeler
Carol McNicholl
Jacqui Poncelet
Richard Slee
Janice Tchalenko
Hans Coper
Bernard Leach
Lucie Rie
Frank Stella
Beth Lapides
Eric Fischl
Anne Howeson
Russell Mills
Liz Pyle
George Hardie
Bush Hollyhead
Tony McSweeny
Peter Till
Ian Wright
Gary Powell
Linda Scott
Krzysztof Wodiczko
Les Levine
Silvia Kolbowski
Sherrie Levine
Yve Lomax
Richard Tuttle
Joe Fish
Stephen McKenna
Mikey Cuddihy
Ingrid Pollard
Brenda Agard
Maud Sulter
Sutapa Biswas
Sonia Boyce
Jennifer Comrie
Marlene Smith
Veronica Ryan
Claudette Johnson
Chila Burnaus

1986
Adolf Loos
Wendy Smith
Stephen Willats
Terri Frecker
Zara Matthews
Sue Morris
Alan Grimwood
Henry Pimm
Yoko Terauchi
Louise Blair
Hannah Vowles
Glyn Banks
William Furlong
Michael Archer
Bill Culbert
Michael Peel
Jenny Matthews
Ex-Triptych Ballet
Lee Friedlander
Mark Francis
Marina Abramovic and Ulay
Richard Artschwager
Christian Boltanski
Tony Cragg
Gilbert & George
Giulio Paolini
Gerhard Richter
David Salle
Sol LeWitt
Jean-Paul Sartre
Mark Skinner
Werner Buettner
Georg Herold
Albert Oehlen
Gary Stevens
Caroline Wilkinson
Caroline Evans
Georgina Carless

1987
Anselm Kiefer
Carlo Maria Mariani
Imants Tillers
Michael Nelson
Peter Dunn
Loraine Leeson
Miriam Cahn
Geoff Dunlop
John Wyver
Donald Rodney
Jennie Moncur
Olaf Metzel
Gerd Rohling
Ina Barfuss
Thomas Wachter
Bernard Faucon
Stuart Davies
Michael Sandle
Sheena Wagstaff
Jean-Luc Vilmouth
Patrick Tosani
Franz Xavier Messerschmidt

1988
Sue MacKinnon
Lucy Casson
Martha Russell
Andy Hazell
Linda Brown
Mineo Aayamaguchi
Deyan Sudjic
Graham Young
Fischli & Weiss
Clifford Possum Tjapaltjarri
Julie Brown-Rrap
Jeff Gibson
Bill Henson
Jacky Redgate
Bernd and Hilla Becher
Gunther Forg
Jean-Louis Garnell
Craigie Horsfield
Suzanne Lafont

Thomas Struth
Stephen Taylor Woodrow
Nigel Holland von Klier
Ron Arad
Nigel Coates
Doug Branson
Future Systems
Zaha Hadid
John Pawson
Claudio Silvestrin
Daniel Weil
Gerard Taylor
Fred Scott
Jane Dillon
Rodney Kinsman
Tom Dixon
Andre Dubreuil
Jasper Morrison
Mary Little
Katharina Fritsch
Rosemarie Trockel
Kate Malone

1989
Nigel McCune
Erik Bulatov
Mark Francis
Ilya Kabakov
Peter Wollen
Astrid Klein
Iwona Blazwick
Linda Brandon
Shelagh Alexander
Jamie Reid
Malcolm McLaren
Guy Debord
Constant
Giuseppe Pinot-Gallizio
Peter Halley
Meret Oppenheim
Veronica Ryan
Sacha Craddock
Jon Thompson
Nicholas Logsdail

1990
Rosemary Alexander
Vanessa Robinson
Bernard Brunon
James Lingwood
The Smithsons
Andrea Schlieker
Michael Duerden
Colin McCahon
Cildo Meireles
Johanna Mahlangu
William Wegman
Alex Katz
Robert Gober
Tishan Hsu
Patty Martori
Jennifer Bolande
Nancy Shaver
Laurie Parsons
Emma Dexter
Cady Noland
Jon Kessler
Dustin Shuler
Christian Marclay
Miroslaw Balka
Stephen Balkenhol
Jean-Marc Bustamante
Asta Groeting
Juan Munoz
Thomas Schuette
Franz West

1991
Maciej Stelmach
Willie Doherty
Mark Mason
Leyla Ali
Art & Langugae
Cheri Samba
Mark Wallinger
Judith Barry
Klaus Von Bruch
Marianne Brouwer
Franz Kaiser
Alastair McLennan
Glenn Brown
Victoria Aldred
Henry Obuabang
Alan Charlton
Jannis Kounellis
Rudi Fuchs
Jean-Francois Chevrier
Bethan Huws
Bruce Nauman
Damien Hirst

1992
Guy Days
Carole Child
Toshikatsu Endo
Callum Innes
Mike Kelley
Anya Gallacio
Lee Miller
Genevieve Cadieux
Larry Johnson
Karen Kilimnik
Raymond Pettibon
Jack Pierson
Jim Shaw
Mark Dion
Renee Green
Peter Fend
Dominique Gonzalez-Foerster
Liam Gillick
Paul Mittleman
Mark Dion
Jean Nouvel
Emmanuel Cattani
Michel Jacques
Jane Withers

1993
Andrew Grassie
Marina Warner
Gang Chen
Russell Coleman
Siobhan Davies
Tacita Dean
X K Deiroff
Katherine Dowson
Francesca Fuchs
Angela Gill
Jasmine Green
Permindar Kaur
Andrea Lansley
Theresa Limbrick
Johnny Magee
Parul Modha
Anne O'Brien
Barnaby O'Rourke
Joanne Pearson
Ines Rae
Lisa Richardson
Louise Short
Josephine Thom
Tanya Ury
Eugenio Dittborn
Rirkrit Tiravanija
Gabriel Orozco
Andrea Zittel
Lincoln Tobier
Gavin Brown
Steven Pippin
Marlene Dumas
Nicole Eisenman
Sue Williams
Rachel Evans
Nan Goldin
Dorothy Cross
Jimmie Durham

1994
Deva Palmier
Fiona Rae
Mik Flood
Pepe Espaliu
Charles Ray
Stan Douglas
Claude Cahun
Virginia Nimarkoh
Jeremy Millar
Christine Borland
Henry Bond
Angela Bulloch
Matt Collishaw
Jeff Koons
Thomas Ruff
Fiona Banner
Jake and Dinos Chapman
Graham Gussin
Peter Fraser
Jessica Diamond
Fischli & Weiss

1995
Nick Copcutt
Abigail Lane
Anita Timlin
Luc Tuymans
Lizzie Barker
Isaac Julien
Eddie George
Trevor Mathison
Steve McQueen
Marc Latamie
Lyle Ashton Harris
Glenn Ligon
David Bailey
Gary Hume
Christine and Irene Hohenbuechler
Heidemarie Hohenbuechler
John Currin
Siobhan Hapaska
Ingrid Swenson

1996
Nahoko Kudo
Michael Curran
Johnnie Bassett
Jaki Irvine
James van Werven
Keith Tyson
Samantha Andrews
Gillian Wearing
Jake and Dinos Chapman
Kathleen Rogers
James Turrell
Vija Celmins

1997
Andrea Tarsia
Andreas Gursky
Paul Thek
Chris Ofili
Kerry Stewart
Stephan Balkenhol
Carsten Holler
Mariele Neudecker
Alice Stepanek and Steven Maslin
Dick Bengtsson
Annika von Hausswolff
Jean-Frederic Schnyder
Kathleen Schimert
Mark Manders
Paul de Reus
Liza May Post
Marie-Ange Guilleminot
Jean-Michel Alberola
Tania Kovats
Ceal Floyer
John Frankland
Paul Noble
Peter Doig
Elizabeth Wright
Billy Name
Darren Almond
Jarvis Cocker
Steve Mackey
Sarah Lucas
Jorge Pardo
Phil Poynter
Katy England
Patrick Whitaker
Martin Green
Tobias Rehberger
Hilary Lloyd
Piotr Uklanski
Gregor Muir
Kate Bush
Vanessa Beecroft
Paolo Colombo
Stefano Arienti
Mario Airo
Maurizio Cattelan
Bruna Esposito
Miltos Manetas
Margherita Manzelli
Eva Marisaldi
Franco Silvestro
Grazia Toderi
Vedovamazzei
Liliana Moro
Helen Storey
Dr Kate Storey
Philip Treacy
Lucia Simon
Sarah Taylor
Articular
muf

1998
Simon Hillier
Tim Dawson
Richard deCordova
Jennifer Bornstein
Christine Atha
Miles Coolidge
Rebecca Preston
Rineke Dijkstra
Alison Senior
Sarah Dobai
Toby Taylor
Olafur Eliasson
Anna Gaskell
Sharon Lockhart
Rut Blees Luxemburg
Esko Mannikko
Florence Paradeis
Jorg Sasse
Paul Seawright
Elisa Sighicelli
Hannah Starkey
Jan Kaplicky
Amanda Levete
Sarah Sze
Okupi
Lari Pittman
Chad McCail
Lily van der Stokker
David Shrigley
Janice Kerbal
Kai Althoff
Richard Wright
Shahin Afrassiabi
Matthew Antezzo
Gillian Carnegie
John Chilver
Keith Farquhar
Ewan Gibbs
Luke Gottelier
Thomas Helbig
Emma Kay
Paul Morrison
Simon Periton
Manfred Pernice
Alessandro Raho
David Rayson
Richard Reynolds
Katy Schimert
Nicholas Usansky
Chris Warmington
TJ Wilcox
Jun Hasegawa
David Thorpe
Peter Davies
Martin Maloney
Steven Gontarski
Jane Brennan
Caroline Warde
Michael Raedecker
Dexter Dalwood
Gary Webb
Shaun Roberts

1999
Puneet Sulhan
David Ellis
Georg Baldele
Michael Williams
Michael Marriott
Liam Cahill
Tony Dunne
James Hatt
Fiona Raby
Donna Hay
Michael Anastassiades
Lee Curran
Ann-Sofie Back
Caitriona Donaldson
Tord Boontje
Catrin Williams
El Ultimo Grito
Tim Anderson
Rebecca Brown
Geraldine Walsh
Mike Heath
Alex Rich
FAT
Bump
British Creative Decay
The Light Surgeons
Shin and Tomoko Azumi
6876
24/Seven
Claire Catterall
Rem Koolhaas
Pope & Guthrie
Mark Dean
Mongrel
Scanner
Tonne
Rachel Baker
Andy Long
Szuper Gallery
Inventory
Mark Leckey
Heath Bunting
Kate Glazer
Christian Jankowski

Matthieu Laurette
Ben Kinmont
Peter Rataitz
Graham Ramsey
John Beagles

2000
Philip Owens
Urs Fischer
Miriam Backstrom
Katya Garcia-Anton
Kasper Konig
Matthew Higgs
Mario Gabrielli
Jane Wilson
Claire Odupitan
Jane and Louise Wilson
Vissey Safavi
Sune Nordgren
Mark Harrison
Andrew Stewart
Liz Arnold
Duncan Smith
Rosalind Arratoon
Martin Boyce
Rachel Cottam
Roderick Buchanan
Philip Dodd
Caroline Moore
Lucy McKenzie
Benjamin Parsons
Stephen Murphy
Chloe Mercier
Rose Hempton
Hayley Newman
Kelly Slade
Tina Davis
Cathy Wilkes
Florence Tyler
Ernesto Neto
Lynne Wilson
Christopher Brellis
Jhan Stanley
Will Warren
Aeronout Mik

2001
James Doherty
Jeremy Deller
Ruby Aspinall
Lucy Shanahan
Lucy Gunning
Rita Wanogho
Gavin Gooddy
Jonathon Monk
Joanne Shurvell
Ross Sinclair
Emma Pettit
Laura Karacic
Jessica Green
Keith Coventry
Rob Bowman
Dominic Martin
David Powell
Greg Pope
Jemima Stehli
Fabienne Audeoud
Simon Bill
David Burrows
Brian Griffiths
Dan Holdsworth
Gemma Iles
DJ Simpson
Tim Stone
Clare Woods
Zadie Smith
Richard Flood
Katerina Gregos
Anthony Fawcett
Hans Hemmert
Thomas Scheibitz
Adam Kobe
Juliane Duda
Oliver van den Berg
Roland Boden
Paschutan Buzari
Frank Coldewey
Raphael Danke
Tobias Dunke
Katalin Deer
Katja Eydel
Sabine Hornig
Petra Karadimas
Achim Kobe
Takehito Koganezawa
Karsten Konrad
Pauline Kraneis
Axel Lieber
Andre Reuter
Les Schliesser
Geralyn Huxley
Jack Goldstein
Oliver Payne and Nick Relph
Mike Nelson
Pierre Huyghe
M/M
Philippe Parreno
Francois Roche
Stephanie Lavaux

2002
Simon Wallis
L A Raeven
Alexis Johnson
Annika Larsson
Theresa Aldriges
David Cotterrell
Kiri Jones
Toby Paterson
Christopher O'Brien
Kirsten Glass
Angelica Fernando
Dan Perfect
Amy Busfield
Paul Hosking
Jasleen Anand
Neil Rumming
John Dunning
Rachel Lowe
Chloe Stewart
Hideyuki Sawayanagi
Toby Webster
David Lintern
Lisa Coffey
Tom Wood
Steven Blackwell
Mark Francis
Michael Cross
Saskia Bos
Simon Benson
Vivienne Gaskin
Harland Miller
Julio Pereira
Marianne Faithfull
Charles Poulet
Jeroen de Rijke
Willem de Rooij
Fergus Greer
Leigh Bowery
Richard Kern
Lothar Hempel
John Baldessari
Gilbert & George
Robert Morris
Yoko Ono
John Lennon
Edward Ruscha
Hannah Wilke
Steven Leiber
Simon Boswell
Gebhard Sengmueller
Martin Diamant
Gunter Erhart and Best Before
Street Vision

2003
Sara Squires
Jens Haaning
Patrick Waters
Julia Hamilton
Aleksandra Mir
Jennie Sharpe
Deborah White
Rebecca Finkel
Rosie Allerhand
Vincent Van Gogh
Joe Wilson
Joseph Schneider
Katie Pettitt
Russell Heron
Jejinder Jouhal
Lee Johnson
Nick Crowe
Sean Garland
Lucy Skaer
Jon Levene
Nicola Coween
Carey Young
Huw Aveston
Alan Currall
Joanna Foster
David Sherry
Steven Henry
Bernd Behr
Jamie Eastman
Rosalind Nashashibi
Francis Upritchard
Yvonne Salt
Russell Ferguson
Colette Meacher
Maria Lind
Gemma Starkey
Hans Ulrich Obrist
Jitan Patel
Michael Landy
Linda Huckstep
Marina Abramovic and Ulay
Gary Cargill
Vito Acconci
Dos Reis Chaia
Ocean Mims
Dara Birnbaum
Iona Scott
Claire Lloyd
Joan Jonas
Jen Thatcher
Melanie Rimmer
Paul McCarthy
Samantha Punt
Willoughby Cunningham
Tony Oursler
Ferdinand Kiggundu
Pipilotti Rist
Richard Serra
Bill Viola
Klaus Biesenbach
Barbara London
Chrisopher Eamon
Alejandro Zaera Polo
Farshid Moussavi

2004
Jens Hoffman
Larushka Ivan-Zadeh
Haluk Akakce
Jackson Pearce-White
Tonico Lemos Auad
Saul Bogdevicius
Simon Bedwell
Ros Fowler
Ergin Cavusoglu
Mara Rebelo
Andrew Cross
Ilona Cheshire
Saskia Olde Wolbers
Marcus McSweeny
Imgoen Stidworthy
Alexander Houghton
Hayley Tompkins
Nathaniel Mann
Nicoline van Harskamp
Beth Louise Vyse
James Anthony Corner
Katrina Brown
Ruth Barnes
Dan Cameron
Simon Humm
Anjana Janardanan
Philippe Parreno
John Boal
Brian Eno
Giorgio Sadotti
Victoria Smith
Chloe Vaitsou
Claude Leveque
Eli Kleppe
Didier Marcel
Mika Nakayama
Olivier Mosset
Claire Fitzsimmons
Shimabuku
James Harkin
Dan Walsh
Sam Welton
Ian Wilson
John Summers
Mathieu Copeland
Benjamin Green
Pawel Althamer
Rachael Booth
Eleanor Antin
Paul Shottner
Emma Bennett
Jonathan Clabburn
Victoria Benjamin
Elmgreen & Dragset
Gemma Donohue
Natasha Plowright
Andrew Bala
Mestre Bimba
Brian Jungen
Roy Nnawchi
Ilya & Emilia Kabakov
Oki Uhure
Tim Lee
Nicola Cunningham
Rahel Habtegiorgis
Jonathan Monk
Mariko Mori
Charlotte Neal
Kate Street
Yvonne Rainer
Bradley Grimshaw
Anri Sala
Ben Songhurst
Yinka Shonibare
Sarah Kaldor
Natasha Vickers
Art & Language
Eija-Liisa Ahtila
Ghada Amer
Janet Cardiff
Martin Creed
Eberhard Havekost
Koo Jeong-a
Cildo Mereiles
Vik Muniz
Rivane Neuenschwander
Cornelia Parker
Tino Seghal
Gary Hill
Fred Sandbank
Lygia Clark
Fischli & Weiss
Narcisse Tordoir
John Bock
Meg Cranston
Reverend Ethan Acres
Terry Allen
Jo Harvey Allen
Brienne Arrington
David Askevold
Lillian Ball
Cindy Bernard
Andrea Bowers
Delia Brown
Edgar Bryan
Chris Burden
Mary Ellen Carroll
Erin Cosgrove
Sam Durrant
Katharina Fritsch
Jonathan Furmanski
Jeremy Gilbert-Rolfe
James Gobel
Scott Grieger
James Hayward
Micol Hebron
Mark Kelley
Martin Kersels
Nicholas Kersulis
Martin Kippenberger
Rachel Lachowicz
Norm Laich
Liz Larner
Louise Lawler
William Leavitt
Barry Le Va
Jen Liu
Thomas Locher
Daria Martin
T Kelly Mason
Rita McBride
Carlos Mollura
J P Munro
Jennifer Nelson
Eric Niebuhr
Leonard Nimoy
Catherine Opie
Simon Patterson
Hirsch Perlman
Luciano Perna
Renee Petropoulos
Paul Pfieffer
Nicolette Pot
Rob Pruitt
Jonathan Horowitz
David Reed
Victoria Reynolds
Susan Rothenberg
Nancy Rubins
Glen Walter Rubsamen
Allen Ruppersberg
Pauline Stella Sanchez
Kim Schoenstadt
Gary Simmons
Alexis Smith
Yutaka Sone
Thaddeus Strode
Diana Thater
Mungo Thomson
Thorvaldur Thorsteinsson
Jeffrey Vallance
John Waters
Marnie Weber
Benjamin Weissman
James Welling

Eric Wesley
John Wesley
Chris Wilder
Christopher Williams
Stephen Wong
Mans Wrange
Mario Ybarra Jr

2005
Seraina Mueller
Seke Chimutengwende
Lali Chetwynd
Adam Wyner
Luke Fowler
Erica Burton
Ryan Gander
Renee Callahan
Christina Mackie
Francesco Cerminara
Timothy Chipping
Donald Urquhart
Seth Cohen
Wolfgang Tillmans
Richard Gill
Cerith Wyn Evans
Colin McLean
Jessica Morgan
Charlie Meyrick
Louise Neri
Linda Samuels
Beatrix Ruf
Adele Tomlin
Adam Carr
Louise Hojer
Dale Adcock
Robert Anderson
Diann Bauer
Simon Glendinning
Dave Beech
Kristi Harris
Pierre Bismuth
Emma James
Corine Borgnet
Carey Jewitt
Andrew Bracey
Annette Mees
Caroline Pelletier
Tom Chaffe
Amber Sealey
Jan Christensen
Jasper van der Kutjp
Adriana Marques
Layla Curtis
Jonny Blamey
Erica Donovan
Alexander Saphir
Matthew Green
Alan English
Sarah Emerson
Iram Quraishi
Michele Fletcher
Khalid Almaini
Tue Greenfort
Alexei Salikhov
Lorenzo Appetecchia
Rachel Goodyear
Iain Shields
Sam Gordon
Matthew Cook
Ellen Harvey
David D'Albis
Hrafnhildur Halldorsdottir
Tom Woolner
Michael Heym
Helen Nisbet
Richard Hughes
Elizabeth Leese
James Hutchinson
Martha Pym
James Ireland
Michael Cooter
Henrik Plenge Jakobsen
Fabio Paiva
Lawrence Lane
Ekow Eshun
Jim Lambie
Natasha Jacoby
Kit Lawrence
Toby Chris Messer
Cedar Lewisohn
Emma Quinn
Tor-Magnus Lundeby
Sian Gardiner
Paul McDevitt
Helen Mason
Adam McEwen
Sergio Gabriel
Jim Medway
Nick Luscombe
Jo Mitchell
Guy Perricone
Adrian Hermanides
Motomichi Nakamura
Lena Nix
Jeroen Offerman
Jennifer Byrne
Jonathan Parsons
Sarah Scarsbrook
Richard Priestly
Nicole Elias
Magnus Quaife
Redmond Entwistle
Ian Rawlinson
Neil Shields
Andrea Salvino
Merlene Walcott
Mark Titchner
Stefanie Pisu
Martin Vincent
Douglas Belford
Johannes Wohnseifer
Lianne Rooney
Neil Zakiewicz
Avril Furness
Toby Ziegler
Cristina Natalicchio
Nicola Chambers
Kathleen Meyts
Tom Morton
Catharina Patha
Gilane Tawadros
Catherine Wood
Pablo Bronstein
Sarah Carrington and Sophie Hope (B+B)
Catharine Patha
Richard Battye
Pablo Leon de la Barra
Christopher Keller
Josh Smith
Christopher Wool
Edgar Schmitz

2006
Kevin Bucknall
Jo Robertson
John Colbeck
Lucy Stein
Joe Schneider
Patrick Davies
Stefan Bruggemann
Max Perkin
Flavia Muller Medeiros
Samuel Perriman
Seb Patane
Max Rayner
Olivia Plender
Josh Redmond
Simon Popper
Fred Rowson
Jamie Shovlin
Jonathan Saffron
Daniel Sinsel
Tom Stewart
Matt Stokes
Samuel Verbi
Sue Tompkins
Andrew Brand
Bedwyr Williams
Mark Innes
Rajeev Seghal
Pamela Furness
Andrew Inkpin
Margaret Jackson-Roberts
Laurence McDonagh
Janánne Al-Ani
Marc Camille Chaimowicz
Jo Noble
Alexandre da Cunha
Michelle Papalios
Godfried Donkor
Annette Wookey
Ivan Grubanov
Katie Guggenheim
Bettina Brunner
Runa Islam
Stanley Glendinning
Matt Packer
Oswaldo Macia
Nadine Monem
Anna Hyde
Uriel Orlow
Sylvia Goodman
Zineb Sedira
Lee Scrivner
Joao Penalva
Kee-Nic Li
Hiraki Sawa
Alan Smith
Raqib Shaw
Clare Evans
Ben Woodeson
Andrea Jespersen
Erika Tan
Harriet Wailling
John Baldessari
Doug Aitken
Jussi Brightmore
Matthew Barney
Angelo Madonna
Mark Addams
Deirdre Kelly
Larry Clark
Pamela Jahn
E Fenton
Mark Hauenstein
Thomas Demand
Kate Wallace
Astrida Grigulis
Kelly Saxton
Raul Ortega Ayala
Olafur Eliasson
Viniita Moran
Danny Birchall
Douglas Gordon
Rodney Graham
Martine Rouleau
Beth Leese
Thomas Hirschorn
Charlie England
Patrick Coyle
Carsten Hoeller
Paddy Kernohan
Herbert Wright
Anish Kapoor
Richard Osborne
Ilya and Emilia Kabakov
Kate Crutchley
Christopher Rainbow
William Turner
Trevor Hall
Paul Sammut
Petya Manahilova
Ella Robson
Colm O'Reilly
Takashi Murakami
Ava Grauls
Isaias Pena Samboy
Olivier Castel
Chris Ofili
Kerry Andrews
Alasdair MacGregor
Elizabeth Peyton
Simon Noble
Soka Kapundu
Neo Rauch
Sion Parkinson
Rod Howells
Steven Lawrie
Catherine O'Connor
Santiago Sierra
Anna Privitera
Indi Davies
Rirkrit Tiravanija
Jessie Swisher-McClure
Kara Walker
Claire Gascoyne
Klaus Burgel
Lucy Brown
George Vasey
Corinne Calder
Hamad Butt
Rachael Maddocks
Laylah Ali
Marepe
Anna Schori
Edgar Cleijne
Ellen Gallagher
David Huffman
Hew Locke
Henna Nadeem
Kori Newkirk
Mario Ybarra Jr

2007
Tino Sehgal
Mark Sladen
Charles Atlas
Bodymap
Kate Cowcher
James Barnard
Lohan Emmanuel
Tim Hale
Michael Clark
Lora Findlay
Pat Gilbert
Duvet Brothers
Andrew Bainbridge
Nathaniel Cramp
Claire Jackson
Justin Hood
Gorilla Tapes
Silvia Tramontana
Anna Wood
Maria Georka
Mark McCullam
Simon Houghton
Sandra Lahire
Jane Dawson
Linder
Rebecca Gray
Stuart Marshall
Nesreen Hussein
Neil Bartlett
Alain Miller
Emma-Jayne Taylor
Neo-Naturists
Ruchama Hoed
Martin Bardell
Jon Savage
Deniz Unal
Jan Hofmann
Mark E Smith
Eleanor Reid
Elsa Aleluia da Costa
Trojan
Jennifer Milor
Daniel Somerville
Michael Bracewell
Yung Kha
Stefan Kalmar
Isabel Cruz
Ian White
Kenji Takahashi
Lida Abdul
Nathaniel Barbier
Kieran Begley
Roberto Ocete de Lima
Nick Edwardson
Chris Evans
Ivylin Hainsley
Matias Faldbakken
Marc Marazzi
Harrell Fletcher
Shelley Metcalfe
Sophie Risner
Erik van Lieshout
Andrew Lee
Nate Lowman
Amy Thomson
Michaela Miese
Roman Ondak
Katie Arnold
Collier Schorr
Keith McDonnell
Sean Snyder
Gemma Tortella
Jalal Toufic
Sarah Boris
Klaus Weber
Robin Andrews
Keith Wilson
Tomas Tokle
Samantha Morton
Martha Heiland-Allen
Sara Knowlands
Beth Ditto
Leah Lovett
Gareth Pugh
Andrea Dettmar
The Dirty Three
Graham Coxon
Richard Birkett
Mika
Michael Crowe
Idris Khan
Ian Bunney
Conrad Shawcross
Anna-Sophie Springer
Matthew Gordon
Zelda Cheatle
Grayson Perry
Dr Mike Phillips
Enrico David
Peter Hujar
Emily Wardill

2008
Abigail Ramsey
Christoph Schlingensief
Isla Leaver-Yap
Artur Zmijewski
Vicky Steer
Phil Collins
Karen Wong
Alys Williams

Barbara Visser
Francesca Astesani
Dora Garcia
Dominka Klimas
Joe Scanlan
Samuel Wilkin
Donelle Woolford
Ruggero Pantaleoni
Claire Bishop
Amy Budd
Loris Greaud
Thomas Jones
Kim Coleman
Amy McKelvie
Jenny Hogarth
William Davies
Boyle Family
Ania Vilinsky
Babak Ghazi
Zoe Franklin
Nina Canell
Anna Pinaka
Robin Watkins
Terence Lee
Aileen Campbell
Emilie Bell
Nicola Gallani
Scott Ramsay Kyle
Hardcore is More Than Music
Alastair MacKinven
Cristina Tarpey
Seamus Harahan
Michael Connors
Matthew Darbyshire
Tom Cox-Bisham
Maria Benjamin
Julia Dalby-Gray
Ruth Hoflich
Joel Trill
Clunie Reid
Trevor Giles
Anja Kirschner
Pol McLernon
David Panos
Marcia dos Reis
Jesse Jones
Martyn Francis
Emma Hart
Susan Friesner
Benedict Drew
Marcela Hajek
Alexander Heim
Graham Hudson
Mike Cooter
Ann Hunter
Anna Colin
Piers Jamson
Joe Scotland
Sarah McCrory
James Johnson
Emily Pethick
John Kamel
Nina Beier
Catherine Lawson
Marie Lund
Nikki Marsh
Claire McKeown
Andy Hewitt
Claire Moore
Mel Jordan
Beata Stelmach
Jurg Lehni
Penny Sychrava
John Tiney
Emily King
Heather Ward
Juliette Blightman
Devan Wells
Andrea Buttner
Chris Bird
Ian Evans
Alec Steadman
Sean Edwards
Thomas Kratz
Andrew Hunt
Erik Blinderman
Michael Eddy
Jonty Lees
Dr Paul O'Neill
Mick Wilson
Andy Wake
Will Holder
Kev Rice
Dave Smith
Thom Winterburn
Sally O'Reilly
Ben Roberts
Mel Brimfield
James Richards
Tris Vonna-Michell
Stephen Connolly
Iain Hetherington
Ursula Meyer
Lorna Macintyre
Ruth Beale
Hannah Rickards
Ilya and Emilia Kabakow
Michelangelo Pistoletto
Sarah Pierce
Giles Round
David Osbaldeston
Stephen Sutcliffe
Junior Aspirin Records
Ben Rivers
Maria Fusco
Alun Rowlands
Francesca Gavin
Eileen Simpson
Ben White
Matthew Noel-Tod
Mark Aerial Waller
Kathrin Bohm
Roberto Cuoghi
Garrett Phelan
Ruth Ewan
Gail Pickering
Torsten Lauschmann
Fiona Jardine
Duncan Campbell
Maya-Victoria Kjellstrand
Frances May Morgan
ELECTRA
Support Structure

This list of names has been compiled from ICA bulletin archives held at Tate (1948–1987) and from accountancy documents (2002–). It includes every person documented by the institution as having exhibited or worked within it, listed chronologically from the start date of the engagement. This list is incomplete and will be updated by the institution for as long as it can manage. Special thanks to Richard Birkett, Amy Budd, Alexander Dynan and Marcus Werner Hed at Pundersons Gardens, Pamela Jahn, Isla Leaver-Yap, and Elizabeth Manchester.

Essays

These essays were first published in the six *Nought to Sixty* magazines, in this order, between May and October 2008.

Some paradoxes and parameters

by Lisa Le Feuvre

At the heart of the Institute of Contemporary Arts is a paradox that has been embraced since its inception some sixty years ago. The ICA came into being in 1947, imagined by its founders – Herbert Read, Roland Penrose, ELT Mesens and Peter Watson – as a discursive site that would operate as "a laboratory rather than a museum".[1] The organisation deliberately positioned itself as both generative *of* and responsive *to* the present, existing as a hub of potential with an orthodoxy of disagreement and counter-argument. Naming itself, in an apparently contradictory way, as both an 'institution' and as 'contemporary', the ICA set out to be an alternative to what was deemed the dominant culture – at that time conceived largely as the Tate Gallery, the British Council and the Council for the Encouragement of Music and the Arts. The difficult double role of being a thorn in the side of the establishment while being a clearly identified institution has continued to define the ICA.

Initially the ICA used temporary venues for its activities, striving to challenge the conventions of art display – the first exhibition, *40 Years of Modern Art: A Selection from British Collections*, was held in the basement of the Academy Cinema on Oxford Street. In 1950 a building in Mayfair's Dover Street provided the organisation with its first permanent home, including offices, a library, meeting spaces and a small exhibition venue, while films and concerts continued to be staged offsite. During the 1950s the Independent Group were at the centre of the ICA's activities, coming together in 1952 as a result of debate over the organisation's visiting lecture programme.[2] This self-defined 'young group' – which included Richard Hamilton, Nigel Henderson, Eduardo Paolozzi, Alison and Peter Smithson and William Turnbull – started to invite writers and thinkers from a diversity of disciplines to develop questions, rather than answers, about contemporary culture in its broader context.

The exhibition *This is Tomorrow*, held at the Whitechapel Art Gallery in 1956, retrospectively drew together the Independent Group's concerns, and in the catalogue Lawrence Alloway boldly made the claim that the aim of the exhibition was "to oppose the specialisation of the arts... An exhibition like this ... is a lesson in spectatorship, which cuts across the learned responses of conventional reception".[3] Their intention was to break institutional conventions and challenge visitors' expectations in order to redefine a sense of the present. The group's experiments at the ICA – for example the 1953 exhibition *Parallel of Life and Art*, which displayed over a hundred uncaptioned images culled from heterogeneous sources – have now become historicised, but have continued to assert their influence on subsequent versions of the contemporary.

In 1968 the ICA moved to its current premises in Nash House, still holding strong to the laboratorial impulse and courting failure, instability and the unknown in an attempt to define the contemporary. Can, though, an institution really be contemporary? An institution is a collection of conventions, assumptions and behaviours that follows a preordained set of values, and institutions are famously slow-moving and mired with bureaucracy. There is an irony in associating the phrase 'nought to sixty' with an institution: it is generally used as a comparison for accelerative power, operating as a standard measurement of time for a vehicle to move from standing still to 60 miles per hour. The Ford Escort, for example, apparently takes 6.5 seconds and the Mini Cooper 8.9 seconds. Not necessarily an accurate tool, the phrase has slipped into vernacular in spite of inherent contradictions: the circumstances under which the measurement is taken will be rarely, if ever, replicated with normal driving. The 0–60 test has no interest in what happens before the countdown; the condition of the car after the experiment is irrelevant and the exhilaration of the driver and spectators merely a symptom.

How fast does one have to go to reach the contemporary? Once captured in language, the present is, tautologically, no longer contemporary – while the past is a dynamic concept constantly redefined through the present. As John Cage stated: "People still ask for definitions, but it's quite clear now that nothing can be defined. Let alone art, its purpose, etc. We're not even sure of carrots (whether they're what we think they are, how poisonous they are, who grew them and under what circumstances)."[4] Describing the present, or the contemporary, is an impossible task that involves a translation of individual experience, via language, to enable another to experience a moment in time indirectly. Such a communication will always be unsatisfactory.

Gertrude Stein speaks of the continuous present, suggesting that the world, and our knowledge of it, can only possibly exist in the present. Rather than creating constancy, this makes every experience unique and extended into space and time. Cage was a great admirer of Stein, and through his own extension of musical structures he created work that had no beginning, middle or end; instead he would initiate fields of sonic activity within which the listener would be called on to play an active role – in other words, a constant existence in the present. In a 0–60 test where does the present lie?

It surely cannot be at zero, as this is a moment of standing still, of certainty. Neither can it be at the moment where the mythical '60' is reached, as this is another predictable end point. The ambiguous present lies somewhere between the two poles, yet the present has no need to be defined in terms of progress – indeed in our contemporary present a celebration of progress seems obsolete.

If the 'C' for contemporary is impossible to define, can the 'I' for institute be discussed with any more certainty? In 1971 the artist Robert Morris developed a solo exhibition at the Tate Gallery that is a curious case study of the relation between these two concepts. The exhibition consisted of two parts – one an anthology of existing works and the other a series of objects for use that were "not primarily for looking at but for pulling and pushing, balancing on and climbing over, through or up".[5] After five days, 1,964 people had seen the exhibition, only for it to be closed as a result of overzealous participation – it subsequently reopened as a standard retrospective. Reflecting on this incident, the director of the Tate Gallery, Norman Reid, mused on whether Morris' experiment with objects was indeed too contemporary for the museum, suggesting "the [Tate] Gallery must adapt its methods, techniques and ways of dealing with the artist to the demands that the art raises, so long as it remains compatible in some degree with the purpose for which the Gallery exists".[6]

The stock characteristic of an institution is bureaucracy. The power of bureaucracy is in its emphasis on the *how* rather than the *what* of production, as encapsulated by the pair of copy clerks in Gustave Flaubert's 1881 novel *Bouvard and Pécuchet*. Following the inheritance of a fortune, the pair set out to increase their knowledge and, taking up residence in the countryside armed with an expanding library, they try their hand at experiments that include farming, medicine, museology, love, garden design and distilling alcohol – each one costing more than it should and ultimately ending in complete failure as they swallow reference books whole, refusing to analyse information or synthesise conflicting positions. Eventually their thirst for knowledge settles on the task of copying and cataloguing everything that comes into their possession, with no desire or use for any engagement with the content. (The emphasis on the 'how' can also be disruptive, of course – take, for example, the title character in Herman Melville's *Bartleby, the Scrivener* (1853), who responds to his institutional demands with variations of the phrase "I would prefer not to", in an incessant passive resistance to required and prescribed behaviours.)

An institution can be defined as a set of behaviours that have become normalised and accepted over time, and such conduct is often symbolised by a building-based organisation – a museum, school or hospital, for instance. The artist Andrea Fraser has described how "the institution is inside of us" – whereby the 'us' will always include the individual perceiving or producing the work of art.[7] Through habit and repetition, certain beliefs come to be perceived as facts and are oftentimes left unchallenged. However, if the institution cannot be avoided, it does not necessarily follow that to operate within a symbolic institution means a loss of urgency or agency. If the institution is to be considered an attitude, or set of attitudes, then it is imperative that ideas are constantly challenged. Flaubert's scribes take comfort in replicating institutional behaviour, and fail as a result. Could it be, though, that conditions of conduct have shifted to a place where an institution can be generative and responsive, where parameters are simply a point zero and agency is encouraged? The question today is less "how can the institution of art be avoided?" and more "how can it be shifted to something more productive beyond its own ends?"

At the time of writing, *Nought to Sixty* is still largely unknown other than by its basic parameters. It is a season across time as well as space, stretching from May to November 2008 and presenting solo projects by sixty artists based in Great Britain and Ireland. There will be exhibitions, events and interruptions – all demanding the attention of potential visitors for six months and including events on every Monday night within this period. It is a programme claiming to be a partial and subjective reading of the contemporary rather than a definitive measure, with announcements about participants made only a month in advance. The selected artists may contest, celebrate, annoy, extend, comply, make difficult, return elsewhere, disappear, replay conventions and create replacement conventions.

This experiment at times may not work, and may leave an audience standing around feeling a little embarrassed before rushing off to the bar. Some of the Monday night events may just have three people in attendance (although future historical anecdotes may tell a different story); others will have a line of impatient visitors snaking down the Mall trying to gain access. Visitors may get bored of their Mondays being booked up and declare that there is nothing new to be seen. The programme may confirm what people think they already know, or generate something quite unexpected. All that is known now is a set of institutional parameters, within which potentially anything can occur. So begins this subjective narrative of what the contemporary present might be.

Notes

1 See Tate Archives, which holds the archive of the ICA from 1947 to 1987.
2 See Anne Massey, *The Independent Group*, Manchester University Press, 1995.
3 Cited by Lynne Cooke, 'The Independent Group: British and American Pop Art, A "Palimpcestous" Legacy' in *Modern Art in Popular Culture*. M. Greenberg. New York, Museum of Modern Art, 1990, pp. 192–216.
4 John Cage, 'Diary: How to Improve the World (You Will Only Make Matters Worse)', *Aspen* number 4, 1966.
5 Press release for the exhibition, Tate Archives.
6 Barbara Reise, 'A Tale of Two Exhibitions: the aborted Hans Haacke and Robert Morris shows', *Studio International* 1971, pp. 30–39.
7 Andrea Fraser, 'From the Critique of Institutions to an Institution of Critique', *Artforum*, September 2005.

Notes on art criticism as a practice

by Pablo Lafuente

In a philosophical context, after Immanuel Kant, critique has come to identify a type of philosophy that does not search for causes or grounds, but tries to determine the possible conditions for a particular faculty or activity. If applied to the criticism of art, this 'critique of critique' would not result in art criticism itself, but in a philosophy of art that delimits what can be said about art or its experience or both.

This philosophy could establish what the object of art criticism might be (artworks, whatever might qualify as such, and their display in the form of exhibitions; or an aesthetic experience that constitutes its object as art); it would then determine what art criticism can and cannot do with this object; and it would conclude by constituting art criticism as a discipline in opposition to other disciplines and practices such as art history and theory, curatorial practice, art journalism, or film and theatre criticism. Having done this, a new canon could then be constructed, the discipline taught within an academic framework, and supporting structures developed for the professional practice of the discipline. Such structures would then defend the discipline from both external and internal attacks. However, none of this seems close to happening, and the level of disagreement about the object, methods, function, state and goals of art criticism remains extreme.[1]

At present art criticism is just a practice – one with an empirically given domain, engaging a considerable number of people who play more or less specific roles within a cultural sector that has significant business ramifications. Those practising art criticism often consider themselves to be in a professionally precarious situation, affected by working conditions that reproduce the flexibility of post-Fordist capitalism, and occupying a position of irrelevance (common complaints among art critics today are their loss of influence and lack of audience). The transformation of this practice into a discipline might establish foundations from which to address those working conditions, although that is far from guaranteed. These conditions are no worse than those affecting academically certified disciplines, both in the scientific and the cultural field, and they are considerably better than those from other professional sectors. Whether a 'disciplined' art criticism would bring with it a renewed influence and a wider audience is even more uncertain.

But perhaps this 'doubling-up' of critique in order to constitute art criticism as a discipline is wrong. Maybe it is best for art criticism to remain a practice. What is the point of embarking on a process of clarification, definition, stabilisation and institutionalisation of art criticism, precisely when art is involved in a process of blurring demarcated lines and eliminating distinctions? At the turn of the nineteenth century, early German Romanticism and French literary realism set up the grounds for a tendency that continues today by which the criteria for distinguishing art and non-art, and therefore those for distinguishing 'good' from 'bad' art, have vanished, despite recurring attempts to construct linear historical narratives and tight definitions[2]. Today anything can be art, and it can be art in any way. With the disappearance of criteria, the possibility of defining an audience disappears too. The bourgeois audience able to decipher codes and distinguish between 'good' and 'bad' is replaced by an 'anybody' who can experience the text, image or any other material if he or she is willing to do so. Knowledge is no longer the main factor, mere will is. As a consequence of this, everyone has in principle equal access to art, and equal ability to decide what qualifies as such and how it should be approached.[3]

However, after more than 200 years, this principle of equality has not done away with inequality within the field of contemporary art, as certain factors continue to define levels of access and identify the authorised voices. These include the definition of a modernist canon by art theorists in conjunction with cultural and governmental institutions and private capital, Anglo Saxon cultural and market dominance, or, more generally, a system of education, exhibition, exchange and discourse production shaped by public and private institutions and different interests in specific times and locations.

As participants within this system, the producers of art criticism today face practical questions with ethical and political implications – many of which are shared by others involved in contemporary art. They not only have to find a style, approach and genealogy to their practice, but also reflect on their desired level or autonomy in relation to art, its producers and others financially or institutionally invested in it. They have to guarantee an income (not necessarily from writing alone), while simultaneously discerning the role of art within society. They must decide who they are writing for but, before that, find a willing publisher. They have to work out what relationships to establish with art, artists and others involved, as well as determine the legitimacy of such associations, blindly guessing the effects any discursive material would have on art's production and reception. They must avoid exhaustion and, ideally, they should learn how to be truthful to the principle of equality by taking a position within concrete situations of inequality.

Is there a notion of critique that corresponds to this task, one that doesn't circumscribe what is possible but rather opens it up? Perhaps critique as intervention, as clarification of a critical point, and the establishment of a relation between this clarification and a decision. What is interesting about this conception is that it begins with a situation of crisis that demands intervention. The crisis is not something that takes place in a specific period or place within a linear history, but the permanent state of culture itself, as well as politics. If applied to the context of art criticism, this notion would displace the focus of critique from a task of definition and theorisation to one of action. And, through implied notions of crisis and productive/disruptive engagement, it would also dismiss any rhetorical lamentations for the current irrelevance of art criticism as a consequence of the dismantling of the bourgeois public sphere.

This text is clearly unable to offer an exhaustive account of the specific traits of this notion of criticism and address its implications in detail. Instead, it attempts to define the grounds of this practice and identify various approaches it opposes:

Independence and engagement

When used in the context of art criticism, the term 'independent' often stands in for 'freelance'. The financial constraints that a freelance critic experiences are different, but comparable, to those that a staff writer faces. Professional engagement with either the public or private sector results in a series of compromises that may have an influence in the practice of writing. However, these don't necessarily invalidate claims to a critical position. Perhaps this is a risky assertion at a time when advertising pages in art magazines have multiplied exponentially; publications are associated to commercial ventures; and some writers also work as museum and school directors and advisors to private collections. But the notion of the independent writer effectively functions as a screen to camouflage the real conditions of the practice. Instead of acting independently from the process of production and distribution, art criticism should be developed from a position of engagement with that process, establishing alliances and performing rejections. Engagement here doesn't mean continuity: the task of writing about the work is not the same as the task of making it or exhibiting it. In fact, the work made by the artist is not exactly the same work written about by the critic – the critic makes the work appear other than it is, producing a new work.

Division of labour and hierarchy

Recognition of the specific character of criticism does not imply a division of labour between artist, critic, curator or art historian. In fact, art criticism can be practised by anyone in the absence of any privileged positions. Different knowledge, sensibilities and approaches result in different criticisms, but no academic degree, no level of familiarity with the process of making, and no amount of knowledge alone makes one type of criticism preferable to another. (Art criticism, like art practice or politics, should be grounded on the assumption of the equal intelligence of all those looking at art, as well as those reading the text.)

Styles and methods

Accordingly, no particular linguistic tropes should be privileged over others. The 'knowledge effect' produced by academic writing is no better than the 'reality effect' that phenomenological or confessional writing brings forth, nor the 'communication effect' that journalistic writing aims at. The practice of one instead of the other is simply a matter of choice – perhaps by the editor as often as the writer – and none can be deemed to fall out of the remit of art criticism. Perhaps, and only because it betrays the principle of equality, mystifying writing of any kind should be rejected. This includes hermeneutic writing that looks for a hidden meaning, since it translates the artwork into something other than itself and limits its understanding to the search for a single meaning; normative criticism, which considers the artwork always preceded by an ideal model to which it must be referred back, therefore dismissing the work's specificity; or ethical writing, which proposes a debt of writer to artwork, artist or reader, moralising what is in reality a matter of will and turning art criticism into authoritative pedagogy.

Specificity and change

Choice of style, just as choice of subject, should be a function of the specific situation where criticism takes place. The crisis that art criticism is compelled to respond to is always concrete, as are artworks themselves. The response to the artwork and the situation of crisis around it must avoid universalisations, instead always accounting for that specificity. Criticism should not be an exercise in reporting, archiving or advocating either the old or new, but a productive contribution that constructs the subject of its discourse and aims to produce change. As an activity criticism is continuous with that of the artist who makes it, the curator or gallerist who exhibits it, the institution that hosts it and the audience that looks at it. And like each of these positions it produces a new version of the artwork, modifying its status and reach possibly in disagreement with the versions produced by the others. As the principle of equality implies, this change always already relates the art that is written about to its surroundings. Perhaps one of the key features of art, as defined by the tendency identified above, is that it constitutes a privileged place for showing how things can be different. Sometimes it can even do so by effecting change itself. Art criticism can play an important role in that process, not only by pointing at what art makes possible, but also by helping it in the process.

Notes

1 This is very clearly reflected by *The State of Art Criticism*, Eds. James Elkins and Michael Newman. London and New York, Routledge, 2008.

2 This conception is proposed by Jacques Rancière in books such as *La Parole muette. Essai sur les contradictions de la littérature*. Paris, Hachette, 2005; and *The Politics of Aesthetics: The Distribution of the Sensible*. London and New York, Continuum, 2004.

3 This democratisation of the field of art is parallel and contemporaneous to a democratisation of politics, when, after the French Revolution, the masses, the anybody – rather than the aristocrats, the property owners or the citizens – become the subjects of politics.

Emergence

by Paul O'Neill and Mick Wilson

Curatorial discourse and the contested trope of emergence

Dave Hickey, in a recently printed roundtable transcript, declares that his position on curating is that "the meaning of the show emerges from the show itself. The curator is a more or less inspired art herder".[1] He goes on to assert that "this is what curators are doing: they are flying around to national capitals, taking government-paid tours to look at government-approved artists that are biennial-friendly. Curating is a very corrupt discourse".

There are two issues of interest in Hickey's provocations. Firstly, there is the posited antagonism between art criticism and curatorial discourse as rival modalities in the discursive recuperation of art practice: curatorial discourse, as presented by Hickey, is in the ascendant position and therefore in need of debunking. Secondly, curatorial discourse is presented as aligned with the dynamics of a globalised art world, within which various national interests compete with each other for the attentions of highly mobile trans-national bearers of symbolic capital – this scenario is signalled through the figure of the travelling curator and the ubiquitous biennial.

However, there is a further point of interest in Hickey's remarks, and that is the way in which the rhetorical topos of 'emergence' operates as an anchor for authenticity. While curatorial discourse is declared corrupt, the self-actualising process of meaning-formation that emerges "from the show itself" is construed as uncontaminated: what is self-generated or emergent is the counterpoint to the inauthentic machinations of the 'art herding' curator.

Ironically, contra Hickey, this figuring of authentic culture as emergent and self-organised – rather than commissioned, prescribed or authored from elsewhere – is precisely one of the most important themes within the curatorial discourse of the last two decades, particularly in a European context. While it would be a gross distortion to present curatorial discourse as univocal and monolithic, it is still appropriate to note the recurrence of certain themes across the divergent debates and practices of curators in recent decades. One such theme is precisely the trope of emergence and the dialogical negotiation of artworks into public existence through the organic, open-ended co-production and conversation of artists, curators, artist-curators and other players. However, privileging the emergent as the locus of the authentic pre-dates the appearance of curatorial discourse itself.

In *Marxism and Literature* Raymond Williams constructs a triumvirate of "dominant, residual, and emergent" cultural moments.[2] While the dominant may be taken as read, residual cultural elements are those that operate at some distance from effective dominant culture but are still part of it. The residual comprises those cultural elements that derive from a grand tradition and are employed in legitimating contemporary social relations, while operating in a largely marginal space. Williams argues that this incorporation of the residual through "reinterpretation, dilution, projection, discriminating inclusion and exclusion" is the work of selective tradition. On the other hand, emergent cultural innovation comprises new practices that produce new meanings, values and kinds of relationships. Emergence is thus not the mere appearance of novelty: it is the site of dialectical opposition to the dominant – the promise of overcoming, transgressing, evading, renegotiating or bypassing the dominant – and not simply delivering more of the same under the blandishments of the 'new'.

Truly emergent practices, Williams argues, are difficult to distinguish from those that are simply new phases in the dominant culture and thus merely 'novel'. Practices that are emergent in the strict sense provide real alternatives to sanctioned cultural experiences, behaviours and values. What matters for Williams in emergent culture, as distinct from residual or dominant culture, is that – while it will always depend on finding new forms or adaptations of form – it contains an element of implicit or explicit critical dissent. There is of course a longstanding co-option of the rhetoric of emergence by the art market, as evidenced in the cliche of 'emergent artists'. This co-option makes the discernment of the 'truly' emergent all the more complex, engaging the uncertain dynamics of authenticity as both a point of resistance and a point of sale.

Arguably, curatorial discourse – or rather a specific sub-formation within curatorial discourse – has functioned as an important cultural matrix in recent decades. Curatorial discourse has enabled a range of critical innovations that contest the dominant culture across a number of institutional sites and practices – art education, art museums and galleries, biennials, public art programmes, urbanism and art publishing to name only some of the most prominent. In order to understand how curatorial discourse operates as an engine of emergence, it will help to consider the growth of curatorial discourse in its own right.

The emergence of curatorial discourse

Curating – a cultural practice once associated primarily with the care and selection of works for display, usually in the context of a gallery or museum – emerged in the late 1960s as a creative, semi-autonomous and individually authored form of mediation (and production). By the time Harald Szeemann curated Documenta 5, *Questioning Reality, Pictorial Worlds Today* (1972), the position of the individual curator had already opened up to wider international debate. This debate was accompanied by a shift of emphasis in the criticism of art: away from the primary critique of the artwork as an autonomous object of study; towards a mode of curatorial criticism in which the curator becomes a central subject of critique. The critical response to Documenta 5, for example, focused on Szeemann's alleged overemphasis of his own curatorial concept rather than on consideration of the artworks in the exhibition.

The idea of a curatorial remit operating above and beyond the interests of the artist, or the notion of the discrete art work, opened up a space of critical contestation – one which, ironically, reflected how artists were increasingly concerning themselves with mediation and the language of mediation, as they turned towards conceptual strategies – and began to address the curated exhibition as a cohesive cultural text. In this sense, the analysis of curating that developed in the 1960s, founded on the demystification of the art system – originating in opposition to the dominant order – became a discussion about the work of exhibition construction and its production of meanings and values. While for some, curating, even now, is yet to be fully established as an historical discourse and academic field of enquiry, it is clear that by the late 1990s the institutionalisation of curating was well underway: with the appearance of curatorial study programmes; the rise of nomadic über-curators, linked to the rising international biennial curatorial market; and the creation of a range of formal spaces for the discussion of curating. In the 1990s, in the English-speaking world, one of the main features of this new era was the development of publications specifically examining the histories of curatorial innovations and models, as well as their potential links to an evolving practice.

During this time, individual curators became the subject of discussion and a process of historicisation began to take shape, at the same time as major transformations were realised in contemporary curatorial praxis. As Helmut Draxler argued in 1992, the early 1990s were already being recognised as a period of institutionalisation for the curator, with the flourishing of curatorial training programmes following an initial "institutional shift in the course of the sixties, which [came] from a certain uneasiness with respect to the inescapability of museums as well as other exhibition institutions to react to new forms of expression in art".[3] What Draxler could not have foreseen was that the institutionalisation of the curator's function was only the first stage in the development of an expansive curatorial discourse – and an accompanying publishing industry – led by, and for, a new generation of self-conscious and reflexive curators.

In their introduction to *Thinking About Exhibitions* (1996), Bruce Ferguson, Reesa Greenberg and Sandy Nairne highlighted what they called "the emergence and consolidation of a new discourse on art exhibitions" and stated their intention to "bring into debate a range of issues at play in their formation and reception".[4] Their eclectic selection of texts focused mainly on twentieth-century exhibition histories – curating, exhibition sites, forms of installation and spectatorship – in an attempt to demonstrate how the discourse around exhibitions had changed dramatically since the 1980s and to show how, in the 1990s, "focus on art exhibitions was indicative of the political and cultural agency of so many of the debates centred on and fostered by exhibitions".[5] The impact of key exhibitions on the history of art had already been highlighted by Bruce Altshuler a couple of years earlier, when he claimed that the history of the avant-garde – from the early twentieth-century avant-garde through the vanguard of the 1960s – was characterised by a dialogue between a community of artists and the public, one based on acceptance and rejection, with "all participants enmeshed in systems of personal and economic relations".[6]

For Michael Brenson, the curator's moment had truly arrived by the mid-1990s, with the emergence of biennials, organised international meetings and curatorial summits:

> After listening to heads of international biennials and triennials speak to one another for three days about their hopes and concerns, it was clear to me that the era of the curator has begun. The organisers of these exhibitions, as well as other curators around the world who work across cultures and are able to think imaginatively about the points of compatibility and conflict among them, must be at once aestheticians, diplomats, economists, critics, historians, politicians, audience developers, and promoters. They must be able to communicate not only with artists but also with community leaders, business executives, and heads of state … The texture and tone of the curator's voice, the voices it welcomes or excludes, and the shape of the conversation it sets in motion are essential to the texture and perception of contemporary art.[7]

The expansion of curatorial discourse was accelerated by the advent of curatorial training programmes in the early 1990s. Students and programme leaders began to look at existing exhibition models and a relatively small number of established curatorial precedents, focusing on exhibition history and scrutinising the curatorial component instead of the artwork(s). Thirdly, since the 1990s, the discourse around the figure of the biennial curator has created a market for a nomadic type of global curator, during a time when new associations were being attached to curating, as a potentially creative form of cultural practice and as a possible career choice for artists, art historians, critics and art administrators.

The 1990s saw an attempt to formulate a new lexicon and rhetorical armature for curating as a diverse, internationalised practice. Through these articulations the individualised curatorial act became a central concept, but did so in a manner that also troubled the authorial function of the curator. Curating by the late 1990s and through the early 2000s had come to be represented as an adaptive discipline, using inherited codes and rules of behaviour. There is now a long list of metaphors that attempt to reconcile diverse modes of practice, with the curator envisaged as editor, DJ, technician, agent, manager, platform-provider, promoter and scout, or – more absurdly – as diviner, fairy godmother and, even, god.

Since the late 1990s, the discussion around curating has acknowledged the subjective and authorial nature of exhibition-making and the importance of a growing awareness of the curator's part in shaping exhibitions.[8] It is indicative of this that art magazines, over the past five years, have begun to focus on curatorial practice as one of their major subjects for discussion: discussions which have, in turn, largely been led by invited curators. One explanation for this focus may simply be that many critics and professional art writers are now primarily curators, but there are also other factors in play.

A parallel publishing industry has developed around the curator's enhanced visibility. The ubiquity of the curator, the relative absence of published material on the subject of curating and, most significantly, the growth of a new audience has meant that an ever-increasing number of curators, curatorial students and graduates are now in search of relevant material – thus generating a significant readership. The period of professionalisation experienced in the 1990s by curators and artists alike generated a new market and a newfound field of study, one centred upon the medium of the exhibition and those involved in its mediation. However, curatorial discourse remains diverse, so that the mainstreaming of this discourse does not exhaustively dictate its possibilities.

Curatorial discourse as an engine of emergence

One might be tempted to assume that this narrative of the appearance of curatorial discourse, and its newfound accommodation within the art journals, should now culminate in a moment of cultural dominance; however, this would be premature. Indeed, this is where Dave Hickey's declarations against curating are at their weakest: they are lazy and largely inattentive to the diversity of strategy and engagement manifest in the range of actual curatorial practice (it is notable again and again that in art criticism the curatorial function is crudely reduced to exhibition-making). For, if one looks, however summarily, at the diverse strategies that curatorial discourse has opened up, it is apparent that the discourse has operated as a rhetorical matrix providing for the appearance of a range of new and critical practices. And here we return again to this trope of emergence and the associated values of self-organisation and, indeed, the search for notions of authentic agency that escape the dead-end heroics of avant-gardism.

The argument we propose is that curatorial discourse has acted as an engine of emergence for a set of contemporary practices, ones that do not simply rehearse the marketing of inconsequential novelty. Curatorial discourse has done so by providing a diverse rhetoric of agency, which overcomes the flawed creator-genius machismo and heroic individualism of avant-gardism, while reinstating a sense of individual and collective agency through a range of animating metaphors and theoretical positions: from DIY culture to DJ culture; postproduction to informal networking; dialogical aesthetics to discursive practice. While the extensive and seemingly unending arguments of curatorial discourse have at times seemed tediously self-regarding, it is very important to reassert the potency of this speech in re-establishing, or at least bolstering, a coherent sense of agency in contemporary art practice; and in fostering frameworks for greater interaction with other disciplines and cultural practices.

This is not to say that curatorial discourse has been, or continues to be, a uniformly 'good thing'. Rather this is to assert that within the multiplicity of curatorial discourse many possibilities have opened – however temporarily and with whatever fragility – for cultural practitioners to forge practices of self-organised cultural dissent and creative contestation. In part these possibilities have been created by the emergence of alternative reputational economies that are not circumscribed by the market, and which are not necessarily destined to be 'cashed-in'. Paradoxically, these practices of self-organisation have been enabled in part by their ability to feed precariously from the margins of the market. The precariousness of dissent within a largely market-driven culture and society has required us to generate new rhetorics of impurity and contingency: curatorial discourse has generated – and will continue to generate – these enabling figures, metaphors and tropes.

Notes

1 *The State of Art Criticism*, Eds. James Elkins and Michael Newman. London and New York, Routledge, 2008.

2 Raymond Williams, *Marxism and Literature*, Oxford and New York, Oxford University Press, 1986 [originally 1977], pp. 121–26.

3 Helmut Draxler, 'The Institutional Discourse', *Meta 2: A New Spirit in Curating*, Stuttgart, Kunstlerhaüs Stuttgart, 1992, p. 18.

4 Reesa Greenberg, Bruce Ferguson and Sandy Nairne's 'Introduction,' in *Thinking About Exhibitions*, eds. Bruce Ferguson, Reesa Greenberg and Sandy Nairne, London and New York, Routledge, 1996. p. 2.

5 Ibid. pp. 3–4.

6 Bruce Altshuler, *The Avant-Garde in Exhibition: New Art in the 20th Century*, Berkeley and London, University of California Press, 1994. p. 8.

7 Michael Brenson, 'The Curator's Moment – Trends in the Field of International Contemporary Art Exhibitions', *Art Journal*, 57: 4, (Winter, 1998), p. 16.

8 Catherine Thomas, 'Introduction', *The Edge of Everything: Reflections on Curatorial Practice*, ed. Catherine Thomas, Banff, Canada, Banff Centre Press, 2000. p. ix.

We spoke about hippies
by Sarah Pierce

"At the risk of seeming ridiculous, let me say that the true revolutionary is guided by great feelings of love." —Che Guevara[1]

Recently I was with a curator friend and we were speaking casually about upcoming projects when she said, "Nonknowledge is my next thing." I realised that by 'nonknowledge' she meant it was the subject of an exhibition. As I listened to her plans for nonknowledge – the exhibition and her convictions regarding its promise – it struck me how certain institutional work requires us to project a level of certitude, despite our doubts about how to proceed. I have been struggling with a research topic for over a year, winding through an archipelago of ideas connected by rugged proximity rather than any grounded analysis. The institutional impulse to thematise difficult concepts and deliver them with ease, to effectively synthesise and 'do' knowledge without undoing *how* we know, is at the heart of this struggle. The longer I remain stuck in my archipelago, the more I want to disown this type of certitude in favour of multifaceted, complex ways of knowing. With this in mind, I am hoping to convey some persistent thoughts following a recent symposium at the ICA on the 'educational turn' in art.[2] Paul O'Neill and Mick Wilson organised the event. I was part of the panel. That it is difficult to adequately navigate this topic is at the core of my understanding of the potential of the educational turn. How we come to recognise this potential – without closing down its meaning – is what I hope to unfold here.

As an introduction to the issues in the symposium, Mick Wilson identified the educational turn in art as a piqued interest in contemporary art in education, defined as a preponderance of projects, exhibitions and ancillary activities that take on paradigms found in pedagogy to elaborate a cultural practice. Mick presented these as a counterbalance to mainstream art education. As formal art education in Europe undergoes a largely bureaucratic makeover, another space in contemporary practice outside the academy is making an appeal to alternative notions of the pedagogical. Instances of such appeals came in the form of large-scale projects, such as Manifesta 6, which initiated a temporary art school in Cyprus and was subsequently closed by the city of Nicosia; and Documenta 12, which cited education via one of the exhibition's three leitmotifs. In addition, Mick made reference to a rise in visibility of small-scale engagements concerned with pedagogy as a group encounter or durational space beyond the timeframe of an exhibition. The evening's discussion was proposed as an opportunity to take account of this activity as it was taking place, specifically to think about what is at stake in the turn to an informal educational praxis.

The panel consisted of five speakers: Liam Gillick, Andrea Phillips, Dave Beech and myself, with Adrian Rifkin as the respondent. Early on, Liam signalled a problem. The problem, to paraphrase, is this: *The productive potential of this educational turn does not rest on the moments when we stop to take account of it. Its relevance lies elsewhere, in other discussions.* It's not that we can't recognise an educational turn. We can. It's not that this educational turn doesn't call for analysis. It does. It's that when asked to account for its productive potential, we lose sight of our subject. We pivot our observations around formalised encounters like art education and we enlist what we know. We forget that this educational turn is not one thing. It is not one place or one time. In taking account, we circumvent what is at stake: *other discussions, elsewhere*.

In the August issue of the *Nought to Sixty* magazine, Emily Pethick referred to a number of projects that resist institutionalisation through an emphasis on discourse and exchange rather than on presentation.[3] I believe, as we enter a discussion of the educational turn, it is important to make a similar distinction between projects where education is a motif in an exhibition and those where the mechanisms of engagement are less easily recuperated as 'art'. Here, we can dismiss a whole set of projects where education appears 'on display'. While this might seem like a huge sweep, it is crucial to understanding exactly how prevalent this educational turn actually is or isn't. For example, although the curators of Documenta 12 identified education as a concern, it remained for the most part a thematic subordinated within the formalised structures of the exhibition. Yes, some kind of learning was taking place, but this rather facile observation weighs in lightly against extensions of informal education in contemporary art that dissent from the primacy of exhibitions. If we consider for just a moment what happened to Manifesta 6, we can begin to grasp just how precarious, how hard to come by and how lacking in support other, less visible activities actually are. Despite what appears to be a prevalence of activity, it is important to remember that we have to fight for the cultural, economic and political structures that support this activity; sometimes, despite our demands, the battle is lost.

When we discharge education as a curatorial 'trope' or aesthetic, we begin to understand the relevance of projects in contemporary art that are serious about the types of exchanges that are not possible, are effectively unavailable, through art's dominant mechanisms of 'display'. Not coincidentally, here we could simply expand on the list named by Emily of projects that resist institutionalisation, whose emphasis, as she puts it, "lies in discourse and exchange rather than presentation". I'll follow Emily's lead and extend the varied intellectual and non-academic paradigms set up through projects like 16 Beaver and Sarai, and by artists like Wendelien van Oldenborgh and Annette Krauss, to include a range of engagements that find the terms for locating social change in how we mediate learning and how we negotiate spaces for speculation and reflection. And suddenly, we are no longer just talking about contemporary art. We are opening our discussion to an expanded network of non-aligned projects that inhabit education as a *transformative practice*. The very behaviours by which we come to 'know' education begin to shift away from institutionalised notions of pedagogy and instruction towards something more convivial and expansive. It is perhaps useful to consider 'conviviality' as set forth by Ivan Illich, the Austrian thinker known for his polemical work on informal education, who enlists the term 'conviviality' to describe *a range of autonomous and creative exchanges among people*.[4] For Illich, conviviality is the opposite of manipulation, which is the dominant type of institutional treatment. Conviviality is humble and spontaneous, interpersonal and facilitating. It is here, in a distilling of the institutional impulse into something more mutual, reciprocal and interdependent, that we can recognise the productive potential of an educational turn in contemporary art.

I first began to feel this potential in 2004 with Annie Fletcher, when we began to think – without knowing at the outset what this might mean – about modalities and potentials in 'paraeducation' as a way to proceed through an exhibition. For us, paraeducation was a way to gather around certain urgencies without confining ourselves to an a priori event. As a counterbalance to debates that occur within institutional and educational settings – which hinge on the distance between speakers and listeners – paraeducation hinged on common points of reference reinforced as collectiveness. Pursuing the question of whether education is an activist position and thinking about how artists might organise in different situations, the Paraeducation Department developed along the lines of an affinity group. Affinity groups are self-sufficient support systems of about 5–15 people. A number of affinity groups may work together toward a common goal in a large action, or one affinity group might conceive of and carry out an action on its own. Sometimes affinity groups remain together over a long period of time, existing as study groups and only occasionally participating in actions. Affinity groups serve as a source of support and solidarity for their members. Feelings of being isolated or alienated from the movement, the crowd or the world in general can be alleviated through familiarity and trust, which develops when an affinity group works and acts together. Every affinity group must decide for themselves how they will make decisions and what they want to do. This process starts when an affinity group forms.[5]

In 1996, Tom Finkelpearl, then director of New York City's Percent for Art Program, interviewed Paulo Freire, the Brazilian educator and philosopher who emphasised informal education and dialogue as key components of a transformative 'educational process' – outlined in his seminal work, *Pedagogy of the Oppressed*. Finkelpearl noted the broad influence of Freire's methodology – not just on education but also on art (an influence that endures with even greater impact today) – and he asked Freire if he experienced problems with the application of his notions of 'dialogue' in other fields. Freire responded: "[T]he only way for one not to have this kind of experience is not to produce and not to think. The moment you make a proposal you risk both understanding and misunderstanding, distortion and respect."[6] Freire also noted that the response to misunderstanding is not for the speaker, in his words, "to commit suicide", but rather to use misunderstanding productively, as an opportunity to recompose one's ideas and declare one's position. This process of re-understanding requires testing information in both directions. Here, analysis is not the end point of a process, but proceeds somewhere in the middle of an ongoing exchange between speakers and listeners. A process of education based on dialogue involves thinking, shifting, producing, reflecting, imagining, displacing, observing, translating, leading and following in a generative manner that does not always move along one path; there are u-turns, diversions and distractions along the way.

As we negotiate what is at stake in the educational turn, perhaps we should think about the moments when we gather to take account of its productive potential. It still seems important to resist the institutional imperative to measure 'potential' through this type of legitimating exercise. At a certain point in the discussion at the ICA, the term 'nostalgia' came into play. First, it was in reference to exhibitions that use a pedagogical aesthetic to signal the kinds of reclaimed, equalised spaces found in popular education. Then, when Dave Beech cited civil disobedience as an example of grassroots organising that has particular resonance in art practice, one member of the audience wondered if this too tended towards nostalgia. What soon became clear was that nostalgia was a pejorative. It was a way to regulate certain expressions of desire in need of correction. This left us somewhat bereft. It seemed that nostalgia befit any practice that identified with education on any level. It is hard to answer why we needed to read the kinds of productive potentials we were dealing with as misguided *misreads* of past political situations. Was it to make their outputs more legible or less relevant? Either way, we obscured other perhaps more relevant and compelling conflicts in these practices. In the moments that we disavowed those who desire *other discussions, elsewhere*, we simultaneously dismantled our own productive potential.

Which brings me to a poignant moment in the evening, which Adrian Rifkin introduced, and which I will name here as:

The Marxist vs. the hippy

The Marxist arrives with politics intact, prepared and knowing the correct course of action to follow. The hippy arrives chaotically, unprepared, unknowing and distracted. Yet, really, the hippy knows everything and the Marxist knows nothing. With a sense of displaced nostalgia, Adrian longs to be the hippy, the one inscribed with the anticipation of not knowing anything while knowing everything. He mused, "I'm faintly nostalgic for what happens *next*, which is tomorrow ... because I want to see what it will contain and how we can rethink art and education in their unfixed and changing relations." What if we were to read the productive potential of an educational turn in anticipation of *what we may find out*, as opposed to *what we already know*? How might this allow us to speak about the things we love and believe in without feeling embarrassed, retrograde or fanatic?

While sitting outside on the UCLA campus last April, I observed a small group of students convene and begin an anti-war demonstration against the US occupation of Iraq. Carrying placards and with a megaphone at hand, they took turns calling out several rounds of chants as they strolled along the pathway that encircles the Arts quad. After a while, they concluded the protest and dispersed, giving each other hugs and kisses and high-fives. I suddenly felt like I was watching Epic theatre. Like a band of actors in Brecht's *Galileo*, the protesters momentarily suspended the scene of the academy, demonstrating the political as anachronistic ritual, available and remote at once. I was drawn in and confused: Do I get up and join the demonstration? Do I stay where I am? I happened to be on the campus to interview Mary Kelly for my research in relation to *Nought to Sixty*. Specifically, I wanted to ask her about *The State of British Art* debate, held at the ICA in 1978. In speaking about the event, which she remembered well, Mary noted that it was always acceptable in those settings to situate your political thought in Marxist theory, but as soon as someone tried to shift this to include gender, it was like a bombshell had been set off in the room.

As I write, I wonder about several projects that take on the tensions between pedagogical strategies and enabling fictions that condition how we know what we know – projects like Catherine David's *Contemporary Arab Representations*, Maria Lind's programme at the Kunstverein Munich between 2001–04, and Ute Meta Bauer's 2004 Berlin Biennial. Behind each of these extended curatorial projects is a tenacious insistence on shifting yet potent durational frameworks that involve research over a long period of time. Their focus is on minimally articulated, less visible and less visually orientated radical examples of political debates as they occur in *other discussions, elsewhere*. As with Manifesta 6, each of these projects is fraught with contradictions and questions that expose the inequities and territories of our own plurality. These questions, which Manifesta 6's curators invoked before being shut down, implicate all of us in the politics we deplore. It is not lost on me that each of these examples has been cast in some instance as a 'failure'. I suspect this has little to do with their inherent organisation and more to do with conventions of power that persist in contemporary art, where clearly demarcated and authored visibility makes for better career prospects. In a text that introduced the International Summer Academy in Frankfurt 2004, Marius Babias and Florian Waldvogel described the political motivation behind their idea of education as firmly grounded in a sociopolitical realm, where "knowledge has always been closely associated with conventions of power, institutions, pedagogy, ethics, and politics".[7] These associations are equally present in the socio-political realm of the art world.

During our interview, I mentioned to Mary the demonstration I had witnessed a few hours before. She smiled, which I read as approval. Not just for what the students were protesting, but for their organised presence on campus. It was our take on the students' experience of course, but we decided protest is better when it's fun.

Notes

1 Che Guevara, 'Socialism and man in Cuba', 1965, *The Che Reader*, Melbourne, Ocean Press, 2005.

2 Paul O'Neill and Mick Wilson, 'You talkin' to me? Why art is turning to education', 14 July, 2008, ICA, London.

3 Emily Pethick, 'Resisting Institutionalisation', *Nought to Sixty*, issue 4, August 2008, Institute of Contemporary Arts, London.

4 Ivan Illich, 'Tools for Conviviality', http://clevercycles.com/tools_for_conviviality [originally published New York, Harper & Row, 1973].

5 Sarah Pierce, 'Organising and Art Practice', *The Paraeducation Department Reader*, eds. Sarah Pierce and Annie Fletcher, Belfast, Interface, 2006.

6 Tom Finkelpearl, 'Paulo Freire: Discussing Dialogue', *Dialogues in Public Art*, ed. Tom Finkelpearl, Cambridge, MIT Press, 2000, p. 284.

7 Marius Babias and Florian Waldvogel, 'Political Art Practice', http://www.internationalesommerakademie.de/sak2004/en/03/00_01.htm

Resisting institutionalisation

by Emily Pethick

One of the described intentions of the *Nought to Sixty* programme is to focus on practices that are rarely represented in the institution, usually because they are 'conversational' and more closely linked to self-organised activity. This notion of conversation is closely related to some of the projects realised at Casco – Office for Art, Design and Theory, in Utrecht – during the time I worked there; these projects functioned as a way of thinking through different models of interaction, participation and collaboration.

Conversation generates forms of exchange that are not fixed or static but rather sustain ongoing processes of engagement, responsiveness and change. As Brazilian artist Ricardo Basbaum (who realised the project *Re-projecting (Utrecht)* with Casco in April 2008) describes:

> 'Conversations' are a way of thinking, where the self opens to the outside, producing a special social space where no single language of truth is prevalent. It enables the transformation of the voice of the other… 'Conversations' are a sort of dialogue that have their own dynamics, always surprising the participants… 'Conversations' succeed as a play-like situation, and involve a certain practice on how to keep yourself in a permanent state of awareness and change (flexibility). There's nothing specific to be achieved in a conversation, except that when the participants feel they are out of it – that is, when they finish a particular dialogue – they just cannot go back to the same places they left before (some transformation might have happened). Therefore, 'conversation' is a modality of movement.[1]

On the international cultural landscape there are a number of small-to-medium-scale contemporary art institutions whose emphasis lies in discourse and exchange rather than presentation. Artist-led organisations such as Sarai,[2] New Delhi, the recently closed Copenhagen Free University,[3] and 16 Beaver,[4] New York, are all examples of progressive models for small organisations. These spaces are sites for sustained critical inquiry, where the activities of artists, writers, researchers and other cultural practitioners can intersect, where discourse may build up over time and where new reflexive practices, methods and ideas can be developed in order to address the contemporary condition and to think about (or sometimes even enact) the possibilities for change, if only on a micro level. Perhaps the main qualities that distinguish these spaces – and other artist-led or grassroots organisations and small institutions – from more mainstream institutions is their commitment, sustainability and flexibility. These are also qualities that are fundamental to the makeup of Casco, both as I inherited it and continued to run it, and which I will continue to pursue with my new directorship at The Showroom in London.

Nina Möntmann has written about these types of organisations in relation to opacity, where the institution is a site of research and analysis that does not have to be immediately visible but is continuously at work in the background. As an attempt to work between engagement and autonomy, we tried at Casco to combine this kind of opacity with forms of openness by realising projects with artists that had multiple points of entry and layers of resonance. A number of projects had very public moments, or direct forms of activity that were often embedded in the city or were formed through collective processes that mixed publics. These sometimes began with a theoretical proposal or led to critical reflection, creating forms of feedback between practice and theory.

Copenhagen Free University described their activity as working with "forms of knowledge that are fleeting, fluid, schizophrenic, uncompromising, subjective, uneconomic, acapitalist, produced in the kitchen, produced when asleep or arisen on a social excursion – collectively". This approach is close to that of a number of Casco's projects that employed experimental or collective research processes and produced what might be described as unstable forms of knowledge. In particular, works produced through the involvement of many voices or forms of input – as opposed to the singular voice of the artist – were open to conflict, forms of disagreement and uncertainty, wherein conversation becomes a way of preventing a fixed representation.

Wendelien van Oldenborgh's *Maurits Script* (2006), produced by Casco, examined Dutch colonial history in North East Brazil and the often contradictory stories that surround the period. Van Oldenborgh's script comprises conflicting historical accounts of Maurits' governorship, and the film was shot in the renowned Dutch museum Mauritshuis, the house of Johann Maurits, governor of North East Brazil in the early 1600s. The actors, who each had a different relationship to the history of colonisation, read their scripted roles. However, during the screening of the film, which also occurred in Mauritshuis, these same actors appeared on the other side of the room, engaging in a live conversation about their own relationships to the legacies of colonial history. Participation in this discussion was open to the museum's public and, during this second staging, a new script was written. With the input of multiple voices, this second script was, at times, a contradictory reflection on the personal experiences of a multicultural society – it did not produce one single truth or perspective. In some respects this project performed what Irit Rogoff describes as "smuggling – an embodied criticality,"[5] where critical practice shifts away from a distanced, analytical mode and moves towards an inhabitation of a problem that is open to participation – in this case entering into the museum and destabilising its official narrative from within through conversation.

This sense of inhabiting a problem and opening it up through a conversational process also informed Annette Krauss' *Hidden Curriculum* (2007), produced by Casco. The project looked at forms of school-based learning generated outside the official curricula. During the three-month collaboration, two groups of teenagers critically addressed their own behaviour in the school environment. The outcomes of their investigations were then used to develop actions and interventions in the school and in public spaces. These actions sought to counter the normal routines of both environments, expose the hidden rule structures that exist in public and institutional spaces, and reveal codes of conduct of which students were previously unaware. In one example the students looked for a space in the school that was previously unacknowledged in their habitual use of the building. The students then entered the space and documented what they found, thus finding a parallel to the grey areas and holes in the forms of knowledge that they were investigating. This was extended to actions in public space, where students used their bodies to create barriers. Sometimes without realising it, members of the public were forced to alter their routines, sometimes in an imperceptible way that had an effect on others' movements. In this resistance to normalisation processes, *Hidden Curriculum* explored and exposed the boundaries of received ideas, both in terms of knowledge and common behaviour. What was important was not only the critical process of unpicking these codes, through a collective process within the school in order to find these unexpected spaces of learning, but also the way that the project emphasised the potential of challenging and changing the rules.

Dave Hullfish Bailey's project *What's Left to its own Devices (On Reclamation)* (2007), produced by Casco, also attempted to unravel conventional patterns in the way we read spaces and places. Bailey researched the manner in which public spaces are formed and the relations between the public and private spheres. The project drew comparisons between the highly structured city centre of Utrecht and Slab City, an ad hoc squatters' camp in the California desert. Bailey's experimental geography initially examined the role of hydrological processes in creating specific spaces of sociability and private retreat. This approach led him to find similarities between the narratives of individual freedom and communal living associated with Slab City, and the historical development of Utrecht, a city that arose from the collective task of managing a system of canals, and which has also been cited as an early model of democratic political organisation.

In Utrecht, Bailey discovered instances of people creating individual ways of inhabiting or occupying space. He discovered that an old man had been living in a van and a boat around the corner from Casco for over 30 years. Gerrit Rietveld's infamous Schröder House, meanwhile, was built on the outskirts of the city centre in the 1920s, in the style of de Stijl. The product of a collaboration between Rietveld and his commissioner Mrs Schröder, the ground floor was structured according to planning regulations, but Rietveld and Schröder designated the second floor as an 'attic', giving themselves freedom to experiment with utopian ideas of how to live.

Bailey focused on such micro-sites in both Utrecht and Slab City, drawing them together using non-linear heuristic methods to forge links across a range of subjects, both social and geographical, that were as varied as forms of sedimentation and accumulation, water diversion structures, barricades as tools of spatial control, DIY culture, and the social functions of books and libraries. The project highlighted the way in which things collect or gravitate towards one another, be they people, detritus or books, as well as ways in which people realise their individual freedoms within existing structures. Bailey's findings were tested in Manual Intuition and Makeshift Fashion, a group workshop that experimented with constructing devices that altered existing relations between public and private space, and examined what other ambiguous or unstable positions might be opened up. Not only did this challenge how the structure of public space is understood, it initiated a collective, speculative thinking-by-doing. As a consequence the project formed an activity-driven process, generating alternative ways of conducting research in opposition to purely cerebral, analytical or planned approaches.

These three aforementioned projects each negotiate institutional structures – whether those of the museum, an official history, the school or public space – rethinking existing relations and acknowledging that nothing is stable or fixed. Bailey describes his practice as an approach in which he disorganises and reorganises information in order to find new connection points. This activity of creating non-standard links between art and other fields is common in art practice, yet many art institutions have remained relatively isolated. Simon Sheikh describes the art institution as the "in-between, the mediator, interlocutor, translator and meeting place between art production and the conception of its 'public'."[6] Sheikh writes further, I would suggest, that we take our point of departure in precisely the unhinging of stable categories and subject positions, in the interdisciplinary and intermediary, in the conflictual and dividing, in the fragmented and permissive – in different spaces of experience, as it were. We should begin to think of this contradictory and non-unitary notion of a public sphere, and of the art institution as the embodiment of this sphere.

A definitive feature of Casco is that it is not conceived of as a gallery but as an open space, where many different kinds of activities and forms of work can happen both in and outside of the space – each changing the organisation and lending it a different character. At the beginning of a project there was no directive as to what form it might take, where it would resonate or its duration. In this sense we resisted any form of standardisation that might close down the possibility of what we could do. The funding situation in the Netherlands – where one has a starting budget for the programme – made this process much easier. In the UK, institutions have to fundraise for a much larger percentage of their income, as well as to satisfy the different demands of public funding bodies, private patrons and marketing departments. In some cases this has led to organisations becoming less flexible and more institutional. However, I believe there are ways to work within these circumstances creatively. It is possible to learn from artistic practices and self-organised, socially based networks, as well as other types of practices and debates. One is able to generate different types of relationships and forms of engagement with artists, publics and other collaborators, avoiding habit and routine through constant rethinking and reinvention. Certainly this is something that The Showroom will take as a challenge. With an imminent change of space, a move to a new area and many new sets of relations to explore, let us see what is possible.

Notes

1 Ricardo Basbaum, *Re-projecting(Utrecht)*. Utrecht, Casco, 2008.

2 Sarai – "a space for research, practice and conversation about the contemporary media and urban constellations."

3 The Copenhagen Free University opened in May 2001 in the flat of Jakob Jakobsen and Henriette Heise in Copenhagen. It was an artist-run institution dedicated to the production of critical consciousness and poetic language.

4 16 Beaver Street – a network of artists, curators, writers, thinkers and activists who converge on a regular basis at a space in Lower Manhattan to discuss issues, exchange ideas and raise questions.

5 Irit Rogoff, 'Smuggling – An Embodied Criticality', 2006, www.eipcp.net.

6 Simon Sheikh, 'Public Spheres and Functions of Progressive Art Institutions', 2004, www.republicart.net.

Not about institutions, but why we are so unsure of them
by J.J. Charlesworth

Anniversaries, especially those of institutions, often become opportunities for taking stock. This is true of the ICA in its 60th anniversary year; the programming of *Nought to Sixty* has sought to implicate itself in the dynamic of critical reflection and self-questioning that the arrival of the ICA's seventh decade has prompted. That process of critical reflection has been both explicit and implicit; explicit in the various events of dialogue and discussion that have been a key part of *Nought to Sixty*'s programme; explicit in the texts, like this one, published every month. And that process of critical reflection is implicit in the form of the programme itself – "60 projects, 6 months" – which, quite apart from being a good catchphrase, prompts a variety of questions: Why 60 projects? Why 'emerging artists'? Why shows that last a week? Why openings on a Monday night? In short, why present a programme of art like this and not any other way? And by extension, *Nought to Sixty* asks a bigger question: Why an institution of contemporary art(s) like this and not any other?

How to be an art institution today seems beset by a huge range of uncertainties and conflicting demands. Sixty years ago, there was not one institution in London that explicitly championed contemporary art. Today, it is the great galleries of old art that seem out of place and anachronous, and everywhere is a space for contemporary art. So the project that was the ICA – an institution explicitly committed to artistic culture that was speculative, independent and current, rather than hidebound by tradition and dominated by the sanction of the academy – is one which now seems to have been realised, and the ICA has become a victim of its own success. Instead of being driven by the need to represent forms of cultural practice ignored and unrepresented by the institutions that represented art, the ICA now finds itself to be just another 'venue' for that thing which it set out to make visible in the first place.

So, how to be not just another venue. If *Nought to Sixty* presents 60 projects in six months, this points to an ongoing critical dilemma about the function that institutions of contemporary art now perform. What does it mean to represent already current artistic practice today? This is no easy job, when much of the most self-consciously critical art of the last decades has called into question the relationship – between art and its public – that is produced and perpetuated by this thing called the art institution. In her essay for *Nought to Sixty*, curator Emily Pethick describes her approach to her job as curator of Casco in Utrecht, the defining feature of which "is that it is not conceived of as a gallery but as an open space, where many different kinds of activities and forms of work can happen."[1] Her discussion of the projects she developed there shows how far one can go from the standard idea of a 'gallery', where particular objects and works produced elsewhere are brought for presentation to a public.

Nevertheless, the presentation of works produced elsewhere is still, by and large, what goes on in these spaces we once used to simply call art galleries. Yet one paradoxical aspect of the debate over alternative definitions of what can go on in an art gallery, or 'art space', is that such alternatives inevitably return to being 'presentations', however much they attempt to redefine the relation between work and public *away* from presentation and spectatorship. 'Presentation', it could be argued, isn't a relationship produced between people and certain types of *artwork*, but is rather a type of relationship between people and an *institution*, produced, in largest part, by the institution itself. That's why the ability to present is itself a form of power.

That power, however, is rarely alluded to explicitly. To a cynical observer of the art world, it can appear as if all institutions that 'present' are involved in a similar business of inclusion and exclusion. While the power of that business is an unspoken given; institutions appear merely as passive presenters of what is 'best' or 'most innovative' in artistic practice, while obscuring or hiding the fact that institutions make choices about what not to present, exerting power over how artistic practices are made visible.

This 'behind the scenes' character of presentation is the actual relation of power that exists between artist, institution and public. It's this form of relationship that leads institutions to various habits of deferral of responsibility in the way they explain the choices they make. Often this responsibility is passed to some other institution – artist X has had previous shows in one or other major exhibition / biennial / museum, which becomes justification for another show elsewhere. This form of serialised artistic career, where an artist can move from one institutional presentation to another, highlights how homogenised the culture of presentation of contemporary art has become, in the sense that many institutions replicate the same attention to certain artists once their significance has become unquestionable. (In this regard, the reputation economy of much of the art world uncannily mirrors that of the art market, where artworks are seen as investments whose value should only go up, not down.)

The active aspect of institutional choice becomes more visibly unstable, however, when it addresses that thing called the 'emerging artist'. What is an 'emerging artist'? Where do they emerge from and what do they emerge into? This is an obvious preoccupation for a programme such as *Nought to Sixty*, which offers itself as a mediator of a thriving scene of artists in the UK and Ireland who have not had "significant commercial exposure". *Nought to Sixty* draws instead "on a network of artist-run initiatives". Again, the legitimacy of such a programme is based on the sanction of a constituency elsewhere – the network of artist-run initiatives – and the process of presentation becomes a job of facilitating the communication of this pre-existing constituency to another one; that of the ICA's public. There is of course a lot of truth in this, even though what remains unspoken are the many exclusions and omissions that are always part of such programming. But the paradoxical aspect of such formulations of art as 'emerging' is that responsibility for art emerging is assigned to itself, or to any other agency other than the institution that in fact enables its emergence. We could argue that nowadays the institutions of presentation of contemporary art are strangely uncomfortable with openly declaring the power that they do in fact wield. I may be wrong, but the Independent Group, so central to the establishment of the early ICA, did not claim for itself the description of 'emerging art'. What it did claim was the legitimacy that came from championing an art that related to contemporary experience, rather than the institutionalised conventions of a culture rooted in the past.

Emerging art only emerges if powerful institutions allow it to. It is obvious, for instance, that art that cannot be sold will not emerge out of the 'institution' of the commercial art market. Public institutions have the option to either merely reflect the conditions of presentation of the commercial art system, or instead to sponsor and support different forms of artistic practice and presentation. Since the late 60s, ambitious art has massively extended the definition of what can be presented within the institutional sphere of art; that expansion of artistic possibilities was assisted by – is in fact synonymous with – the progressive expansion of semiautonomous public venues for new artistic production such as the ICA. The acknowledgement of the role of the contemporary art institution in *producing* an art scene, and not merely representing an already existing one, lies behind many recent discussions regarding curatorial practice and the role of the curator, especially the role of the curator-as-author.

But curiously, what is largely absent from those discussions is an acknowledgement of the curator as someone who wields power and makes substantial decisions of inclusion and exclusion. Curator-as-facilitator, curator-as-DJ, curator-as-artist – what these well-worn tropes have in common is the persistent disavowal of the purely *institutional* character of the curator's power. It may be that an artist can curate and that a curator can make art, but – until all artists are in charge of their own personal art space – the categorical distinction between artist and curator remains an institutional one, governed by an inequality of access to resources. This is the real power of the already-existing institutions of contemporary art. It was the concentration of power in the hands of certain institutions that provoked the formation of the ICA (and subsequently the Independent Group). A couple of generations later, it was a similar concentration of power that drove the explosion of artist-run initiatives that characterised the London art world of the 1990s. With the rising cost of property in the last decade, that dynamic has largely disappeared from the London art scene, shifting from non-commercial spaces to commercial spaces, and from the artist-run space to the artist-run event – including the performance evening or screening programme. It is not coincidental that the period of decline of the artist-run space is also the period in which the role of the curator has expanded. But it also the period in which institutions of art presentation have become increasingly homogenous and interchangeable, directed to an increasingly mainstream public, while the process of decision-making becomes increasingly professionalised and opaque. This is no coincidence either. What distinguishes the art institution today is its relative distance from the community of practising artists (or rather, the separation of *the latter* from those institutions that directly represent them). In contrast to earlier institutional formations such as the original ICA, the usual contemporary art institution's programme is no longer governed by a close association with a group of artists or mutually interested practitioners.

As the ICA goes through a period of self-scrutiny and revision, how might it rethink itself, in a crowded market of identikit public spaces for contemporary art that its own long history has helped to shape? Staying close to young artists, being implicated in their 'emergence', and acting as a first port of call for ambitious new art is a good place to start. But if that process is to distinguish itself from the 'scene' of other similar institutions – each with their programmes of presentation that appear ready-made, and yet all strangely similar – it needs to go further. Rather than merely present the emergent as if the institution has no hand in the matter, the case should be made for an institution that is argumentative, that openly discusses the choices it makes and the art it chooses to represent.

Rather than a taste-maker institution that serves up its own version of the 'contemporary' to an otherwise casual public, this imagined institution would not only present, but re-present: shaping the attention of practitioners and non-practitioners alike through discussion of the questions that drive the shifting tendencies of the art scene; and harbouring what it disagrees with, as much as what it agrees with. Such strategies would openly reveal the power and partisanship that all institutions wield, rather than hiding them behind a false and inscrutable neutrality. In these ways the institution would avoid becoming 'institutionalised'. Recomposed of active, conflicting publics of practitioners and non-practitioners, a forum for opinion and opinion-former, it might solve the apparent contradiction of being an institute for the contemporary.

Notes

1 Emily Pethick, 'Resisting Institutionalisation', *Nought to Sixty*, Issue 4, August 2008, Institute of Contemporary Arts, London.

Gazetteer

Artist-run, independent and non-profit spaces, publications and organisations have long been fundamental to the emerging art scenes in Britain and Ireland, and much of the research for Nought to Sixty *was informed by the work of such organisations and the knowledge of the individuals who run them. These bodies are often financially precarious or deliberately transient, but their activities are of great importance in defining a territory distinct from commercial galleries and regularly-funded institutions. Documenting projects across the two countries, and written by those involved, the listings below offer a partial map of a highly diverse network of activities and resources.*

ARC
www.artcardiff.com

Artist Resource Cardiff (ARC) is an artist-led, non-profit web hub for anyone with an interest in contemporary art in Cardiff. Created as a response to a wealth of unrecognised initiatives and isolated groups, ARC helps promote artists' activities, facilitate collaboration and develop new networks nationally and internationally. ARC sees the flux of ideas and their development as vital for a creative ecology. The organisation does not acknowledge any hierarchies; it nurtures the aspirations of the visual arts community through a free online resource. Launched in February 2008 – with a Contemporary Art Pub Quiz by artist Louise Short – ARC is currently developing a programme for critical debate on contemporary art in Wales.

auto-italia
1 Glengall Road, London SE15 6NJ
T: 07748 505172
www.autoitaliasoutheast.org
info@autoitaliasoutheast.org

auto-italia is run by three artists and is in its second temporary site, a large disused car showroom on the Old Kent Road. This space has been donated for a couple of years, and is used as studios, living space and a gallery. auto-italia programme one show each month. For the remainder of the time the space is negotiated between the artists working with auto-italia. We host talks, screenings, shoots, and have flexible studio space for projects while remaining a free resource, with no need to fulfil funding criteria or to sell work in order to operate. The first show in this new space – *EPIC* – was a cross-section of 50 artists involved in this critical peer network, examining the space as a future context for making work, and as a starting point for new networks.

A.Vermin
5 Oban Court, Flat 3/1 Glasgow
T: 0141 946 4468
www.avermin.org
info@avermin.org

Initiated in 2006, A.Vermin is an ongoing artist project, a curatorial venture and a platform for emerging artists. Under the pseudonym A.Vermin, Alhena Katsof hosts site-specific exhibitions of new work by artists who do not typically work in this mode.
A. Vermin's programme functions as a platform for conversations about current contemporary practice and our everyday relationship to art. The act of hospitality is an essential part of A.Vermin – it elevates the creative process implicit in bringing people and ideas together through a series of social experiences grounded in visual practice. Exhibitions primarily take place in the A.Vermin flat and, during Glasgow International 2008, in The State Bar. Recent exhibitions include work by Baldvin Ringsted, Ben Merris and Stina Wirfelt; a recent project featured work by Amélie Guérin-Simard and Anna Mields.

Aye-Aye Books
c/o CCA: The Centre for Contemporary Arts
350 Sauchiehall Street
Glasgow G2 3JD
T: 07946 643 757
www.aye-ayebooks.com
martin@aye-ayebooks.com
A contemporary art publisher and bookseller based in Glasgow and Salford, Aye-Aye's aim is to propagate publications that are independent, intemperate, indigenous and intercontinental. In 2006 Martin Vincent moved to Glasgow from Manchester, where he had been co-director of the International 3 gallery and i3 Publications. In Glasgow, he found a city with plenty of galleries, loads of artists, but no specialist art bookshop. i3 was re-branded as Aye-Aye Books, and, in collaboration with Sapna Agarwal, Vincent opened Aye-Aye Book Depot – a year-long independent bookshop/project space at Glasgow Sculpture Studios. With one foot in England at the Aye-Aye Sorting Office, Islington Mill, Salford, Aye-Aye's transnational publications programme has recently dispensed books by David Mackintosh, Rachel Goodyear, Edwina fitzPatrick and Esther Shalev-Gerz. It now has a new retail base, Aye-Aye Book Kiosk in Glasgow's CCA, and a new website under development, which will provide a comprehensive resource of books by Scottish artists. Aye-Aye's next project is to build some more shelves.

Bad Bad Boys Club
42 Blinshall Street
Dundee DD1 4JJ
www.badbadboysclub.com
mail@badbadboysclub.com

Seeking to go beyond the confines of institutional structures, Bad Bad Boys Club is an independent contemporary art organisation that supports artists in project-specific enterprises. Currently self-funded, BBBC abstains from the typical economy of the artist-led organisation. Founded in Rotterdam in 2005 by artists Steven Cairns and Andy Wake, BBBC works with artists and collaborative groups at various stages in their careers to facilitate the production of new work in a range of environments. It supports artist residencies and collaborates on curatorial projects with other organisations. Running parallel to its ongoing programme, BBBC is producing a publishing portfolio comprising visual, audio and textual research in relation to its exhibition programme and those of associated artist organisations. Recent projects include Conal McStravick, BBBC's artist-in-residence, and a screening featuring work by Luke Fowler and Henry VIII's Wives.

Between Bridges
223 Cambridge Heath Road
London E2 0EL
www.betweenbridges.net

Between Bridges is a non-commercial gallery in Bethnal Green located in the entrance of Wolfgang Tillmans' studio. It primarily, but not exclusively, exhibits artists who through their work show a strong interest in the larger society they live in and who have used their voices as artists to get politically involved. Between Bridges also sees its role to exhibit artists whose work might not be shown in commercial galleries or established institutions. Previous shows include Wolfgang Breuer, David Wojnarowicz, Sister Corita, Charlotte Posenenske, Isa Genzken's *Ground Zero (2)*, The Center for Land Use Interpretation and Wilhelm Leibl.

Black Dogs
www.black-dogs.org

Set up in Leeds in 2004 as a reaction against art-school inertia, Black Dogs is now an expansive regional project open to anyone who wants to celebrate the minor and the absurd in everyday life. Self-funded and wholly independent, the group seeks to promote dialogue between artists and audiences, and to establish constructive relationships with local communities. Most recently, the Dogs held *Gallery Giveaway*, an audience-led participatory event at The Dazed Gallery, London; and an exhibition of ongoing solo projects at 42 New Briggate Gallery, Leeds. *Consequences* (produced in association with Axisweb) was the group's first foray into the murky work of internet-based art; *The Black Dogs Almanacs* provide a printed record of group work; while *I can do it* – recently published for the launch event of the Leeds Independent Music Exposition – is a DIY manual extolling the virtues of ostensibly minor skills and personal pastimes.

Blaengar
www.blaengar.org

Blaengar is an Aberystwyth-based not-for-profit arts organisation, whose principal objective is to provide a forum for dialogue and collaboration. Formed in 2006 by a small group of emerging artists, Blaengar aims to stage events and exhibitions outside the traditional gallery space, and the projects – which include performance, installation and new media – take place in the landscape and built environments of mid-Wales. Previous projects include *Interaction*, an exhibition of public art surrounding Aberystwyth's promenade and museum (which will be continued in summer 2009); and *Spoilio*, a site-specific work at Llywernog Silver and Lead Mine near Ponterwyd. More recently Blaengar staged a site-specific installation in partnership with Ceredigion Museum and a local youth group; and an international project with three Balkan artists, touring to Croatia, Serbia, Italy and Wales.

Broadcast
Portland Row, Dublin Institute of Technology, Dublin 1

Broadcast is a Dublin-based gallery set in Dublin Institute of Technology (DIT) School of Art. Programmed by a team of DIT staff members – including Mark Garry, Ronan McCrea, Linda Quinlan and Jesse Jones – Broadcast enables a situation in which criticality and learning are fluidly integrated into the educational process. Programmed workshops and lectures parallel the concerns of the artist presenting work, with a specific focus on concepts of knowledge and how artists occupy the space of research. A presentation of Anja Kirschner's film *POLLY II* (2006), for example, prompted a conversation between the artist and Maeve Connolly, creating an opportunity to discuss the politics of speculative development and artists' strategies within commissioning processes.

Butcher's
http://butchersprojects.org
butchersprojects@gmail.com

Founded in July 2008 by curators Ben Borthwick and Cylena Simonds, Butcher's provides a platform for a network of artists, designers and other creative producers to develop projects, share resources, and exchange services using the economic model of bartering. There are no fixed members or sites of presentation, but shifting affiliations depending on available resources. Projects may materialize as exhibitions, performances, publications or any other format depending on the aesthetics and concept. As the name suggests, Butcher's is committed to working with the high street as part of the everyday fabric of communities. Projects in 2008 included works by Tim Etchells and Brazilian artist Marcos Chaves in a shopfront window in Camden. In December 2008 Butcher's presented *A Brush for Robben Island*, a sound installation by Emma Wolukau-Wanambwa.

Canal
canalonvyner.blogspot.com
canalonvyner@gmail.com

Canal formed in May 2006 with the aim of presenting a range of activities including discussions, screenings and performances. Originally based in a dedicated space on Vyner Street, East London, it is now a peripatetic organisation hosted by different venues according to the project in hand. As an informal group of artists and curators, Canal acts as a framework to generate a programme which is not exhibition-led, and which incorporates practitioners from other fields in addition to the visual arts. Canal is Anna Colin, Matthew Darbyshire, Sarah McCrory and Olivia Plender. It has worked with Simon Martin, Phyllida Barlow and Elinor Jansz among others. Hosted by venues including Peer, Between Bridges and AK28, Canal worked on a series of projects for the Whitechapel Gallery's one-year offsite project, *The Street.*

Catalyst Arts
2nd Floor 5 College Court, Belfast BT1 6BS, T: 028 9031 3303
www.catalystarts.org.uk
catalystarts@gmail.com

Catalyst Arts was formed 15 years ago and – despite chronic underfunding – is one of Belfast's most significant artist-led organisations, best known for challenging the formal structures of curatorship. Realising experimental projects that break the mould of the artist-audience relationship, the organisation presents art as something to engage with or react to rather than something to consume. Catalyst runs the oldest biennial performance art festival in Europe, and during its existence it has hosted over a thousand artists at varying career stages from Northern Ireland and beyond. Catalysts' ethos is fundamentally non-profit and members-based. The gallery is run on a voluntary basis by a committee of co-directors. A directorship lasts two years, ensuring Catalyst's vibrant and youthful energy. Thus, Catalyst never learns from its mistakes and completely avoids stagnation. Recent and forthcoming presentations include *Open Studios* (November–December 2008), a solo show from Ursula Burke (April 2009) and *Fix09* (September 2009).

Cell Project Space
258 Cambridge Heath Road
London E2 9DA, T: 020 7241 3600
www.cell.org.uk

Cell is a self-funded organisation based in Bethnal Green, founded and run by artists Milika Muritu and Richard Priestley. Cell's studio complex includes an exhibition space; and as part of the organisation's commitment to the professional development of artists, Cell's key aims include offering a high level of curatorial, administrative and practical support to exhibitors; while hosting a range of talks, screenings and events which run alongside its exhibition programme. Increasing links with institutions and galleries overseas, Cell has realised projects from the Netherlands, Korea, Japan, Poland, Germany, Denmark, and the USA. As part of a unique collaboration, Cell has also hosted the Jerwood Artists Platform, showcasing ambitious solo exhibitions and site-specific projects.

Centrefold
www.rezaaramesh.com
info@rezaaramesh.com

Centrefold is a limited edition publication in scrapbook format, with a print run of no more than 60 copies. Born in 2003 from a curatorial project entitled *Wooden Hearts*, *Centrefold* is a low-tech cut-and-paste production. For each issue artists are invited to treat one or two pages as their own scrapbook; while a writer/historian/curator or artist is usually invited to produce the centrefold. All the pages are then complied, formatted, and designed – the latter by Reza Aramesh, or in collaboration with a guest artist. *Centrefold* attempts to record a non-linear (local) art history through the view of an artist (Aramesh), rather than echo how art is recorded and fictionalised by art historians. The title of each scrapbook is taken from a socio-political issue at the time of its production.

The Changing Room
Tolbooth Jail Wynd, Stirling FK8 1DE
T: 01786 274005
www.stirling.gov.uk/changingroom
changingroom@stirling.gov.uk

Established in 1997 in response to the growing network of contemporary arts organisations within Scotland, The Changing Room is the only organisation of its kind outside the main cities in Scotland's central belt. The gallery focuses on supporting emerging practice while also bringing work by more established artists to Stirling. The Changing Room's programme has featured early career solo exhibitions – with artists such as Nathan Coley, Victoria Morton and Duncan Marquiss – alongside group projects such as *Tender Scene* (2007), with Fiona Jardine, Alex Pollard, Clare Stephenson and Gregor Wright and *Concrete Shadows* (2008) with Kate Davis, Lucy Skaer and Catherine Street. The gallery's location offers a unique critical space for artists from the UK and further afield to develop new work, and the organisation supports professional development for local artists, runs an education programme and commissions critical and creative writing. The forthcoming programme includes Katy Dove and Luke Fowler's research project, using the University of Stirling archives of filmmakers John Grierson and Norman McLaren.

City Projects
www.cityprojects.org
info@cityprojects.org

A visual art commissioning agency and research centre based in Homerton, East London, City Projects was set up to facilitate ambitious research-based or long-term projects by contemporary artists and organisations. Run by Dan Kidner and Kate Parker, past commissions include Chris Evans and Graham Fagan. City Projects' most recent commission is a film by Phil Coy, *Wordland* (2008), screened in London and Norfolk, which features a live soundtrack composed and performed by Alexander Tucker.

Collective Gallery
22–28 Cockburn Street, Edinburgh EH1 1NY, T: 0131 220 1260
www.collectivegallery.net
mail@collectivegallery.net

The Collective Gallery was established in 1984 as an artist-run space that supported and promoted emerging practice. Since then the organisation has become a pioneering exhibition, commissioning and development agency that supports new work and connects artists with diverse communities. Over two decades the Collective has built a reputation for its consistent support of relevant, socially-engaged and challenging projects through its regular exhibition programme: including *New Work Scotland Programme*, which spots and supports new ideas by emerging artists; and *One Mile*, a three-year programme introducing groups and individuals – who live or work within a one-mile radius of the gallery – to artists, in order to facilitate work of mutual interest.

Commonplace Amateur Projects
10 Burgh Quay, Dublin 2
www.commonplace.ie
commonplaceprojects@gmail.com

Commonplace Amateur Projects (CPAP) is a multiple-use project space located in Dublin's city centre. CPAP allows artists time and space to articulate interests that go beyond notions of amateurism and productive behaviour. Founded by artist Sally Timmons, the organisation has three areas of programming, including a city centre meeting and workspace, regular workshops and projects. It began commissioning artists' editions in September 2007; has featured solo projects by artists Karl Burke, Andrew Salomone and Paul Timoney, as well as the group project *Take me back to Trinidad*; while future projects include Projector Collective, Human Resources, David Beattie and Sarah Browne. Artists and curators visiting Dublin are encouraged to use CPAP as a base for meetings or projects.

Eastside Projects
86 Heath Mill Lane, Birmingham B9 4AR, www.eastsideprojects.org
info@eastsideprojects.org

Eastside Projects is an artist-run, non-profit experimental public space. As an incubator for ideas and forms, it develops a new type of physical space alongside a complex evolving programme of commissioned works and events based on radical historical positions. Eastside Projects is examining the potential of cumulative projects across its programme, within a constantly evolving architectural space and in collaboration with invited artists and the founding members. Eastside Projects was formed by artist-curator Gavin Wade, artists Ruth Claxton, Simon and Tom Bloor, designer James Langdon and architect Celine Condorelli.

Elysium Artspace
41 High Street, Swansea SA1 1LT
T: 01792 641 313
www.elysiumgallery.com
elysiumgallery@yahoo.co.uk

Elysium is a volunteer-run artists' space situated in the rundown high street of Swansea city centre. Opened in September 2007, the gallery is committed to exhibiting and promoting the work of emerging artists from diverse disciplines. Elysium fills a cultural gap in Swansea, which now has a base for artists to promote freedom of expression, experimentation and critical appreciation. There are two exhibition spaces: the basement for experimental studio and film projects, and the main gallery space on the ground floor. Elysium accepts proposals for exhibitions, one-off events, film, music, performance, installation – and all ideas! Elysium Artspace is a non-profit organisation, sponsored by nobody and therefore answerable to nobody.

The Embassy
www.embassygallery.co.uk
embassygallery@hotmail.co.uk

The Embassy is an Edinburgh-based, non-profit, artist-run space dedicated to supporting emerging artists; it has worked with artists such as Jenny Hogarth, Kim Coleman, Alasdair Gray, Marcus Coates and Brandon Vickerd. Through the gallery's diverse programme of exhibitions and events, it provides a platform for inspiring local and international artists to exhibit and meet. Run by a rolling committee that changes biennially, continual change fuels the gallery's development. As The Embassy prepares to move to new premises, the gallery's reputation as a dynamic Edinburgh art space is central to the current committee's vision. The relocation is an opportunity for The Embassy to redefine and develop, not only as a gallery, but also as a resource for an active audience.

E:vent
96 Teesdale Street, London E2 6PU
T: 020 7613 0300
www.eventnetwork.org.uk
info@eventnetwork.org.uk

E:vent was established in 2003 as an artist-led project space with the aim of presenting contemporary culture including art exhibitions, installations and performances, music, film and video, art research projects, workshops and talks. Located in the East End of London the project attempts to exploit the potential of the experimental event focusing on the role of agency and action to find alternative and progressive ways of communicating art. E:vent's fundamental politics are microscopic, migrating, minimal gestures; instances of talk and encounters; and the diagrammatic nature of spatial potentialities (towards architecture and abstraction, the non-figurative, and the musical score).

Exhibitions Department
Duncan of Jordanstone College of Art and Design, 13 Perth Road
Dundee DD1 4HT
T: 01382 385330
www.exhibitions.dundee.ac.uk
exhibitions@dundee.ac.uk

Based in Duncan of Jordanstone College of Art and Design, Dundee, Exhibitions Department is dedicated to working with contemporary artists, designers and cultural practitioners from the UK and abroad, while supporting teaching activity and developing significant opportunities with staff and students. Run by curator Jenny Brownrigg and assistant curator Laura Simpson, it manages a number of spaces, including Cooper Gallery, which features four major curated shows each year and comprises emerging and established contemporary practitioners; meanwhile Lower Foyer Gallery is committed to student-led projects. The innovative programme of exhibitions, performance, seminars, artist talks and outreach aims to explore the creative, social and educational impact of contemporary arts practice. Previous shows include Tim Knowles and Torsten Lauschmann's *The Autonomy of the Object* (2007); and *I Gave You Life* (2007), with Erica Eyres, Nathalie Djurberg, Eri Itoi and Kirsty Whiten. Exhibitions Department, with School of Fine Art, is currently co-hosting a two-year residency for *Map* magazine.

Feint
feintis@gmail.com

Feint is an artists' fanzine that commissions writing and reviews alongside new artworks. Published by Vaari Claffey and edited together with Isabel Nolan, *Feint* often includes gifts of original artworks. It operates using a system of exchange – no money changes hands. *Feint* has featured artists and writers such as Liam Gillick, Garrett Phelan and Falke Pisano, while previous issues include 'Keep Plugging Away – Action and Commitment' and 'Yes Yes Yes No No No – Commitment and Ambivalence'. Recent inclusions are 'Vanity Fair City' and 'Sorrow', the motivating quality of sadness and depression, and *Be not solitary, be not idle*, a series of two-person exhibitions. *Feint* is published sporadically rather than periodically and favours the personal over the professional. It is supported by graphic design agency Language.

Fieldgate Gallery
14 Fieldgate Street, London E8 1NG
www.fieldgategallery.com

In early 2006, artist-curator Richard Ducker and Sonya Park transformed a 10,000-sq-ft disused warehouse in Whitechapel into one of the largest artist-run contemporary art project spaces in London. With the aim of showing emerging artists alongside more established names, Fieldgate Gallery has presented a series of diverse and dynamic shows. Although unfunded, the gallery supports the artists and curators it works with in kind, including a comprehensive website. Being a non-commercial space, the gallery allows ambitious, experimental projects to be realised. Recent exhibitions include *Bass Diffusion Model* (May–June 2008) as well as work by Terry Atkinson, Stuart Brisley and Tim Head (June–July 2008).

Fire Station Artists' Studios
9–11 Lower Buckingham Street, Dublin 1, T: 353 1 8069 010
www.firestation.ie

Located in the North East district of Dublin's inner city, Fire Station Artists' Studios was established in 1993 by the Arts Council to address the needs of professional visual artists. It provides combined live/work studios for Irish and international artists, sculpture workshop facilities for large-scale work, as well as training, talks and master classes for artists. Uniquely placed on the doorstep of Dublin's city centre, Fire Station is an integral part of the local community, delivering projects that innovatively engage with communities of professional artists and contributing to debate around participatory arts practice. Fire Station encourages visual artists to apply for its residency at the above address and online.

Five Storey Projects
www.fivestoreyprojects.com
fivestoreyprojects@googlemail.com

Five Store Projects is a non-profit curatorial collective that stages exhibitions, events, interventions, and various methods of critical thinking, pursuing an engagement with the spatial environment. *Matter of Time* at James Taylor Gallery (December 2008), was its first exhibition and featured new works by fifteen artists, who were asked to engage with the building's materiality, history and location. Events included a sound piece, talks and walks by artists and a panel discussion with leading art critics.

Flax Art Studios
44–46 Corporation Street, Belfast BT1 3HA, T: 028 9023 4300
www.flaxartstudios.org
info@flaxartstudios.org

An artist-run organisation founded in 1989, Flax Art Studios is located in the heart of Belfast's creative quarter. Supporting contemporary practice through the provision of subsidised physical resources and a unique working context, Flax Art is funded by the Arts Council of Northern Ireland and Belfast City Council. In June 2003 Flax Art's premises in Edenderry Industrial Estate were destroyed by fire. This disaster – which completely destroyed the contents of the building, including facilities and artwork – was not the end for the organisation. Instead it was taken as an opportunity to take stock and move on. Six programmes now take place each year: the International Artist in Residency Programme, hosting four artists annually by open submission; an exchange programme with the Institute for Contemporary Arts in Celje, Slovenia; an exchange programme with KHOJ in New Delhi, India; a Graduating Student Residency programme; as well as ongoing research and community outreach projects.

Focal Point Gallery
Southend Central Library
Victoria Avenue, Southend-on-Sea
Essex SS2 6EX, T: 017 025 34108
www.focalpoint.org.uk
focalpointgallery@southend.gov.uk

From its unassuming setting on the second floor of Southend Central Library, Focal Point Gallery (initiated 1991) is transitioning to a regional curatorial laboratory exploring the potential of the wider Thames Gateway. With an accent on lens-based media within the expanded field of contemporary art, the gallery presents projects which aim to scramble history and memory, questioning the current status of 'the centre' and 'the periphery'. Artists for 2009 include Alastair MacKinven, Clunie Reid, Milly Thompson and Tris Vonna-Michell. Interrogating forms of recalcitrant optimism, and with local and international partners, Focal Point Gallery aims for a paradigm shift in its audience's perception of contemporary social and political reality. They urge you to run from London and join them.

FormContent
347 Beck Road, London E8 4RE
www.formcontent.org

FormContent, a curatorial project space situated under the railway tracks in the East End of London, was founded in 2007 by Francesco Pedraglio, Caterina Riva and Pieternel Vermoortel. Occupying a space of about 40 sq m with a 5m-high brick arch, FormContent has been shaped as a testing ground both for the curators and for the artists involved. The programme has comprised solo exhibitions, collaborative projects and group shows, with a pace of approximately one new project every six weeks. It is a process-based endeavour and often practicalities can shape the conceptual focus of the projects. The urgency to tackle curating and the importance of developing a dialogue with the invited artists are at the core of FormContent's intentions.

FOUR
119 Capel Street, Dublin 1,
T: 086 365 1256
www.fourdublin.com
fourgallery@gmail.com

Since its inauguration in November 2005, FOUR has been devoted to the development of an uninhibited exploration of ideas, discourses and trends in contemporary art. The organisation's function is to promote and support the artists and curators who take part in its evolution. FOUR recently acquired a new space on Capel Street, Dublin, which will feature a bookstore and a video and audio archive. The new site houses two gallery spaces. For 2009 FOUR will present solo projects by Lyndsay Mann and Mark Hamilton and a curated show by Caoimhín Mac Giolla Léith.

Framework
frameworkcontact@yahoo.co.uk
www.myspace.com/
frameworkswansea

Framework is a Swansea-based artists' collective, which was launched in February 2007 with *Bring Music Bake Bread*, a social action at Mission Gallery, and which has since staged exhibitions, residencies and artists' discussions. Framework seeks to build a sense of community for artists in the South Wales area, and to facilitate support for individual practices. *Framework Social*, a monthly event held in a working men's club, provides a space to show multidisciplinary live and interactive work. Framework encourages small, grassroots activity in Wales, and favours a sustainable art scene. Its recent endeavour has been *Annexe*, an exhibition of unselected work from 2008's National Eisteddfod in Cardiff.

g39
Mill Lane, Cardiff CF10 1FH
T: 029 2025 5541
www.g39.org
post@g39.org

g39 is an artist-run organisation based in the heart of Cardiff. Part gallery, part community and part resource, it was founded by artists Chris Brown and Anthony Shapland in 1998. g39 has organised 60 exhibitions to date, both at its main location and in temporary sites throughout the city. The organisation has curated projects internationally at other galleries, acting as an important showcase of work from Wales, as well serving as a conduit for work from further afield. The space has recently developed WARP, an artists' resource programme, under the direction of Sean Edwards. The g39 anniversary show, *If You Build It, They Will Come* in 2008 – a retrospective (of sorts) of the last ten years – featured new works from Gordon Dalton, Jennifer Savage, Bedwyr Williams and George Henry Longly, among others.

Gallery of Owls
27 Woodbridge Road, Moseley
Birmingham B13 8EH
www.galleryofowls.org
galleryofowls@googlemail.com

Gallery of Owls is an artist-run, non-profit initiative directed by art group Owls. Following their difficulties in finding spaces to make and exhibit work in Birmingham, Owls decided to use short-term spaces and to adapt to changing environments, anticipating that one day the gallery will find a permanent space. Owls is dedicated to having creative input with each event and generates unconventional collaborative exhibitions that bring more activity and excitement to the Birmingham art scene. Its current method of creating events is to absorb new artists into the group with each project, and create work that is spontaneous and circumstantial. Consequently Owls is a fluid group – anyone working within the Owls context is an Owl. Owls also release a regular fanzine entitled *GZEAN*, which showcases a variety of illustrative, collage and photo imagery. Gallery of Owls currently resides in Moseley, Birmingham, and will be moving to occupy various venues throughout the city.

Generator Projects
25–26 Mid Wynd Industrial Estate
Dundee DD1 4JG
T: 01382 225 982

Generator Projects is an artist-led initiative that has been an integral part of the Dundee art scene for 12 years. The project is run by a rolling committee of volunteers that is refreshed biennially – precluding any 'house style' – and is partially funded by Dundee City Council and the Scottish Arts Council. Generator assists emerging artists by facilitating the production of new work, providing a vital support network and a space to create and exhibit. A non-profit organization, Generator is able to ensure that participating artists have complete creative freedom and are able to make work that stretches the boundaries of contemporary art and culture.

Glasgow Sculpture Studios
145 Kelvinhaugh Street
Glasgow G3 8PX
www.glasgowsculpturestudios.org
info@glasgowsculpturestudios.org

Glasgow Sculpture Studios (GSS) is a centre for research, production, presentation and dissemination of contemporary sculptural practices. Established in 1988 as a membership organisation, GSS now plays a crucial role as a resource and forum for artists, providing subsidised studios, production and research facilities. Complimented by exhibition and residency programmes, GSS hosts talks and artist-led projects both on and off-site, supporting a community of emergent and established artists. Recent programmes includes residencies with artists Beagles and Ramsay and AHM (aka Sam Ainsley, David Harding and Sandy Moffat) alongside graduate fellowships.

Grey Area
31 Queens Road, Brighton BN1 3XA
www.thegrey-area.blogspot.com

Grey Area is an independent artist-run gallery in the centre of Brighton. Established in a dilapidated basement in March 2006, it has become a platform for experimental art events. The gallery's rapid programme explores concepts of squatting, fictional space, historicism, and sites of Otherness. Artists who have exhibited at Grey Area include Delaine Le Bas, Cathy Lomax, Mally Mallinson and Shaun Doyle, Pil and Galia Kollectiv, and Bob and Roberta Smith. Events at Grey Area are listed on the website and in *Vacuum*, an art paper that was formed in partnership with the Permanent Gallery.

Hats Plus
101b Kings Cross Road, London WC1X 9LP, Hats Plus is open on Fridays, Saturdays and Sundays

Hats Plus is not a gallery
Hats Plus likes parties
Hats Plus likes the Rebel
Hats Plus is open from 12–6
Hats Plus also functions as an artist's studio
Hats Plus is a not-for-profit space
Hats Plus likes Marcus Selg
Hats Plus does not like most East End galleries
Hats Plus likes some
Hats Plus does not like Munters
Hats Plus likes JJ
Hats Plus is at 101 Kings Cross Road
Hats Plus is run by artists
Hats Plus likes Isa
Hats Plus is free
Hats Plus likes Woolf
Hats Plus likes boys
Hats Plus likes Natalie Price
Hats Plus likes music
Hats Plus likes film
Hats Plus exists
Hats Plus is not a platform to somewhere else
Hats Plus is a nice place to be for a time

The Hex
27 Sandgate House Pembury Road
London E5 8JH, T: 020 7165 4699
www.hexprojects.org
hexprojects@gmail.com

The Hex is a project space located in the spare room of a flat in the Pembury Estate, Clapton. Each show is a solo commission, with new work produced for the space. The artists can then invite others to take part, and they are free to use any part of the flat for their exhibition. During the course of the programme, the shows take place both within the flat and in the surrounding environs of the estate. The programme also features a number of offsite projects which have run concurrently with the main shows. Artist's projects featured at The Hex include Vanessa Billy with Alex Heim and Carl June, Charlotte Thrane and Anthea Hamilton, Sam Porritt and Tom Chamberlain, and Anne Lowe.

iam
www.informationasmaterial.com
simon@informationasmaterial.com

information as material was established in York in 2002 to publish work by artists who use extant material: who select and reframe such material to generate new meanings; and who, in doing so, disrupt the existing order of things. iam's catalogue includes books, prints, documentary film and audio works, and its imprint activities involve exhibitions, online projects and lectures. Alongside several new book works are a one-hour documentary film, *Making Nothing Happen*, on the work of Czech artist Pavel Büchler, which will be released in 2009. iam's publications are edited by Simon Morris and Nick Thurston, and distributed internationally by Cornerhouse (UK) and SPD (USA).

i-cabin
Clarendon Buildings, 11 Ronalds Road, London N5 1XJ
Bransford Hollow, Worcestershire.
T: 07813 764937
www.i-cabin.co.uk
info@i-cabin.co.uk

I regularly contribute, on i-cabin's behalf, to the debate on current exhibition practice and I am often asked to comment on the notion of the artist-run space. It seems that the term is sometimes used as a substitute for a serious attempt at a worthwhile artistic agenda in that it acts as a synonym for 'alternative' or 'emerging'. In our increasingly lightweight creative culture the latter two terms read as inherently valuable in the search for the next big thing. Organisations believe that credibility can be gained by being seen to be, or to support, artist-run and emerging practices. I want to be clear that artist-run spaces, in many cases, fail to be any better than other galleries in nurturing artistic strategies of cultural importance and are not in themselves a sign of something important taking place. However, thanks to the research by Elena Serpotta, I am now beginning to remember that artist-run spaces are an economic and managerial scenario based on absolute necessity and artists' entrepreneurial drive to improve things for/by themselves. —*Sebastian Craig*

Intermedia
350 Sauchiehall Street
Glasgow G2 3JD

Intermedia gallery plays an unusual but vital role in the Glasgow's visual arts scene. Opening in 1992 on King Street, next door to Transmission Gallery, Intermedia is now based in the CCA. Run by Glasgow City Council (now Culture and Sport Glasgow), Intermedia stands apart from other organisations in the city. In the past 16 years, Intermedia has shown artists such as Kate Davis, Fiona Jardine and Alan Michael.

Irish Artist-led Archive
www.theartistledarchive.com
info@theartistledarchive.com

The *Irish Artist-led Archive – Sustainable Activism and the Embrace of Flux* is an archival project, touring exhibition and online resource conceived and developed by Megs Morley, a practicing artist and curator. The project forms an ongoing investigation into artist-led initiatives in Ireland over the last 30 years. Posing an alternative approach, it examines the development of the visual arts in Ireland through a turbulent era of political, social and economic change. The project uses a variety of live archiving strategies to initiate dialogue and debate about artist-led culture, including roundtable discussions, performance artworks and word of mouth. Through the process of dialogue and exchange, artist-led groups have the freedom to continually develop and engage an evolving representation of their activities, rather than presenting a fixed definition of themselves within a permanent archive.

Locws International
16 J Shed, Kings Road
Swansea SA1 8PL
www.locwsinternational.com

Locws International works with international artists to create temporary visual arts projects for public spaces across the city of Swansea, projects in which place and context are integral, and which employ a broad variety of locations. Recent projects include Locws Projects 08, in which Wales-based artists Jennie Savage and Richard Higlett created new works for the Swansea Festival of Music: Savage presented audio stories from the city in response to the expansive Swansea Bay; while Higlett put together a canine choir to perform a musical concert to commemorate local hero Swansea Jack. Locws International 4, planned for Spring 2009, will see ten international artists create temporary works in public sites.

Lowsalt
www.lowsalt.org.uk

Lowsalt is an artist-run, non-profit organisation that has been occupying alternative spaces in Glasgow since early 2006. Based primarily on an ongoing 'open call for submissions', Lowsalt's programme aims to capture the spirit of an independent, creative community by encouraging artists and collectives to take greater control of the infrastructure and context of each project. Recent Lowsalt projects include a free screen-printing workshop, a drawing battle on overhead projectors, inflatable sculptures in Glasgow's public spaces, and an experimental promenade street theatre. Lowsalt's goal is to promote the processes of multidisciplinary art within the context of a broader cultural scene and to build new relationships among the diverse creative activities and identities in Glasgow and beyond. Lowsalt is run by artists Krisdy Shindler and Rebecca Anson.

Mermaid & Monster
www.mermaidandmonster.com
mail@mermaidandmonster.com

Based in Cardiff, Mermaid & Monster is the first and only contemporary art agency in Wales, formed in January 2007 by artists Gordon Dalton and Richard Higlett. Representing artists at various career stages, both locally and internationally, Mermaid & Monster develops gallery and off-site projects, takes artists to international art fairs and works with them to produce limited edition prints. Recent presentations include Year 07 at County Hall, London; *Loners' Island*, at g39 Cardiff; and the *Rotate* exhibition at the Contemporary Art Society, London.

Miss B's Salons
www.ruthbeale.net/salons

Cher Monsieurs et Madames – mes amis et collègues of great refinement. Miss B's Salons are discussion events which might, at different times, entail presentations, recitals, readings, film screenings and workshops. There is a loose theme around self-initiated projects, DIY approaches and artist-curators. The first series of six salons, supported by Artquest's Forum programme, welcomed a core group of invited artists and curators such as Melanie Carvalho, Ben Roberts and Spartacus Chetwynd. Miss B now works in collaboration with different hosts at each venue – galleries, pubs, homes and studios – to curate each event. Victuals and libations are provided where possible. Attendance is generally by invitation, but new guests will also be received. Past locations include Limoncello, Transition and the Wenlock Arms. Miss B welcomes offers and ideas to collaborate from potential hosts. *Salutations distinguées.*

Moot
1 Thorseby Street, Nottingham NG1 1AJ, www.mootgallery.org
mootinfo@gmail.com

Opening in October 2005, Moot was keen to establish its outward-looking perspective by working with local and international artists, combining a program of solo and group exhibitions, off-site activities, and publications such as *The Long Take*. Moot seeks to act as a middle ground between discovery and gallery representation, working with artists such as Jack Strange, Jonty Lees, Sean Edwards, Morag Keil and S Mark Gubb. Established as a not-for-profit organisation, money from sales goes back into the exhibition and commissioning programme. Moot recently opened its new space in the ground floor of a grand four-storey warehouse. Working alongside Stand Assembly, three floors are dedicated to workspaces for artists and curators. The building is the first artists' workspace in Nottingham since the legendary Midlands Group to combine such diverse practice and activity in the city.

no.w.here
1st floor, 316–318 Bethnal Green Road, London E2 0AG
T: 020 7729 4494
www.nowhere-lab.org

Formed in 2004, no.w.here is an artist-run project space. no.w.here's screenings, debates, publications and exhibitions engage artists in thinking about their practice, and create a dialogue between the moving image and other art forms, ideas and contexts. no.w.here's East London lab supports artists with a unique set of film facilities and equipment, along with workshops and residencies. Recent projects include *Cinema of Prayoga* – a major touring programme of Indian artists' film/video, *Instructions for Films* at Zoo Art Fair 2007, and collaborations with Camden Arts Centre, The British Library, Yorkshire Sculpture Park, Tate Modern and Serpentine Gallery.

Occasionals Studio
15.3 1–15 Cremer Street
London E2 8HD
www.occasionals.co.uk
info@occasionals.co.uk

Organised by Philomene Pirecki, Occasionals is an artist-run project space where artists, writers and curators present their work in a single day or in an evening event. Including work still in the making as well as previously unexhibited, Occasionals offers an opportunity for participants to show work and test out ideas in an informal but public situation. Previous participants have included Juan Cruz, Ian Whittlesea and Andrew Chesher.

Ointment
www.ointment.org.uk
post@ointment.org.uk

Formed in 2001 and based in West Wales, Ointment is an itinerant artists' collective – of six visual artists, performance artists and dancers – that responds to environmental and rural change. Over the last six years the organisation has developed a place-sensitive language of ideas, performance and images, in conversation with local and international audiences. Projects have been presented and performed in milking barns, the Preseli Hills and the coastline, and alongside farmers, GM protesters and the public.

OUTPOST
www.norwichoutpost.org
questions@norwichoutpost.org

OUTPOST is an artist-run gallery founded in November 2004. Based in Norwich, OUTPOST is committed to the development of emerging contemporary art practices. The organisation has a core programme of twelve exhibitions per year (selected both from the members' archive and a wider pool), and a programme of events that includes film nights, artists' talks and critical discussions. OUTPOST is run by its artist members, eight of whom form a steering committee and manage the gallery in a voluntary capacity. As the organisation approaches its 50th month-long exhibition, recent programmes have featured a typically broad range of practices, with *Plastique Fantastique: Protocols for Deceleration*, a solo show by Lucy Harrison, *Members' Show* selected by Andrew Hunt, as well as shows by Steve Bishop and Peter Coffin. OUTPOST is supported by Arts Council England East, Norfolk County Council, Norwich City Council and Norwich Gallery.

Parade
Unit A, Enterprise House, Tudor Grove
London E9 7QL
www.paradespace.com
pmd@paradespace.com

Parade opened in 2006. The gallery was initiated to maintain involvement in art production and to explore the process of exhibition-making. Established with the traditional intention of offering artists a space to realise exhibitions, it also has an interest in the meeting and developing of a community of artists, curators and art professionals. Parade has worked on a sporadic programme of shows developed through dialogue, support and promotion. The recent programme includes: *Three works in September*, a solo show by Dan Rees; a group show by Matthew Darbyshire, Djordje Ozbolt, Alexander Tucker; and, in late 2007, *The Death of Affect*, curated by Matt Williams and featuring Keith Connolly, Alastair MacKinven and Hannah Sawtell. In May 2008, Parade presented a group show of new paintings by Stuart Andrew, Philip Caramazza and Gabriel Hartley.

Permanent Gallery
20 Bedford Place, Brighton BN1 2PT
www.permanentgallery.com
info@permanentgallery.com

Permanent Gallery is an independent artist-run gallery and bookshop set up in 2003. The organisation's guiding principle was discovered through articulating what it was already doing: working responsively with emerging artists and curators to realise experimental exhibitions. Projects are complimented by specially-commissioned texts published in booklet form, and an events programme which includes artists' talks, film nights, and the discussion forum *Armchair Critics*. Previously, performance group These Horses inhabited the gallery for two weeks, ceramicist Keith Harrison held live-firing events across two sites, and renowned photographer Jason Evans culminated five years of practice with his first solo show. Recent exhibitions include *On Overgrown Paths* by Ben Rivers – a 16mm film installation across two sites (November–December 2008).

Plan 9
Bridewell Island, Bridewell Street
Bristol BS1, www.plan9.org.uk
info@plan9.org.uk

Plan 9 is an independent contemporary art project which was established in 2005. Currently operating a gallery and studio complex in Bristol's city centre, Plan 9 aims to provide a platform for individuals or groups to realise projects, and to expand critical engagement through contextual programming. Projects include *In the Beginning* (October–November 2008), an exhibition featuring artists from London, Leipzig and Bristol, and *Somewhere Here* (November–December 2008), a citywide poster installation. The programme structure is extending to include the formation of the Plan 9 Trade Union, which provided art workers for an offsite project initiated by the Arnolfini in Bristol (plan9tradeunion.blogspot.com) and the workshop/talk *What is an Organisation?* (facilitated by the curatorial group What, How and for Whom, based in Zagreb).

Project Space Leeds
Whitehall Waterfront, 2 Riverside Way, Leeds LS1 4EH
T: 07930 236383
www.projectspaceleeds.org.uk
info@projectspaceleeds.org.uk
Project Space Leeds (PSL) is an independent, artist-led contemporary art space, founded in 2006 by artist-curators Pippa Hale, Kerry Harker and Diane Howse (working in partnership with property developer K W Linfoot Plc). Based on the waterfront in Leed's city centre, PSL stages exhibitions of modern and contemporary work across all art forms and by artists from the UK and abroad. Associated events such as talks, seminars and education workshops complement the exhibition programme, engaging diverse audiences and aiming to develop awareness of the contemporary visual arts in the city. By working with curators from outside Leeds, PSL aims not only to bring established artists to the city and provide opportunities for native talent, but also to position Leeds on the national and international radar.

Publish and Be Damned
www.publishandbedamned.org

publishandbedamned@gmail.com
Surveying an abundance of independent publications, Publish and Be Damned demonstrates individual experimental approaches to making and distributing the work of artists, writers and musicians outside of the commercial mainstream. Initiated by curators Kit Hammonds and Emily Pethick in 2004 for Cubitt, London, it now stages publishing fairs, a touring archive and occasional events run by Sarah McCrory and Joe Scotland. The annual fair provides a much-needed and previously non-existent network, profiling publications that do not have wide distribution. The project also exists as an archive of material collected during the fair, including publications that have been specially sourced or donated.

Redux Projects
www.reduxprojects.org.uk
plewis@reduxprojects.org.uk
T: 020 898 11014

Redux opened on Commercial Street, London, in November 2003 with two projects by Giorgio Sadotti. Its remit was to re-present works that may have been overlooked in the ten-year period since the London art scene has been the focus of international media attention.
Inviting a new generation of artists and curators to present projects, Redux offered a space for thinking about the construction of myth. Projects with the likes of Peter Suchin, Urban Drift and Shezad Dawood extended the invitation to curators and critics, while off-site projects included: Zoo Art Fair, London; Magazin 4, Bregenz, Austria; and Utopia Display Platform, NABA, Milan. Publications such as *Transmission* and *Slimvolume* were launched, complementing the exhibitions programme curated by Peter Lewis and Makiko Nagaya at Commercial Street until 2006.
Redux Projects is also the London base of the MA Curating Contemporary Art Programme, Leeds Metropolitan University.

Rêl Institiwt-Real Institute
www.realinstitute.org
mail@realinstitute.org

Founded in Wales in 2000, and in direct response to the paucity of independent cinema in the region, Rêl Institiwt stages regular alternative film nights and one-off events involving a variety of art forms. Deliberately without permanent residence, Rêl Institiwt's unofficial philosophy is this: "The popular notion that the best of contemporary art can only successfully occur in areas of high population density and that rural areas should be left with a blend of unambitious mediocrity is twaddle and dangerous twaddle at that." Previous projects include *Really Restrictive Shorts*, *Soporific* and *Un-Wanted Djs*.

Rhys & Hannah Present
15 The Arcade, Broadmead, Bristol
BS1 3JA, http://rhysandhannahpresent.blogspot.com
rhysandhannahpresent@hotmail.com

We are two artists who recently graduated from the Fine Art School in Bristol, and our collaboration is called Rhys & Hannah Present. After exhibiting in New Contemporaries 2007 we were inspired to find a way to promote young and emerging Bristol-based artists, and to make the work of other artists from outside Bristol more visible in the city. Using temporary sites, Rhys & Hannah Present organised *A Birthday Art Show* and *what we'd buy if you buy (our t-shirts)*. After this we obtained a short-term lease on an old shop in the heart of Bristol's commercial centre, where we have subsequently organised *The Big Art Draw* and *Clouds*, and hosted an exchange with the Manchester-based exhibition exchange *o p e n e n d e d*. Recent activities include *Window*, a two-part project in November 2008, and hosting artist-run spaces from across the country (December 2008), including Blackpool Museum for Contemporary Art, Eastside Projects and Royal Standard.

The Royal Standard
Unit 3, Vauxhall Business Centre
131 Vauxhall Rd, Liverpool L3 6BN
T: 0151 236 1919
www.the-royal-standard.com
info@the-royal-standard.com

The Royal Standard, which was founded in 2005, is an artist-led group, studio, gallery and social workspace that is currently based in an old print works on the northern edge of Liverpool's city centre. The organisation seeks to offer the city's artistic and cultural community a location for meeting, talk and engagement. The Royal Standard showcases innovative projects and events from the UK and abroad, hosting exhibitions by art college graduates, emerging artists and established practitioners, as well as artist-initiatives. In 2008 the exhibitions included *Navigator* (a group show of UK-based artists exploring themes of landscape, mapping and re-location) and *Mr Democracy* (an ambitious international project exploring trade, democracy and globalisation). In October 2008 The Royal co-hosted *The Winner Takes it All?*, an international artist conference aiming to explore and debate the Capital of Culture in Liverpool.

Scolt Head Screenings
The Scolt Head, 107a Culford Road
London N1 4HT
www.thescolthead.co.uk
scoltheadscreenings@gmail.com

Scolt Head Screenings was established in the Scolt Head pub and restaurant in North-East London by Isobel Harbison and Vanessa Desclaux in early 2007. Programmed into different series of six monthly events, the free screenings take place on Sunday evenings. For each screening, an artist is invited to show a particular work on video or film, and to recommend a feature film to be shown afterwards. Highlights from the recent third series include Anya Kirschner's *Supernumeraries* (2003) accompanied by Hiroshi Teshigahara's *Pitfall* (1962). The presence of the artists at each screening is intended in part to provide an alternative context for understanding individual practices, and also provoke informal discussions about the development of artists' works on film and video. Listings available from www.lux.org.uk.

Sierra Metro
22 West Harbour Road, Edinburgh
EH5 1PN, www.sierrametro.com
info@sierrametro.com

Sierra Metro is an independent, not-for-profit artist-run gallery currently housed in a disused testing facility in Granton, Edinburgh. A largely industrial area in the north of the city, Granton is in the early stages regeneration – a gentrification that will ultimately dictate Sierra Metro's tenure of the building. The organisation showcases and supports emerging artists in a climate of flexibility and experimentation. The current space allows a much larger area for exhibiting than usually available to early-career artists, and the setting provides a useful focus for the artists. Open to change and collaboration, Sierra Metro is a welcoming and democratic place for discussion, development and exchange surrounding diverse practices in Scotland and beyond. Past exhibitions include solo presentations by Neville Rae and Cara Tolmie.

Southside Gallery
17 Westmoreland Street, Glasgow
G42 8LL, www.southsidestudios.org
info@southsidestudios.org

Set in the heart of a vibrant community of emerging artists, Southside Gallery (formerly Fridge Gallery) has been committed to showing diverse and challenging work since its inception, and has recently crystallised a longstanding dedication into a more muscular and focused agenda for the future. Taking the idea of generosity as its impetus, forthcoming exhibitions will facilitate unique opportunities for early career artists to show alongside established names. The programme, curated by Gregor Johnstone, has already included an eight-week artists' film and cinema season which opened with Luke Fowler in summer 2008, and the 2009 gallery programme includes a group show featuring David Shrigley, Billy Teasedale and Alan Stanners.

Space Station Sixty-Five
65 North Cross Road, London SE22
9ET, www.spacestationsixtyfive.com,
spacestationsixtyfive@btopenworld.com

At artist-run Space Station Sixty-Five, we continue to curate the contemporary art we love in accessible venues, unswayed by fashion, trends and the whims of government funding. In 2008 this included *The Marquis of Camberwell* at a Camberwell pub; and *Carney Town* at The Portman Gallery. Recent window installations include *Smile More, Laugh Now,*

Cry Less by Counterproductions and *The Gift and the Message, a Norwegian Gift of Light* by Jan Kjetil Bjørheim. After six years, our East Dulwich shop front gallery and project space is undergoing exciting architectural development as part of an expanded organisation.

Springhill Institute
www.springhillinstitute.org

Springhill Institute was established in 2003 with the simple intention of bringing people together in constructive dialogue. The programme began with a series of lectures in which artists were invited to talk on a subject of their choosing; while exhibitions such as *Time and Breakfast* (2004) – which opened at 6am with a free fried breakfast – created an alternative platform for social interaction. From 2004 to 2006 the institute hosted seven international artist's residencies, in which each participant made an ambitious project in an intensive two-week process, while living in an apartment in the Victorian factory that houses the institute's studio and gallery. Springhill Institute is now in a process of reconfiguration, establishing a structure to support our present activities, extend our terms of collaboration and increase our mobility.

Standby
www.standbyprojects.wordpress.com
standbysolutions@hotmail.com

Standby, an artist-led organisation based in Edinburgh, hosts spontaneous exhibitions and events and collaborates with artists, curators and producers. It is a fluid organisation which takes an alternative approach to exhibition coordination. Without a permanent location, Standby inhabits various spaces – from retail units to apartments – and adapts to suit each environment, providing a dynamic programme of events and exhibitions dominated by site- and time-specific work. Recent projects include a residency in the Guest Room of Collective Gallery, Edinburgh; and a series of events, exhibitions and publications organised for the Edinburgh Annuale.

Star and Shadow Cinema
Stepney Bank, Newcastle upon Tyne NE1 2NP
www.starandshadow.org.uk
info@starandshadow.org.uk

Star and Shadow Cinema is a collective of volunteers who run a venue in Newcastle upon Tyne. It aims to show a truly independent programme of inspirational films as cheaply as possible, as well as provide a venue for artists and musicians of all varieties. It is a cosy venue that provides a haven from the mundane mainstream of film and music, and it is a nursery for independent creativity and thinking. Recent programme have included a Fred Wiseman film programming season, Northern Lights Film Festival, a storytelling evening by David Campbell, and talks by Portia Rankoane.

studio1.1
57a Redchurch Street, London E2 7DJ, T: 07952 986696
www.naimad.co.uk/studio1-1
studio1-1.gallery@virgin.net

studio1.1 collective began in July 2003 with no particular battle plan. We have evolved with a range of shows as diverse as possible, presenting artists at any stage of their career, from any country, in any discipline. Our commitment is to the work itself, and to fostering the three-way relationship between artist, artwork, and viewer; looking for what Cage, in another context called "the quality of encounter". Art isn't a distraction, or an act of consumption, but a relationship. Or, as Richard Foreman said, "Art attempts to evoke something that you are not yet. Entertainment only talks to that person that you are now."

Studio Voltaire
1a Nelsons Row, London SW4 7JR
T: 020 7622 1294
www.studiovoltaire.org

Studio Voltaire is the only artist-led gallery and studio complex in South-West London. Established in 1994, the organisation has developed a reputation for supporting artists at a pivotal stage in their careers through an ambitious public programme of exhibitions, commissions, live events and offsite projects. Studio Voltaire recently worked with Spartacus Chetwynd, Chris Evans, Thea Djordjadze, Emma Hedditch, Dawn Mellor, Jimmy Robert, Ruth Ewan, Joanne Tatham and Tom O'Sullivan and White Columns, while the exhibition programme for 2008–9 includes solo projects by Donald Urquhart, Thomas Ravens, Nairy Baghramian, Maria Pask and Cathy Wilkes. Studio Voltaire also runs an innovative and wide-reaching education programme producing artist-led projects and activities for individuals and communities within the local area.

temporarycontemporary
www.tempcontemp.co.uk
www.metropolis-rise.co.uk
www.MrGross.com

temporarycontemporary is a nomadic project space, run by artists Anthony Gross and Jen Wu, exploring the intersections of contemporary art and social production. Originally based in Deptford, gallery exhibitions have now been replaced by activities like poker-games-as-group-shows, video events in pubs and Tate Modern, occasional art fairs and roving exhibitions in China. temporarycontemporary's *Event Horizon* programme formed part of the Royal Academy's GSK Contemporary season (October 2008–January 2009). The latter programme took the form of a temporary occupation of four neo-classical spaces and included major new commissions, performances and events radiating from a free-for-all slacker-lounge-café-bar.

«ten til ten»
First Floor, 60 Tradeston Street,
Glasgow G5 8BH
60tradestonstreet@gmail.com
www.tentilten.co.uk

«ten til ten» is a project space based in Glasgow and run by Lindsey Hanlon and Rocca Gutteridge. Artists are selected for their aesthetic and philosophical ideas, as well as their capacity for exploring concepts that engage with postmodernism and a rethinking of conceptual art. There is a dedicated focus on poetic dialogue between the artist, work and audience. «ten til ten» was established in December 2007 in Tradeston, Glasgow, and privileges public accessibility and international and national exchange. Past exhibitions include *Reading Public*, and *To be Alert is To be Decorative*, which received British Council Funding to travel to Paris. «ten til ten» is currently organising a residency programme for artists.

Trace
26 Moira Place, Cardiff CF24 0ET
T: 02920 407 338
www.tracegallery.org
tracegallery@aol.com

TRACE is an art space in a terraced house in Cardiff. Dedicated to researching and disseminating performance art, TRACE has a regular exhibition programme that displays documentation, residues and partial objects created through the process of performance. Since 2000 it has presented 56 live solo performance artworks, 28 of which were produced as part of external events and international exchange projects in Wales, Québec, the US and China. In 2006 the organisation initiated publications on performance art through Samizdat Press, including *What's Welsh For Performance Art* by Heike Roms. TRACE is also home to Trace Collective – a group of artists who focus on living performance activity.

Transmission
45–49 King Street, Glasgow G1 5RA
T: 0141 552 7141
www.transmissiongallery.org
info@transmissiongallery.org

Transmission provides a place where artists can meet, talk and exhibit. Artist-run and committed to reflecting the needs and concerns of artists in Scotland, the gallery provides a crucial context for practice to develop and broaden outside the pressures of a commercial art world. Established in 1983, Transmission maintains a commitment to a collective ethos and continues to focus on serving a community of which it is intrinsically part. Membership is open to anybody, and members receive a regular newsletter and entitlement to submit work to the annual members' exhibition. They are also invited to submit work for inclusion in the gallery archive that is available for view by visiting curators and researchers. Recent projects include *Moot Points*, a month long agenda of events and publications featuring contributions by Cinenova, Dexter Sinister, Emma Hedditch and others.

Washington Garcia
Arch 24, 1 Eastvale Place
Glasgow G3 8QG
www.washingtongarciagallery.com
washingtongarciagallery@gmail.com

Washington Garcia is a Glasgow-based gallery initiative directed by artists Kendall Koppe, Ruth Barker and Douglas Morland. With no permanent base, it retains the flexibility of utilising the city's unique variety of venues in order to reveal artists' practices in distinctive and challenging contexts. The gallery focuses on presenting high-quality work by artists, both from the UK and abroad, at various career stages. Occupying a unique position within the contemporary landscape, the gallery curates a programme that encourages dialogue between institutions and individuals operating within the city's dynamic art community and beyond. Past exhibitions included work by artists Claire Barclay, Kalup Linzy and Miranda Whall, in spaces as varied as a tenement flat, a working riding school, and an empty Victorian retail space.

The Wayward Canon
www.waywardcanon.com
mark@waywardcanon.com

The Wayward Canon, founded by Mark Aerial Waller in 2002, is a platform for event-based interventions in cinematic work, and is a test ground for concepts in development in Waller's gallery-based video practice. Audience, space and editing are re-organised to discover new directions. Past events have included *Simon and the Radioactive Flesh*, a portmanteau film with disco transitions, produced in collaboration with Giles Round, 2007; and an all-night collision between exhibition space and epic television serial, *My Kleine Fassbinderbar*, 2002. Activities include *La Societe des Amis de Judex*, at Objectif Exhibitions in Antwerp, Belgium, May 2008; and an event at France Fiction, Paris, June 2008. The Wayward Canon publication *The Flipside of Darkness* features an interview with The Wayward Canon by Stuart Bailey.

Whitechapel Project Space
20 Fordham St
London E1 1HS
T: 020 7377 6289
www.whitechapelprojectspace.org.uk
info@whitechapelprojectspace.org.uk

Whitechapel Project Space was initiated as a non-profit artist-led gallery space in 2002, aiming to commission and facilitate projects from art practitioners on an open basis that allows for experimentation. This loose structure emphasises the realisation of exhibitions and events through relationships with individuals, as opposed to large group projects. As such the organisation represents a commitment to long-term dialogues with artists, curators and other practitioners, and sees the gallery as a social and shared critical context. Artists who have been involved with Whitechapel Project Space include Juliette Blightman, Pablo Bronstein, Sebastian Buerkner, Elliot Dodd and Brian Moran, Babak Ghazi, Melanie Gilligan, Charlotte Ginsborg, Iain Hetherington, Anja Kirschner, Craig Mulholland, Alex Pollard, Simon Popper, and Giles Round and Luke Dowd.

Index of artists / list of works

Numbers after an artist's name indicate:
project number within overall sequence (first);
page number for project text (second)

Stephen Connolly (36) p. 161

The Whale, 2003
16mm film, 9m

Great American Desert, 2008
16mm film, 16m

Más Se Perdió (scratch), 2008
16mm film, 14m

Mike Cooter (16) p. 112

Original Intent, 2007
Installation, including works as follows:

Untitled (Falcon...Bork), 2007
Photograph

Production Design (Maltese Falcon), 2007
Bespoke film stills offset in mount

Re: Maltese Falcon, 2006
Five letters

Untitled (Reeded Glass), 2007
Reeded glass, metal, fluorescent tubes

Glass / Falcon, 2007
Archival photograph

Untitled (Intervention), 2007
Replacement of all exterior glasswork with ½ inch reeded glass

Also shown:
Interview footage, Channel 4 News (ITN UK), 27 October 2005

Matthew Darbyshire (3) p. 85

BP p.l.c. Headquarters (reception), 1 St James's Square, London SW1, May 2008
Green LED ropelights installed in ICA foyer

Christ's Church Spitalfields (building façade), Commercial Street, London E1, May 2008
Magenta lamps and gels installed in ICA stairwell

Hackney Community College (entrance), Falkirk Street, London N1, May 2008
Purple lamps and gels installed in ICA entrance

The Orange Shop (wall coffers), Fulham Broadway Retail Centre, London SW6, May 2008
Orange lamps and gels installed in ICA concourse

Vauxhall Cross Underpass, Vauxhall Cross Transport Interchange, London SW8, May 2008
Blue lamps and gels installed in ICA toilets

Selfridges & Co (upper level windows), 400 Oxford Street, London W1, May 2008
Colour-changing backlights installed in ICA windows

Sony Pictures, 25 Golden Square, London W1, June 2008
Colour-changing backlights installed in ICA windows

Odeon Cinema, Panton Street, London SW1, July 2008
Colour-changing backlights installed in ICA windows

Adidas Concept Store, Earlham Street, London WC2, August 2008
Colour-changing backlights installed in ICA windows

Virgin Softroom Upper Class Lounge, Heathrow Airport, September 2008
Colour-changing backlights installed in ICA windows

Sean Edwards (27) p. 139

turning it around, slowly, in the light
Installation, including works as follows:

An Evans Gambit, 2008
Framed magazine

In the light, 2008
Cardboard boxes

Lap Steel, 2008
16mm film, 2m

Practice Table (ICA), 2008
MDF plinth and various objects

Snowing like a Checkerboard, 2008
C-print

Untitled, 2008
Veneered wardrobe off-cut, cardboard, surface filler and glue

Untitled, 2008
Cardboard box

Untitled, 2008
Thread and masking tape

Redmond Entwistle (22) p. 128

Skein
Event, ICA Cinema, 7 July 2008

Ruth Ewan (47) p. 189

Fang Sang, 2008
Booklet and audio CD
Edition of 4000

Six Feet of Earth, 2008
Video projection, 6m 37s

Freee (9) p. 95

Protest Drives History, 2008
Photograph; billboard poster, ICA Bar; billboard poster, Hassard Street, London

Maria Fusco (44) p. 182

Event, ICA Nash/Brandon Rooms, 15 September 2008

Spume
Texts broadcast by Bluetooth from ICA, 15 September–2 November 2008

Babak Ghazi (2) p. 83

Model, 2008
26 digital prints on canvas

Guestroom (11) p. 104

The Librarians, 2008
Videos, monitors

Reading Room
Event, ICA Nash/Brandon Rooms, 2 June 2008

Seamus Harahan (7) p. 92

Valley of Jehosephat / Version – In Your Mind, 2007
Two-screen video projection (loop)

Hardcore Is More Than Music (4) p. 87

The Cut collaborative magazine, produced May–November 2008, with launch event in ICA Nash/ Brandon Rooms, 27 October 2008

Emma Hart and Benedict Drew (15) p. 111

Untitled 5.
Event, ICA Theatre, 16 June 2008

Alexander Heim (17) p. 114

a, 2008
Glazed stoneware, red glass

b, 2008
Stoneware, blue glass

des, 2008
Earthenware, brown glass

es, 2008
Glazed stoneware, red glass

f, 2008
Glazed stoneware, white glass

g, 2008
Glazed earthenware

Doves, 2008
Papier-mâché on cardboard

Three Seasons, 2007
Video projection, 12m

Iain Hetherington (32) p. 155

Composite Picture 1 (Diversified Cultural Worker), 2008

Composite Picture 2 (Diversified Cultural Worker), 2008

Composite Picture 3 (Diversified Cultural Worker), 2008

Culturally Competent Opinion, 2008

Culturally Competent Opinion 2, 2008

Design for Public Monument to Sir Francis Galton, 2008

Diversified Cultural Worker 2, 2008

Diversified Cultural Worker 5, 2008

Diversified Cultural Worker 6, 2008

All works: oil on canvas except *Composite Picture 3*: acrylic on canvas

Will Holder (29) p. 143

Bachelor Party
Event, ICA Nash/Brandon Rooms, 28 July 2008

The Hut Project (28) p. 140

Old Kunst, 2008
Every work ever made by The Hut Project and members of The Hut Project, 1971–2008

Works in this exhibition included:
The Hut Project, *Lead*, 2006/7
Courtesy Beat Raeber and Ryan Gander

Alfred Johansen, *Untitled*, 1966
Courtesy Alfred Johansen Estate and Studio Elmgreen & Dragset

William Hogarth, *Time Smoking a Picture*, 1761
Courtesy Andrew Edmunds Prints and Drawings and Nick Livesey

Fiona Jardine (57) p. 211

(For Patrick), 2008
Four framed collages (all *Untitled*, 2008), carpet tiles, paint

Jeffrey Charles Henry Peacock Gallery (24) p. 132

Pecuniary Proposal
Proposal delivered by hand to ICA, 19 February 2008

Pecuniary Proposal
Invitation card printed and distributed by ICA, July 2008

Pecuniary Proposal
Invitation card printed and distributed by Jeffrey Charles Henry Peacock Gallery, July 2008

Jesse Jones (14) p. 110

The Spectre and the Sphere, 2008
16mm film, 12m 30s

Junior Aspirin Records (40) p. 174

Event, ICA Theatre, 1 September 2008
Including performances by DJ Jerome, Socrates That Practices Music, God In Hackney, Skill 7 Stamina 12, Bob Parks

Anja Kirschner and David Panos (12) p. 107

Trail of the Spider, 2008
Video projection, 53m

Thomas Kratz (20) p. 119

Strawberry Camouflage, 2008
Event, ICA Nash/Brandon Rooms, 30 June 2008

Torsten Lauschmann (54) p. 206

Dead Man's Switch, 2008
High definition video projection (loop), light-switching programme, wall painting

Feral, 2008
High definition video projection (loop)

Jonty Lees (23) p. 131

Looking for Love in All the Wrong Places, 2008
Videos, newspaper clippings, photographs, shelf, invigilator, chair, chocks, gilded-rubber, powered toy, plane, wooden ramps

Lorna Macintyre (37) p. 164

Arcadia, 2008
Plywood, gloss paint, wood, glass jar, wild flowers

In the evening there is feeling, 2008
Silver gelatin print

In the morning there is meaning, 2008
Silver gelatin print

Untitled, 2008
Mirrors, rosewood

Alastair MacKinven (8) and (23), p. 93 and 131

Solo project:

Et Sic In Infinitum Again, 2008
This exhibition included the following works:

Andway Isthay Oreverfay, 2008

Andway Sick In Infinitumway, 2008

Double Pointless Perspective, 2008

Et Sick In Infinitum, 2007

Et Sic In Infinitum, 2008

Et Sick In Infinitum [Sic], 2008

Etway Icsay Inway Infinitumway, 2008

Etway Sic Inway Infinitum, 2008

Et Sic In Oreverfay, 2008

All works: oil on canvas

Crutch, 2008
Resin, aluminium, bronze powder

Hairway To Steven, 2008
Aluminium, steel

Group project:

Time Shifter, Sailor Killer, Moth Fucker, 2008
Video projection, bamboo pole, duct tape, vanity mirror, photographs

Macroprosopus Dancehall Band (58) p. 213

Event, ICA Theatre, 2 November 2008

Ursula Mayer (38) p. 165

The Crystal Gaze, 2007
16mm film (loop)

Matthew Noel-Tod (52) p. 202

Blind Carbon Copy, 2008
Event, ICA Cinema, 6 October 2008

Matthew Noel-Tod's *Blind Carbon Copy* is a Film London Artists' Moving Image Network and Picture This co-production and was produced as part of the Bristol Mean Time residency

Open Music Archive (49) p. 192

Free-to-Air
Event, ICA Theatre, 29 September 2008

David Osbaldeston (45) p. 184

The Pleasure of Your Company, 2008
57 framed drypoint etchings
All works: no. 1 in an edition of 1 (with 1 artist's proof)

Garrett Phelan (48) p. 191

IT, is not IT
Installation, including:

Interruption. Or between two ITs – Part 2, 2008
Metal, paint, fabric, wood

IT is dead, 2008
Photograph

IT is dead, 2008
Used batteries

IT will bring you light, 2008
Cement, radio, cable

Gail Pickering (55) p. 208

Brutalist Premolition, 2008
High definition video projection (loop)
Actors: Raji James, Babita Pohoomull.
Assistant: Liz Bowley
Camera: Adrian O'Toole, Bernd Behr
Family: Mr Anwar, Jewell Kahn, Salma Kahn, Salman Raza

Repo Rehearsal, 2008
Plywood

Robin Hood Nook, 2008
Painted plywood, drawing

Gail Pickering's *Brutalist Premolition* is a Media Art Bath commission with support from the Henry Moore Foundation

Sarah Pierce (41) p. 175

"It's time, man. It feels imminent", 2008
Video, monitor, fluorescent tubes, plinths, slides, photographs, letters
Slides, photographs and letters courtesy ICA collection, Tate Library and Archive, Hyman Kreitman Research Centre

Clunie Reid (13) p. 108

SHE GETS EVEN HAPPIER!, 2008
Mixed media on foamboard

James Richards (33) p. 156

Active Negative Programme, 2008
Video programme

Untitled Merchandise (Lovers and Dealers), 2008
Six machine-knitted nylon blankets

Hannah Rickards (30) p. 145

To enable me to fix my attention on any one of these symbols I was to imagine that I was looking at the colours as I might see them on a moving-picture screen.
Printed text, *Nought to Sixty* magazine, August 2008

He was trying to speak about the difficulty of painting air.
Printed text, *Nought to Sixty* magazine, September 2008

One can make out the surface only by placing any dark-coloured object on the ground.
Printed text, *Nought to Sixty* magazine, October 2008

Ben Rivers (43) p. 180

The Coming Race, 2006
16mm film, 5m

We The People, 2004
16mm film, 1m

Giles Round (42) p. 178

Strange days and nights of mystery and fear mixed with excitement and wonder strange days and nights strange months and years, 2008
Installation, mixed media

Alun Rowlands (51) p. 200

Communiqué § 4, 2008
Pamphlet

Support Structure (60) p. 221

Curtain as declaration of desire for change of function, 2008–ongoing
Various manifestations, including: video on plasma screen, ICA foyer, 2008, and printed text, *Nought to Sixty* catalogue, 2009

Stephen Sutcliffe (46) p. 188

Green Tea, 2008
Wall drawing

Untitled, c.1968
Photograph from the artist's collection

No good on Sundays, 2008
Video on monitor, 56s

"O come all ye faithful", 2007
Video on monitor, 47s

Six Essential Books, 2008
Video on monitor, 1m 34s

Untitled, 2008
Video on monitor, 16s

Vacillation, 2008
Video on monitor, 35s

We'll Let You Know, 2008
Video on monitor, 58s

Tris Vonna-Michell (35) p. 160

hahn/huhn
Event, ICA Cinema, 11 August 2008

Andy Wake (26) p. 137

The Storming of the Bastille
Event, ICA Nash/Brandon Rooms, 21 July 2008

Mark Aerial Waller (53) p. 205

Resistance Domination Secret
Event, ICA Theatre, 13 October 2008, including works as follows:

Resistance Domination Secret, 2007
Video, 7m

The Flipside of Darkness, 2007
Video, 12m

The Children of the Night, 2008
Video, 6m

Writers

Mark Beasley is Curator at Creative Time, New York. His recent curatorial projects include *Hey Hey Glossolalia* for Creative Time, and *Sudden White (after London)* for GSK Contemporary, London. He is a contributor to publications including *frieze, Dot Dot Dot* and *Artforum*.

Richard Birkett is Assistant Curator at the ICA, and formerly co-organiser of Whitechapel Project Space, London.

Andrew Bonacina is a curator and writer based in London. He is a regular contributor to *frieze, Art Press* and *Untitled*, and is a contributing editor of *UOVO* magazine. He recently co-founded Almanac, a curatorial studio and independent imprint.

JJ Charlesworth is a freelance critic and Reviews Editor of *ArtReview*. He has written extensively on contemporary art, with an emphasis on the political and institutional dimensions of artistic practice. He is Tutor in Painting at the Royal College of Art, London.

William Fowler is Curator of Artists' Moving Image at the BFI National Archive, London, where he has produced the DVD *Peter Whitehead and the Sixties* and where he is currently restoring Jeff Keen's films. Fowler curated the film programme *Visionary Landscapes* for LUX, London, and is a contributor to www.keepmovingimages.com.

Melissa Gronlund is Associate Editor of *Afterall* and the *Afterall One Work* book series. She is a critic and a regular contributor to *frieze, Afterall, Art Monthly, Dot Dot Dot*. She is a visiting tutor at the Ruskin School of Drawing & Fine Art, Oxford University.

Isobel Harbison is a writer and curator who has contributed to a number of publications including *Circa, Untitled*, and *ArtReview*. She is founder of Scolt Head Screenings and Assistant Curator of Hayward Touring.

Pablo Lafuente is Managing Editor of *Afterall*, and Associate Curator at the Office for Contemporary Art Norway.

Isla Leaver-Yap is Exhibition Organiser at the ICA, and editor-at-large of *MAP* magazine.

Nicola Lees is Public Programmes Curator at Serpentine Gallery, London. She curated the exhibitions *Left Pop* for the Second Moscow Biennale 2007, and *Exquisite Corpse* at IMMA, Dublin, 2008.

Lisa Le Feuvre teaches on the postgraduate Curatorial Programme at Goldsmiths and is Curator of Contemporary Art at the National Maritime Museum. In 2010 she and Tom Morton will co-curate the British Art Show 7.

Coline Milliard is an art writer based in London. She is a regular contributor to *ArtReview, Modern Painters, Art Monthly, frieze.com* and *Art Press*, and has also written for *Contemporary, Flash Art International, Untitled, Metropolis M, MAP* and *Afterall Online*.

Neil Mulholland is a writer based in Scotland. He is Director of the Centre for Visual and Cultural Studies, and Reader in Contemporary Art Theory, at Edinburgh College of Art.

Paul O'Neill is an artist, curator and writer. He is GWR Research Fellow with Situations at the University of the West of England, where he is leading the international research project *Locating the Producers*.

Emily Pethick is a curator and writer. She is Director of The Showroom, London. From 2005–08 she was the director of Casco, Office for Art, Design and Theory, Utrecht.

Sarah Pierce is an artist and organiser of The Metropolitan Complex. See page 175.

Emma Ridgway is Curator at the Arts and Ecology Centre, Royal Society of Arts, London. She edited the book *Experiment Marathon*, Reykjavik Art Museum, 2009, and curated *Beings and Doings* for the British Council, New Delhi, 2007.

Jennifer Thatcher is Co-Director of Talks at the ICA, and a regular contributor to *Art Monthly* and *ArtReview*. She is also a founding member of the Art Critics' Curry Club.

Matt Williams is Curator of International Project Space, Birmingham. His other projects include *The Death of Affect*, Parade, London, 2007; *Dracularising*, Galerie Neue Alte Bruecke, Frankfurt am Main, 2007. He is co-editor of *Novel*.

Mick Wilson is an artist, educator and writer. He is Dean of the Graduate School of Creative Arts & Media, Dublin.

Tony F Wilson is a London-born writer and musician based in Oslo. His recorded work includes collaborations with members of Slowdive, Sonic Youth and Loop, and he regularly produces events with Norwegian artist and musician Are Mokkelbost. He is a regular contributor to *frieze*.

Nought to Sixty magazine, designed by Sarah Boris

Published as a record of *Nought to Sixty*
Institute of Contemporary Arts
5 May–2 November 2008

Nought to Sixty was an ICA project supported by the Scottish Arts Council, Culture Ireland and The Henry Moore Foundation. Support from premium Japanese lager, Kirin Ichiban.

Nought to Sixty was organised by Mark Sladen, Richard Birkett and Isla Leaver-Yap.

Editors Mark Sladen, Richard Birkett, Isla Leaver-Yap
Copy editors Melissa Dunn, Charles Gute
Editorial assistant Melissa Faulkner
Designer Sara De Bondt studio
Printer Die Keure, Belgium
Publisher ICA, London
Distributor Cornerhouse Publications, Manchester, www.cornerhouse.org

ISBN: 978-1-900300-59-9

ICA
Institute of Contemporary Arts
The Mall
London SW1Y 5AH
United Kingdom
T: +44 20 7930 3647
www.ica.org.uk

The ICA would like to thank all of the artists and their representatives for their help in the preparation of this project. We would like to thank the following for their help and advice: Laura Aldridge, Alfred Johansen Estate, Andrew Edmunds Prints, Susanna Beaumont, Charlie Blightman, Jenny Brownrigg, Jo Bruton, Steven Cairns, Anna Colin, Stuart Comer, Benjamin Cook, Sasha Craddock, Sorcha Dallas, Clementine Deliss, Darren Flook, Melissa Faulkner, Konrad Fischer, Ryan Gander, Marianne Greated, Tessa Giblin, Daniel Kennedy, Marie-France Kittler, Eric Liknaitzky, Nick Livesey, Maureen Mahony, Elizabeth Manchester, Sarah McCrory, Anna McNally, Paul O'Neill, Stephen Palmer, Alex Pollard, Beat Raeber, Soraya Rodriguez, Joe Scotland, Mike Sperlinger, Studio Elmgreen & Dragset, David Thorp, Sally Timmons, Keith Wilson, Jen Wu.

We would like to thank the following patrons for their continued support: Joan and Robin Alvarez, Charles Asprey, Ayling & Conroy, Robert Beat, Kathy Burnham, Dimitris Daskalopoulos, Fred Dorfman, Denise Esfandi, Jules and Barbara Farber, Sam Hainsworth, Marc and Kristen Holtzman, David Kotler, Martha Mehta, Monica O'Neil, Maureen Paley, Nicola Plant, John Scott, Rumi Verjee, Jay Verjee, Andrew Warren and Alison Wiltshire.

Credits
All pictures courtesy of the artists, and as listed hereafter. Nina Beier and Marie Lund: Laura Bartlett, London, and Croy Nielsen, Berlin. Juliette Blightman: HOTEL Gallery, London. Andrea Büttner: Hollybush Gardens, London. Duncan Campbell: HOTEL, London. Nina Canell and Robin Watkins: mother's tankstation, Dublin. Mike Cooter: ZINGERpresents, Amsterdam. Matthew Darbyshire: Herald Street, London. Sean Edwards: Limoncello, London. Ruth Ewan: Ancient & Modern, London. Seamus Harahan: Gimpel Fils, London. Alexander Heim: doggerfisher, Edinburgh, and Galerie Karin Guenther, Hamburg. Iain Hetherington: Mary Mary, Glasgow. The Hut Project: Limoncello, London. Anja Kirschner and David Panos: Hollybush Gardens, London. Torsten Lauschmann: Mary Mary, Glasgow. Lorna Macintyre: Mary Mary, Glasgow, and Kamm Galerie, Berlin. Alastair MacKinven: HOTEL, London. Ursula Mayer: Monitor, Rome, and Juliëtte Jongma Gallery, Amsterdam. David Osbaldeston: Matt's Gallery, London. Garrett Phelan: mother's tankstation, Dublin. Clunie Reid: MOT International, London. Stephen Sutcliffe: Galerie Micky Schubert, Berlin. Tris Vonna-Michell: Cabinet, London. Mark Aerial Waller: Rodeo, Istanbul.

All installation images: photography by Stephen White. All images of events: photography by BenedictJohnson.com except as listed hereafter. Page 36: Juliette Blightman, photography by Melinda Gibson. Page 38: Thomas Kratz, photography courtesy the artist. Page 41: Andrew Hunt, photography by Alastair Fyfe. Page 96: Freee, photography by Danny Birchall. Page 116: Juliette Blightman, photography by Marcus Leith. Page 130: Andrew Hunt, photography by Andrew Hunt. Page 135: Nina Beier and Marie Lund, photography by Åbäke. Page 142: The Hut Project, photography by Thomas Cuckle. Page 165: Lorna Macintyre, photography by Jens Ziehe. Page 166: Ursula Mayer, photography by Tim Brotherton.

Institute of Contemporary Arts

Scottish Arts Council

culture ireland
cultúr éireann
promoting the arts abroad
cur chun cinn na n-ealaíon thar lear

The Henry Moore Foundation

LUX

ArtReview:

Afterall

JAPAN'S PRIME BREW
KIRIN ICHIBAN

ARTS COUNCIL ENGLAND